Sex, Family & Fertility in Haiti

Sex, Family & Fertility in Haiti

by

Timothy T. Schwartz

2nd Edition published January 2011

ISBN 10   146812966X

ISBN 13   9781468129663

Table of Contents

Tables

Figures

Chapter 1

Introduction

Fertility

I have three objectives in this book: First, to explain why fertility decline in rural Haiti has not come about. At 5.0 childbirths per mother, birthrates in towns and rural areas, where 70 percent of the population live, are among the highest in the Western hemisphere; in Jean Rabel county, where I conducted much of the research presented below, they are among the highest in the world. Significant effort and research funds have been devoted to trying to explain why contraceptive campaigns in Haiti have largely failed, but to date no researcher has satisfactorily answered that question. On the contrary, it will be seen that explanations for the lack of fertility decline in rural Haiti have become increasingly obscure, confusing, and unverifiable.

Anthropologists explained high fertility in Haiti with "love" and "prestige," "absence of contraceptives," and "tradition" (Herskovits 1937: 89); "the desire to live with reason, and to die with dignity" (Lowenthal 1987: 305); "fear of abandonment in women" and "strong tenets . . . rooted in the culture" (Maynard-Tucker 1996: 1387). Others have argued that it is lack of knowledge and an ineffective health care system (Jennie Smith 1998: 11), old age security (Murray 1977), and even land redistribution mechanisms (Murray 1977). It will be shown that in doing so, in turning to immeasurable variables, remote causation, and value-based explanations, anthropologists have often contradicted their own data.

Table 1.1: Total fertility rates in Haiti (TFR)

Year	Source	Rural TFR	Rural and urban
1971	Census	6.26	—
1971–1975	Demo Survey	5.56	—
1977	HFS	6.10	—
1994	EMMUS I	5.90	4.8
2000	EMMUS II	5.80	4.7
2006	EMMUS III	5.00	4.0
2007	CIA	—	4.9

Source: Allman 1982b; EMMUS I 1994/1995; EMMUS II 2000; EMMUS III 2005/2006; CIA 2007.

Kinship and Family Patterns

My second objective is to show that the same logic underlying family patterns in contemporary Haiti can be generalized to the rest of the traditional Caribbean and that doing so resolves questions about Caribbean family patterns that have puzzled anthropologists for over half a century: The anthropology of the Caribbean has been called "the battleground for competing theories regarding family structure" (D'Amico-Samuels 1988: 785). Different areas of the region were differentially influenced by native Arawaks and Carib Indians, French, Dutch, British, and various Asian cultures as well as the many African groups that came to prevail in the region. Despite these multicultural origins—what historian William Green (1977: 509) called a "cockpit of conflicting cultures"—there emerged a distinct pan-regional family structure such that M.G. Smith (1962: 244) identified twenty-three features common to 20th century Caribbean families. The most confounding, those that Western anthropologists found most challenging to explain, were late age at marriage, high rates of births to single women, matrifocality, child dispersal, *de facto* polygyny, and what Ho (1999: 37) called "brittle" conjugal unions, meaning that individuals readily took on new spouses or engaged in extramarital relationships in the absence of their primary spouse.

Thus, in "the battle" to explain Caribbean family structure, victory presumably would have come with a convincing causal model for the behaviours described and an explanation for the degree to which, despite their multicultural origins, these behaviors prevailed throughout the region. Yet, after more than half a century of intensive research and debate, no unifying explanation emerged. Similar to explanations for high fertility, scholars most often turned to the values of the people they studied, often with a decisive ethnocentric bent. During the 1940s and 1950s they dismissed Caribbean family patterns as "disintegrate" (Simey 1946), "uncivilized" (Matthews 1953: 302), "normless" and "distorted" (Smith 1996: 35, 54), "promiscuous" and "dysfunctional" (Smith and Mosby 2003). Since the 1960s, many scholars have recognized that family patterns are consistent with the poverty prevalent in much of the region (Brown 2002). But a comprehensive explanation has yet to be achieved such that Blackwood (2005: 14) could convincingly indict both feminists and more traditional anthropologists working in the Caribbean for casting "a long shadow over the theories of kinship, marriage, and the family."

NGOs and Paradigmatic Shift of Anthropology

My third objective is to deal with why I have to address these issues at all. More precisely, why have many social scientists, and especially anthropologists, increasingly turned away from empirically demonstrable material explanations for social phenomenon and instead favored explanations that blame impoverishment and high birth rates on the impoverished people themselves, on their values, cultures, and traditions? I believe that I can show that the answer is that governments, international financial organizations and corporations that fund our studies and the nongovernmental organizations (NGOs) that receive, redistribute, and partake in absorbing those funds refocus social-scientific inquiries and influence our conclusions in a manner conducive not to understanding and explaining, but rather to their own political and economic agendas. In understanding why and how, it is necessary to look at the post-WWII shift in funding sources. Before the advent of overseas "development intervention"— as I try to restrict myself to calling it in this book—most social scientists, and anthropologists in particular, went to the field to document the subsistence strategies and cultures of the people who live there (albeit with the hope of furthering colonial objectives). The criteria for success were accurate knowledge, data, and convincing explanations for patterned behavior. Today most anthropologists go to the field not simply to document and explain behavior, but as part of endeavors to change it (in more subtle ways and with more humanitarian rationales than our colonial predecessors). They work for internationally funded "intervention" organizations—NGOs—and have become agents of "value campaigns" targeted to promote specific Western morals and politico-economic "development" programs designed to modify modes of production and markets.

Jean Rabel and the Sociocultural Fertility Complex

To make my case I take a close look at one of the poorest, least developed, and most aided places in Haiti, a place called Jean Rabel, a commune, or what in the United States is known as a county, where I lived, worked, and intermittently conducted research for eighteen years. Jean Rabel is made up of 467 km^2 of one of the most geographically remote areas of Haiti and peopled by 130,320 men, women, and children who are primarily engaged in agriculture, animal husbandry, and to a much lesser degree fishing.[1] Despite close proximity to the United States, heavy migration, and the long presence of NGOs, the people there lead a daily life remarkably independent of the world economy.

At the time of the most intense survey research, 1996 to 2001, there were no televisions and only 15 percent of households had a radio. There were only three private vehicles in the entire commune. Less than 1 percent of households had a member who owned a motorcycle and only 5 percent had a bicycle. Eighty-seven percent of people in the area inhabited houses that had dirt floors and 82 percent of houses had a thatch roof. Animal husbandry and the planting of gardens were the principal livelihoods but only 2 percent of farmers used fertilizers, and pesticides were used with even less frequency. Farmers did not select seed stock and they made only feeble attempts to irrigate. Only hoes and machetes were employed in planting and harvesting crops; there was not a single tractor or any other type automated farm equipment in the commune. Animals were not corralled but tethered. Most people did not bother to vaccinate their animals and, except for occasional vitamin and protein supplements for pigs, industrial products or processed animal feeds were unknown. Fishing was carried out exclusively with bamboo traps, hand lines, and hand-woven nets. Boats were built entirely from local materials and propelled with wooden oars and sails that were patched together from used clothing. For medical care, people in the area overwhelmingly depended on herbal healers, called *leaf-doctors*, and shamans. Only about 50 percent of pregnant women visited the fifteen foreign-sponsored rural health clinics in the region.

The impoverishment and regional economic autonomy being described are accompanied by extremely high birth rates. Fertility among Jean Rabel farmers is perhaps the highest rate biologically possible given the prevalence of infectious diseases, low-calorie diets, high rates of female malnutrition, high female labor demands, and high rates of male absenteeism. It will be seen that at 7.1 births per woman, the TFR in Jean Rabel is, despite all these limiting factors, equivalent to the second-highest country birth rate in the world and almost as high as 19th and early 20th century Hutterites, who had the highest sustained fertility levels ever documented. This high fertility is reinforced by a general rejection of modern contraceptives, something that exists despite more than a decade of internationally funded educational campaigns and contraceptive giveaways. Only 4.5 percent of the reproductive-age female population use contraceptives, ranking the commune of Jean Rabel, if it were a country, among the four lowest contraceptive use rates in the world.

The reason for underdevelopment, poverty, and a rejection of contraceptives in Jean Rabel is emphatically not a lack of influence from state or foreign governments and institutions. Since the first Catholic clergy came to the region (1704), through the first U.S. military occupation of Haiti (1915–1934), and through the past fifty years of intensive Protestant missionary activity and costly foreign-sponsored development interventions, Jean Rabeliens have been exposed to a l/ong history of attempts to change the behaviors described above. Yet, as we have seen, little has changed.

No one seems to know why. Why have rural Haitians, and in this case Jean Rabeliens, shrugged off fifty years of foreign and state efforts to promote the use of modern technologies and why do they remain so desperately impoverished? As with the scholarly interpretations of fertility and kinship seen earlier, the Western-trained agronomists, economists, medical practitioners, and anthropologists who come to the area as specialists and international consultants in the field of foreign aid are generally perplexed by the persistent aversion to contraceptives, the insistence on giving supplements to infants within days of birth, the wholesale refusal to make any additional investments in cropping strategies or livestock, the apparent prevalence of sexually promiscuous patterns of behavior, polygynous unions, high rates of illegitimate births, sky-high fertility levels, and the intellectual tenacity with which Haitians cling to folk medicines, beliefs in sorcery, and other mystical phenomena. In an effort to understand and explain the behavior of the people they are trying to help and to rationalize the shortfalls of foreign development interventions, visiting experts typically resort to an eclectic array of explanations: resistance to technology is usually ascribed to laziness; promiscuity to the lack of economic opportunity available to women; resistance to contraceptives and belief in supernatural phenomena to tradition and an inferior educational system. L. E. Harrison, a former branch director of USAID in Haiti, typified this attitude when he wrote, "To repeat, the principal obstacles to progress in Haiti are cultural: a set of traditional attitudes and values. . . . The solutions must focus on obstacles in the Haitian mind" (Harrison 1991).

I believe that I can offer a better explanation. I am not claiming that I can explain all of Haiti or all of Haitian behavior. But what I try to do in this book is focus on high fertility and family patterns to offer an alternative explanation for hitherto perplexing behaviors found in the rural areas of the commune of Jean Rabel, elsewhere in Haiti, and in the Caribbean in general. In doing so, rather than resorting to the immeasurable inner workings of the Haitian mind or some progress-obstructing aspect of Haitian culture, I focus on external, observable environmental and economic conditions: most importantly, the contribution to survival that children make to impoverished families.

The Research

I first went to Jean Rabel as a graduate student in 1991 and 1994 to study missionaries and later illegal migrant boat voyages. I returned in September 1995 and between that time and June 1997, I spent fifteen months living in the thatch and tin roofed fishing hamlet of Makab (a pseudonym). I then worked and conducted research in the region of Jean Rabel until 2001. [2]

Early on, I lived in homes of impoverished farmers and fishermen. Later in my research, when I was employed, I maintained several residences, one in the city of Port-de-Paix, the capital of the Department de NordOuest, one in the village of Jean Rabel, and two in rural areas. I always had people from my research sites living with me: children attending school in the city, women who worked as cook or caretaker for the children, visitors looking for work, and itinerant female marketing women. My continued relationship as friend, sometimes guardian, and often "patron" made research easier than it would otherwise have been. When home writing up research results, if I did not understand something or needed to verify a fact about a person or family, I could simply turn to the person next to me for clarification.

In addition to living with Jean Rabeliens for the better part of six years, the major surveys I conducted and draw on in this book are the following:

The Baseline Survey

A one-in-fourteen systematic random sample of all 22,827 households in the commune. The survey was also called the Nutritional, Health, Agricultural, Demographic, and Social (NHADS) Survey because questions and measurements covered all these issues, from interviewing mothers about feeding practices, to weighing mothers and children, to developing profiles of the household membership and detailing information regarding farming practices.

The survey took three months to complete. Survey staff included twelve full-time interviewers, three full-time supervisors, another twenty house counters, cooks, and messengers. The total sample size was 1,586 households; of this figure 46 households were either vacant or interviewers were never able to locate the necessary respondents for at least one of the questionnaires.

The household head or spouse of the household head was the required respondent for the farming portions of the survey; the female head of the household or the spouse of the man identified as the household head answered nutritional and demographic survey questions. In 4 percent of cases no household respondent was located. A household was defined as a building in which people sleep; household members were defined as people who reportedly sleep in the house more than they sleep elsewhere. Households were counted and physically marked with a number. From the resulting lists, one in every fourteen households was systematically chosen using a random starting point. Longitudinal and latitudinal coordinates of the selected households were subsequently recorded using Global Positioning System (GPS) devices. Loading the information into SPSS spreadsheets involved some 1.5 million separate entries (observations). The original data entry was accomplished in the first two weeks of December 1997 by the survey staff and secretaries working for the local NGOs. With help from hired assistants, data were subsequently entered a second time during the period January to May 1998.

The Opinion Survey

This survey took nine days to complete and involved me and four full-time interviewers—two male interviewers and two female interviewers, all residents of the area and hired based on competency demonstrated during the Baseline Survey. We revisited 136 (~9%) of the households in the Baseline Survey. The sample was selected by dividing Jean Rabel County into twelve geographical zones; five zones were selected randomly and an approximately equal number of households were randomly chosen from each of the geographical clusters (~twenty-eight households per cluster). The sample was stratified by gender. In sixty-eight cases the female household head or the spouse of the male head was interviewed and in sixty-eight cases the male head or spouse of the female head was interviewed. Male interviewers visited male respondents and female interviewers visited female respondents. Only one respondent was chosen per household. Interviewers recorded responses to key questions on cassette tapes. I traveled and stayed with the interviewers and, using the cassette recordings, monitored interviewer performance daily. Transcription of the interviews began in the field and continued for several weeks after the survey ended. Fifty percent of the recorded interviews were reviewed; approximately 30 percent were transcribed.

Household Labor Demands Survey

In an effort to develop ethnographically dependable profiles of household labor demands and needs, I visited and conducted qualitative research in each of five Jean Rabel *lokalites* (rural neighborhoods). The *lokalites* were chosen for ecological variability: (1) dry foothill, (2) dry mountain, (3) humid mountain, (4) humid plain, and (5) dry coastal zone. One to three days were spent per visit in each *lokalite*. Information was gathered by the old-fashioned anthropological technique of hanging out, tagging along, watching, and "whying" people to the point of annoyance.

Livestock and Garden Survey

The Livestock and Garden Survey was carried out in two communities, one in a semi-humid mountainous community (n = 50) and another in a humid plain community (n = 56). The goal was to measure the strength of the relationship between the number of children and the number of animals and gardens per household. I decided this survey was necessary because: (1) in the Baseline Survey and the Opinion Survey farmers gave obviously misleading reports regarding livestock and crop yields (Jean Rabeliens have come to expect that if they report to visitors that they own nothing, then gifts may be forthcoming), and (2) we discovered that respondents in the Baseline Survey were including in their enumeration of household members children who were away at school in the village or in the city—the inclusion of these children led to a misrepresentation of the actual number of available child laborers—and (3) it is important to my argument to provide a concrete measure of the role of children in household livelihood strategies (so that I can provide tests of the relationship between the number of children present in particular households and the number of livestock and gardens tended by household members).

In order to correct these shortcomings and obtain dependable data, two communities were chosen not at random but because they were the home communities of a Baseline Survey supervisor's parents. The supervisor and his family knew everyone in these two communities and they were able to independently verify details relating to livestock, gardens, and the number of children present in the house. Expected crop yields were also measured during this survey.

Polygyny Survey

De facto polygyny is widespread in Jean Rabel and I hypothesized that it is somehow related to the value of children and therefore an important issue in the research. But inquiry into trends in polygyny was inadequately addressed in both the Baseline and the Opinion Surveys. In the Baseline Survey, a question regarding current polygyny was included but there was no question regarding past polygyny. Past and present polygyny were measured during the Opinion Survey but only men were asked about past polygyny—wives were not asked about their husbands' past polygynous behavior—and the sample was too small to give a statistically reliable image of polygyny over the course of a Jean Rabel man's lifetime. Thus, a three-hundred-respondent polygyny survey was carried out using the same supervisor and in the same two communities as the Animal and Garden Survey.

Two other small polygyny surveys were carried out, one focusing on forty-one skilled craftsmen and another among sixteen male shaman (known as *bokor* or alternatively *hougan* or, in the approximately 10 percent of cases where the subject is female, *mambo*). The areas for these surveys were chosen as a matter of convenience. Being familiar with people in the area, I was able to confidently substantiate reports by consulting with more than one local informant.

Clinics and NGO Reports

Data on interbirth intervals, contraceptive use, and health status were also garnered from local clinics, hospitals, churches, and NGOs working in the area. The most notable resource for regional health data was Faith Medical Clinic in Mare Rouge, physically outside the commune of Jean Rabel but with some 50 percent of its clientele coming from within the borders of the commune. Health care workers with the French NGO Initiative Developpement (ID) also provided health information and made reports available, as did the directors of PISANO (Projet Integre de Securité Alimentaire Nord-Ouest) and AAA (Agro Action Allemande). Staff at CARE International also provided access to reports and information on food aid and ongoing projects.

There were three survey reports that were especially important for comparison and validation of the data collected in the field. CARE International previously performed two large surveys in the region. The first, conducted in 1994, was a 1,400-household, twenty-six-cluster random survey covering the entire Northwest Department of Haiti (which includes Jean Rabel). The second CARE survey, in 1996, was a followup to the earlier survey. The third report was by PISANO (German Government NGO) and was based on a 1,300- household, five-cluster random survey in 1990 that largely covered the commune of Jean Rabel (PISANO 1990). The references for the respective survey reports are listed in the bibliography.

Overview of the Book

The book is comprised of nineteen chapters. The present chapter provides the introduction and description of the field research and methods used to gather the data presented in subsequent chapters. The following chapter provides a review of the literature regarding Caribbean family patterns and fertility, most importantly on the peculiar denial of the labor utility of children, an issue that I argue is at the base of understanding Caribbean family patterns. In chapter 3, I introduce the county of Jean Rabel, its people, the local history, and present conditions, including the environment and the importance of the role of the State and what others have called development organizations but I am calling foreign-sponsored intervention institutions.

In chapters 4 through 6, I introduce and describe the central topic of the book, what I am calling rural Haiti's *pronatal sociocultural fertility complex*. Jean Rabel women achieve what are among the highest birthrates in the world and they do so despite high incidence of disease, low-fat diets, intense work regimes, scarce resources, low male-to-female sex ratios, and high geographic mobility of both women and men, all factors that militate against pregnancy and childbirth. This high fertility is associated with aversion to the use of contraceptives and abortion, and the prevalence of pronatal laws, customs, and patterns of sexual behavior and beliefs that promote high fertility.

Chapter 7 through 10 are the beginning of an effort to achieve a holistic understanding of the underlying causes of high fertility and pronatal belief systems and behaviors in Jean Rabel and to lay out the conditions that underlie kinship and family patterns found there. I describe and analyze local livelihood survival strategies, and the importance of the household as the organizational framework within which most productive and survival activities are carried out.

In chapters 11 and 12, I show how the livelihood strategies described above translate to high labor demands and the tasks that must be accomplished to sustain a household and its members. Also examined are the sexual division of labor and how labor demands and the lack of alternative energy sources such as electricity and mechanized labor-saving devices mean that contributions Jean Rabel children make to the household labor pool are indispensable for survival. Chapter 12 ends with statistical correlations between household prosperity and number of children, but it is acknowledged that, alone, the data are insufficient to show a causal relationship between fertility and labor demands. To resolve this issue, chapter 13 includes a statistically representative analysis of the opinions of Jean Rabel men and women. The analysis demonstrates that children not only appear to be important to household security based on labor needs and the tasks they accomplish, but also Jean Rabel farming men and women conceive of children as an absolute necessity.

Chapters 14 and 15 covers the mode of reproduction, which here includes an examination of childrearing practices and reproductive unions. I link the mode of reproduction with the mode of production to show how it is that family and kinship in rural Haiti are conditioned by demand for child labor. The analysis is carried out in light of the necessity of children established in earlier chapters. The labor utility of children is shown to be reflected in—if not a principal conditioner of—childrearing practices, paternity, godparentage, the loaning of children, corporal punishment, and ultimately, conjugal unions—including *de facto* polygyny. In chapter 16 I show how the system is maintained and perpetuated and whose interest it is; specifically, I show how mature market women, those who control homesteads and dominate the regional marketing system, earnestly promote high fertility and seek to gain control over the children whose labor make homesteads productive.

In chapter 17, I demonstrate how my study of the sociocultural fertility complex in Jean Rabel and the insights garnered from studying it can be generalized to the rest of the Caribbean to clarify the determinants of kinship and family systems. Prior to the recent growth of the tourist industry and modernization of Caribbean economies, family and subsistence patterns throughout the lower-income social strata of the West Indies resembled those found in Jean Rabel and the extensive ethnographic record reveals the same causal patterns and dependency on household livelihood strategies and child labor.

Picking up on the importance of child labor as a conditioner of social patterns, in chapter 18 I examine one of the great demographic mysteries of the Caribbean—the irony of increasing birth rates when fewer men were present, i.e., fewer men, more babies—to demonstrate the applicability and causal significance of my argument.

In chapter 19 I return to the points touched on at the beginning of the book: why scholars never highlighted the importance of child labor as a determinant of social and demographic trends in the Caribbean, and why, despite overwhelming data to the contrary, they downplayed the economic contributions of children. The reason for this shortcoming, I argue, is because our research has been couched in "value campaigns"— part of massive "foreign aid" programs funded by powerful States—particularly those of the United States, Canada, and Western Europe. The programs are carried out in alliance with monetary policies of international financial and political institutions—such as the World Bank and International Monetary Fund, both controlled by the United States and European allies—but they are largely executed by multinational corporate charities that compete for the right to carry out specific interventions and in doing so manage the funds earmarked for such projects. Social science research has been embedded in these processes. In the service of these organizations, anthropologists have become agents of "value campaigns." These include the first anthropologists working in the Caribbean, the structural-functionalists of the 1940s and 1950s and 1960s working in the service of colonial governments that sought to modify behavior of the impoverished people living in the region; in the 1960s to the present, feminist scholars, also funded by agencies interested in changing behavior, focused on empowering women; other anthropologists worked as part of antinatal and procontraceptive campaigns; others were embedded in substance abuse campaigns, promotion of gay marriage coming out of queer anthropology, and child value campaigns that sought to export changing U.S. values toward children.

Conclusion and Importance of the Research

Understanding the impact that concrete and measurable conditions have on social organization and particularly on reproduction, kinship, and family patterns is important in the struggle to assist people in Haiti and in other impoverished regions of the Caribbean and the world. For more than half a century, Jean Rabel has been the target of intense foreign-sponsored intervention, most of which has met with indifference. But entrenched poverty and high fertility are not consequences of Jean Rabel inhabitants' nostalgic clinging to a rustic way of life, nor some shortcoming in the collective Haitian psyche or culture, as suggested by former USAID director Harris. Jean Rabel farmers conceptualize farming as the lowliest of occupations, virtually all rural Jean Rabeliens would prefer to migrate out of Jean Rabel and preferably out of Haiti, and many women interviewed in the surveys conducted for this book stated quite frankly that they would prefer not to have many children but, as will be seen, they must have children because they believe that children are necessary to survive.

Thus, in the struggle to maintain their living standards, those Haitians who cannot escape by emigrating are trapped in a system of spiraling population growth, declining soil conditions, and stagnant technology. It is a system beyond their control. There is currently no active State presence in rural Haiti; and local community organizational structures are often functionally nonexistent beyond the level of the household. The system, however, is not beyond the control of foreign-sponsored international intervention agencies working in the area. I hope this book contributes to changing their practices in a way that helps rural Haitians.

Notes

. Generally called *peasants*, presumably because of their tenuous and limited participation in the world market, I refer to rural Jean Rabel men and women throughout this book as farmers. The reason I use the term farmer rather than peasant is because *peasant* strikes me as too thoroughly imbued with a historic association to the disparaging, semi-slavery status of the medieval European serf. A difference in terms also seems to suggest that the impoverished Jean Rabel cultivator is somehow intrinsically different than the developed world "farmer." I prefer to use the same, less disparaging term, *farmer*, and emphasize the environment as the source of behavioral differences (see Dalton 1974 for controversy surrounding the term).

2. My initial fieldwork was sponsored by the Curtis Wilgus Foundation. Field work in 1996–1997 was sponsored by the College of Liberal Arts and Sciences at the University of Florida and a grant from the National Science Foundation and institutional support from IICA. The 1997 Jean Rabel baseline survey was sponsored by the German GTZ project, the German NGO AgroActionAlemande (AAA), and the French NGO Initiative Developpement (ID), the directors of which graciously granted permission to for the data to be used in academic publications.

Chapter 2

Review of the Literature:
The Neglected Half of Chayanov's Rule

Introduction

The basis of my arguments is that children are useful on the nonindustrialized farm because they work. The point might at first seem trite and obvious, but in recent decades social scientists have so rigorously denied the economic utility of children in developing areas that the denial itself is fascinating. Moreover, I believe this denial is the smoking gun in understanding why social scientists have failed to satisfactorily explain Caribbean family structure, kinship, and courting practices. To illustrate my point I want to begin by going back to an earlier time, before the modern worldwide fertility decline, to early 20th century social science, when the small farm in the developing world was intensively studied by a different but no less attentive generation of social scientists.

The Neglected Half of Chayanov's Rule

Any economic unit, including the peasant farm is acquisitive—an undertaking aiming at maximum income. . . . But in the family farm, apart from capital available expressed in means of production, this tendency is limited by the family labor force and the increasing drudgery of work if its intensity is forced up.

(Alexander Chayanov 1925)

From the quote above was derived Chayanov's rule: "the amount of time peasants devote to work is proportionate to the household dependency ratio of consumers to producers." Marshall Sahlins (1972) brought the "rule" to the fore of U.S. anthropological discourse in *Stone Age Economics*, an ethnographic *tour de force* in which he expounded on the way members of nonindustrial societies, limited by the domestic mode of production (production organized around the household), maximize leisure time rather than profits or productivity. But also inherent in Chayanov's rule was a principle that bears directly on the thesis of this book: small farmers dependent on nonindustrialized technologies and "limited by the family labor force" use high fertility to increase the size of that labor force.

The point was not lost on other social scientists. The economic value of children among small farmers and the impact that value had on fertility was widely accepted and rigorously substantiated as a basic tenet of anthropological and demographic theory up to and through the 1970s (Notestein 1945; Liebenstein 1957; Becker 1960; Freeman 1962; Boserup 1965). Mahmood Mamdani (1973: 14) conducted research in an Indian village and summarized what became a consensus among many scholars when he wrote that "People are not poor because they have large families. Quite the contrary: They have large families because they are poor." At about the same time, White (1973, 1976, 1982), Nag et al. (1978), and Cain (1977) carried out similarly renowned studies empirically demonstrating that impoverished families, particularly those engaged in farming-oriented household livelihood strategies, deliberately use high fertility to maximize the household labor force.

Demographer John Caldwell (1976) took the point to its logical conclusion, setting up what should have been the beginning of a florescence of explanations for family, kinship, and courting patterns focusing on the importance of child labor among small farmers. In his theory of intergenerational wealth flows, Caldwell (1982: 33) defined wealth as "money, goods, services, and guarantees that one person provides to another," and he argued that when wealth flowed from children to parents—as for example, when children were a valuable source of labor—fertility would be high as would the emotional and cultural reinforcements that encouraged high birthrates. This is, as I show in subsequent chapters, precisely what can be seen in rural Haiti today. Rural Haitians are radically pronatal; the entire rural Haitian social-kinship system and associated attitudes, opinions, and emotions are adapted to maximizing high birthrates and child survival; and the economic value of children in terms of their contributions to household productivity cannot and never has been *empirically* disputed—not in Haiti. Moreover, this same extreme pronatalism and economic value of children was, I will show, abundantly evident elsewhere in the Caribbean before the growth of the tourist and industrial sectors transformed most regional economies. But first, returning to the issue of economic explanations for high fertility, on the scholarly front something subsequently went strangely awry.

Social scientists began to steer clear of explanations that gave child labor contributions a determinant role in high fertility and the formulation of social and kinship patterns. New studies contradicted earlier ones, concluding that children were rarely if ever a net value to the parental generation (Das Gupta 1994; Lee 1996). Others focused on old-age security as the principal economic advantage of offspring, effectively making the intergenerational flow of wealth from children to parents so remote that it became, at best, a secondary determinant variable (Hugo 1997; Schellekens 1993; DeLancey 1990; Lillard and Willis 1997; Lee et al. 1994). This was not simply a trend among scholars new to the argument. John Caldwell also changed his emphasis, explaining resistance to fertility decline in sub-Saharan Africa with reasons that are "cultural and have much to do with a religious belief system" (Caldwell and Caldwell 1987: 409).

The new trend—that of denying the economic utility of children—can be linked to a shift in our Western value system of which most anthropologists are a part (Lancy 2007). In her study of the evolution of child-adult play. Adriana Zelizer (1985: 171) concluded, "while in the nineteenth century a child's capacity for labor determined its exchange value, the market price of a twentieth century child was set by smiles, dimples and curls"; and in a study by Gary Cross (2004: 4), "Today, as never before, we are obsessed with kids. We come close to worshipping them." David Lancy (2007) suggests that it was in fact developed Western governments that imposed these new values on poor countries. Post-WWII institutions founded to export the new values included the United Nations Children's Fund (UNICEF, founded in 1946), Compassion International (1952), the International Association for the Child's Right to Play (1961), Children Incorporated (1964), Child Defense Fund (1973), and the Alliance for Childhood (1997).

The rise of Western child worship and the well-funded institutions that exported the new values became part of the failure to explain why fertility in much of the world was high in the first place. It is a classic example of how anthropology has been undermined by the same forces that drive the discipline—funding agencies. Lancy captured the relationship when he explained:

> With modernization, fertility dropped, demand for child workers dried up, and suburbia mushroomed. Gone were the extended family, the "mother ground" where children played [and worked] under the casual supervision of adults in the vicinity, and the large brood of sibling playmates. In their place we have the image of the carefree young mother pushing her toddler on a swing in the backyard. An image that owed much to mass media and marketing became enshrined in academic discourse as well. (2007: 277–78)

I return to this issue of funding agencies in chapter 19 where I show how the new values were promoted in developing countries, but here I want to stay focused on the scholarly negation of the economic utility of children in the face of overwhelming evidence to the contrary. A close look at how this denial of child labor occurred in the Caribbean and in Haiti demonstrates the extremity of the trend and accents why, in order to understand kinship systems and family patterns, it is so important to rectify it.

Pronatalism in the Caribbean

Documentation of children in the nonindustrialized Caribbean and their important role as contributors to traditional household livelihood strategies abounded in the ethnographic record. On the island of Montserrat, "in the terms of the day-to-day household activities . . . the child is a definite asset." (Philpott 1973: 138). In Jamaica, "life is very strenuous for a peasant child . . . there are innumerable tasks to be done around the yard" (Kerr 1952: 47–48). In Trinidad, "a child is expected to help with a variety of tasks . . . as soon as the child 'has sense,' or as soon as he 'can walk and talk'" (Rodman 1971: 83). Among the Black Carib in British Honduras, "children help with household tasks, doing such things as carrying water, running errands, sweeping the house and compound. . . . Children of three or four may carry out many of these activities" (Gonzalez 1969: 53). In St. Vincent, "Young children were also perceived as economically useful. Children help around the house by performing chores, caring for smaller children, rearing livestock, running errands" (Gearing 1988: 236). In Barbados, "At five . . . [children] start caring for the 'stocks,' carrying water from the pipe, and 'cleaning the wares.' Boys . . . care for the animals, cut 'meat' [grass], carry water and help on the land. Their sisters learn to cook, wash clothes, clean the house, and shop with mother" (Greenfield 1966: 106). In Barbuda, "When six years old, boys and girls alike begin to carry water and look after the younger children. They run errands, scrub, and go to the shop . . . do laundry and cook. . . . help sow, weed and harvest (Berleant-Schiller 1978: 259). In St. John, "Children were sent to the spring to get water when they could carry a pail on their head . . . to find firewood in the bush . . . sweep the yard and help with food preparations . . . watering and re-staking daily the animals that were kept in the bush. They helped cultivate the provision ground and burn the coal, and often had to 'hold water' [keep the boats in position] when the fish pots were being hauled (Olwig 1985: 118–19).

Congruent with child labor contributions, pronatalism was an outstanding cultural feature of the traditional nonindustrialized Caribbean. People wanted children and customs, beliefs, and behaviors encouraged high birth rates. In St. Vincent, for example, it was believed that a woman who could not have children was, "tragic, sad, and pitiable" (Gearing 1988: 235) and as with women, "a man who could not have children is equally scorned, and his masculinity and virility are called into question" (Gearing 1988: 237). In Jamaica, "a child is God's gift"; "nothing should be done to prevent the birth of a child"; "no woman who has not proved that she can bear a child is likely to find a man to be responsible for her"; and "just as a woman is only considered 'really' a woman after she has borne a child, so the proof of a man's maleness is the impregnation of a woman" (Clarke 1966: 95, 96). In summarizing the results of 1,600 interviews from the extensive Women in the Caribbean Project (WICP 1979–1982), Olive Senior (1991: 68) concluded that, "there is an almost universal impulse to mothering," "Virtually all women are mothers. . . . Childless women are scorned," they are "mules" and they are "beyond the pale of society."

In addition to the general desire for children and the censure of childless individuals, there were beliefs that militated against birth control. Physical and mental disorders were associated with contraceptive use, abortion, and childlessness. In rural Suriname, if a woman did not have the destined number of children she might get "cancer" (Buschkens 1974: 223). In Jamaica "she will be nervous, have headaches, and even go insane" (Kerr 1952: 25). Young Jamaican girls were instilled with "horror" regarding abortion, and told things like the child's head and nails remain in the womb (Blake 1961: 200). Even *coitus interruptus* was abhorred, as illustrated by Blake's informant who equated it with murder, explaining that:

When the liquid is coming you can get up and throw it away but at the same time it is your blood you dashing away, and for that reason I don't like it. It is a sin, because you are destroying your blood, it is like killing a child. (Blake 1961; 201)

When explaining this pronatal complex of customs and behavior—extreme desire for children and aversion to contraceptives—one would expect that social scientists, especially anthropologists, would have turned to the child labor contributions that were so assiduously documented in the ethnographic literature. As a rule they did not.

Despite overwhelming evidence to the contrary, social scientists working in the Caribbean contradicted their own reports and denied the economic utility of children; and they did this much earlier on than the rejection of the utility of children found elsewhere.

Judith Blake (1961), co-author of the most influential demographic paradigm of the 20th century—the proximate and intermediate determinants of fertility (Davis and Blake 1956)—asked a sample of sixty-five Jamaican women, "What is your idea of a good son?" Fully 95 percent of the women interviewed replied, one who "helps" with productive household tasks. The next most common response (36%) was a son who "obeys," which according to Blake meant "he heeds instructions . . . willingly helps in domestic chores," "thinks of his parents all the time . . . considers in every way he can help them." Only 11 percent of respondents mentioned "love or affection." Yet, despite her informants clearly telling her the contrary, and despite acknowledging that "the child in the poorer strata of Jamaican society appears to lead a fairly burdensome and chore-ridden life," (62) Blake decided that high fertility in Jamaica had little or nothing to do with child labor contributions. It was, according to Blake, "a means to non-economic ends" (250–51).

This tendency to note the critical economic contributions children made to the household while at the same time downplaying child labor as a determinant of pronatalism or high birth rates was not the oversight of a select few social scientists; it was and is representative of the entire body of anthropological, sociological, and demographic literature on the Caribbean. In her summary of findings from the Women in the Caribbean Project and exhaustive review of Caribbean ethnographies, Olive Senior summarized:

Where there is no piped water, children are assigned the task of carrying water from a river or spring some distance from the house. Where there is no cooking gas or electricity or other easily available fuel, seeking firewood—sometimes at a great distance—is a major daily task. Where there is no refrigeration and the family income arrives in a fragmentary way, running to the shop for basic items as needed is a constant activity. Caring for domestic animals and garden plots, helping with laundry, cooking, cleaning and other housekeeping tasks and caring for younger siblings are all regarded as the duties of children.

(Senior 1991:34)

Quoting Brodber (1986: 60) in Jamaica, Senior drove the point home:

Children are seen as appendages of elders and have little existence of their own; rarely can they find occasions to slip away to play with neighboring children. . . . As their parents hire no help, and as there are no labor saving devices, their human energy is very highly valued and is not frittered away in play.

(Senior 1991: 34)

But having said this, Senior subsequently summarized explanations from the Caribbean ethnographic literature, presenting children as a maternal burden, wanted because childbearing is the way that a woman "proves herself to a man," the way she "completes a family," the way she achieves "social recognition," the result of the "widespread belief in the biblical injunction to be 'fruitful and multiply,'" and thus bearing children is "a good thing to do," an activity that "makes you feel like a woman" and allows women to "realize their self-image" to derive "psychic satisfaction" (Senior 1991: 67–69). In all of Senior's discussion of the causes of pronatalism, the only material factor cited is that woman want children because they are useful as "minders in old age" (Senior 1991: 67). Nothing is said about the benefits of young children as contributors to household production, benefits that, as seen, Senior herself noted are of major significance.

Illustrative of the point is also Penn Handwerker, deservedly among the most respected contemporary anthropologists in the field of fertility, a scholar who has provided the social sciences with our most powerful cross-cultural statistical model for fertility decline (see Handwerker 1989). When referring to the islands of St. Lucia, Barbados, and Antigua, Handwerker (1993) explained that the economic value of children for women consisted not in labor utility but in the fact that "childbearing was a singularly effective way to secure their future material welfare [a reference to old age] and to establish the relatively permanent ties to men that improved their immediate material welfare" (1993: 45).[1] Handwerker (1989: 87) made a similar argument with regard to Barbados, saying that "the probability a woman could adequately support herself through her own employment was close to zero." The reason women had children in the first place was that "young women overtly traded sex for financial support. Pregnancies and children occurred as mere byproducts of that exchange" (Handwerker 1989: 87–88).

As with many scholars, Handwerker's focus was on economic opportunities that would have been expected in upper-class Western industrialized societies, specifically "employment" and outside economic opportunity. But he gave little attention to the household as a woman's realm of productive activity or to other nonformal work activities and, most importantly, to the value of children in accomplishing such work. And he did this despite noting that:

> All children began working when they were capable of helping. . . . As early as five or six, girls began to sweep, dust, straighten, to wash, dry, and put dishes away. To fetch water, put water on for tea, to look for eggs, feed the chickens, collect firewood, and to wash, iron, and dry clothes. Boys too were assigned tasks at early ages . . . their tasks were primarily outside chores—boys took care of the stock and helped their fathers. (Handwerker 1989: 81–82)

Anthropologist Ann Brittain is another example. Brittain (1990) made the counterintuitive and demographically startling observation that fertility rates on the islands of St. Barthelemy and St. Vincent and the Grenadines (1991a) increased with male migration (fewer men but more babies)—something that flies in the face of conventional demographic wisdom, but that, as will be seen in chapter 18, is tantamount to a demographic rule in the traditional Caribbean and has befuddled a host of other anthropologists. Having discovered this demographic oddity, Brittain offered a tentative explanation and in doing so deemphasized the value of child labor in favor of preeminence of contributions, not from young children, but from adult offspring who twenty years after they were born might seek remunerated employment on distant islands and share it with their mothers:

> The most likely explanation for the connection between the crude rate of emigration five years earlier seems to be that parents were not acting directly in response to the loss of children through death or migration, but anticipating the emigration of some of their offspring when they reached adulthood. . . . Children provide valuable labour in farming families but the presence of adult offspring may be even more important as a support of old age.
>
> (Brittain 1990: 57)

The point is not that the cited scholars did shoddy research. Senior, Handwerker, and Brittain have produced some of the most commendable anthro-demographic studies on family and fertility in the Caribbean. The point is that they illustrate how social scientists have, for whatever reason, glossed over the significance of child labor contributions to household livelihood strategies and, as I will attempt to demonstrate, in doing so have fallen short of explaining the determinants of high fertility and family patterns in the region. Despite their own data, they attributed birth rates to causes such as the desire to feel like a woman, biblical injunctions to "be fruitful and multiply," inadvertent byproducts of sex, and the value of grown offspring; at the same time scholars were often insistent about viewing young children as a burden. Although they often provided the data that showed otherwise, they paid little attention to the role that children played in making households productive and little attention to how female engagement in extra-household marketing activities depended on child labor contributions.

Child Labor and Pronatalism in Haiti

Concerning the literature on rural Haiti, an area with perhaps the richest history of ethnographic accounts and currently the largest and one of the few remaining bastions of traditional nonindustrialized Caribbean lifestyles, emphasis on the importance of child labor co-present with a rejection of its role as a determinant of pronatalism has been the norm. Similar to other regions of the Caribbean, children in rural Haiti are highly prized. They are the mark of adulthood and they bring the individual respect. As one of the very first ethnographers in Haiti, George Simpson (1942: 670) reported that "the peasant couple wishes to have children, and to have the largest number possible." Simpson recognized that Haitian pronatalism derived from the value of child labor, which he said is of such "great assistance to the family" that rural Haitians say, "if it is necessary to choose between a large fortune without children and a large family without money, one must not hesitate to choose the large family without money." (Simpson 1942: 670).

But virtually all other ethnographers at the time and since have wavered on the issue. Melville Herskovits (1937: 101) wrote that in Haiti, "at about the age of seven or eight the children's play-life is invaded by the serious work which they must assume."

But when it came to pronatal attitudes and high fertility, Herskovits never mentioned child labor activities, preferring instead to explain the desire for children and high fertility with factors such as "love" and "prestige," "absence of contraceptives," and "tradition" (Herskovits 1937: 89).[2] Thirty years later Gerald Murray (1977) spent twenty-one months living in a low-altitude plains community in central Haiti and he carried out what is among the most exhaustive systematic investigations of Caribbean farmers' opinions regarding fertility ever conducted. One of the questions Murray asked his sample of 227 farming men and women was, "why they liked to have children/didn't like to remain childless." When interpreting his data Murray concluded that, "the data strongly suggest that the current utility of children in the ongoing domestic economy has come to play a secondary role" (1977: 273). Murray preferred to explain the "primary role" as the result of sociocultural evolutionary processes that, through selective advantages, had given way to the emergence of costly funeral rites: families were forced to sell off property to cover the costs of funerals for deceased elders, the forced sale of the property functioning as a societal mechanism for the redistribution of land. But, although Murray's argument is fascinating and his contributions to the ethnographic literature on Haiti arguably exceed in breadth and quality that of any other scholar, his ranking of the reasons people gave for wanting children was flawed. Murray split the response *itil* (useful). When coding his open-ended questions, he created two categories for the term: One for the 30 percent of farmers who said they wanted children because children were *itil* ("useful") but did not specify why ("unspecified useful"); and another category for the 32 percent of farmers who said that children were *itil* and added that the reason was because they helped accomplish agricultural and domestic tasks. But in the investigations I conducted in northwest Haiti, investigations detailed in later chapters, informants used *itil* as a catchall term to refer to the usefulness of children in accomplishing chores, whether those chores were helping around the house, helping with the animals, in the gardens, or running to the market. There was no ambiguity in this regard. Thus, if the same were true for informants in Murray's research area—and Murray gives no reason to believe otherwise—then the "current utility" of children was not "playing a secondary role," rather, with a total of 62 percent respondents, it was playing the primary role. Of Murray's 277 respondents in Kinanbwa, Haiti, 67 (30%) said children were *itil* (agricultural and domestic), 72 (32%) said *itil* but didn't specify, 108 (48%) said old age and sickness, and 123 (54%) said burial (Murray 1977: 273). (Respondents could choose more than a single category.)

Another highly respected and excellent anthropological work on life in rural Haiti was that of Ira Lowenthal (1987), who spent four years living in a village on Haiti's southern peninsula. Lowenthal titled his dissertation *Marriage is 20, Children are 21*, a proverb that has nothing to do with age—as it might intuitively seem to outsiders—but rather highlights the value Haitian farmers attach to children. The proverb means that while marriage is a prestigious behavior—it gets a high number—having children is of even greater importance—it gets an even higher number. Thus, the very title of Lowenthal's dissertation emphasized the desire for children among the rural Haitians he was studying. In supporting this notion of the importance of children among his farmer informants, Lowenthal reported that "children's multifaceted labor *contributions* to the household, from a relatively early age through early adulthood, cannot be gainsaid" (1987: 303; the italics belong to Lowenthal). Yet, similar to Murray, Lowenthal did not believe these contributions could be used as a rationale for high fertility, saying that "despite the absence of hard data on the topic, peasants . . . definitely see children as a financial burden, not an economic asset" (1987: 394). Lowenthal (1987: 305) concluded that "progeneration" among the people at his research site was the means by which people fulfilled "the desire to live with reason, and to die with dignity."

Even more recently, anthropologist Gisele Maynard-Tucker (1996) reported on a three-part sample of 2,383 impoverished rural and urban Haitian women. Maynard-Tucker's objective was to address the problem that despite massive contraceptive giveaway programs financed by USAID (United States Agency for International Development), programs that date back to the 1970s, Haiti continued—and continues—to have the lowest rate of contraceptive use in the Western hemisphere. Her principal finding was that both rural- and slum-dwelling Haitian women were not using contraceptives simply because they did not want to use them. They wanted more children: When asked "why they did not want to use contraceptives?" the most common reason given, after "pregnant" or "breastfeeding," was precisely "wanting additional children" (1996: 1385). Not only were informants telling Maynard-Tucker they wanted children, but Maynard-Tucker herself noted the economic utility of children, saying that, "in the countryside children fetch water and carry water and help with the cooking, cleaning, child care, gardening, and animal care" (1996: 1381). In the slums "children are taught at an early age to sell and trade goods in the streets or to do menial work, carry water, goods, watch property" (1996: 1381). So important was child labor that, according to Maynard-Tucker (1996), only one-third of both slum and rural children were sent to school (she explicitly explains this as a consequence of the economic activities of children, 1996). Yet, in spite of this clear recognition of the economic utility of children, Maynard-Tucker downplayed the utility of children, forming conclusions such as that the popular Haitian saying, *ti moun se riches* ("children are wealth") is not derived from the current utility of children, but "probably based on colonial times when children were needed to work the fields for their parents who had to produce for the 'colonial masters'" (1996: 1381).

In fact, during colonial times the master often controlled and directed child labor activities; and slave women bore an average of less than one child per woman. The point is that Maynard-Tucker, like other anthropologists, forsook pursuing the obvious notion that high birth rates may actually be an adaptation to the "living standards" that are "the lowest in the Western hemisphere; most living quarters have no piped water, electricity or sanitation facilities . . . . Job opportunities are scarce and every day brings a new search for food and survival" (Maynard-Tucker 1996: 1379). And similar to Murray and Lowenthal before her, Maynard-Tucker (1387) reached for immaterial and nondemonstrable explanations, indeed nonexplanatory explanations, saying that "the lessons learned in Haiti are that strong tenets about the importance of children are rooted in the culture." In other words, there were no lessons at all to be learned, Haitians are having many children simply because they are Haitian.

Another excellent ethnography, and the latest to deal with pronatalism in Haiti, is that of Jennie Smith (1998: 7) who spent three years living in a rural mountain hamlet in northern Haiti. She too noted the importance of child labor with regard to the rejection of contraceptive use, explaining that for the rural Haitian household, "the tasks to be done are never-ending" and "without several children it seems impossible for a family to function well." She (1998:11) built on her observation of the economic utility of Haitian children, saying that the primary reason why intervention practitioners have been so unsuccessful in their efforts to promote family planning in Haiti is because, "they are simply proposing the preposterous!" (punctuation belongs to Smith). But Smith then went on to disregard her own insights when she subsequently attributed low contraceptive use, not to her observation that parents need children to accomplish the "never ending" labor tasks of daily life in rural Haiti, but to shortcomings in the local health care system. To her credit, Smith concluded with a self-reflective comment that very neatly sums up the essence of scholarly conclusions regarding the causes of high fertility in the nonindustrialized Caribbean:

> Most scholars asking questions about why family planning initiatives have not been accepted by the people of Haiti seems to reflect crucial (though often tacit) preconceptions. Not only do these scholars tend to assume that if people were more educated about the issue and more aware of their options, and if these options were more accessible to them, then they would choose to accept family planning. They also tend to imply that *this compliance would be good for them.* (Looking back over the pages above, I find that I myself, however unwittingly, also seem to hold that underlying assumption.) (all punctuation in the original: Smith 1998: 24) [3]

Thus, similar to both the cross-cultural and the Caribbean literature regarding fertility decline and the economic utility of children, an interesting if not academically astonishing facet of the Haitian ethnographic record is the contradictions that we, as social scientists, have made ourselves.

Conclusion

Reflecting trends in Western demographic theory at the global level, researchers in the Caribbean have left a record of stark denial. We have often ignored the determinant role of material conditions as our informants reported them to us, and specifically, in this case, the value of child labor. In the following chapters I want to show how reinserting the importance of child labor can resolve some of the most perplexing issues that have confounded anthropological research, specifically persistent high fertility in Haiti and the determinants of what many have considered the Caribbean's unique courtship, family, and kinship patterns. To do so, I take the reader to Jean Rabel, Haiti, one of the few regions left in the Caribbean where traditional livelihood strategies continue to prevail and where there are ample data to demonstrate the mechanics and underlying causes of kinship and family patterns that prevail there.

Notes

1. Handwerker (1986) provides the most successful model available for fertility decline. His model explains over 95 percent of the variance in a very large sample of country d/ata, demonstrating that fertility decline is a consequence of increasing economic opportunities. However, explaining why fertility declined does not resolve the issue of why it was high in the first place and, like many contemporary scholars, Handwerker prefers not to emphasize the labor value of children when they are young.

2. The full quote from Herskovits is as follows:

The love of children, and the prestige which a man gains as head of a large family are factors that go far to explain the desire for numerous progeny. In this not only is he aided by his own sophistication in matters of sex...but his desire is furthered as well by the absence of contraceptives, and the emphasis laid by Church, State, and African traditions on the desirability of many offspring.   (Herskovits 1937: 89)

3. Also important but for editorial reasons omitted is Glen Smucker's (1983) excellent ethnography on peasants/farmers in the north of Haiti. Smucker does not attempt to evaluate the importance of child labor as a cause of pronatalism and thus the insight he provides does not fit into the literature review in the main text. Smucker's work is, however, among the most thorough and instructive resources written on rural life in Haiti and he does make frequent mention of the economic utility of children, as for example:

After children learn to walk, they are expected to help with domestic tasks, carrying water, gathering wood and running errands. When they are old enough, boys go to the fields with their father, and girls take greater responsibility for household domestic tasks and marketing. As they approach adolescence, boys are assigned their own gardens and livestock. (1983: 232–33).

Chapter 3
The Commune of Jean Rabel

Introduction

The commune of Jean Rabel has had a sometimes glorious and prosperous past. It was home to the most socioculturally complex Indians in the Caribbean, the Classic Taino, and one of the first places that Christopher Columbus landed in the new world. It became a refuge of pirates and buccaneers, it was a prosperous quarter of the French colony of Saint Dominigue, the first New World home to some ten thousand African-born slaves, a strategically important site during the Haitian wars for independence, and it was an area that produced and exported significant quantities of rum and plantains during the mid 1900s. But in recent decades Jean Rabel has experienced deteriorating environmental, economic, and social conditions. The presence of the State is feeble at best, and no local community organizations exist capable of confronting the devastating social, economic, and ecological problems that affect the area. International NGOs have been operating in the commune for fifty years and are presently the only effective suprahousehold community help organizations and the only real providers of institutional healthcare, agricultural, and social security services to the 130,320 residents of the region.

Today, contemporary farmers living in Jean Rabel survive in the face of harsh cyclical environmental conditions exacerbated by the rapid degradation of their natural resource base and periodic hurricanes, droughts, and floods. The absence of assistance from the State in the form of an agricultural extension service, price support during market gluts or disaster, aid in storing crops and moving them to markets, or assistance with infrastructure such as roads and ports mean that, with the NGOs aside, Jean Rabel families have had to adapt to harsh environmental and economic conditions on their own. Disease, malnutrition, chronic food shortages, and scarcity of potable water have been making life even more difficult. To most observers, the primary force driving the disaster is exponential demographic increment. But as I argue, it is precisely the demographic increment that is the primary adaptive mechanism.

Geography

The commune is half mountain, half plain, and includes approximately thirty-five kilometers of Atlantic coastline. Beginning in the humid three-thousand-foot inland mountains and moving northward toward the sea, the landscape transforms in a quick seven to eight kilometers into foothills and then fertile plain. The plain runs the entire length of the Jean Rabel coast but a smaller range of drier low-slung, wind-sheared desert mountains separates the plain from the ocean. Rainfall varies from one thousand mm in the high inland altitudes to four hundred mm along the coast (see figures 3.1 and 3.2 below). Rainfall on the drier plains occurs most often in the autumn and winter months and rain in the mountains falls most heavily in the spring (see chapter 11, figure 11.1, p. 119). The plains both benefit and suffer from the mountain runoff, which provides temporary irrigation and, at times, crop-devastating floods.

Deforestation and Erosion

All of Jean Rabel is largely deforested. In the mountains there are pockets of mature trees such as avocados, and colonial introductions such as mangos and breadfruit. The plains contain mostly scrub bushes and stubby, native acacia trees. The low, coastal mountains are covered with thorny xerophytic vegetation and cacti. Scenes of erosion are one of the most spectacular features of the landscape. At higher altitudes one occasionally finds single bodies of earth, some encompassing hectares of land, slipping down mountainsides. But it is gully erosion that residents and local intervention workers consider to be the primary soil control problem in Jean Rabel. Low-altitude gullies can appear in several weeks and the course of a single stormy night. Some of the gullies are a spectacular ten and fifteen meters deep. They cut roads and footpaths, forcing people to take new routes, and in a few short years they divide neighborhoods into separate communities.

Droughts and Hurricanes and Adaptation

Jean Rabeliens are primarily farmers, and the greatest danger to their livelihood is droughts and hurricanes—both called *siklon* by locals. Hurricanes are not as severe because tuber crops such as manioc, sweet potatoes, and arrowroot survive and even benefit from the abundant rainfall. Prolonged droughts are different. Crops stop yielding and livestock begin to die off. People who are old or sick are more likely to die at these times. Stricken families begin moving, going from house to house begging morsels of food. People typically ridicule and humiliate them, but some give. Banditry increases. Desperate people hide themselves in the brush by trails and charge unsuspecting voyagers, hurling rocks and screaming, driving the traveler away from her donkey and seizing her merchandise.

Locals give the *siklon* names like *dekore* (unleashed) and *twa ribon* (three ribbons—a reference to the strips of cloth that hungry people tie around their stomachs to squelch the pangs of starvation). Since 1921 there have been at least three major hurricanes that devastated the region and severe drought has struck at least nine times during that same period.

Table 3.1: Major natural disasters in Jean Rabel since 1921

1921: Drought (name forgotten).
1931: Unnamed hurricane devastated crops and killed livestock.
1938–1939: Severe drought called *twa ribon*. Elders remember banditry, gangs of people watching roads and paths to steal whatever supplies a traveler might be carrying.
1950: Drought (no details).
1954 (October 12): Hurricane Hazel wrecked crops and killed livestock. Locals called it *douz oktob* (October Twelfth), and it is a major milestone in temporal reckoning for people in Jean Rabel and all over Haiti.
1956–1957: It is not clear if this was really a crisis year. Several old-timers in Jean Rabel remember the year as a drought period and report going to the nearby island of La Tortue to buy manioc for relief. An earthquake occurred in 1956, but reportedly had little to no effect on the gardens. Pasture Brown of UFM (Unevangelized Field Missions) gave tents to displaced villagers and the Red Cross came in to evaluate the situation.
1965: Drought that is poorly remembered because of the severity of the ensuing drought in 1967–1968.
1967–1968: Drought called *dechouke* (Uproot) and *plan dijans* (Emergency Plan). The latter name stuck because food aid was distributed in the form of a road project that opened a direct route to capital city of Port-au-Prince. The food some report was *rapadou*, a crude sugar that comes wrapped in banana leaves.
1975: Drought called *goldrin* after a *blan* named Gordon who was reportedly responsible for regional food relief under HACHO.
1979: Hurricane David devastated crops, tore roofs off houses, and caused flooding in low-lying areas. The incident is not recollected by most farmers.
1991–1993: A drought called *dekore* (Let Loose) and *twa zorey* (Three Ears). Some people at the time called it the *dèziem imbago* (the second embargo—the first embargo being imposed by the United Nations in 1992, this second embargo was imposed by God). Reportedly much banditry occurred. USAID/CARE relief effort began in earnest toward the end of the drought.
1997: Drought—no name.

Figure 3.1: Historic Regional Rainfall by year (1921-1950)

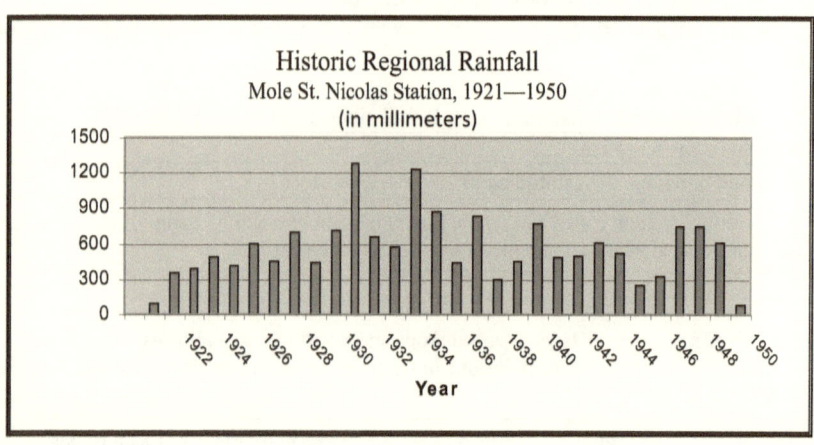

Figure 3.2: Historic Regional Rainfall by year (1965-1969, 1978-1996)

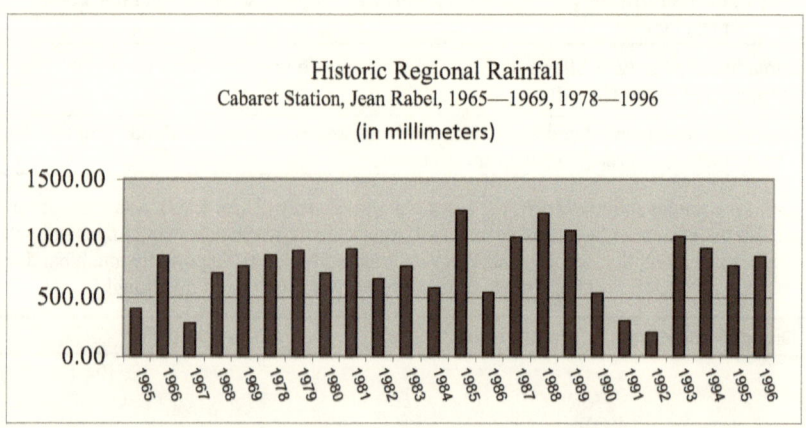

Note: 1993 is from NOAA global precipitation data

While difficult, the prudent farmers, those who have saved money and those who have planted sufficient security crops like cassava, yams, and sugarcane, come through crises relatively unscathed, for the crops planted by Jean Rabel farmers are uniquely suited to surviving drought. Plants such as sweet potato go into a state of dormancy during drought and then come back vigorously at first rain and may yield as much as twelve metric tons per acre on as little as four inches of rainfall. But the more it rains, the more the vine produces (see Bouwkamp 1985; Onwueme 1978). Or there is cassava, a close competitor with sweet potatoes for the most productive tropical food plant in terms of calories produced per square meter. It needs more rain than sweet potatoes to grow, but it is more tolerant of drought, easily surviving dry periods longer than six months. Further, unlike sweet potatoes, cassava has the unique ability to be stored in the ground and is hurricane proof because it can lose all its leaves and its branches may break but the root, which is where the food is, will not die. After drought or hurricanes the plant draws on carbohydrate reserves in the roots to rejuvenate itself (see Toro and Atlee 1980; Cock 1985). Or pigeon peas, a bush-like plant with roots reaching six to seven feet beneath the surface, deeper than cassava, making the plant highly drought resistant. When drought does strike, pigeon peas shed all their leaves and go into a state of dormancy just like cassava, coming back to life when the rains return (see Nene et al. 1990). Or sorghum and millit, both crops that yield with minimum rainfall. The roots reach more than eight feet beneath the surface, enabling the plant to withstand over two months of drought. When the crop is entirely lost to drought or has been harvested, the stalks can be cut back and the plant will begin growing again (see Nzeza 1988). Peanuts are even more drought resistant than sorghum, and in Jean Rabel they are planted in sandy soil and in the *kadas* where only cacti and xerophytic plants are found. It is also the premier high yield cash crop in the mountains, taking over the role that corn and beans fill on the plains (see Nzeza 1988).

The other lesser but still important crops all fit into an agricultural strategy that is clearly selected more for eking out a living in the face of an unpredictable market and natural environment than for participating in the world economy: Lima beans, which are inter-cropped with corn, are nitrogen fixing and begin to yield two to three months after harvest and continue to yield for as long as there is sufficient rainfall. Pumpkins and squash also yield continually as long as there is rain. The most popular yam in the mountains of Jean Rabel (*yam reyal*) can be planted during dry spells and will begin to grow with the first rains. Like cassava, it can be stored in the ground indefinitely, serving as an important food during droughts and other crises. Sugarcane endures for years, propagates itself without human intervention, can be harvested at any time after it is mature, and will grow back after being cut. Perhaps most importantly with regard to sugarcane, the hard fibrous exterior locks in water while the roots extend some eighteen feet underground, making it a completely drought-resistant source of water and high-energy food for both people and animals.

During the most severe dry spells, people traditionally purchase cassava and *rapadou* (a gummy crudely refined brown sugar wrapped in banana leaf) on the nearby island of La Tortue, an area with three times the average annual rainfall of Jean Rabel. People also resort to eating boiled green mangos, and a variety of wild plants, including a yam and several types of seedpods. Livestock are sold or slaughtered and eaten as they succumb to the drought.

Infrastructure

Jean Rabel is one of the poorest communes in Haiti. For whatever reason—lack of funds, corruption or apathy—the Haitian State has only a marginal presence and provides few public services. There is no electricity, no indoor plumbing, and no sewers. In 2000, the State sponsored a small hospital staffed by four Haitian doctors and two visiting Cuban doctors, but the facilities permit only minor surgery. The police force consists of eighteen national police officers who are usually absent from their posts. Even when they are present, they do little more than sit huddled around their two-room headquarters in the village playing cards and dominoes (albeit it is difficult for them to do anything else as they have no vehicles—no truck, no motorcycle, not even a mule). There are no State irrigation works and no State-supported maintenance services. In the past forty years the State has built only one hundred yards of drainage canal and no new roads. Older roads in the region are maintained by international intervention agencies.

The Village

The village, or *bouk* as locals call it, which continues to be the administrative seat of the commune, is like a place time and progress forgot. The streets are laid out in an orderly grid—a vestige of the village's colonial origins—and are made of dirt with muddy drainage ditches running down both sides. As late as 1992, a spiked colonial cannon still lay discarded by the roadside. The center of the village is a cluster of several hundred rusty tin roofs, rickety wooden two-story houses built in the 1930s and 1940s, and a few cement ones built in the 1990s, evidence of the latest "boom" in NGO intervention activity. Some of the older single-story houses at the edge of town have been all but swallowed by a creeping lava-like flow of mud that pours down the eroding hillsides during rainy season. Vehicles have to ford a shallow river to arrive or leave, and once outside of town the streets fizzle their way out, becoming winding, rural, rock-strewn and gully-ridden roads and footpaths.

Houses, Settlement Patterns, and Transportation

Beyond the hills surrounding the village, up in the mountains, across the plain, and along the coast is where most of Jean Rabel's 130,320 inhabitants live, in isolated homesteads and tiny hamlets. Not much has changed for these people over the past two centuries. More than half the adult population has no education, none. Over 80 percent of all houses are made of sticks, rocks, and mud, clay, or lime. The floors are dirt and the paneless windows protected only by wooden shutters that can be opened during the day. There is no access to any form of electricity, water service, or any other utility. Animal and foot traffic remain the primary modes of transportation: 89 percent of households own one or more donkey, 19 percent own at least one horse and 10 percent own at least one mule, the Mercedes Benz of rural Haiti (data on transport animals is taken from the Polygyny Survey; see table 3.2). Less than 1 percent own motorcycles and about 5 percent own bicycles.

Figure 3.3: Years of school for respondents over eighteen years of age

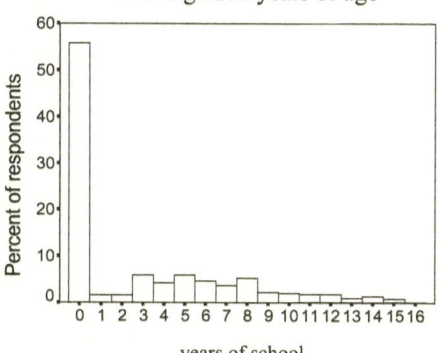

years of school

There are only three privately owned noncommercial vehicles in the entire commune, and the only public transportation for the 130,320 residents is provided by approximately twenty pick-up trucks, sixteen larger trucks, and two school buses, all privately owned. When traveling to the distant urban centers of Gonaives and Port-au-Prince, people in Jean Rabel pay H$10 to H$20 (US$3–$US6) to squeeze aboard the overloaded trucks, brightly painted in colorful designs and bedecked with lights and ornamentation. Bleating goats and squawking chickens are strapped to the roofs and bumpers as the top-heavy vehicles totter their way along, ever so slowly, often inching through river beds and down rocky and washed out roads. It takes them ten to twelve hours to reach the capital by bus.[1]

Table 3.2: Transport vehicles

Vehicle	Household Survey (n = 1,509)
Bicycle	4.7%
Motorcycle	0.8%
Car	0.0%

Pack Animals	Polygyny Survey (n = 300)
Donkey	89%
Horse	19%
Mule	10%

Malnutrition and Disease

Despite the occasional natural disasters, the deteriorating environment, absence of modern utilities, and the poor educational opportunities, life in Jean Rabel might not be so bad, except for the scarcity of potable water and the high prevalence of infectious diseases. To begin with, potable water sources are few and far between. The average round trip walking distance from a Jean Rabel household to the nearest water source is seventy minutes (see chapter 11, table 11.4). During droughts, many springs dry up and the distance to the water often doubles and can be as much as three or four times as far. Foreign employees of the French NGO Initiative Developpement report that only 65 percent of the springs in the region qualify as safe drinking water. After heavy rains, many springs become polluted with runoff and are unsafe to drink. Locals often resort to digging holes in river beds and areas where there is ground seepage, something that also exposes them to contamination from animal and human feces.

Most Jean Rabel households make two hot meals a day. People also eat fruit, avocados, bread, peanuts, and a series of other inter-meal snacks. But by U.S. standards, 15 to 20 percent of Jean Rabel children are malnourished, and a 1990 study found that 26 percent of women were mild to severely malnourished (PISANO 1990). Chronic food scarcity has intensified recently with the deteriorating environment and with the rise in food aid, something that is arguably a principal cause of increasing poverty (Richardson 1997). Food aid lowers market prices for staple foods, reducing the income farmers get for their own produce, which, in lieu of the fact that other household expenses do not change, lowers household cash reserves for food purchases during the off season.

Complicating the problem of scarce drinking water and malnutrition—or perhaps largely as a consequence of these factors—are high rates of infectious diseases. The exact rates are difficult to ascertain. No one is keeping count of the sick and less than half the population uses the fifteen NGO-sponsored clinics in the region (the estimate is courtesy of clinic staff who fail to keep the records). By any measure, at least 10 percent of infants die in their first year of life and 25 percent of children do not survive past the age of five. Interviews with sixty-four women revealed that in the twelve months prior to the interview, twenty-two (34%) had at least one bout with a debilitating disease that left them bedridden for several days to months, and as seen in the following chapter, at any given time about 5 percent of adult Jean Rabel women suffer from a sexually transmitted disease.[2]

Table 3.3: Offspring deceased by children born (per mother)

		Number of children deceased					
		0	1 to 2	3 to 4	5 to 6	7+	Total
Number of children born	1 to 2	87.8%	12.2%	.0%	.0%	.0%	100.0%
	3 to 4	72.3%	27.4%	.3%	.0%	.0%	100.0%
	5 to 6	52.4%	39.9%	7.3%	.3%	.0%	100.0%
	7+	20.6%	44.6%	21.5%	7.8%	5.4%	100.0%
	N =	835	551	167	53	36	1642

Migration

Many Jean Rabeliens desperately try—and many have succeeded—to escape to the city and to neighboring countries, to the United States, and to Europe. For example, the migration of the village elite, from whose ranks come political leaders and people in positions of public trust and power, is alarming. Since the early 1980s the number of village residents has grown from 3,294 to the current estimate of 8,000 people (out of the total commune population of 130,320). But longtime Jean Rabel residents explain that more that 80 percent of the villagers who were present in the early 1980s are gone.

In an attempt to corroborate these reports and to measure the extent of migration out of the village, I took a list of village residents from a 1960 open letter to then President Francois Duvalier that I found in a Port-au-Prince newspaper (*Nouvelliste* 1960). The letter was a plea for aid after a storm had washed out the local cemetery, uncovering graves and sending coffins and cadavers floating through the streets. There were 178 signatures on the letter. Using local informants, we were able to identify eighty-two of the individuals listed in the letter, all the rest presumably having long ago left with their entire families. For sixty-nine of the individuals, information was obtained on the number of children they had and the current whereabouts of these children. Of the individuals, thirty-one had left Jean Rabel; twenty-one of these had immigrated to Miami. Of the 287 offspring identified, 76 percent had left Jean Rabel and 57 percent had immigrated to the United States.[3]

The same trends are evident in rural areas. In a 1992 random sample of two rural areas near Jean Rabel, I compared tin-roofed households (a sign of higher income) to thatch-roofed houses (a sign of lower income).[4] None of the sixty-nine heads of thatch-roofed households had any children in the United States and only three had a sibling in the United States. In contrast, seven of twenty-seven tin-roofed household heads had siblings and four had children living in the United States (Schwartz 1992).

It is not that migrant families have more money because they have migrants. It is the inverse. As one moves from the poorest rural areas into those zones where there is a relative concentration of wealth, migration becomes the dominant theme. In one of the only irrigated zones in the region I found that 74 percent of all children of the largest landowners had left the region. Thirty-one percent (31%) were reported as being in the United States, and this percentage did not take into consideration the age of the children and the fact that some were still very young and hence had not yet emigrated (see tables 3.4 and 3.5).

Table 3.4: Migration of the offspring of owners of irrigated land

| | | Location of Children | | | |
		U.S.	Urban	Local	Total
Amount of land	3 or more	23	32	19	74
(1 *kawo* = 1.29	1 to 3	14	11	17	42
hectares)	Less than 1	3	34	5	42

Source: Schwartz 1992

Table 3.5: Current location of circa 1960 villagers and their offspring

	Jean Rabel	Elsewhere [a]	Miami
Signors (n = 82)	51	31	21
Offspring (287)	69	218	165

[a] = total number of individuals in category who have left Jean Rabel
Source: Schwartz 1992

Population Growth, Fertility, and Contraceptive Campaigns

While migration has been spectacular in terms of the number of people leaving the region, it has done little to offset population growth. In the past few decades, population growth in Jean Rabel has reached juggernaut proportions. In the first century following Haitian independence, the Jean Rabel population grew at the slow rate of 0.36 percent per year. Perhaps as a result of medical interventions associated with the 1915–1934 United States military occupation of Haiti, the population growth rate increased substantially during the 1900s. Between 1919 and 1971 the population growth rate averaged 1.6 percent; and between 1971 and 1997, the rate was 3.7 percent, putting the current estimated Jean Rabel population at almost three times what it was in 1971, the same year the Haitian government initiated an internationally funded national contraceptive program (Allman 1982a).

The fertility control campaign reached Jean Rabel in the mid 1980s, when international intervention organizations began trying to veer Jean Rabeliens from a collision course with overpopulation, stagnant technology, and ecological catastrophe by, among other things, making contraceptives available to women.[5] Currently the French, U.S., and German governments, along with the European Union and the United Nations, all promote family planning through the fifteen health facilities—three of which are outside the commune— and three NGO programs in the region. Condoms are given away and other contraceptives are sold for nominal service fees.[6] But efforts to get women in Jean Rabel to use contraceptives can be summed up as a failure. In the 1,586-household Baseline Survey, 82.2 percent of women were aware of contraceptives and where to get them.[7] Of these, 1,131 women (6.3%) reported not using contraceptives for religious reasons; 11.5 percent reported their husband objected; 27.6 percent reported a belief that contraceptives would make them ill; and 54.6 percent explained they did not use contraceptives simply because they did not want to.

Table 3.6: Contraceptive knowledge and use

Knowledge and Use		No	Yes	Total
Women who have ever heard of family planning and know where to get it	Count	245	1,131	1,376
	Percentage	17.8%	82.2%	100%
Women who have ever used family planning	Count	922	209	1,131
	Percentage	81.5%	18.5%	100%

Currently, only one clinic in the region reports artificial contraceptive methods being used by more than 5 percent of reproductive-age women in its service area, and this figure is skewed by the fact that over 50 percent of the patients listed are actually tubal ligation patients who visited the clinic over a period of fourteen years. Twenty percent of the tubal ligations were performed because of medical complications that made pregnancy a dangerous or life-threatening condition for the woman. Most of the women had over five children. And many of the patients reported as having received tubal ligations actually came from outside the clinic service area as this particular clinic was one of the few institutions in Far-West Haiti that offered the operation.[8]

Table 3.7: Women using contraceptives in Far-West 1998–1999 (15 to 49 yrs) [9]

	Region[a]		
	Mare Rouge[b]	Jean Rabel[c]	Zone 3[d]
Reproductive-age women	12,000	26,200	7,000
Injection, implants, and pills	660	1,125	281
Surgically sterilized	422	60	0
Total contraceptive use	9.1%	4.5%	4.0%
Chemical contraceptives only	5.5%	4.3%	4.0%

Overall, reproductive-age women in the Jean Rabel commune have a 4.5 percent rate of contraceptive use, which is one-fourth the rate for Haiti as a whole (18%), one-seventh that of the lowest country rate in the Caribbean (Guatemala at 31%), and one-thirteenth the level of contraceptive use for Latin America and the Caribbean as a whole (59%). The contraceptive use rate in Jean Rabel is compatible with the four lowest country rates in the world—Mozambique at 2 percent, Ethiopia and Niger at 4 percent, and Eritrea at 5 percent (see the UN 2000).

Thus, today, while technology remains virtually unchanged from what it was two centuries ago—indeed, more rudimentary—Jean Rabel is inhabited by 130,320 residents, an average of 279 people per km^2 or 724/$mile^2$. Forty-six percent of Jean Rabeliens are children under fifteen years of age and 57 percent of residents are under twenty years of age (see figure 3.1). Very few women are interested in using

contraceptives and if the current fertility rate continues, the population of Jean Rabel will double in the next twenty years, reaching 260,000 people, 1,548 people per square mile.
[10]

Table 3.8: Population of Jean Rabel in the years 1780–1997*

Year	Pop.	# of years	Pop. increment	Mid-point pop.	Rate of increase	Pop. density (km^2)	Source
1780	12,000	—	—	—	—	26	Moreau
1919	14,802	139	2,802	13,401	0.15%	43	Census
1950	33,372	31	18,570	24,087	2.49%	71	Census
1971	46,378	21	13,006	39,875	1.55%	99	Census
1982	67,925	11	21,547	57,152	3.43%	145	Census
1997	130,320	15	62,395	99,123	4.20%	279	NHADS

*Rates calculated from previous population estimates. Rate of population increase estimate = midpoint population/ (total population increment/number of years)

Conclusion

Droughts, hurricanes, periodic famine, declining soil productivity, and spectacular and catastrophic erosion would seemingly militate against high birth rates but, as will be seen, while large numbers of children may be illogical from the standpoint of the population as a whole, it is logical from the standpoint of the family and, more importantly, from the standpoint of the women who are the owners and managers of households, the primary productive units around which labor is organized in Jean Rabel. But before getting to that, I want show how the high fertility seen above is accomplished in the face of an array of factors averse to high birth rates, specifically disease, malnutrition, intensive labor regimes, conjugal unions interrupted by male absenteeism, and a scarcity of men with the financial resources to care for young children.

Notes

1. During the Baseline Survey, 35 percent of household respondents told interviewers they own at least one donkey, 8 percent reported owning a horse, and 7 percent percent of households owned a mule. But this later data was skewed by the drought that was occurring and so I have used data from the Polygyny Survey carried out two years later and in which questions regarding pack animals were included. Intuitively, I believe the Polygyny Survey results reflect general conditions in Jean Rabel but it focused on only two communities, one in the mountains and one on the plain, and therefore must be interpreted with this in mind.

2. The interviews were conducted at the Nan Sentren Clinic by missionary Carol Ann Truelove. Of the women interviewed, thirty-four were visiting the clinic because they were pregnant or nursing mothers and of these, ten had experienced a debilitating illness in the previous year; thirty of the interviewees were currently sick at the time of the interview, and ten of these had experienced a prior debilitating illness within the previous twelve months.

3. The identification of "prestigious" is simply those individuals who were most easily recognized, about which informants had no questions, and were double-checked without

complication.

4. These samples were chosen from lists made in two neighborhoods. Beginning at a random starting point, every fifth household was chosen from the lists.

5. Promotion of contraceptives began with the opening of the Protestant-funded Nan Sentren clinic and accelerated in the later 1980s, when the French NGO InterAid began taking over regional clinics that the Catholic Church sponsored and managed.

6. The organizations that actually do the promoting, funding, and/or supplying of contraceptives are Profamil, PROMESS, EEU, USAID, CARE, PISANO, ID, and MSPP. AAA plans to join the effort in 2000. The fees for contraceptives are 25 *gdes* (US$1.50) to place Norplant, 25 *gdes* (US$1.50) to remove Norplant, 5 *gdes* (US$0.30) consultation fee for all other chemical contraceptives (Depo-Provera, Noristat, and pills). Condoms are given away at clinics and sold in rural stores at three condoms for 2 *gdes* (US$0.12). Tubal ligation is 50 *gdes* (US$3.00). Charges account for the cost of service and not the cost of contraceptives, which are considered gratuitous.

7.

Table 3.9: Knowledge of contraceptive methods (N = 1,132)

Contraceptive Methods	No	Yes
Depo-Provera	99 (8.7%)	1033 (91.3%)
Pill	149 (13.2%)	983 (86.8%)
Norplant	862 (76.1%)	270 (23.9%)
Surgery	924 (81.6%)	208 (19.4%)
Condom*	916 (80.9%)	216 (19.1%)
Other	1088 (96.1%)	44 (3.9%)

* Condoms are not generally thought of as a contraceptive method by Jean Rabeliens, but rather as a means of avoiding sexually transmitted disease

8. The figures in the table have been adjusted to account for skewing by the fact that over 50 percent of the patients listed are actually tubal ligation patients. The codes are as follows.
[a] Regions are based on clinic zones and do not coincide with commune boundaries.
[b] Population estimate based on census by missionaries responsible for the Faith Medical Clinic, Mare Rouge Medical Clinic, and Kote d'Fer Medical Clinic.
[c] Population estimate based on 1997 Baseline Survey; represents 70 percent of population in the commune of Jean Rabel.
[d] Mole St. Nicolas, Temps Perdu, Kot d'Fer, and La Montagne; only La Montagne (population of reproductive age women = 2,910) is within the commune of Jean Rabel.
There were 24 vasectomies in the region, all in Nan Sentren.

9. The average age of the women was 34.5; the average number of children ever born was 6.0; and the average number of living children was 5.15.

10' From the time of the revolution to the time of the end of U.S. military occupation, the population in Jean Rabel grew very little. Ostensibly this was because of high death rates that began declining in 1915 with the occupation of Haiti by the U.S. Marines. As seen, just prior to the wars in 1789, Moreau had recorded a population of twelve thousand in the commune; nine thousand of these people were slaves who would likely have stayed in the region after independence had been won. In 1919, a priest named Marcel Simonneau visited Jean Rabel and reported there were 20,000 people in the commune. But it is not clear where Simonneau got this estimation and I have deferred to the 1919 US Marine Corps census, which placed the population at 14,802. Simonneau did report that there were one thousand baptisms a year—something the priest should well know—which translates to a gross fertility rate of about sixty-seven births per thousand people. This is too high. It is twenty-two births higher than Hutterites and eighteen births higher than the highest crude birth rate recorded during the 1990s. Thus, perhaps Simonneau was correct in estimating a population of 20,000. Verschuren reports that in 1936 there were thirty-five thousand inhabitants and this looks like an estimation based on the 1919 figure and would fit well with a population growth of about 4 percent—derived from the gross fertility rate of fifty. But, again, it is not stated where these data came from and the census of 1950, fourteen years later—when the population should have increased by at least another 50 percent—found only 33,372 people living in the Commune—less than Veschueren estimated in 1936. The most prudent course of action seems to be to eliminate the 1936 estimate and go with the 1950 census if for no other reason than they are censuses. That is what I have done here. Nevertheless, the important point is that, whichever population estimates are used, population growth has been much higher since 1919 and it has steadily increased throughout the century.

The population growth rate estimate appears and probably is slightly too high and this could very well be caused by undercounts in early censuses. However, with the youthful population structure of current Jean Rabel—something that typically results in a low death rate—and, as will be seen in a later chapter, with a total fertility rate of more than seven children per woman and completed fertility rates of about eight children per woman, population growth rates above 3 percent are not simply possible but likely.

Chapter 4

Extremely High Fertility

Introduction

High fertility seen in the previous chapter is a spectacular demographic feat. If Jean Rabel were a country, then at the time I carried out the research for this book it would have had the second highest total fertility rate (TFR) in the world: 7.1 births per mother. The achievement is startling because in the endeavor to reproduce, Jean Rabel women face extreme adversity. High rates of infectious diseases, low-fat and low-calorie diets, high rates of female malnutrition, demanding exercise regimes, and a high rate of male absenteeism diminish the probability of pregnancies and weigh heavily against the likelihood of high birth rates. Yet, Jean Rabel fertility rates measure up impressively to that of the early 20th century Hutterites, people who had the highest sustained fertility levels ever recorded. Thirty-two percent of Jean Rabel women equal or exceed the median ten births attained by early to mid 20th century Hutterite women (Eaton and Mayer 1953; Larsen and Vaupel 1993; Nonaka et al. 1994). In this chapter I compare Jean Rabel women to their Hutterite counterparts to show how remarkable high fertility is and how efficacious are the customs that make it possible.[1]

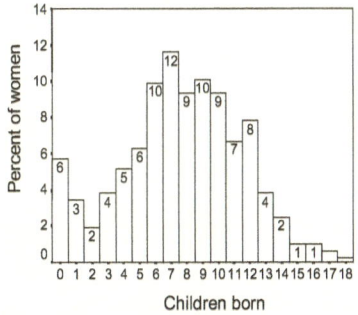

Figure 4.1: Completed fertility in Jean Rabel for
women over 45 yrs

Factors that Dampen Fertility

High incidence of diseases, widespread malnutrition, intensive physical exertion and labor regimes, and the disruption of unions through male absenteeism are all factors associated with low birth rates. All are also factors conspicuous in the lives of Jean Rabel women.

Data from the Baseline Survey indicate that 5.7 percent of Jean Rabel women never succeed in carrying a pregnancy to full term, a figure close to the median of 4.2 percent reported for all developing countries (Vaessen 1984). But clinic records for pregnant women also indicate that, at any given time, 5 to 10 percent of women in the region suffer from sexually transmitted diseases such as chlamydia, HIV/AIDS, and syphilis—maladies that interrupt and sometimes prematurely end reproductive careers. As seen, other widespread and debilitating diseases such as malaria, typhoid, and hepatitis annually leave over 30 percent of women in the region bedridden and sexually incapacitated for months and sometimes years. [2]

Malnutrition and high levels of physical exertion are also factors known to lower fertility by inducing amenorrhea—the suspension of menstrual cycles for three or more months. In the Baseline Survey, women were found to generally consume low-fat, high-carbohydrate diets (see table 4.1). And 26 percent of Jean Rabel women were found to be slightly to severely malnourished. [3]

Table 4.1: Most commonly eaten foods in Jean Rabel (N=1,483)

Foods	Every day	2 to 3 times weekly	Total
Cooking oil	90.2	7.9	98.1
Bread	63.9	32.9	96.8
Beans/peas	47.6	49.1	96.7
Citrus	33.6	50.6	84.2
Rice	26.4	71.3	97.7
Corn	20.5	76.2	96.7
Plantain/banana	15.2	75.0	90.2
Mango, papaya, avocado	15.0	66.4	81.4
Meat	9.6	82.3	91.9
Greens	6.1	73.7	79.8
Dairy (milk and eggs)	5.3	76.5	81.8
Pasta	4.7	77.8	82.5
Millet	4.6	72.2	76.8
Manioc and sweet potato	2.6	69.0	71.6

The average Jean Rabel woman also leads a physically demanding life. Fetching household water requires daily walks to water sources often located more than one half hour from the household. The return trip involves carrying a filled five-gallon bucket balanced on top of the head. Women also walk an average of six hours per week to make market purchases and sales for the household.

Figure 4.2: Completed fertility in Jean Rabel

for five-year age groups

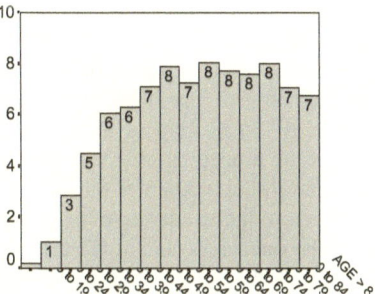

An average of six hours per week is also spent picking produce from the gardens, and another twelve to twenty-four hours are spent walking back and forth from the nearest water source to hand scrub clothes. This total exercise regime certainly matches or exceeds the five miles of jogging per week that induced amenorrhea in 6 percent of the U.S. subjects studied by Feight et al. (1978) and is probably closer to the weekly physical exertion of women in the same study who ran forty-five miles per week inducing amenorrhea in 43 percent of the cases. Extended breastfeeding, necessary in the absence of high-protein baby formulas, is also known to suppress ovulation (WHO 1999); and 63 percent of women in the Jean Rabel Baseline Survey reported breast feeding their last child for eighteen to twenty-seven months (see figure 4.3).[4]

Figure 4.3: Duration of breastfeeding

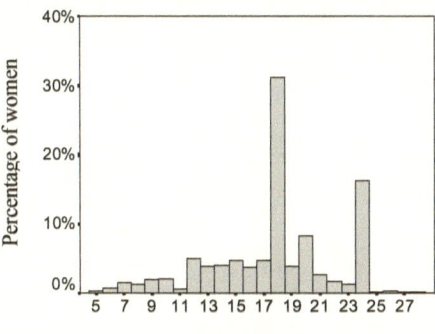

Months breastfeeding

Another factor researchers have identified as a determinant of low fertility is reduced exposure to the risk of pregnancy through late entry into union or disrupted union through factors such as wage migration (Bongaarts and Potter 1983; Williams et al. 1975; Blake 1954). Male absenteeism is part of the rural Haitian demographic profile. Males in Haiti migrate to larger Haitian cities and overseas to the Bahamas, the United States, and the Dominican Republic at a significantly higher rate than their female counterparts. The result is lower male-to-female sex ratios. In the Baseline Survey, 10 percent of Jean Rabel men in the twenty- to forty-nine-year-old age groups were reported as being absent and no longer considered as members of the household from which they originated. Furthermore, in the Opinion Survey, 26 percent of men in union reported having been away from home for at least 30 of the preceding 365 days (see table 4.3). Congruent with male transience, 52 percent of Jean Rabel women in the twenty- to twenty-four-year-old age group and 26 percent of women in the twenty-five to twenty-nine-year-old age group were not in union at the time of the interview, and at least 26 percent of women abandon or are abandoned by their first spouse during the course of their reproductive careers (see table 4.4).

In a society with strongly enforced values regarding monogamy and premarital pregnancy, the type of male absenteeism and transience being described would disrupt ongoing conjugal union and force a minority of women to remain out of union and childless. Yet, according to respondents in the Opinion Survey, the average age at first union for Jean Rabel women is 21.7 years and the average age at first childbirth is 22.3 years. These averages for Jean Rabel women are not unusually high or low. For example, the average age women in the remote rural Dominican Republic first enter into unions and give birth is significantly lower than the averages cited for Jean Rabel (McPherson and Schwartz 2001). Nevertheless, entry into union at moderate age and the high birth rates are accomplished despite high rates of male absenteeism.

Table 4.2: Mean age of follow-up survey respondents

	Male	Female	Male/Female
Mean age at	26.0	21.7	23.7
marriage/*plasage*	(n=60)	(n=67)	(n=127)
Mean age at birth of	24.1	22.3	23.2
1st child	(n=63)	(n=66)	(n=129)

Table 4.3: Temporary male migration in Jean Rabel

		Number	Percentage
Men who report having worked	Yes	17	26%
in the city or overseas for at	No	49	74%
least 30 of the past 365 days	Total	66	100%

Table 4.4: Individuals still with first spouse

		Gender		
		Men (n = 68)	Women (n = 68)	N
Individuals	No	15%	26%	28
still with first	Yes	85%	74%	108
spouse	Total	100%	100%	136

As will be seen in the following two chapters, Jean Rabel society has adapted to male migration with an array of customs, beliefs, and behaviors that, with respect to fertility, allow women to overcome the problem of male absenteeism.

Jean Rabel Women vs. Hutterite Women

Despite all the preceding factors that work against high fertility, Jean Rabel women measure up impressively against the Hutterites of North Dakota and Canada, the healthy, well-fed, and fecund world champions of high fertility. Jean Rabel women on average eat two and sometimes only one cooked meal per day and meals rarely include meat or dairy foods (see table 4.1). Hutterite women eat three meals per day, every day, and meat, dairy products, or sometimes both are included in virtually every meal (Hostetler 1974: 353). Further, while Jean Rabel women are members of what is among the most disease-ridden populations in the Western hemisphere and at any given time upwards of 5 percent of Jean Rabel women are suffering from an STD—to say nothing of other infectious diseases—the incidence of infectious diseases among Hutterites is even lower than their healthy Canadian neighbors, something that Ross and Cheang (1997) attribute to a genetically superior immune system. When Eaton and Mayer (1953) surveyed the Hutterites during the 1940s they found virtually no deprivation or interruption of Hutterite unions resulting from imbalanced sex ratios, wage-migration, or divorce. There were 106 men for every 100 women in the twenty- to forty-nine-year-old age range. Only 33 percent of Hutterite women in the twenty- to twenty-four-year-old range were not in union; and only 7 percent of those in the twenty-five- to thirty-year-old age group were not in union. In comparison, 52 percent and 26 percent of Jean Rabel women in the same age groups were not in union (see table 4.5, following page). Eaton and Mayer (1953) noted that:

> Hutterite couples are never separated after marriage. In the history of the group since 1875 there has been only one divorce and only 4 desertions. We know of one other case where husband and wife separated temporarily to live in different colonies. (p. 223)

Thus, while reproductive-age Jean Rabel women are faced with a 10 percent deficit of men, Hutterite women are outnumbered by men. And, as might be expected, there was an average of 13 percent more reproductive-age Hutterite women in union than there are in contemporary Jean Rabel.[5, 6]

     But despite all of the limiting factors, including the absence of many Jean Rabel men and the physiological factors mitigating against high fertility, 32 percent of contemporary Jean Rabel women who have completed their childbearing careers equal or exceed the median ten children born per Hutterite woman in the years 1880 to 1950. Contemporary Jean Rabel fertility levels are 13 percent higher than contemporary Hutterites (Eaton and Mayer 1953; Larsen and Vaupel 1993; Nonaka et al. 1994).[7]

Table 4.5: Hutterites vs. Jean Rabeliens: Percentage of women in union per five-year age group and sex ratios (includes widows)

	Jean Rabel				Hutterites			
Ages	Women in union	Age-specific fertility[a]	Femal pop. (n)	Sex ratio (m/f)	Women in union[b]	Age-specific fertility[c]	Female pop[d]	Sex ratio[e] (m/f)
15–19	12%	.02	387	0.96	6%	.06	198	.91
20–24	48%	1.01	378	0.91	67%	1.16	176	.98
25–29	76%	1.83	285	0.89	93%	1.92	129	.98
30–34	85%	1.65	216	0.85	99%	1.95	98	1.00
35–39	90%	1.56	214	0.92	99%	1.73	85	.89
40–44	89%	.24	170	0.93	97%	1.04	68	1.4
45–49	87%	.80	144	0.93	100%	.21	42	1.13
50 +	81%	—	532	1.10	—	—	—	1.08
Total	—	7.11	2,326	0.96	—	8.07	796	1.00

a=mean children born for all five years, b=1940, c = 1946 thru 1950, d = 1940, e = 1950
Source: Hutterite data from Eaton and Mayer 1953

Conclusion

Fertility in Jean Rabel is extremely high despite nutritional, epidemiological, and social factors that work against it. In the following chapter I want to show that this extremely high fertility is not the inadvertent consequence of people helplessly procreating while lamenting the burden of more children. On the contrary, this high fertility in the face of adverse conditions is made possible by a specific array of interrelated beliefs, customs, and behaviors that promote childbirth.

Notes

1. Jean Rabel's TFR of 7.1 is 48 percent higher than Haiti's overall country TFR of 4.8 children and 20 percent higher than the rural Haitian TFR of 5.9 children per woman (EMMUS 1994/95). The Hutterites had a sustained overall TFR of 8.0 to 8.5—the commonly cited Hutterite fertility rates are median completed fertility and the TFR of married women, one of which is discussed in the text. The highest birth rate in the UN data base, year 2000—date of the Jean Rabel Baseline Survey--was Niger at 7.25 births per mother (see the UN web site).

2. Infecundity is deduced from the number of women who have completed their childbearing years without bearing children (age > 45) (see Vaessen 1984). There was no relevant clinic data available in Jean Rabel. The records that have been kept at the hospital are sporadic and unreliable. More often than not, nurses failed to record the results for STD tests. The observation is generalized from data collected at the Bombardopolis clinic, which is in the Far-West but outside the commune of Jean Rabel, and there is little reason to believe there is a difference between the communes. Other epidemiological data are similar.

3. The determination of malnutrition was based on a brachial measure of less than 18.5 centimeters. The size of the sample was 770 women.

4. There might be a way around suppression of ovulation through breastfeeding. The suppression of ovulation is apparently a reflex response to suckling. According to a research review by Larsen and Vaupel (1993), a woman must nurse her infant at least four times a day for a minimum of twenty minutes each time. By conscious design or simply custom, Hutterite women only allow their babies to nurse for ten minutes or less. Further, supplementary foods are introduced early and by six to seven weeks the infant is fed before it is given the breast. Interestingly, while it is not known how long Jean Rabel women allow infants to nurse, they too introduce foods extremely early, often within days of birth, a practice that healthcare workers have ardently and with little success tried to overcome.

5.. Eaton and Mayer (1953) only found evidence of ten illegitimate births in the Hutterite population between 1875 and 1950, indicating that few births occur before marriage. The age-specific birth rate in 1950 for women twenty to twenty-four was 1.4 births.

6. Hutterite women during the period 1880 to 1950—when their fertility was highest—entered union at 22 years, only .3 years later than among Jean Rabel women, and bore their first child a mean thirteen months later, at 23.1 years of age—about ten months later than Jean Rabel women.

7. Jean Rabel women between the ages of fifteen and forty-five years old have an overall average birth interval of 50.5 months—one child every 4.2 years. But in a sample of eighty-nine women who have already begun childbearing, the average interbirth interval was thirty-two months—one child every 2.7 years.

The latter data on interval birth intervals was obtained from a Nan Sentren clinic run by missionary Carol Anne Truelove. The clinic has records on female birth histories dating back to 1984 when the clinic was first opened. The clinic serves a population of approximately sixty thousand, half within the commune of Jean Rabel and half outside of the commune boundaries (the population estimate is based on a census by clinic staff carried out in 1991; the extrapolation was based on 3 percent estimated population growth). Records were chosen based on the presence of information for the first and last child born to the mother—some women had begun their childbearing career elsewhere or had left the region. There were thirty-two women who had used contraceptives, with an average interbirth interval of 37.1 months and a standard error of the mean of 2.3 months (95% CI = 32.5 – 41.6 months). There were fifty-seven records for women who had never used contraceptives, with an average interbirth interval of 29.6 months and a standard error of the mean of 1.3 months (95% CI = 28.3 – 30.9 months).

Chapter 5

The Pronatal Sociocultural Fertility Complex

Introduction

The extremely high fertility seen in the previous chapters is made possible by what I call rural Haiti's pronatal sociocultural fertility complex, an array of social behaviors that allow Jean Rabel women to overcome high disease, poor nutrition, and scarcity of financially eligible reproductive-age males. Jean Rabeliens want children for themselves, for family, for friends, and for neighbors. The merits of having numerous children are a commonly discussed topic, even with strangers. The farmers generally regard childless people with suspicion and derision. Contraceptives are thought to make women sick, even to cause death, and women who use them, particularly young women, are thought of as immoral. Abortion is abhorred as a grievous crime and a sin, and women revealed to have had an abortion are publicly humiliated, their families are fined, and they may face imprisonment. In contrast, pregnant and postpartum women are relieved of heavy work, fed unusually large amounts of choice foods, cared for and waited on by family and friends, and massaged daily by a paid attendant. Overall, this pronatal complex of behaviors articulates with a series of sexual beliefs and behaviors seen in the following chapter to function as a catalyst of high fertility despite malnutrition, intensive work regimes, and disease.

Pronatal Attitudes, Customs, Beliefs, and Behaviors

For a Jean Rabelien not to have children is tragic. Childless people, especially women, are pitied, even criticized as *millet* (mules), and sometimes suspected of being *lougawou* (witches) or having sold their unborn children to demons (*li te manje yo*).[1]

With parenthood comes adulthood and respect. As one man once remarked to me; "it is children that bring you respect" (*se ti moun k-ap fe moun respekte ou*). Another man explained, "a woman needs children or her husband will not respect her" (*yon fi bezwenn ti moun paskè san ti moun gason ki rete ave-li l-ap manke respè*). People who have not yet borne children are considered children themselves, no matter what their age. Not to have children at all is a far greater shame than having children outside of a union or with someone who is considered disreputable.

Not only do Jean Rabeliens want children, but they want everyone else to have children as well. The first question a rural Jean Rabelien asks a stranger is, "how many children do you have?" (*kombyen pitit ou genyen?*). Responses to childlessness almost invariably go as follows: "why don't you have children?" (*pou ki sa ou pa gen pitit?*); "you are supposed to make children" (*ou sipoze fe pitit*); "you are supposed to make lots of children" (*ou sipoze fe anpil pitit*); "you are supposed to make children when you are young" (*ou sipoze fe pitit jen*); "children are a good thing" (*ti moun se yon bon bagay*); "children can help you" (*ti moun ka ede ou*).

Most women are eager to bear children. Childless women in their early twenties who are not in school will lament their barrenness, "I need to have a child" (*m bezwenn fe yon timoun*), and their age "I am beginning to get too ripe" (*m presk mi*). A woman who cannot get pregnant visits leaf doctors and clinics. She might make costly pilgrimages to distant sacred sites to ask for help from the Virgin Mary or a Catholic saint.[2] In a commonly occurring phenomenon known as *perdisyon*, discussed in greater detail in the following chapter, the woman may blame *kolegs* (co-wives) and other jealous rivals for magically tying her fetus up, in vitro, arresting the pregnancy. To overcome the affliction she goes to the spiritual healer (*bokor*) to ask for help, she visits the local mid-wife (*matwon*) who tapes her stomach to hold the imaginary fetus in place, and she goes to massage specialists who arrange (*ranje*) the imaginary fetus in a position to grow.

Attitudes toward Contraceptives

Jean Rabeliens are suspicious of contraceptives. Many believe that using them is immoral and that they may bring on disease. Even women professing to want to use contraceptives insist they don't because of the risk of illness. As one woman told the author, "it is contraceptives themselves that kill people" (*se plannin menm kap touye moun*). Many of those Jean Rabeliens who believe HIV/AIDS really exists attribute the disease to sorcery, while others are convinced it is a fiction contrived by foreign governments wanting to trick Haitians into using condoms, thereby averting pregnancies and limiting the population of black people on the planet. Due to their association with disease, condoms are thought of as something dirty and demeaning. Contraceptives are also commonly associated with loose women (*bouzen*) and infidelity. A Jean Rabel man once explained to me that contraceptives are useful only "when a women has a husband, he's not there. . . . She takes something so she won't get pregnant" (*Tankou lè yon fi gen yon mari ki pa la. Li vle al fe bouzen. L-ap pran yon gren pou li pa fe pitit*).[3]

Abortion

Despite the overwhelmingly pronatal attitudes, there are still some young Jean Rabel women who are reluctant to begin their reproductive careers. In May 1997, a fifteen-year-old girl in the village of Jean Rabel tried to abort an unwanted pregnancy by popping fourteen antimalarial pills (chloroquin) into her mouth and washing them down with raw rum (*kleren*). An hour later, while waiting at the village spring, in the midst of a crowd of other children sent to fill water buckets for their households, she fell dead.

There are other girls who steadfastly disavow that they are pregnant right up until the time their bulging stomachs make denial impossible. In an incident that took place in the summer of 1997, I carried a convulsing sixteen-year-old rural girl to the Jean Rabel hospital. Unbeknownst to everyone, including her siblings and parents, the teenager was eight months pregnant, a condition she had concealed by tying torn strips of cloth around her stomach. The French doctor who treated the young woman told me that the stomach tying had almost killed her. She spent the entire following month being cared for in the hospital until giving birth to a healthy baby boy.

But while some young women try to avoid first pregnancies, most succumb to social pressures that bear on young women reluctant to begin childbearing. A twenty-five-year-old woman explained to me, "my mother said that if she caught us taking birth control pills she would club us to death" (*mama-m di si li jwenn nou pran gren li tap tiye nou anba baton*). Social pressures against abortion are even stronger. Mothers, grandmothers, sisters, and female friends are quick to condemn abortion and older female confidants counsel young girls against abortion by explaining that it will rot their vaginal canals, making them disgusting to men, and that they will burn in hell for having committed the "greatest of all sins" (*pi gwo pech*). Men, too, have something to say about abortion. In an Opinion Survey subsample, forty men were asked what they would do if their wife had an abortion, and 62.5 percent responded that they would abandon their wife and another 25 percent said they would have her arrested. Only one man said he would do nothing. Of responses falling into the category of "other," one man said "I would sit down and talk to that woman to see what the hell was wrong with her." The three remaining men responding "Other" said they would kill their wives with sorcery.[4]

By law, women are supposed to be imprisoned for aborting pregnancies. In reality, imprisonment is rare. But women are, nevertheless, ridiculed and publicly disgraced. In an instance witnessed by a U.S. missionary working in the Jean Rabel area, a fifteen-year-old girl who had allegedly aborted a fetus was tied to a post in a busy market while a civil servant spent his day standing nearby announcing her crime over a handheld loudspeaker. In the spring of 1998, in the thatch-roofed, seaside hamlet of Makab, where my research began, fishermen found a fetus floating in the sea. The news spread quickly and literally hundreds of people descended from the hills into the tiny village. The police were summoned. Houses were searched, and eventually the still-bleeding sixteen-year-old mother was discovered hiding under a sheet in the corner of a friend's house. As the police led the humiliated girl away, the crowd chanted her name, "Viki! Viki! Viki!" [5]

Pregnancy

The typical Jean Rabel woman does not understand the female menstrual cycle in a way that would permit her to avoid pregnancy. Many young women are taught by their mothers or other female elders that pregnancy occurs most readily during or just after menstruation, and many young women believe they cannot become pregnant as the result of a single sexual encounter. But older women in rural Jean Rabel understand very well that missed menstrual cycles may mean pregnancy, and they carefully track the dates of their and their daughter's menstrual cycle so they can act swiftly to defend against sorcery that may arrest development of the fetus and so they can begin to care for and nourish the gestating fetus.

When a woman knows that she is pregnant, she takes up the habit of spitting, supposedly to spare the fetus the ill effects of bile but something that also informs others of her special condition. Family and friends relieve her of heavy work and attend to her needs. If she is a young woman, she is encouraged not to travel, mount pack animals, or ride on the back of motorcycles. She is encouraged to eat nutritious and fatty foods and she should never be refused a food of her choosing. The stingy individual who refuses food to a pregnant woman is menaced with the belief that a boil will erupt on his/her eye.[6]

The new mother remains confined in the house for five days, during which time female family members and often a paid midwife attend to her. She is given hot ginger tea twice a day, once in the morning and once at night. Each morning she is bathed with warm water. Each afternoon she is given a sweat bath, for which she sits on a steaming pot of water with a sheet draped over her head. Instead of the usual two meals a day and rare portion of meat, she is fed three meals a day, all including the luxury of meat, especially goat and chicken slaughtered specifically to feed her. [7] After five days, the mother may leave the house, but for the first two months she must not engage in heavy work, not leave the homestead, never go out at night for fear the cold (*fredi*) will make her sick, bathe only with warm water, and not speak loudly or do heavy work.[8]

Conclusion

High fertility in Jean Rabel is indisputably bound with the beliefs seen above. The association of pregnancy and childbirth with duty; the concern with conception and the care and rewarding attentiveness toward pregnant women; the abhorrence of contraceptives and abortion; the misinforming of young women concerning the mechanics of pregnancy; and the censuring of childless individuals all act to promote conception among Jean Rabel women. In addition to these blatantly pronatal attitudes, high fertility is further reinforced through local customs and belief systems that remove social, legal, and moral barriers to pregnancy, values associated with what I want to call the sexual moral economy, the subject of the next chapter.

Notes

1. Several women in the survey illustrated this point, one woman for example saying, "If you don't have children, there is a name they call you, they curse you *mule*." (*Si ou pa gen ti moun, gen yon non yo konn di ou, y-ap joure ou millet si ou pat fe ti moun*).

Witch is here meant in the anthropological sense of being the incarnation of antisociety and it is a very widespread if not pancultural ideological phenomenon. Mischief caused by witches is usually peculiar to the society. A witch is conceptualized as a threat where the society is most vulnerable. Thus, pastoralists often believe witches suck the milk and blood from their animals at night. Agriculturists often conceptualize witches as destroyers of crops. Haitians fear witches as the eaters of children—usually manifest in the form of disease but also as the causal agent in accidents. The supposed behavior of the Haitian witch, the *lougawou,* is testimony to a strong pronatalist tendency in Haiti and a dependency on children.

2. There are a series of sacred sites throughout Haiti. Some of these sites are associated with voudou deities and some with the sighting of the Virgin Mary or the presence of a saint. There is a sacred rock in Mare Rouge, just on the outskirts of the commune of Jean Rabel. The rock is called Marie Noel and people leave written prayers in the crevices of the rock. The next nearest sacred site to Jean Rabel is Anse-a-Fleur, where people visit once a year for an annual voudou festival. If my understanding is accurate—and in this instance there is a good chance it is not—several years ago a doll was found and elevated to the status of a manifestation of Saint Anne. The doll is kept in a shrine in the yard of a *mambo* (female spirtual practitioner).

3. Even many well-educated rural Haitians believe that AIDS is caused by sorcery—as when one person goes to a *bokor* ("witch doctor") to kill another person—and that venereal diseases are caused by jealous spouses who *ranje* (magically fix) their partners so that other lovers will fall ill.

4. *M ta chita pale a fi sa pou we sa li genyen.*

5. "Viki" had until only days before the incident been away to school in the village. "Abortion" is, according to the only civil judge in Jean Rabel during 1999, the worst crime known (*Sa se pi gwo krim ki ka genyen*). It is considered voluntary homicide. A woman can be given life in prison as can anyone who participated in the abortion. In practice, it is not always if ever like this. Police and judges do tend to arrest everyone who might be involved in an abortion and there is usually a grand interrogation. But fines rather than prison tend to be the rule. Although humiliated, neither of the girls whose abortion stories were told in the body of the text spent time in jail. In the village and in the department seat Port-de-Paix, abortion services are reportedly available for H\$50.00 and by western-trained medical doctors. During a chance encounter in the city, a judge of a neighboring Jean Rabel commune once told me he was in town to help a fifteen-year-old girl he had impregnated locate a doctor to abort the fetus. Further, in rural areas there are leaf doctors known to specialize in abortificants. Nevertheless, there is a definitive ideological horror associated with abortion and a very public disapproval of it, particularly among the truly rural people of the region.

A couple of ethnographic examples to note: In the early summer of 1997, in the incident where a fourteen-year-old girl in the village died after trying to abort a fetus with a dose of fourteen chloroquins washed down with rum, the police commissioner ordered the arrest of the twenty-two-year-old man who had prescribed the medicines, but he was subsequently released. Between 1996 and 1998, at least two girls in nearby Mole St. Nicolas were caught aborting viable fetuses—one of which lived to be adopted by a UN medic in the area with a project to repair the local high school. Neither of the girls served time in prison.

Mention should also be made of *la djablesse*, the Haitian boogeywoman. All over Haiti *la djablesse* are believed to live alone in caves. They are giant female, human-like creatures, with breasts sagging to the ankles, extremely long hair, moss and weeds hanging off their bodies. *La djablesse*s are associated with fertility. A *la djablesse* is thought to hunt men and if she gets hold of one, she leads the man back to her cave, where she forces the man to impregnate her. The sexual appetite of a *la djablesse* is thought to be insatiable. Simpson (1942) explained that in Plaisance in the north of Haiti, *la djablesse*s were thought to be young girls who died before having sex and were caught in the netherworld of spirits. Simpson reported that because of the fear that a deceased virgin could become a *la djablesse*, cadavers of young girls were deflowered with a stick before burial. Their were no reports of this practice in Jean Rabel and local farmers explained *la djablesse* as a human-like animal rather than a spirit.

6. See Harris and Ross (1987; 5, 164–67) for a cross-cultural discussion of nutritional deprivation of pregnant mothers.

7. Plantains are also an important element in the postpartum mother's diet. She may eat red and black beans but white beans and rice are considered dangerous as they are cold (*fret*) foods that can make the woman ill. A partial list of other dangerous versus not dangerous foods follows:

Healthy	**Dangerous**
Corn	Sweet potato
Taro	White beans
Banana	
Flour	
Corn	
Goat	
Chicken	

8. During confinement, only those people who were present during the actual birth may enter the house. All is applicable even if the baby dies. If the child is a boy, restrictions may apply for as long as three months and if the baby is a girl, restrictions may be lifted as early as 2 months. Boys are thought of as harder to bear and thus it takes longer to get over the birth.

Chapter 6

The Sexual Moral Economy

Introduction

The attitudes, customs, beliefs, and behaviors seen in the previous chapter are complemented by a specific econo-sexual patterns of behavior found throughout rural Haiti. Rural Haitian women assiduously negotiate sexual acquiescence to men and they do so with the goal of material gain. Ira Lowenthal (1984: 22) first described this behavior in detail when he reported that women in his research community referred to their genitals as *intere-m* (my assets), *lajan-m* (my money), or *manmanlajan-m* (my capital), in addition to *tè-m* (my land); a common proverb was, *chak famn fet ak yon kawo te—nan mitan janm ni* (every women is born with a parcel of land—between her legs). Lowenthal (1984) described this type of female commoditization of sexuality as a "field of competition" wherein women are at a socially constructed advantage: men are conceived of and taught to think they need sexual interaction with women, while women portray themselves and are taught to think of themselves as able to get along without sex and thus are able to exact material rewards for sexual contact with men. Called "gendered capital" by Richman (2003: 123), these sexual-material values are universal in rural Haiti and apply whether the woman in question is dealing with a husband, lover, or more casual relationship.

Jean Rabel is no different, and in later chapters I show that the commoditization of womanhood being described is linked to a sexual division of labor and rights and duties associated with control of the household, children, extra-household income, and female marketing activities; but here I simply want to describe "gendered capital," or what may alternatively be described as rural Haiti's sexual-moral economy, and show how it combines with the pronatal sociocultural fertility complex seen in the previous chapter to make extremely high fertility possible despite conditions aversive to conception. In accomplishing this I will illustrate my points with songs that rural adolescent girls in Jean Rabel compose, sing, and act out in theatrical performances called *téat*. Reminiscent of Jorge Duany (1984: 186), who stated that the traditional song "cannot fail to create and recreate the most important social values of the group that produced it," and John Szwed (1970: 220), who wrote that "song forms and performances are themselves models of social behavior that reflect strategies of adaptation to human and natural environments," the songs I present below highlight the uniform sexual-material-domestic value system found throughout rural Haiti.

Girls' Téat Songs

Girls' Theater

When school is out for the summer, girls in rural Jean Rabel neighborhoods form dance troupes called *téat* (theater). The troupes are formed by the girls themselves. There is no adult sponsorship or leadership. The girls are all prenuptial, have not yet borne children, and are generally aged ten to twenty years. Older girls appoint themselves troupe directors and instruct the younger girls in daily practices. The girls dress in short skirts and sing while performing the latest erotic dances such as the *buterfli* (butterfly), a dance in which the girls gyrate, opening their legs wide and rocking their abdomens out toward the impromptu audience as they descend lower and lower toward the ground. The songs are improvised from bits of other songs and spiced with the girls' own creative additions. The most popular songs are imbued with sexual connotations, such as the following, in which the girls celebrate their own budding sexuality with respect to the sexual bravado of men:

Look here, it is mango season	*Vwasi lè mango,*
Look here, the mangos are sweet and beautiful	*Vwasi lè mango, yo dous e yo koket*
	Bon swa madamwazel mwen di ou bon swa
Good day young lady, I say to you good day	*Se yon banan ki vini pou-l sikre*
It is a plantain that has come to make things sweet	*Se pepsi kola m bwe, se koka kola m bwe*
	Se pepsi kola m bwe, se koka kola m bwe
It's Pepsi Cola I drink. It is Coca Cola I drink	
It's Pepsi Cola I drink. It is Coca Cola I drink	

As can be seen, the song relies heavily on metaphors. In this particular song, informants explained that mangos, ubiquitous in Haiti and the all-time favorite fruit, symbolize the girls' budding young breasts. The eroticism of fruit and particularly a mango with its soft juicy flesh is clear to native speakers, the declaration that "it is mango season," means that it is time to eat mangos, the fruit is ripe, or rather, the girl has come of age and she is ready to engage in sexual relations. The "good day young lady" is an introduction to the young woman. The next line reveals the speaker, a man, represented as another fruit, a plantain, which has come to add sugar (*sikre*). The plantain also happens to be the most phallic shaped fruit in Haiti leaving little doubt for analysis (any remaining doubts are erased by snickering Haitian informants). The references to Pepsi and Coca Cola are metaphors for prestige. In Jean Rabel these are, aside from beer, the most expensive locally available beverages and they have correspondingly high prestige value, representing the speaker as a high roller.

Thus, the songs I use below to illustrate the sexual moral economy all touch on the theme of sex. The songs also, as will be seen, highlight female ideals and aspirations, gender relations, control over resources, parent-daughter relationships, and most importantly of all, the rules, expectations, and norms associated with male-female sexual interaction, all of which, I argue, are interrelated in what might be called a type of sexual-moral economy. The analysis, conducted with the assistance of local informants who helped explain the double and sometimes triple meaning of the words to the songs, begins with a look at a socially constructed problem that Jean Rabel women have and the representation of that problem in *téat* songs.

Male Sexual Aggressiveness

A common expression used by women in Jean Rabel is "men are dogs" (*gason se chyen*); "men cannot get by without having sex" (*gason pa ka rete san fi*). No strong prohibitions exist in Jean Rabel against men seducing young women, and Haitian laws that prohibit sex with girls under fifteen are not enforced. Men in their fifties, sixties, and even men in their seventies are referred to with regard to their sexuality as *jenn gason* (young men), and powerful men may have four or five and even six common-law wives, a source of pride and esteem. Thus, young women are badgered and cajoled by a relatively large pool of socially eligible, sexually active, and highly aggressive men. The most common seduction tactic is for a man to catch a woman on a footpath or while she is alone in the kitchen. He will seize her arm so she cannot get away, playfully trying to pull her near, proclaiming his desire for her and pleading for her sexual affection while whispering promises of money and gifts.

As counterintuitive as it might first seem, females arguably play an influential role in encouraging aggressive male sexual conduct. They take part in propagating the myth that a celibate man can go insane, become ill, and may die. They tease timid boys and ridicule celibate men, taunting them with names like *jay-jay* (retarded) and *masisi* (homosexual); and they goad younger brothers and even sons into pursuing nubile young women with comments that sound to the Westerner like admonitions to rape: "you must bother them, don't let them get away, grab them" (*fo ou jennen yo, pa kite yo ale, fo ou kenbe yo*). The influence of women in conditioning male attitudes begins at an early age, as exemplified by the fondling of the genitals of male infants, toddlers, and boys up to the ages of nine and ten years, something so thoroughly engrained and accepted as to appear to the foreigner to be below the level of awareness. The fondling is made easy by the custom of making prepubescent boys go without pants. Examples of the context in which it occurs include the following: a rural woman nervous about being interviewed distracts herself by fondling a four-year-old's penis all the while she is answering my questions; a nineteen-year-old woman sitting on a bed in a dimly lit hut talking to me reaches beside her and, without ever looking at what she is doing, begins fondling the penis of a naked eight-year-old boy, doing this as nonchalantly as if she had just picked up a pen or any other stray object off the table; a twenty-two-year-old woman excited to see her two-year-old nephew tickles his penis, lifts the boy, swings his body up to her face, and pops his penis playfully into her mouth. The toddlers and young boys are not indifferent to the treatment and react with enthusiasm, smile, and laugh when given the attention and often follow their significant female others around. The song below playfully alludes to, or is at least suggestive of, the active role that Jean Rabel females play in determining male sexual identity and the coy preservation, or at least guarded access, to their own sexuality,

I went to Port-de-Paix	*M ale Pò-de-Pe*
I went to buy a little wooden club	*M-al achte yon ti baton*
Little club, if it falls I will make it rise again	*Ti baton si-l tonbe m-a leve-l*
Two feet tied, two arms crossed	*Dè pye mare, dè bra-m kwaze*
I have a place	*Mwen g'on kote*
I have a place on my body that boys don't know	*Mwen g'on kote nan ko-m ti gason pa konnen*
Where is it?	*Ki kote li ye?*
Below my mound	*Anba ti vant mwen*
Below my mound	*Anba ti vant mwen*

The reference to "a little wooden club" is an obvious phallic symbol (clubs are not something that everyone in Jean Rabel is walking around with and while old infirm people might use a cane, purchasing one is nonsensical). The line "if the club falls" signifies the loss of an erection and this image is reinforced by the next line, which in Kreyol uses the verb *leve* (rise) and *anko* (again)—"I will make it rise again"—rather than *ranmase*, the Kreyol word for "pick up"—"I will pick up the club." The next line, "Two feet tied, two arms crossed," suggests restraint or prohibited access to the woman's sexuality. The remaining lines, "I have a place boys don't know . . . below my mound" are a proclamation of virginity and chastity: "below my mound" is translated from "*anba ti vant mwen,*" it literally means "below my little stomach." In effect, the girl may choose, "buy," a penis to fondle, making it rise again and again, but her own genitals have never been "known" by boys.

Chastity and the Commercialization of Female Sexuality

Although women encourage men to be sexually aggressive and inculcate boys in the association between females and sexual stimulation, they do not present themselves as so willing to comply with the amorous wishes of men. The socially constructed attitudes of Jean Rabel women are contrary to that of men. While admitting that they desire sex, women define themselves as not needing it. Despite the "hot" tone of the songs, they always include restraint, as in the previous song, "two feet tied, two arms crossed . . . I have a place that boys don't know." All Jean Rabeliens know and commonly say "girls do not flirt with boys" (*fi pa konn koze a gason*), it is the boy's job to flirt. A sexually aggressive woman or one who engages in sex for pleasure is criticized, as in "she is such slut" (*tann li bouzen*), or insultingly called "nymphomaniac" (*piten*). A young woman who has not had children and is not in union will always insist she is a virgin, no matter what her personal sexual history might be; and as a matter of identity and pride most Jean Rabel women insist, often and quite publicly when the subject arises, that they can live without sex. They describe themselves as *sipòtan* (able to tolerate abstinence). They maintain an attitude of sexual indifference, describing excessive sexual intercourse as painful, a burdensome service they provide to men, and while admitting that sex can be fun, and even exalt its pleasures, they consider over-manifestations of their own biological interest in sex to be a fault, something evident in attitudes toward vaginal secretions during sex. Commonly thought in Western society as a biological sign of sexual arousal, Jean Rabel women who become more than slightly wet are called *bonbon dlo* (watery vagina), considered disgusting; and women make efforts to dry themselves if the condition manifests itself during sex, even if the sex is with their husbands.

As seen with the studies mentioned from elsewhere in rural Haiti (Lowenthal 1987; Richman 2003), the defining feature of female attitudes toward sexual relations in Jean Rabel is that they view their sexuality as an economic asset. They say that they are born with a *kawo* of irrigated land between their legs (the most valuable asset in rural Haiti) and they refer to their genitalia in exchange terms, *byen-pa-m* (assets/goods), excusing each other for engaging in an affair outside of conjugal union so long as the man reciprocates with material rewards: "She is a woman isn't she? It's her right"; "Getting by is not a sin" (*degaje se pa pech*). Men are acutely aware of the rules, and they commonly say "in order to have a woman you must have money" (*pou gen fi, fo gen lajan*) and "women eat/devour men," meaning they take all a man's wealth (*fi konn manje gason*). A woman's right to exchange sex for financial reward is exalted in the following song, which according to informants is actually a metaphor for sex and a demand for payment.

I need a couple dollars	*Mwen bezwen dè dola*
Why do I need couple dollars?	*Sa pou-m fe dè dola?*
To buy a ribbon, to tie around my waist,	*Pou achte yon ribon pou fe lamayet mache*
to make my hips shake/the dance work	*Lage li nan riyèl la, dè dola*
Just throw it in my alley, two dollars	*Lage li nan riyèl la, dè dola,*
Just throw it in my alley, two dollars	*Lage li nan riyèl la, dè dola*
Just throw it in my alley, two dollars	

This song humorously summarizes the attitudes with which Jean Rabel women imbue their sexuality. As with the other songs, it is a play on words, but words already very sexual. The Kreyol term *lamayet* designates a sexy dance movement, and informants explained that it is combined with the word *mache* (to function, operate, work) to form the implied verb "to hump"—make the dance (*lamayet*) function, or less suggestively, to enable the girl to better shake her hips. *Lage* literally means "to let go" and a Haitian male "come on" is *lage-m nan reyal la*, which means "let me loose in your alley." But in terms of money, a very common colloquialism is *lage sink goud nan min mwen* (let a dollar go in my hand). Thus, *lage li nan riyèl la* is a play on these two expressions and to state it literally it means "just throw the money in my vaginal canal." So the song is a rather ingenious circular play on words that reduced means "I need two dollars. Why? Because if you want me to perform sex that is what it costs to get my hips going. So just throw the two dollars right in my vagina." The Jean Rabeliens who reviewed these songs with me could hear this particular song several times in succession and would laugh hysterically every time.

Conjugal Union and Sex and Infidelity

With the guarded notion that sex begets children, it is considered to be a Jean Rabel woman's God-given right to use her sexuality to acquire material support. If a man wants to claim exclusive sexual access to a woman, he must purchase that right with gifts and promises (or lies). In the event it is a young woman still living in her parents' home, the man must first *fianse* the girl (become engaged), which requires giving a gold chain and gold earrings to the girl. And, as discussed in a later chapter, if the man wants to maintain his right to his wife's sexual fidelity, he must build her a house, plant gardens, and tend livestock for her.

A man who fails to provide continued assistance to his partner can be legitimately cuckolded. However, not unlike the Hutterites, a woman who is in a union with a man who steadfastly plants gardens and tends livestock to support the household must be unfalteringly faithful, even if her partner or husband decides to enter into union with one or a series of other women. Any sign of a woman's infidelity sets neighbors, family, and friends buzzing with gossip and can damage her reputation in the community for life. With an act of infidelity a woman risks destroying her existing union and diminishes the probability of entrance into a subsequent union with a respectable, or at least a financially able, man.

That is the ideal pattern of behavior. In light of the geographical mobility of many husbands and the scarcity of income, it is often not possible to maintain these standards. The sexual mores seen above and desire for children set up a grey area where women are often not able to conform. As will be seen below, fortunately, or perhaps as a consequence, women and their families are able to appeal to myths, fictive illnesses such as arrested pregnancy syndrome, and superstitious rationales that convince men to accept paternity for children that are not biologically their own. Appealing to the same fictions, men readily accept.[1]

Pregnancy, Paternity, Sex, and Sorcery

In Jean Rabel, 29 percent of women and 35 percent of men over forty years of age report having borne children with more than one partner, a suspiciously imbalanced proportion (table 6.1). Moreover, there is the demographic oddity of men reporting an average of more living offspring than that reported by women: 6.3 versus 5.2.[2] The explanation for why the average number of children born to men is greater than the number born to women is that women often assign paternity to more than one man; 13 percent of men in one of the research communities were reported—by friends, family and neighbors—as having been "clobbered-with-a-baby" (*kout pitit*), an expression meaning that they had at least one child who friends and neighbors reported was actually the child of another man. In a later chapter it will be seen that men have a definitive economic interest in claiming paternity for children that are not their own. This interest is manifest in attempts to identify with and appease women. Some men make displays of sympathetic labor and illness when their wife is giving birth; and the most common paternity suits are not women suing for child support but men suing for exclusive paternity.

Table 6.1: Parental partners (age > 40)

Number of Partners	Female (n=714)	Male (n=758)
1	71.3%	65.3%
2	20.0%	23.9%
3	6.7%	7.5
4	1.0%	2.0%
More than 4	.9%	1.3%
Total	100.0%	100.0%

To clarify or explain doubted paternity or controversial sexual encounters, a variety of universally accepted beliefs can be invoked. Women and men explain away sexual infidelity as having succumbed to magic spells purchased from *bokor* (witch doctors), spells that make people fall in love, that stupefy women, that give men the power to take an unwilling girl's breath away so she can not scream, and that make a married man irresistibly attracted to another woman (*kout maji*). A man uncertain that he is the father of an infant has recourse to a blood test; he pricks his own finger and puts a drop of blood on the newborn's tongue. As everyone in Jean Rabel knows, if the man is not the biological father the baby will die instantly.

A belief that deserves special attention is the fictive illness known as *perdisyon*, mentioned above. *Perdisyon* is diagnosed when a sexually active woman who would otherwise expect herself to be pregnant begins to menstruate again (due either to an actual pregnancy ending in spontaneous abortion or some other amenorrheic condition). In search of an explanation, she visits leaf doctors and other specialists, who are quick to tell her what she wants to hear, she has a baby inside. The explanation provided for the failure of gestation to proceed is invariably that a rival or a jealous lover of her spouse— or boyfriend—is using sorcery to prevent the fetus from growing. The phrase *mare nan vant* is used to describe the condition and it literally means "tied up in the stomach."

Perdisyon provides a convenient rationale for the swelling stomach of a woman who has not seen her emigrant husband for more than the preceding nine months. It also provides the woman and her parents grounds to pressure a man into beginning to *swenyen* (care for) her and the imaginary fetus. That the illness is widespread and accepted by both women and men is evident. Only two of twenty-six women interviewed in Makab had any doubt regarding the veracity of *perdisyon* and even men typically responded to the question: "has your wife ever carried a fetus longer than nine months?"

with replies such as "Thank God no, we haven't had that problem yet." [3]

Elsewhere in Haiti, researchers have found similar trends. Murray (1976) found that one-third of the women in his research village had experienced at least one bout of *perdisyon,* and in a large country sample of deceased women Coreil et al. (1996) found that 6 percent of a sample of 1,287 rural and urban women were in a state of *perdisyon* at the time of death—something they explained had nothing to with death but was a reflection of the widespread belief in the fictive illness.

Whether magic charms, spells, "blood tests," and arrested pregnancy syndrome really exist is unimportant. What is important is that accusations of sorcery and magic provide convenient excuses for lustful or financially inspired sexual escapades or infidelity that result in childbirths and hence cannot be hidden away or dismissed—as often is the case in the Western version of the extramarital affair. Belief among the population in the supernatural phenomenon described above is unanimous. As a French doctor who lived in Jean Rabel for three years remarked, "these are not things that farmers in Jean Rabel 'think' occur, they 'know' they occur." [4]

Conclusion

In previous chapters I showed that fertility rates in Jean Rabel compare favorably with the highest rates ever recorded, those of the 19th and 20th century Hutterites. High fertility is achieved in spite of the presence of factors that should suppress fertility, including the absenteeism of men, free distribution of contraceptives by both government and private, nonprofit agencies, and common physiological factors among Jean Rabel women such as STDs, the practice of prolonged lactation, and malnutrition. I linked high fertility to the pronatal sociocultural fertility complex. Both women and men exalt the blessings of having numerous children, caress and laud the pregnant, ridicule the childless, scorn contraceptives, and criminalize abortion. In this chapter it was shown that customs and beliefs in Jean Rabel reinforce the pronatal sociocultural fertility complex: In spite of— or perhaps because of— male absenteeism and male poverty, men are encouraged to be sexually aggressive; women are rewarded and remunerated for sexual intercourse, while confining it to acceptable and financially capable fathers; conflict over infidelity and ambiguous paternity are rationalized with fictive illnesses and appeal to superstition and magic. These patterns of behavior are embedded in a flexible type of sexual-material negotiation between men and women, what other scholars have called "gendered capitalism" as well as part of a "field of competition" and that I referred to as the sexual moral economy. It is this sexual moral economy that can be viewed as a substitute for the stable male breadwinner seen among the Hutterites and not possible in Jean Rabel—not if women are to achieve high levels of fertility.

The questions remain: a) how did these beliefs and behaviors come about, b) what and who sustains them, and c) why, despite the obviously deteriorating economic and environmental conditions and the readily available alternative of using birth control, do Jean Rabeliens continue to avidly favor high fertility and display behaviors and beliefs that promote early and frequent pregnancies among young women? Is it, as foreign experts often suggest, that they are tradition bound, ignorant, unable to let go of deeply embedded values regarding large families? Or is there another, more basic explanation? Could it be the economic utility of children so often denied in the literature? Shedding light on this question requires a closer examination of the material struggle for everyday existence that confronts farming men and women living in Jean Rabel.

Notes

1. The exception is if, when her spouse enters into a union with another woman, the first wife immediately severs the relationship. She then has a right to shamelessly enter into union with another man, but she has sacrificed the house built by the first husband; see chapters 14–15.

2. The figures are from the baseline subsample, n = 136, 68 women and 68 men. In the baseline sample (N = 1,586, missing = 146) the averages were 5.9 children per male household head interviewed (875) and 5.2 children per female household head interviewed (560).

3. Credit for first reporting on *perdisyon* goes to Gerald Murray (1976), who convincingly explained the phenomenon as the only theologically appropriate approach to treating fertility because in Haiti the actual act of conception is entirely a matter for God (*bon dieu*) and, therefore, folk healers must first diagnosis a pregnancy before they can begin to treat the childless woman. When first reading Murray's article as an undergraduate I was strongly tempted to extend his observation to explain *perdisyon* as a belief maintained and reinforced by women in union to justify pregnancy in the absence of their husbands, an especially appealing explanation as Haiti has a history of over one hundred years of male wage migration. And I do not argue with the notion that this may be one function that perpetuates the acceptance of the belief in *perdisyon*. Nor does Murray doubt this occurs (personal communication). In a discussion of the issue, anthropologist Ira Lowenthal affirmed that he knows at least six Haitian women, all in union with men who claim to have experienced *perdisyon* and all invoked the belief in the context of conception in their husband's absence. I too have seen *perdisyon* used this way in at least one instance. In my own research, however, the primary function of *perdisyon* appears, as explained in the text, not to be a rationale for pregnancy but for barrenness. Women typically decide they are experiencing *perdisyon* before they are really pregnant and it is recognition of the condition at this stage that makes it authentic in the eyes of the woman's family, friends, and lovers. The condition is from that point on used to tag the next child born to that particular man with whom she was having relations when *perdisyon* began.

In six of the eight cases of *perdisyon* reported in Makab, it was the woman's first pregnancy, her husband had at least one other *madam* (wife), and she explained her *perdisyon* as being induced magically by one of her husband's other wives. Treatment can get costly. It is understood that Western-trained medical doctors generally do not recognize or believe in the affliction, but there are *medsin* (herb doctors), *matwons* (midwives), *manyè* (massage specialists), and *mambos* and *bokors* (shaman) who specialize in helping women to overcome *perdisyon* and get the fetus growing again.

4. Accusations of magic go both ways. Both men and women can go to the *bokor* for a magic spell or charm. A woman can *jayjay*—tame/brainwash/stupefy—a man with food cooked in water with which she has bathed her genitals or food that has been covered with an unwashed genital rag.

Chapter 7

House, Yard, and Market

Introduction

In order to understand high fertility and the cultural complex of behaviors that reinforce it in Jean Rabel, it is necessary to understand the economy in which it is embedded, for it is the economic exigencies and opportunities that make children important in the struggle to survive in the Jean Rabel harsh environment. Thus, this and the following three chapters describe the local market system, occupations, and income.

It will be seen that despite decades of effort and tens of millions of dollars in development funds described in chapter 3, contemporary Jean Rabel functions largely as an autonomous regional economy with little involvement in the global market. The State provides no significant public services to the population of the region. Houses are simple constructions of thatch, sticks, and mud. The principal income-generating and subsistence activities are agriculture, livestock raising, petty commerce, and charcoal production. Also, approximately 5 percent of the population depends directly on fishing to make a living.

This does not mean, however, that Jean Rabeliens do not seek alternative sources of income outside the household. A dazzling degree of specialization exists in both the production of local material goods and provision of services. A minority of men earn relatively high incomes as skilled craftsmen. Another alternative is seasonal agricultural work and most men at some point in their lives migrate temporarily to urban areas, overseas, or to the Dominican Republic where they work as menial wage laborers. Some women also go to the city and work as maids or cooks, but local and migrant wage opportunities are fewer for women. The primary feminine opportunity is marketing, something that all rural women eventually engage in, and something that has the potential to put women on economically equal footing with men.

But in coming to understand these extra-household income earning opportunities one should keep in mind that prerequisite to pursuing them is membership in a household production unit.. Life in Jean Rabelien—including extra-household endeavors activities—is embedding in a materially simplicity adapted principally to minimizing risk in the face of drought and radically unpredictable market conditions. Jean Rabeliens have no choice but to live in simple houses constructed of inexpensive local materials, to employ inexpensive domestic and transport technologies, and to preserve materially simplistic alternative strategies for meeting subsistence needs. In order to provide for the most basic comforts and conveniences, such as furniture, tin gas-lamps, and labor-saving devices such as graters and coffee strainers, Jean Rabeliens turn to a flourishing regional marketing system. (Unless otherwise indicated, percentages assigned to technologies defined below are based on findings from the 1,586 household Baseline Survey—see chapter 1, p. 5)

Houses

Most houses in Jean Rabel are constructed from local materials. The walls are made of interlaced sticks and are plastered inside and out with clay or lime (83%).[1] Floors are generally dirt (87%) and roofs are thatch (82%) derived from one of several types of palm or one of several types of local grasses.[2] A local vine is used to lash the poles of the house together. On average, the houses contain two rooms (75%), one to six doors (85%), and one to four wooden-shuttered window openings (64%).

It is a man's task to build a house and there are several alternative housing styles and construction methods. A rural house can cost from less than 500 *gdes* (US$30.00) to several thousand Haitian dollars (US$1,000). On the expensive extreme, a man can purchase the land and all necessary construction materials and contract labor for every task involved in building the house. Cement, if used, is the most expensive item, but only the best houses are constructed using cement. On the other extreme, a man with no property and little money is at liberty to build a house on state land and can build the house almost entirely from foraged materials and with his own labor and the help of family and friends. [3]

House Contents and the Yard

The average house in Jean Rabel was constructed nineteen years ago, and was not purchased but built by its owner with varying degrees of paid assistance from local craftsmen. The house is typically twenty feet long and twelve feet wide and, as described above, has two rooms.[4] The room at the front of the house is the dining room (*salon*), which is generally furnished with a locally handcrafted wooden dinner table and wooden chairs. Standing against one wall of the more affluent thatch roof *salon* is a large glass-faced cupboard full of imported utensils, plates, coffee cups with saucers, and juice glasses. Against another wall is a locally made iron frame single bed used for guests. In the corner of most houses sits a large ceramic water jar. The rooms are lit with small oil lamps crafted from discarded cans of condensed milk.

The rear room of the house is used exclusively for sleeping and storage. This room is usually furnished with a locally made wooden frame double bed (70%). Banana thatch sleeping mats are spread on the floor at night for children and are rolled up and stowed in a corner during the day. The only evidence of 20th century mass-produced goods are Goodwill clothing hanging neatly from the rafters. In more cosmopolitan households, torn-out magazine advertisements featuring new cars, radios, vacation spots, and cigarette models adorn the mud walls.

Fifty-two percent of households are built within *lakous* (compounds) in which a yard is shared with at least one other household, that of a parent, sibling, or child. Almost all houses have an outside kitchen (80%). Like the house itself, it is constructed of local wood and thatch. The hearth where the family cooking pot sits is made of three rocks—or often two rocks and a cannonball—the cannonball being there to conduct heat and help the food cook faster. Fifty percent of all houses have some type of latrine, 75 percent of which are simply holes in the ground without any type of enclosure or roof and located some fifteen to thirty meters from the back door. One or more of a variety of fast- growing and malicious vegetation such a dagger-like sisal, cacti, and poison oak are cultivated as living fences (local names for various noxious plants used as fences are *katoch, kandelab, pit, pigwen, bawonet*).

The All-Purpose Yard and Useful Refuse

Many of the items used in and around Jean Rabel households are procured or manufactured by household members from useful plants, trees, and shrubs found in the yard, growing up around the garden, along paths, or in the *kadas* (arid State land). Limes are used as an all-purpose disinfectant and aloe as a hair oil and shampoo. *Galata* and *gayak* leaves, and seeds from the *bawonet* plant, serve as soaps. Rope is woven from sisal and palm thatch. Sacks and saddlebags are fashioned out of thatch and grasses. Baskets are made of grasses and splintered bamboo. Sleeping mats are made from dried plantain stalks. Gourds from the *kalbas* tree provide a range of different sized storage and drinking vessels. Sticks are collected for use as cooking fuel. Flammable coconut husks and dried orange peelings are used to start fires.

Often households do not even own a pack of matches, but must send a child when necessary to borrow a burning ember from a neighbor. Uses are also found for imported industrial refuse: Flammable plastic bottles or packaging serve as fire-starter. Mattresses are fashioned from worn-out Goodwill clothing and sheets. Pigeon houses are made from flattened cans of cooking oil. A scrap bucket lid makes a wheel for a boy's go-cart, a nail is the axle, a stick is the drive shaft, and a sprinting boy is the motor.

Jean Rabeliens regularly consume at least thirteen varieties of wild leaves; a wild olive, which before the recent advent of imports and food aid was an important source of cooking oil; and at least one wild bean. During times of crisis, people eat boiled green mangos, unripe fruit from the corosol tree, at least five types of undomesticated seed pods, two wild yams, and the fruit of a cactus. People in the region also opportunistically eat feral cats, iguanas, and most types of birds—including eagles, hawks, and woodpeckers. They also consume land crabs, fresh-water crabs, and crayfish.[5]

Local Markets and Local Goods

Markets in Jean Rabel are part of a rotating system that provides inhabitants of any particular area walking-distance access to at least two major markets a week. The items sold in the markets are household necessities and are part of a thriving local economy that could, and to a large extent does, exist independently of the global market.

Table 7.1: Regional distribution of market days in and around Jean Rabel

	Sun	Mon	Tues	Wed	Thur	Fri	Sat
Village				+++++			+++++
Lacoma			+++++				
Bab Panyol				+++++			
Beauchaun						+++++	
La Reserve			+++++		+++++		
Paskadebwa		+++++			+++++		
Ma Wouj	+++++		+++++		+++++		
Kot de Fer						+++++	

Figure 7.1: Market Villages

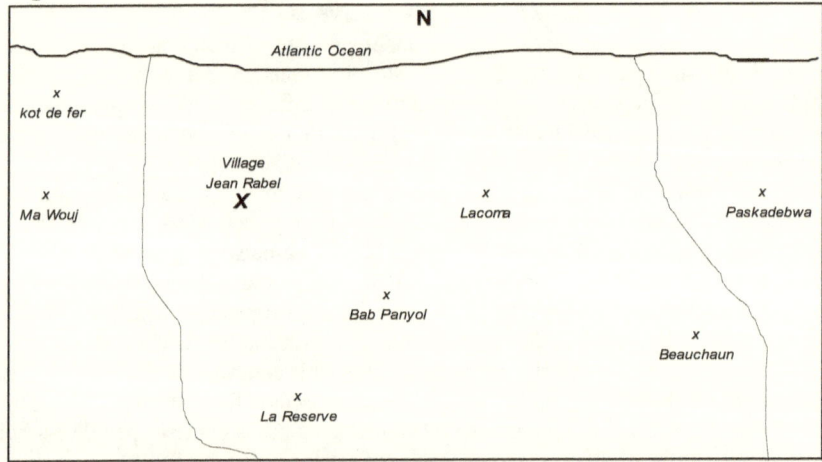

Note: Kot de Fer, Ma Wouj and Paskadebwa fall outside the Commune of Jean Rabel
[- - - -- -- -- --] = Commune boundaries
[_____]   = 10 km.

In Jean Rabel markets one finds not only piles of fruits and vegetables, but locally produced beeswax candles, tin-can lamps, thatch brooms, ropes made of sisal or shredded food aid sacks, tin graters and funnels, cloth coffee and juice strainers, locally crafted wooden mortars and pestles, saddles, saddle blankets, saddlebags, bridles, ropes, baskets, grass sacks, sleeping mats, scrap-iron bed frames, and wooden furniture. Locally produced castor oil is sold as a body lotion and hair relaxer. Bundles of wood are sold as cooking fuel and tiny packets of split pitch pine are sold as kindling. Domestic tobacco is sold in powder and leaf forms. Other locally produced items found include clay pipes, domestic rum concocted with aromatic leaves, roots and spices, homemade sweets made from peanuts, sesame seeds, melted brown sugar and manioc flour, and rolls made with cane syrup and ginger.[6,7]

This is not to say that Jean Rabel markets are stocked entirely with local products. There are also imported staples and necessities that people are able to purchase with their meager earnings: pinto beans, flour, rice, hair ties, used clothing, shoes, wash basins, pots and pans, dishes, drinking glasses, eating utensils, fragrant soaps, machetes, hoes, and kerosene. But whether imported or produced locally, there are very few items sold in the rural Jean Rabel marketplaces that do not relate directly to subsistence. One finds, for example, no bicycles, sporting goods, toys, labor-saving appliances, art, radios, videos, music cassettes, sunglasses, or imported gourmet foods. Nor does one find Hostess Twinkies or Lay's potato chips or items considered necessities by people elsewhere such as toilet paper, tissues, and maxi pads. There are no   even shampoo and deodorant are rarities. In summary, the Jean Rabel economy is not disconnected from the world economy. But corrals of braying donkeys and trains of travelers who have walked for half a day and some overnight to sell their livestock and produce is very much an early 21st century anachronism. And it is very much oriented toward provisioning subsistence needs rather than prestigious or pleasurable wants.

Consumption: Dependency on Household Production vs. the Market

Comparison of results from the Baseline Survey (labled GAFAW) with results from two other large Jean Rabel surveys (PISANO 1990 and SCID 1993) shows that households consume more than they sell for at least four of the six most commonly planted crops.

But the fact that Jean Rabeliens consume much of what they produce should not obscure their dependency on the regional market. In the Opinion Survey, 86.3 percent of all respondents reported getting more of the household food supply from the market than from gardens. And in the spring of 1998, Thomas Hartmanship of the German NGO Agro Action Allemande captured the importance of the market to Jean Rabeliens in a survey in which 128 randomly selected farmers in Jean Rabel were asked, "Where do you most commonly get the produce consumed in your household?" Only in the case of greens and fruits did respondents cite the garden as a more important source of foodstuffs than markets (see tables 7.2 – 7.6).

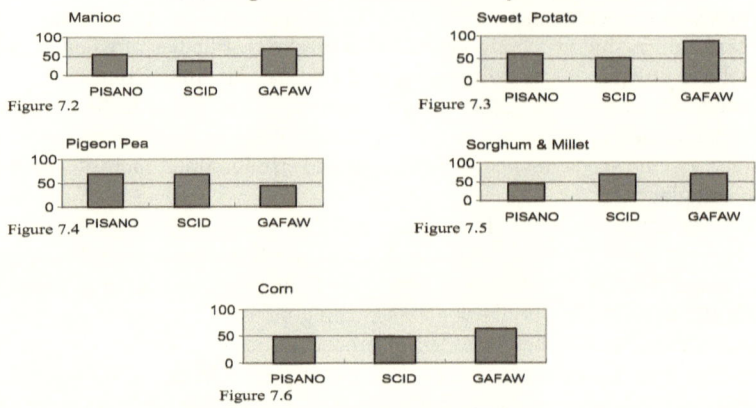

Percentage of harvest consumed by household

Figure 7.2

Figure 7.3

Figure 7.4

Figure 7.5

Figure 7.6

This emphatically does not mean farmers are not producing enough for their own needs. As will be seen below, farmers expect an impressive surplus in at least three out of every four years. The point is that farmers sell their crops and use the money as a storage medium while also rolling the cash over in the market, effectively earning additional income along the way.

Table 7.2: Reports on source of household foods: Gardens vs. markets

	Market	Garden	50/50
Plantain	61%	2%	23%
Greens and fruit	16%	41%	34%
Corn	56%	5%	36%
Sorghum	68%	5%	16%
Manioc, sweet potato, yam	31%	11%	44%
Haricot*	37%	7%	43%
Rice*	70%	1%	0%
Meat and fish	96%	4%	0%

Source: AAA 1998
* 4 percent of haricot and 25 percent of rice were reported as coming from development organizations.

If, for example, a Jean Rabelien is given a bag of rice, he/she will not stash it in a dark recess of the house to be doled out bit by bit over a period of weeks or months. Rather, the rice is sent straight to the market where the woman, her mother, or a younger female

Table 7.3: Parental partners (age > 40)

	Frequency	Percentage
Garden	19	14%
Market	119	86%
Total	138	100%

household member converts it to cash. The cash obtained is then used to engage in other marketing activities and to purchase other foods and provisions as needs arise.

In effect, the market system looms large in local household livelihood strategies. Virtually all households are involved in the market system and while about one-half of most crops are consumed by household members, the other half gets sold and the profits eventually spent on food staples. Thus we can say that Jean Rabeliens are not subsistence farmers but best defined as subsistence-oriented market producers.

Farming

No matter what other skills a person has or what other income-earning activities he or she engages in, everyone in Jean Rabel, except for the very few full-time fishermen, is a farmer. When asked to report the three most significant sources of household income, over 90 percent of Jean Rabel respondents reported agriculture and 50 percent mentioned livestock. Every household head owns or access to at least some garden land and every household has at least a few animals. The farming technologies practiced are those best suited to surviving in the face of an unpredictable environment characterized by drought and hurricane, absence of infrastructure, absence of long-term storage facilities, and absence of effective state-sponsored extension services or crisis management.

Specifically, the strategies are generalized, low-risk and low-investment strategies that provide for household consumption, subsistence expenses, and little more. The point is, no matter how one looks at the issue, farming is the backbone of the Jean Rabel economy, it provides a complex of economic security otherwise unavailable in the face of economic, ecological, and social insecurity, and it depends on social organization focused on the household and family.

Table 7.4: The most commonly planted crops

Crops planted	Origin	% farmers	Crops planted	Origin	% farmers
Corn	Taino/Americas	87.9	Yam	Africa, Asia	2.6
Beans*	Taino/Americas	70.8	Okra	Africa	2.5
Sweet Potato	Taino/Americas	59.1	Arrow root	Taino/Americas	2.0
Cassava	Taino/Americas	44.9	Castor Bean	Africa	1.8
Peanuts	Taino/Americas	39.1	Egg Plant	Asia	0.9
Millet	Africa, Asia	32.1	Carrot	British Isles	0.5
Pumpkin	Taino/Americas	20.6	Tomato	Taino/Americas	0.4
Plantain	Philippines	8.7	Echalot		0.3
Sugar Cane	Asia	7.2	Squash	Taino/Americas	0.3
Watermelon	Africa	6.0	Other		5.6
Sesame	Africa, Asia	3.4			

*All beans and peas were lumped into a single category during the Baseline Survey. This was a mistake and the distinction between beans *rache*—beans harvested at one time which are known in French as Haricot—and pigeon peas, cow peas and lima beans is made elsewhere.
Note: N = 1,539; table illustrates the percentage of Jean Rabel respondents mentioning a crop when asked to report the five crops they most commonly plant.

Agriculture

Agriculture in Jean Rabel is a low-risk and low-input activity. Only 2 percent of farmers in the baseline survey reported using chemical pesticides, and less than 1 percent reported using chemical fertilizers. The only tools reportedly used by farmers were hoes and machetes. No tractors, wagons, or even animal-drawn plows are available for use. Currently, not a single irrigation pump exists in the entire commune of Jean Rabel, and only 40 out of 3,723 (0 .01%) of the plots reported on in the baseline survey were irrigated by a gravity-driven system.[8] As seen earlier, crops planted in Jean Rabel are adapted to harsh environments. Relatively high yields of these crops can be produced with minimal effort in a wide range of soil pH conditions, and they tend to be resilient in the face of unpredictable rainfall patterns, and most importantly, periodic drought. The five principal crops planted are corn, beans, sweet potatoes, cassava, and peanuts—the same five crops most important to the Taino Indians who inhabited the area in pre-Columbian times (Newsom 1993; Rouse 1992). To this basket of Taino domesticates early colonists and slaves added three of the most drought resistant crops on the planet: sorghum, millet, and pigeon peas, crops that continue to be of great importance to Jean Rabeliens, and the lima bean, a quick growing, high yielding legume (Moreau 1797). Most of the crops do not require simultaneous harvesting but rather are crops that yield slowly over a period of several months or year round, making several staples available in the garden in every month of the year (see table 7.5).

Table 7.5: Regional planting cycles on the plain Jean Rabel (H = harvest)

	Jan	Feb	Mar	Apr	May	Jun	Jul	Aug	Sep	Oct	Nov	Dec
Beans		H	H	H								
Cow peas	H	H	H	H	H	H	H					
Lima beans	H	H	H	H	H	H	H					
Pigeon peas	H	H	H	H	H	H	H					
Corn		H	H	H								
Peanuts			H	H						H		
Millet		H	H									
Manioc	H	H	H	H	H	H	H	H	H	H	H	H
Sweet potato	H	H	H	H	H	H	H	H	H	H	H	H
Plantains	H	H	H	H	H	H	H	H	H	H	H	H
Squash	H	H	H	H	H	H					H	H
Sugarcane	H	H	H	H	H	H	H	H	H	H	H	H
Yam		H	H	H	H	H	H	H	H	H	H	H

Fruit Trees

Crop harvesting cycles are complemented by the availability of produce from at least nineteen types of fruit and nut trees, most of which are not planted deliberately but rather selectively permitted to grow and the harvests of which conveniently fall during the leanest months for garden produce. Fruits are sold in the markets for local consumption, they are given away freely among friends and neighbors, and are consumed in abundance by everyone, especially children, and particularly mangos, the unrivaled favorite fruit in Jean Rabel.[9]

Table 7.6: Regional tree cycles (H = harvest)

	Jan	Feb	Mar	Apr	May	Jun	Jul	Aug	Sep	Oct	Nov	Dec
Avocado							H	H	H	H	H	
Mango				H	H	H	H	H	H			
Bread nuts	H	H	H			H	H	H	H	H	H	H
Bread fruit	H	H	H				H	H	H	H		
Kenep							H	H	H	H		
Oranges (sweet)	H	H	H	H				H	H	H	H	H
Gratefruit	H	H	H	H	H	H	H	H	H	H	H	H
Limes	H	H			H	H	H	H	H	H	H	H
Oranges (sour)	H	H	H	H	H	H	H	H	H	H	H	H
Coconut	H	H	H	H	H	H	H	H	H	H	H	H
Papaya	H	H	H	H	H	H	H	H	H	H	H	H
Corosol	H				H	H	H				H	H
Grenadia			H	H	H	H	H	H	H	H	H	H

Livestock

Animal raising is as important a feature of household economic livelihood as agriculture. At any given moment one may encounter households that have no livestock because animals have been sold, stolen, or died off from disease or drought, or been killed by dogs. But all rural households in Jean Rabel raise animals as part of their overall survival strategy. The most important animals in order of prevalence are chickens, followed by goats, sheep, hogs, cattle, and then turkey and guinea fowl. Ducks are numerous in the *bouk* (village) of Jean Rabel but rare in rural areas. Pigeons are also common everywhere in Jean Rabel, a fact that was not investigated in the survey. Table 7.7 below lists the mean number of animals per household as determined in the Baseline Survey. Because the survey was conducted during a period of ongoing drought when many animals had perished, the data are not representative of the typical number of animals people own during normal climatic conditions. Figure 7.7 was derived from data obtained during the three-hundred-household Polygyny Survey—carried out during a non-crisis period—and illustrates the number of households possessing at least one of the larger livestock animals listed.

Table 7.7: Livestock per household, Baseline Survey (N = 1,539)

Livestock species	Animals per household	Std. dev.
Chick	2.27	3.90
Goats	.94	1.87
Sheep	.78	1.83
Hogs	.45	1.47
Cattle	.23	.73

Note: There were two factors that affected reports on livestock: (1) the drought during which the survey took place caused many animals to perish and (2) people often misrepresented the number of livestock they owned in hopes the survey was part of a livestock giveaway project, as ID, AAA, and PISANO have done in the past. For information regarding pack animals—donkeys, horses, and mules—see table 3.2.

Figure 7.7: Household with at least one goat, sheep, pig, or cow
(N = 300)

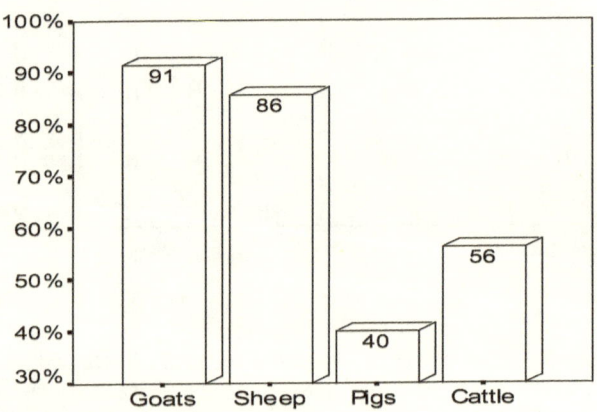

Strategies for raising livestock are similar to those employed in agriculture: minimal costs, minimal risks. The greatest livestock expense most farmers incur, besides actually purchasing the animals, is the cords used to tether them (if the farmer decides to purchase rather than make the cords, they cost 3 *gdes* per animal—US$0.15). Farmers plant clusters of drought-resistant native grass called zeb gine (guinea grass) in their gardens and around their houses to be used as animal fodder. Sugarcane bagasse and leaves, banana leaves, and pigeon pea foliage also provide high protein fodder superior to most grasses. Corn, millet, and bean leaves and stalks are stored on rooftops; when drought strikes, the stored fodder is moistened with salt water and fed to the animals. When market prices are low, surplus garden produce, particularly sweet potatoes, mangos and bread fruit, are fed to livestock rather than sold. Animals are grazed in gardens after harvests or tethered in fallow fields. With the exception of pigs—the one animal sometimes fattened on purchased supplements—farmers only purchase feeds during prolonged crises, and these are invariably grasses or garden refuse found in neighboring ecological zones.[10]

Table 7.8: Reasons for selling livestock[a]

Reasons	Count	Percentage	Cumulative percentage
To buy food or feed hshld	1,558	40.5%	40.5%
School (pay costs)	1,045	27.1%	67.6%
Death (pay for funeral costs)	372	9.7%	77.3%
Birth (pay costs and feed)	342	8.9%	86.2%
Make room for new stock	68	1.8%	88.0%
Marriage, baptism . . .	47	1.2%	89.2%
Overpopulation	9	0.2%	89.4%
Other[b]	412	10.6%	100.0%
Total	3,853	100.0%	100.0%

[a] Respondents were allowed three primary reasons.
[b] The category "other" was almost entirely because the animal was sick or there was a need to buy seeds for planting.

Livestock serves primarily as a cash reserve for the household. When an animal is slaughtered, much of the meat gets sold, primarily to provide for other subsistence needs. In the Baseline Survey, the single most frequently cited reason for both killing and selling animals was so that other food could be purchased with the proceeds from the sale of the surplus meat.[11]

The months most commonly cited as times of animal slaughter and sale are precisely those months householders identify as the hardest/leanest of the year, the same months that crop harvests are at a minimum. The relationship between hard times, animal slaughter, and animal sales only deviates slightly when schools open in September and October and tuition payments come due (see figure 7.8 below).

Figure 7.8: Months animals are sold and slaughtered by lean months

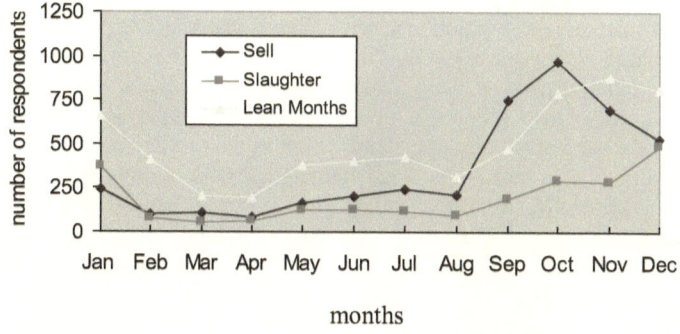

months

Table 7.9: Reasons for killing livestock [a]

Reasons	Count	Percentage	Cumulative Percentage
To buy food or feed hshld	879	40.9%	40.9%
Birth (to feed the mother)	480	22.3%	63.2%
Death (to feed visitors)	318	14.8%	78.0%
Marriage, baptism . . .	209	9.7%	87.7%
Sell	156	7.3%	95.0%
Overpopulation	12	.6%	95.6%
Other[b]	95	4.4%	100.0%
Total	2,149	100.0%	100.0%

[a] Respondents were allowed three primary reasons.
[b] The category "other" was almost entirely because the animal was sick or there was a need to buy seeds for planting.

Conclusion

The opinions of some aid experts to the contrary, the ethnographic fact is that daily life in Jean Rabel is heavily dependent and deeply involved in farming. It is these conditions that, it will be seen, give way to the particular kinship and family structures found in the area, and it is the failure to identify them and accurately understand what they mean for social life that has inhibited an understanding of rural Haitians. Low income levels and the need to maintain a degree of self-sufficiency in the face of impending drought and uncertain market opportunities mean that Jean Rabeliens have little choice but to employ inexpensive domestic and transport technologies and to reserve alternative strategies for obtaining material necessities. They walk or ride pack animals, sometimes for several days, to get where they are going and their houses are simple constructions of thatch, sticks, and mud. In order to satisfy subsistence needs and provide for the most basic comforts and conveniences, such as furniture, tin gas lamps, and labor-saving devices such as graters and coffee strainers, they turn to a flourishing regional marketing system.

The Jean Rabel economy is free from *dependency* on outside goods and services and this autonomy occurs at two levels: the regional level and the household level. At the regional level there is a thriving system of exchange, monetarily based, and characterized by the production of local goods and a rotating market system. At the household level, people do not depend on any public service. Every material item and every service that can be purchased also has a cost-free substitute. Soap can be replaced by special leaves, and a sleeping mat, instead of being purchased in the local market, can be made at home. Even houses, the single greatest lifetime expense for most Jean Rabeliens, can be constructed almost completely independent of nondomestic, paid labor or imported materials. None of this means that Jean Rabeliens live in a system completely shut off from the outside world. Imported staples, for example, can be found in all regional marketplaces, most notably imported rice, beans, and flour, which to varying degrees

Jean Rabeliens purchase and consume; and imported plastic items such as hair berets and perfumes are common in the market. What it does mean is that Jean Rabeliens have recourse to a remarkable degree of autonomy and even self-sufficiency at the level of the household and they are also eager participants in an equally remarkable local economy that can be conceptualized as a regional subsistence market system. In the following chapter, I want to take a look at the income that the most basic household-based livelihood strategies generate, for, in the competition for development funds, aid workers and researchers have often exaggerated and misused income data as well.

Notes

1. Wattle and daub, sticks woven together and plastered with mud, lime or cement. Most kitchens are also constructed in this way but without being plastered.

2. Local names for types of thatch: *kokoye*, *latanye*, and *pay la preskil*. Local names for grasses: *zeb gini*, *zeb kos*, *zeb able*, and *zeb kanna*.

Roofs have to be patched frequently but not uncommonly endure upward of four decades and in at least one instance a grass roof was reported to be seventy years old, albeit it had been added to over the years.

3. The process of building a house usually goes as follows: Branches for house supports and the I-beam that holds the house together are cut from living trees that belong to the man, begged off a friend, or purchased from the market. For the walls, a man gathers rocks or, if the house is going to be wattle and daub, sticks (*galata* is a common source of sticks; see below). For plaster, he makes his own lime by cooking lime rocks, or if he cannot find lime rocks, he uses clay, which is abundant in the area (preferably a white clay). His wife or future wife, mother, grandmother, sisters, and other female relatives, neighbors, and friends will likely carry dirt and sand as needed. The dirt and sand is mixed with lime or clay to make a weak cement. In some areas like La Presque'Ile near Mole St. Nicolas, the man may harvest his own roof thatch or he can use Guinea grass found on State lands. In most areas thatch from the Royal Palm is sold for 2-3 *gdes* per bundle and a typical house can be covered with about four hundred bundles. The vines that lash the house poles together can be gathered in the bush and the poles that form the roof platform are usually from *galata*, a very straight branch derived from a kind of sisal plant that is ubiquitous on the dry State lands (*kadas*). Of course, all the materials can be purchased, but the only materials that typically cannot, if necessary, be foraged are the locally hewn boards used to make window shutters and doors.

To build the house: Neighbors and family, enticed by free rum, are assembled to help erect the frame. The main poles are planted several feet in the ground. Other framing poles are nailed to these. At this point the structure is a standard rectangular house skeleton with a simple A-frame roof. (Friends and neighbors typically fade away at this time, returning to help when the roof is put on.) The doors and windows are then framed, most often by a paid *boss*. The *galata* branches are laid across the roof and lashed with vine to the house frame and then the thatch, strung on lengths of vine, three leaves to a length, is fastened to the house. Then the walls go up. If the walls are rock, the rocks are cemented together with lime or clay mixed with sand and dirt; if the walls are what is locally called *klisay*, then sticks are horizontally interlaced between vertical poles. Doors and windows are then framed and the structure is plastered inside and out with pure clay or lime. The jobs for which bosses are typically employed are framing the house and framing the doors and windows; masonry, if the house is stone; and as mentioned, hanging the doors and windows.

Three examples are given below taken from friends of the author. The first man built a small 9.5 x 15 (ft) house, a typical two-room structure. The man hired both a carpenter and a mason. He was nevertheless able to realize a considerable savings by digging his own clay/mud/plaster, cooking his own lime, and gathering vines himself. The man also gathered poles, *galata*, and thatch from trees growing on his property. He felled a tree for boards and his father, a professional sawyer, sawed the boards free of charge.

Table 7.10: House building costs 1 (prices in *gdes*)

Item/service	Items	Quantity	Cost	Total cost
Carpenter	Labor		350	
	Food		200	
	Rum	3 ka	60	610
Mason	Labor	16 ke	700	
	Food		250	
	Rum		80	1030
Work party				
(fouye/foule)	Food		100	
	Rum		70	170
Work party			100	
(kouvri)	Food			
	Rum		65*	165
Poles			Foraged	
Galata			Foraged	
Thatch			Foraged	
Vines			Foraged	
Lime			Foraged	
Mud			Foraged	
Boards		21	Foraged	
Nails		6 lbs	60	
Hinges		6	60	
Latches		5	40	
Cement		4	500	660
Total				2,635

* price dropped

The second man also built his house almost entirely by himself, spending 2,115 *gdes*. He obtained boards by giving a tree to a sawyer friend of his in exchange for half the boards produced. The house was two rooms and a small 10 x 12.5 feet.

Table 7.11: House building costs 2 (prices in *gdes*)

Item/service	Items	Quantity	Cost	Total cost
Nails	Pounds	4	80	
Boards	Dozen	1	500	
Carpenter	Labor	—	600	
Mason	Labor	—	600	
	Rum & food		240	2,020
Poles			Foraged	
Galata			Foraged	
Thatch			100	
Vines			Foraged	
Lime			Foraged	
Mud (*tif*)			Foraged	
Boards		21	Foraged	
Nails		4 lbs	40	
Hinges		4	40	
Latches		2	15	95
Total				2,115

The house listed below is the other extreme of the rural houses. It is not the grand cement houses as seen in small villages but it is the upper scale of the rural houses and almost all the material and many of the services were purchased. It was built by a woman whose husband was away working in Port-de-Paix but who sent her money to construct the house. It is 10 x 22 feet:

Table 7.12: House building costs 3 (prices in *gdes*)

Item/service	Items	Quantity	Cost	Total cost
Wood poles		Old house	750	
Tin roofing	Sheets	14	1,400	
Nails	Pounds	12	240	
Hinges, etc.			150	
Cement	Sacks	16	1,840	
Boards	Dozen	2	1,250	5,630
Carpenter	Labor	—	1,700	
Mason	Labor	—	1,650	
	Rum & food		160	3,510
Work party (digging sand, dirt and rocks)	Rum & food		300	300
Total				9,440

4. All data, where not otherwise specified, are taken from the baseline survey of 1,586 households; 1,521 actual respondents.

5. The significance of wild plants in the region was partially captured by CARE's 1994 baseline study in which 58 percent of households in CARE's 1,400 household northwest sample reported eating them. It should be emphasized that many plants, and particularly fruit trees, that are considered domesticates, are not deliberately planted by Jean Rabeliens but rather selectively permitted to grow. The seeds propagate easily near households because it is there that people most often throw the seeds. If the people in the household like the tree where it is, they do not pull it up. The types of edible wild plants together with some that are more often thought of as domestic are listed below, some are given in Kreol only:

Wild yams: dala (manje siklon, grate li kom manioc ame), chat, galata
        Wild beans, greens and stalks: piyant (used as a kind of coffee), karaibe, doliv, laman, epina wouj , lyann panye, kou pye, lalo, chou mantad, chou kore, kresan, konkonm, zeb egwi, bondye bay, wild cabbage
Fruits that grow on vines: Militon, Grenadia
        Tree seed pods that are eaten from trees during crisis: bwa fè (grenn), bwa dom (grenn nan kos), bwa blan (grenn nan kos—tankou pistach), tamarin (kouvre grenn nan kos), and brizie (grenn)
Fruit trees: unripened corosol and and green mangos are also eaten during times
        of crisis, guayav, chou palmis, zamond, kenep, papay, korosol zombi, kachima, kayimit (2) pye bwa, manje fri, seriz/cherries, siwal
Wild animals: liza (iguana), chat (feral cat), pentad (guinea fowl), toutril (turtle
        dove), and any other bird they can catch except those listed below:
        Birds not eaten: kwak blanch (cow egret), karanklou (buzzard), serpante, kone–gen gwo, gen piti (unknown)

6. Tobacco was grown abundantly in the region until the last decade when a disease reportedly made planting tobacco unprofitable. One still finds small plots of tobacco but it is not the industry it reportedly used to be. Much tobacco in the region, and in much of Haiti, comes from the Kass market place on the Central Plateau. The Kass market is only three kilometers from the border with the Dominican Republic and it is possible that low grade tobacco is purchased from the Dominicans and sold in Kass and it also possible that some tobacco grown in Kass in sold on the Dominican side of the border. But most people report very little cross border trade in tobacco. The people in the region of Kass explain that Dominican Tobacco is not the same kind as Haitians prefer and vice versa. Further, there is a tremendous amount of tobacco grown nearby on the some fifteen thousand hectares of mud flat that used to be the upper reaches of Lake Peligre—formed by the Peligre hydroelectric dam on the Artibonite river.

7. Up until 1986, rum was distilled locally. Today, raw rum is imported from Leogone. There is little trade with Cape Haitian, the alternative source (another large rum-producing area).

8.

Table 7.13: Crops by use of chemical pesticides and fertilizers

Crops	Pesticide use		Fertilizer use	
	Yes (%)	n	Yes (%)	n
Plantain	1.5%	134	2.2%	134
Okra	0.0%	35	0.0%	35
Sesame	0.0%	48	0.0%	50
Squash	0.0%	313	0.3%	313
Sugar cane	0.0%	100	0.0%	101
Manioc	1.2%	684	0.0%	687
Corn	3.7%	1,356	1.0%	1,367
Melon	1.2%	85	0.0%	85
Sweet potato	0.7%	900	0.1%	902

Peanuts	0.7%	549	0.4%	550
Millet	5.4%	514	1.4%	514
Beans	1.4%	1,079	0.4%	1,081
Taro	0.0%	30	0.0%	30
Yam	2.5%	40	2.5%	40
Total	2.0%	5,867	0.6%	5,889

Note: Units of analysis = crops

9. Mangos originated in India and were introduced sometime during the colonial period. Breadfruit (as well as sisal) came from the South Pacific and is believed to have been first brought to the Caribbean in 1792 by the famous Captain Bligh—three years after his fabled "mutiny on the Bounty" voyage. Avocados originated in the Mexican highlands but by colonial times there was a West Indian variety (see *Encyclopedia Britannica*).

10. Chickens and other poultry are fed grains by owners not to fatten them up but as a means of keeping them near the house (*pou yo pa al lwenn*)—most of what chickens eat is what they find on their own, i.e., insects, grass seeds, and vegetal refuse.

Pigs are the one special case of an animal requiring high investments, such as vitamin and feed supplements, to be profitable. This makes pigs a problem for people disinclined to make monetary investments in their livestock. As one man told the author; *kochon gen plis kob pase tout bet min yo reme mouri twop* (pigs yield more money than all animals but they like to die too much), which makes them a losing investment for most Jean Rabel farmers. Evidence for the lack of interest and the failing success of pig raising in Jean Rabel comes from recent projects promoting investment in hogs.

Table 7.14: Use of veterinary service and medicines

Animal species (units of analysis = animals)	% using veterinary service or medicines (n = 2,789)	Animal species (units of analysis = animals)	% using veterinary service or medicines (n = 2,789)
Donkey	21.4%	Goat	11.9%
Horse	19.5%	Chicken	11.8%
Mule	19.2%	Turkey	2.9%
Hog	27.5%	Guinea Fowl	0%
Bovine	13.7%	Duck	0%
Sheep	12.7%	Total	15.6%

11. People in Jean Rabel do not make cheeses or other products from goat milk, but 36.1 percent of people reported milking goats for home consumption—something the author has never seen and is somewhat skeptical about.

Cow owners do not make cheese, butter, or yogurt from cow's milk—presumably because of low milk fat production related to the lack of high protein feeds and deteriorating quality of grazing land. But, people possessing cows reported milking for home consumption and local sale—something the author has seen often and is not skeptical about. The milk is boiled with cinnamon sticks and salt added.

Chapter 8

Farming and Household-Based Production

Introduction

At the time of this research, the UN listed per capita annual income in Haiti as US$398, making it far and away the poorest country in the Western hemisphere; estimates for Jean Rabel were lower, ranging from US$100.00 per household (UNOPS 1997) to US$350.00 per household (CARE 1996; see also CARE 1997), meaning that with an average of just under six people per household, even CARE's more liberal estimate translates to an annual per capita income of US$60, giving Jean Rabel an income level one-sixth of that of Haitians overall and only slightly higher than the two lowest per capita GDPs in the world—the Democratic Republic of the Congo at US$52 and Sudan at US$59 (Stepick 1982; CARE 1996; United Nations 2000, 2007).

The use of such measurements as indices of human misery, suggesting squalor and the need for intervention, are erroneous. What they measure are remunerated employment and involvement in the world economy. They tell us little about living standards in terms of health, nutrition, leisure time, happiness, and social security. The significance of this will be returned to in later chapters for it is precisely this type of Western-based standards that bias our understanding of life in places like Jean Rabel, where people have gardens and animals, where they forage for plants and small animals and where they have their own thriving internal regional economies and are loath to report income.

Moreover, even when measures of income are based on surveys, such as the cited data for Jean Rabel, these surveys are often conducted with few controls and invariably embedded in fund-soliciting campaigns sponsored by organizations dependent on foreign aid. For example, the estimate of US$100 annual per household income came from UNOPS (United Nations Office of Project Services)—an organization whose employees depend on projects funded by the UN— translating to per capita US$17; a ridiculously low sum of 4 cents per day. How the UN aid workers came up with these estimates is a mystery. They cite no source for the data, and they discuss no systematic study of household income in the region.

The CARE estimate is problematic as well. CARE (the largest multinational charity in the world and the NGO with an exclusive on U.S.-government-funded charity activities in Jean Rabel) was lavishly funded by the U.S. government (more than US$250,000) to come up with the cited household estimate (US$350 per household per year; or 15 cents per day per person). The calculation came from a study of northwest Haiti, and involved a sophisticated, 1,400-household cluster sample in which twenty-six communities were visited by teams of university-educated Haitian interviewers. Focus groups were held in each community and a large number of local households were subsequently visited to interview the breadwinners and obtain precise details regarding household expenses and income. The study was vitiated by an inclination for respondents to conceal their wealth and a lack of initiative on the part of CARE to correct for this. For example, in the fishing hamlet of Makab where I lived for eighteen months, CARE interviewers reported that less than 20 percent of households owned livestock. But when I began my research one year later, there were in fact only two of a total of forty-three households that did not own at least one goat or sheep. One member of the community, a man who villagers report was included in the survey, had upwards of one hundred goats, a detail that was not reflected in the CARE report.[1] Thus, if these findings can be generalized to other communities studied by CARE and UNOPS, the image of Jean Rabel households spending a daily average of US$0.96 is an underestimate. The question is then, how much of an underestimate?

Agricultural Income

In order to estimate income from agriculture we need to first know three things: average holdings, types of garden, and yields.

Average Holdings

The mean garden size in Jean Rabel is .82 hectares and at any one time the average household works 2.8 gardens on a total of 2.3 hectares of land. On the other hand, the average amount of land reportedly owned per household is 1.13 *kawo* or 1.46 hectares (1 *kawo* =1.29 hectares)—the difference being attributable to sharecropping and underreporting of landownership. Almost one-third of respondents, 413 households, reported owning no land; 87.7 percent of households own 2 *kawo* or less; and 1.1 percent of households claimed to own more than 5 *kawo* of land. The number of landless farmers is suspect and probably a consequence of deceptive reporting—some respondents expected that the survey would be followed by food-aid distribution to the poorest households. should not be interpreted to mean that land is concentrated. The largest landholder in the sample owned only 12 *kawo*, and there are no larger plantations or vast tracks of private land in Jean Rabel.

Table 8.1: Total land owned by household

Land in *kawo*	Count	Households Percentage	Cumulative percentage
0	413	29.7%	29.7%
0 to 1	584	42.0%	71.7%
1 to 2	231	16.6%	87.7%
2 to 3	103	7.4%	95.1%
3 to 4	32	2.3%	97.4%
4 to 5	20	1.5%	98.9%
Over 5	16	1.1%	100.0%
Total	1,392	100.0%	100.0%

Note: 1 *kawo* = 1.29 hectares = 3.19 acres

Table 8.2: All types of land tenure (units of analysis = gardens)

Types of land tenure	Count	Percentage	Cumulative percentage
Owned	2,485	67.1%	67.1%
Sharecropped	710	19.1%	86.2%
Rented	410	11.0%	97.2%
On loan	81	2.2%	99.4%
Employed by owner	5	0.1%	99.5%
Other	20	0.5%	100.0%
Total	3,711	100.0%	100.0%

Note: The chart indicates that in Jean Rabel there are basically three ways to access a garden plot: own it (67.1%), sharecrop it (19.1%), or rent it (11.0%). Less important means of accessing land are borrowing and being employed by the landowner (working as a farm hand).

Type of Garden

While the vast majority of land is "dry," there is nevertheless another 4.7 percent of garden land considered "fertile" and "irrigated." On these plots farmers can naturally expect higher and more dependable yields. Table 8.2 above sums up the types of land tenure—i.e., how farmers obtained access to their garden plots.

Table 8.3: Size of gardens by soil type (units of analysis = gardens)

Land in *kawo*	Type of land (%) Irrigated	Fertile	Dry	Total
.01 to .50	62.5%	76.7%	75.6%	75.5%
.51 to 1.0	10.0%	15.8%	18.6%	18.4%
1.1 to 1.5	5.0%	3.0%	1.8%	1.9%
1.51 to 2.0	10.0%	.8%	2.3%	2.4%
2.1 to 2.5	2.5%	0%	.2%	.2%
Over 2.5	10.0%	3.8%	1.4%	1.5%
N =	40	133	3550	3723
Percentage	1.1%	3.6%	95.3%	100%

Yields

Production figures reported in the Livestock and Gardens Survey (n = 104) appear low at first glance. Yields on the plain of Jean Rabel are about one-fifth the world average for corn, five-sixths the world average for beans, and about half the world average for sorghum and millet (see table 8.4). But the fact that farmers in Jean Rabel intercrop means that the figures are not comparable. The same low-altitude hectare that yields 1,116 kilograms of corn is simultaneously planted in pigeon peas, lima beans, pumpkin, drought resistant manioc, sweet potatoes, and okra. Corn and beans do not grow well in the mountains and farmers there reported expecting yields lower than the lowest country average in the world. But mountain farmers only marginally depend on corn and beans. Instead, peanuts are the premier income-generating crop in the mountains and farmers enjoy yields respectably close to the world average (1,273 kilograms per hectare, see table 8.4 below). Furthermore, peanuts are also intercropped with a variety of other plants, including tobacco, castor beans, sorghum, melons, squash, okra, pigeon peas, sweet potatoes, and sesame.

Table 8.4: Yields in kilograms per hectare

Region		Corn	Beans	Sorghum and millet	Peanuts
Jean Rabel	Mountains	172	201	—	1,273
	Plain	1,116	558	372	—
World	Average	4,130	662	758	1,336
	Africa	1,621	688	756	—
Lowest country average		333[1]	236[2]	210[3]	—

[1] Cape Verde [2] Rwanda [3] Botswana *Source*: FAO, 1997.

Figure 8.1 Number of gardens per household
(y = 2.8, sd = 1.6, N = 1,491)

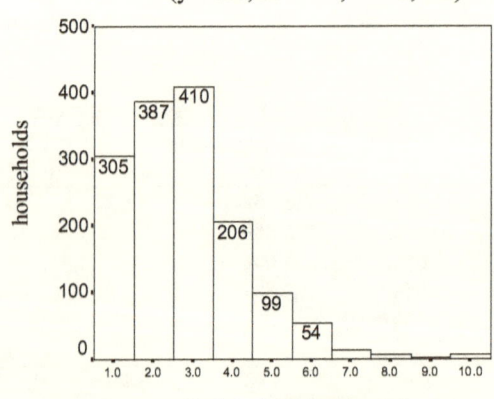

Number of Gardens Planted

Income from Agriculture

If, for the sake of calculation and trying to get a general idea of the income that Jean Rabel farmers can earn, we were to begin by counting only the principal crop cycle (meaning only one planting), putting all other crops aside, and simply assume that Jean Rabel farmers plant only one of the reported average 2.3 garden-hectares (including share cropped property) per household of the cash-crops beans, corn, or peanuts (which are also three of the top five crops farmers most commonly report planting) and we calculate from the prices sold, in a good year, one where there has been sufficient rain, then the typical Jean Rabel household harvests 13,885 *gdes* worth of these crops (US$826). If we assume, as shown in the previous chapter, that the household consumes half of the harvest, then US$413 remains. And again, this is less than half the land cultivated and does not account for sweet potatoes, pigeon peas, sugar cane, cassava, and the various other crops that are also planted and sold.

Nor does this calculation account for differential amounts of land owned, the total amount of land worked through sharecropping and other arrangements, and the quality and productive capacity of particular parcels of land. All of these factors translate into significant annual differences in the amount of income a particular household or individual earns.

The data nevertheless provide an indication of the widespread agricultural income-earning opportunities in the region, opportunities available to households with the labor capacity to work the land, and opportunities that allow individuals to avoid dependency on low-wage employment in the service of larger landholders.

Income from Livestock

Similar calculations can be made regarding livestock. Again, the objective is only to present a general understanding of income possibilities associated with farming. Included are only the most common larger livestock: goats, sheep, cows, and donkeys. The calculations do not include chickens, which are the most common household animal, or pigs, horses, and mules, three of the most expensive animals.

Table 8.5: Estimated average annual income from livestock

Per household	Goats	Mules	Sheep	Cattle	Total
At least 1 animal	91%	89%	86%	56%	-
Average adult animals	3.1	1.1	2.5	0.8	-
Female	81%	63%	78%	77%	-
Average adult female animals	2.5	0.7	1.9	0.6	-
Offspring per female per year	3.0	0.8	3.0	0.8	-
Livestock produced annually	7.5	0,6	5.7	0.5	-
Average price per weanling (gdes)	250	750	200	2,000	-
Est. hshld livestock income (gdes)	1,875	450	1,140	1,000	4,465

In the Polygyny Survey, which included questions on livestock not adequately addressed in other surveys, the average farming household possessed 3.1 adult goats, 2.5 sheep, .8 cows, and 1.1 donkeys. Assuming that goats and sheep can yield a mean three offspring per year (the average is three litters of two kids per litter, every two years) and that a cow or donkey has approximately .8 calves per year, then the typical household earns about 4,465 gdes annually on its weaned livestock (US$266). This figure does not include the most prominent animal in Jean Rabel, poultry, or the most expensive horses, donkeys, and pigs.[2]

Similar to agriculture, livestock provides a broad spectrum of income-earning opportunity among different households. Household earnings from livestock are based on the number of animals a household unit can successfully tend. For the sake of demonstrating these differences, at the bottom of table 8.6 is the tabulated total annual revenue for a household that has one of each animal listed—i.e., one goat, one sheep, one cow, and one hog. The same estimates can be used to calculate projected income from livestock for a hypothetical household with two of each animal, or three, and so on. The calculations are not meant to reflect exact actual conditions—there is, for example, no particular reason why a household would own two goats, two sheep, two pigs, and two cows—but percentages given are based on actual number of animals reportedly owned by households included in the Polygyny Survey, and the figures demonstrate the economic differences that result from one household having the capacity to care for more livestock than another.

Table 8.6: Variation in the number of animals per household

		Number of animals					
		0	1	2	3	4	5+
Goats		8.6%	12.4%	27.6%	20.0%	11.4%	20.2%
Sheep		14.3%	19.0%	23.8%	17.1%	19.0%	6.9%
Cattle		39.3%	36.3%	18.0%	4.7%	1.0%	.6%
Hogs		31.0%	18.0%	28.3%	20.0%	1.7%	.6%
Revenue	Gdes	0	3,700	7,400	14,800	29,600	59,200+
per year	US$	0	220	440	880	1,760	3,520+

Special mention is required regarding pigs, an animal that has tremendous but seldom-realized income-earning potential. Piglets sell for 250 gdes (US$14.88), meaning that a litter of ten can yield the owner(s) a respectable 2,500 gdes (US$148.80), and a single well-fed pig sold in the Port-de-Paix market can fetch as much as 6,000 gdes (US$357.14). But most farmers do not have the capital available to provide feeding pigs nutritionally sufficient quantities of food to breed or to grow to a significant size, and so most pigs are bought, raised, and then sold as stunted adults for approximately 750 gdes (US$50.68). For the latter reason, I have limited the income in table 8.6 calculated for pigs to 750 gdes per animal.

Total Farming Income

Combining agriculture and livestock activities, an average Jean Rabel farming household should be able to generate about US$679 per year, about twice the household income estimated by CARE in 1994. This is still not much revenue—an annual US$116 per capita—and it does not take into consideration losses incurred as a result of thievery, disease, storms, blight, and drought. Nor does it take into account the cost of seeds, ropes, tools, and the purchase of new livestock. On the other hand, although farming is the principal source of income in Jean Rabel for over 90 percent of all households, most households have members simultaneously engaged in several other revenue-generating strategies, the subject of the following chapters.[3]

Conclusion

An analysis of household livelihood strategies and income shows that while people in rural Haiti may be poor, they are not as poor as portrayed neither by intervention experts and charity workers nor as suggested in many reports and statistics submitted by aid agencies. Nor are people in Jean Rabel helplessly sitting around waiting for the next shipment of food aid. On the contrary, they are earnestly engaged in trying to survive and assure security in the face of an unpredictable and harsh environment. The basis of this survival is farming livelihood strategies focused on the household.

The significance of these strategies cannot be gainsaid. There is nothing secure in Jean Rabel beyond the limits of the household. There is no dependable State to provide aid, job security, or unemployment insurance. Foreign intervention agencies, who have come to help, are not there to provide welfare services and the unhappy fact is that even in times of crisis they reach a very small portion of the population; have actually acted as agents of foreign agricultural interests seeking new markets. Individual security, food, and shelter, all depend on being a member of a household. The only people who are not members of a household are a few mentally disturbed individuals called *pov* (poor), easily spotted in their shabby straw hats and scraggly, matted hair; a bowl in hand for begging coins, they wander from market to market, and sleep on the tiny front porches of nicer houses and in churches—and, interestingly, they are very few.

People who sell and purchase in markets are invariably operating on behalf of a household. The produce, livestock, cooked foods, and artisan goods sold are the fruits of the combined efforts of household members, and the vast bulk of the proceeds from the sale of these products will be returned to the household in the form of food purchases and items needed to continue household production—such as saddles, ropes for livestock, seeds, and tools for the garden.

Some households are able to derive greater income from these activities than other households. But although the emphasis thus far has been on the potential economic differences between households, an equally remarkable feature is the general narrowness of these differences. No household for which data was gathered had planted more than eleven gardens and no household owned more than 12 *kawo* of land. The maximum

number of cattle belonging to any of the households visited during the Polygyny Survey
was six; the maximum number of goats, fourteen; the maximum number of sheep, twelve;
the maximum number of hogs, eight. No household owned more than four donkeys, two
horses, or two mules. The explanation for the relatively equal distribution of wealth
among households is simply that, in rural Jean Rabel, despite soil exhaustion and the
declining availability of new land, the balance between the three primary elements of
production—land, labor, and capital—is skewed most heavily by a scarcity of labor, the
subject of a subsequent chapter.

But there is another level of economic activity beyond the household and that
has a determining impact on social life, kinship, and family structure: fishing, specialized
retail marketing, and craftsmanship. I begin with a chapter on fishing to show what
income-generating options are available beyond the household, to what degree people
use them, and how much income they earn, for it is in understanding differences in extra-
household income-generating opportunities that we can get an idea of the causes
underlying specific kinship patterns in Jean Rabel, especially with regard to conjugal
union.

Notes

1. It was also not clear if CARE analysts were aware of the fact that fully 65% of male
household heads in the community had more than one wife with whom they had borne children,
who they continued to help support, and who they considered as a spouse; i.e., they had more than
one family. The wives resided in multiple households, some within the fishing hamlet but most in
other fishing villages and in isolated hillside homesteads. If CARE researchers were aware of this
fact, they did not reveal it nor, of course, did they specify how they dealt with it in their analysis.

2. Chickens are raised for consumption and sale; secondarily for eggs that are eaten and
sold. Depending on its size, a chicken sells for 15 to 100 *gdes* (US$0.89 to 5.95). Goats and sheep
are raised primarily for sale. Kids and lambs sell for 200 to 250 *gdes* (US$11.90 to 14.88); an adult
goat or sheep sells for 300 to 1,000 *gdes* (US$17.86 to 58.52). Both animals are also slaughtered
for consumption, especially goats and especially when a woman has given birth. The meat is often
dried for short-term storage or resale. After chickens, goats are the animal most commonly
slaughtered in association with religious ritual. Pigs fetch the highest price of any livestock raised
for sale. Piglets sell for 200 to 500 *gdes* (US$ 11.90 to 29.76); and an adult pig can sell for as much
as 6,000 *gdes* (US$ 357.14). Pigs are almost always sold rather than slaughtered for consumption
in association with religious rituals. To be profitable, pigs demand large investments in feed and
veterinary services: 27.5% of all pig owners reported using veterinary services and medicines, the
highest use of veterinary services for any animal. Cattle sell for 2,500 to 4,500 *gdes* (US$148.80 to
267.86); a calf sells for 1,000 to 1,500 *gdes* (US$ 58.52 to 89.29). Depending on size, strength, and
age, the price of a donkey ranges from 500 to 2,500 *gdes* (US$29.76 to 148.81). The price of a
horse ranges from 1,000 to 4,000 *gdes* (US$58.52 to 238.10). And the price of a mule, the most
prized pack animal, ranges from 1,750 to 7,500 *gdes* (US$ 104.17 to 446.43). Horses, donkeys, and
mules are the prime means of transportation and are reportedly never eaten or slaughtered. Even a
sick or injured donkey, horse, or mule is simply left to die rather than euthanized.

3. Goats and sheep have a gestation period of 148–150 days and give birth about three
times every two years, meaning six kids. They browse on almost anything, but sheep are reportedly
more finicky and less hardy than goats. At ten months either a sheep or a goat can be bred. They
have twenty-one-day menstrual cycles. Cattle have a gestation period of 280–283 days.

Chapter 9

Fishing

Introduction

Fishing involves a relatively high investment in local materials and craftmanship services. Many of the materials needed must be purchased but some may be procured cost-free by resourceful individuals. Fishermen do not have access to outboard motors, fiberglass hulls, or refrigerated storage. Instead, sails, paddles, and wooden hulls prevail, and fish are salted, dried, and sold in local markets or hauled by boat or pack animal to markets in the provincial city of Port-de-Paix. Nevertheless, based on local standards, fishing is a significant source of income.

Fishing Communities

Fishing-dependent families comprise 4.4 percent of the Jean Rabel population or about 5,800 men, women and children (roughly one thousand households), most of whom are also dependent to varying degrees on their gardens and livestock raising.

They live in two permanent fishing villages in protected harbors on the coast of Jean Rabel (Bord Mer and Port-al-Acu) or in semi-permanent encampments along the arid coastal region stretching from Bord Mer west for approximately seven kilometers. The posts are almost entirely inhabited by people from farming communities who learned to fish by visiting their cousins in fishing hamlets and then struck out on their own, spending the fishing season in the most remote and often most productive sites where they build small lean-to like houses called *joupas*. Some of the men remain full time at the outposts. A steady trickle of wives, children, and cousins of the fishing-farmers come down to the posts to retrieve the fish and carry them back into hillside communities to be sold in the market.

Fishing Vessels

Farmers who fish part time use rudely fashioned one-man kayaks called *topye*. More heavily invested fishermen use *kanots*, row boats that average 11.5 feet in length.

In all of Jean Rabel there are some seventy *kanots* and 350 *topye,* small kayaks that are approximately eight feet in length. The most modern material on boats in Jean Rabel are nails: the smallest vessels are the *topye* kayaks, mentioned above, that are made of three logs lashed and nailed together. Row boats are less common but more important: the hulls are made from locally harvested and hewn oak, avocado, or a wood known locally as *sad*. For a waterproof sealant, fishermen buy a fiberglass-type substance called *brè*, derived from the nut of a local tree. When heated over a fire, *brè* becomes a sticky tar-like paste that cools to a hard glass (*brè* is also used as a coating for iron goods such as latches and hinges, and to repair leaky water buckets). Strips of cloth are dipped in the *brè* while it is hot and then pounded with a wooden mallet into the spaces between the boards from which the boat is fashioned. The entire hull is then coated with the resin. Oars are made of wooden poles with an oval length of board lashed to the end. A corn cob or piece of wood serves as a drain plug; a discarded plastic bowl or *kalbas* gourd is used to bail the boat. On larger vessels—also simply constructed and of which there are only four in the region—a manual bilge pump is fashioned from a length of bamboo or PVC, a wooden pole, and a goat skin, which looks and works like an inverted plunger. Sails are sewn together from used denim. The occasional boat motor in Jean Rabel fishing communities is usually a gift from some overseas relative, but is invariably a short-lived luxury that gets sold or stored away the first time it breaks. There are three compressors in the region but they all belong to the same man, a resident of the Island of La Tortue who supplies Port-au-Prince restaurants with seafood.

Fishing Materials and Technology

Fishing in Jean Rabel is an enterprise based almost entirely on nonindustrial technology and materials. Fish weirs are woven from bamboo and vine. Nets, while made from imported nylon string, are handwoven locally and weighted with rocks or lead from scrapped car batteries. Floats for fishing are made from discarded flip-flops, wood, or flotsam scrounged from the surf, and the nets are made with the buoyant seed pods from the local *moben* tree. Hooks, while often bought, are sometimes made from sharpened wire. Spear guns are made of discarded PVC pipe: wire for the trigger, a piece of wood for the handle, strips of used inner tubes for the charging mechanism, and a length of scrap iron rod for the spear (major fishing techniques used in the area are similar throughout the Caribbean; see Price 1966).

Because of strong winds, rough seas, and the rocky coastline, there are only two seines in the region. A seine is a net measuring several hundred meters used to fish from the shore; they are a common means of fishing in nearby Mole St. Nicolas and throughout the Caribbean. A seine is deployed using a row boat and it is hauled in by teams of from ten to thirty men who stand on the beach in two groups, one at each end of the seine, and they pull the seine in, effectively encircling the fish that are trapped between the position where the seine was originally deployed and the shoreline. Seines are cast during the fishing season when migratory fish pass, and when fish are most abundant, the seine is simply left deployed in the water, one end ashore, the other end tied to a boat. A man waits in the boat looking into the water with a mask or a small window-box that enables him to see under the water. If fish enter he cries *RALE!* (pull) and the *marin,* playing cards under nearby trees or ambling along the shore, sprint to position and pull the net in.

There are also nets strung between reefs or hung in the open ocean, suspended from floats and weighted at the bottom. The most common is the *twa nap*, a three-twine net. The nets are left overnight or fisherman will *bat dlo,* slapping the water in an effort to drive fish into the net.

Nets are more common, but the principal means of fishing is with weirs, of which there are two kinds: the *nas fonn*, which rests on the bottom of the sea, and the *nas flotè* or the floating *nas*. The floating *nas* is more important because for much of the year in Jean Rabel strong easterly winds make the unprotected sea rough and fishing difficult. Weirs not floated are caught up in currents and smashed against the bottom or swept away. The floating trap is buoyed by four one-gallon jugs and anchored to the bottom of the sea by a sack of rocks tied to a cord.

Line fishing and spear fishing are of secondary importance but provide many families in the area with small catches to supplement their diet and income. Both are accomplished from the shore or small outcroppings or from the small *topye* kayak mentioned above. Boys fish for baby balahoo in sandy beach areas, a sport that rivals flying kites but can yield small dividends as well.

Seasons and Fish Types

Because of the winds, fishing activity offshore is most intense from March to June when winds are not strong. But the fishing season, when the migratory fish come, is called the *rekolt* (harvest), and it occurs from July to November. When the fish come in abundance they say they *kase pak* (they broke out of their corral) and many fishermen in fact believe that people *lotbo* (overseas) keep migratory fish in corrals that the fish seasonally break out of during foul weather or when the fish become too many. The primary objective of fishermen are the seasonal migratory, but almost everything in the sea is game, including moray eel, conch, and, beginning at the size of about two inches, most tropical reef fish. Turtles, blowfish, sharks, and rays are also eaten. Local fishermen are not sure what to think of porpoises, although informants in Mole St. Nicolas report having once eaten several of the beached animals in 1994. The enormous humpback whales that are occasionally seen passing the area on their winter migration are regarded with horror.

Income

The principal means of catching fish is with weirs, known locally as *nas*, and fishermen calculate in terms of each weir. The weirs are bamboo, held together with vine. They cost from 30 *gdes* for the smallest to 85 *gdes* for the largest weirs. Fishermen pay other men to transport the weirs from the market to the fishing hamlets—carrying weirs being considered below the dignity of a respectable fisherman—and for a weir to be carried from the market to most coastal settlements costs a maximum of 30 *gdes* for a large weir and 15 *gdes* for a small weir. The weir does not come preassembled but must be woven together with vine (5 *gdes*). A durable waterproof rope is made from the nylon threads of shredded food-aid sacks and is needed to raise and lower the weir (108 *gdes*), and for the floating *nas* four one-gallon jugs are needed (20 *gdes*); four sticks to make a frame so that the weir can be raised and lowered into the sea without collapsing under its own waterlogged weight (4 *gdes*); and a sack of rocks for an anchor (5 *gdes*).

The lifetime of a weir is approximately equivalent to the duration of the fishing season, about four and a half months. But weirs are sometimes swept away by currents, stolen by thieves, and destroyed by big fish and moray eels that get to the catch before the fisherman. All this makes it difficult to estimate how much a weir will yield. The poorest fishermen tend to estimate 150–400 *gdes*, but the wealthiest and most knowledgeable fishermen—some of whom actually keep records—consistently estimate that, lost weirs factored in, a large weir yields on average 1,000 *gdes* over the course of the *rekolt*. This later estimate makes the most sense if one considers the investment in money and time. Deducting the cost of the weir (247 *gdes*), the lifetime yield is 743 *gdes*. Thus for three to six months (average 135 days) the average daily yield per weir is 5.1 *gdes*. A fisherman usually needs at least one helper, which means he must give him some of the fish—usually a fourth to a third of the catch. So before totaling, 30 percent of income must be deducted which brings the income down to 3.6 *gdes* per weir per day. Most fishermen will work a couple weirs during the off season, but during the most intense months of the *rekolt*—September thru November—fishermen who own their own boats typically work twenty weirs, about 72 *gdes* per day (US$4.30).[1] Men without boats, women, and even children will have three or four weirs that are checked by husbands, cousins, or *kanot*-owning neighbors.

Sen (seines), the long nets used for shore fishing, and *filè* (simple nets) that are set farther out to sea or along the cliff-lined coasts, both presuppose that a fisherman has a *kanot*. Owning a *sen* is the economic pinnacle of fishing in the region. Because of the high winds and often violent shore break, there are only three seines within the commune of Jean Rabel, but during the fish *rekolt* some men go to nearby Mole St. Nicolas, where there is a large protected harbor and fishing is significantly different than along the exposed Jean Rabel coast. At the "Mol," there are seventeen seines varying in length from 160 to 400 meters, with an average of 300 meters and a cost of about 50,000 *gdes*.[2]

Based on books kept for five *seines* at nearby Mole St. Nicolas, the average yield per seine in 1998 was 30,000 *gdes* (US$1,786). But 1998 was an off year, and seine owners report an average closer to 40,000 (US$2,381) *gdes* per year . Half of the catch (20,000 *gdes*) goes to the owner of the seine and half goes to the crew. This means that for the approximately 408 men who have a secured place hauling in seines at the Mol every year, their average income from this particular activity is 833 *gdes* (or US$50). For the owners of seines, income is substantially more. With an estimated annual repair cost of approximately 5,000 *gdes* per year, seine owners earn about 15,000 *gdes* (US$893)—of course they have other expenses as well, specifically boats of which they need at least one (US$93 has been deducted as an approximate cost of a boat over its ten+ year lifetime).[3]

Nets are less expensive, shorter than seines, more portable, and do not need a position; hence they are more common, especially among fishermen in the commune of Jean Rabel, who only have a few rarely used seines. Nets are put anywhere that seems opportunistic. They can be left overnight or simply left and checked daily like a *nas*. The average net is about seventy meters long and five meters deep and cost about 1,500 *gdes* (US$90).[4] Serious fishermen earn about 5,000 *gdes* per season per net. During the winter months, when lobster migrate from deeper waters, and provided there are buyers, some net fishermen earn windfalls as high as one thousand Haitian dollars in a single catch. The calculations have been omitted for these unpredictable windfalls. I focus instead on more consistent earnings, specifically, fishermen with nets go on what are called *boukan* (an apparent linguistic survival from the buccaneer era), where they camp out in remote coastal villages. Women also go along and they salt and dry the fish.

On a *boukan* a boat usually has four *marin* (mariners) and a net. The *marin* set the net up overnight and check it in the morning. They sometimes spend the day trying to round fish up by swimming and slapping the water, trying to drive the fish into the net (called *bat dlo*, beating the water, in Creole). As with seines, the catch is split 50/50 between owner and crew—owner gets 50 percent and the crew gets 50 percent—the difference, however, is the owner takes out the costs of damages to the net before the catch is split. On local *boukan* (*Kapafou, Lapreskil, La Grenad, Las Kayo*) a net owner can earn from 250 to 1,000 *gdes. Marin* earn 75 to 350 *gdes*. Boats usually go on two local *boukan* a year, for five to eight days each, in the months of November and December.

In the months of January to May, after the local fishing season is over, many of the full-time fishermen in the region go to the island of La Tortue on the north coast, where they have second or third—and in some cases fourth and fifth—wives. There a *kanot* with a net can reportedly make from 15,000 *gdes* to 25,000 *gde* in a season. This usually means about 9,000 *gdes* for the owner of the net and *kanot*, 3,000 *gdes* for each *marin* and 2,000 *gdes* for damages to the net.

It is important to understand the significance of owning a boat and nets or a *sein*. In general, *kanot* in the region range from 11 to 16 feet long and the regional average is 13.5 feet (a boat longer than 18 feet is called a *chat* and is used for transport). A *kanot* costs from 3,500 *gdes* to 12,500 *gdes*.[5] In Makab, three of twenty-one boats kept there were owned by women. But it is usually men who own the boats and it is always men who fish. The small kayaks mentioned above are only good for small weirs and line fishing and they sell for 500 *gdes*.

A boat is the first and most important ingredient in serious fishing and a significant indicator of wealth and the factors that set one man apart from another. In Makab, the only polygynous man who was not a boat owner was a healer. Most weirs belong to men. Women whose husband or sons fish may invest in weirs and some weirs will be assigned to a child. But it is always a man who raises and checks weirs.

By local standards, fishing is a significant source of income. As seen in table 9.1, a fisherman who owns his own boat, a net, and fishing weirs earns about US$1,268, about twice the US$679 that the average farmer can expect.

Table 9.1: Fishing income

	Fishing technique	Quant.	Months	Income (gdes)	Income (US$)
Owner	Seine	1	Sept–Nov	1,344	80.00
(must	Net	1	Sept–Nov	1,250	74.40
have	Net	1	Jan–May[*]	9,000	535.71
kanot)	Weir	20	Sept–Nov	9,720	578.57
	Total	—	—	21,314	1,268.68
Marin	Seine	—	Sept–Nov	833	49.58
(worker/	Net	—	Sept–Nov	400	23.80
assistant)	Net	—	Jan–May*	3,000	178.57
	Weir	—	Sept–Nov	206	12.26
	Total	—	—	4,439	264.21

[*] Migration to La Tortue

Conclusion

Fishing in Jean Rabel is a technologically basic endeavor in that most resources are procured locally or derived from scrapped industrial goods. Nevertheless, compared to farming it requires a large investment and yields congruently high income. A fisherman who owns his own boat, a net, and fishing weirs, is on a financial level equivalent with or greater than that of farmers and even skilled craftsmen seen in the following chapter. Moreover, although most fishermen are also dependent to varying degrees on farming strategies, the income they earn and the fact that it is earned independently of the household and contributions from other household members—most importantly their spouse—allow many of them to engage in conjugal union with more than one woman. In subsequent chapters I will take a closer look at the relationship between income, how it is earned, and conjugal unions. But first there are several other very important sources of income.

Notes

1. In the 1999 fishing season, six men in Makab—men with *kanots*—had the following number of weirs: Mirabo, twenty; Francois, fourteen; Lanyo, thirty-five; Albè, twenty; Joseph, twenty-two; Antonio, fifteen.

2.

Table 9.2: Cost of 300 meter seine in Haitian dollars (1 Haitian dollar = *gdes*: 1 US dollar (1999) = 16.8 *gdes*)

	Units	Cost/ unit	Unit/ Meter	Cost/ meter	Total units	Total cost
String*	1 roll	9	2	18	600	5,400
Weaving	Per meter	4	2	8	600	2,400
Trim (liej)	Per meter	1	1	1	300	300
Weighting	Per meter	1.5	1	1.5	300	450
Floats	Gallon jug	1.5	2	3	600	900
Cord	Meter	1.5	2	3	300	450
Total Cost		18.5	10	34.5		9,900

Note: Most seines are made with #18 nylon string. They cost H$9 a roll when purchased in bulk. Otherwise, fishermen in the spring of 1999 paid H$12 a roll for any size roll of nylon string.

3. Most financial and catch information on seines is based on Obreun, the largest seine owner in the region. Obreun has a university degree in fisheries. In 1998 he earned 74,900 *gdes* for all five of his seines. Another 74,900 *gdes*—the other half of the catch—went to the 120 *marins* who hauled in the seines. He paid 26,860 *gdes* in reparations. He reports, however, that in a normal year he grosses between 100,000 and 200,000 *gdes* (an equivalent sum going to the *marins*).

Obreun reports that farming is much more lucrative for him, irrigated land he inherited being his biggest earner. Note that the seines do not yield him a great deal; if he makes US$20,000 in a very good year on all five seines and pays US$6,000 for reparations, he is left with US$14,167. Furthermore, this is indisputably among the three wealthiest men in the region, giving one an idea of the upper limits of income.

Note also that, except in the *gran mer* (the ocean), fisherman at the "Mol" do not use the floating *nas*.

4. There are two kinds of *filè: filè twa nap* and *filè sinmp*. A *filè twa nap* is essentially thre layers of netting and the *filè sinmp* is only one layer of netting. The former is made of thicker nylon string (#9 and #36); the latter is made of finer #6 and #9 nylon string:

Table 9.3: The cost of string and weaving nets

String #	Cost per roll (H$)	Cost of weaving per meter (H$)	Meters net per roll
6	45–60	30	4
9	45–60	20	1
15	45–60	15	2/3
18	45–60	20	1/5
36	45–60	10	8

Table 9.4: The cost of weights, floats, and rope

	Units	Cost *gdes*	Cost / unit	Unit/ meter	Cost/ meter
Weights (lead balls)	sack of 50	25	0.5	2.5	1.25
Liez (*kos monben*)	sack of 60	100	1.70	2.5	4.25
Cord	50 dz sacks	1,800	3	1/6	0.50
Weave rope	2 gde per sack	0.33 per mt	—	—	0.33
Total	—	—	—	—	6.33

5. In Jean Rabel, *kanots* are smaller because seines, which require larger boats, are scarce. In Jean Rabel, the average local *kanot* is about 11 feet and the cost is 3,500 to 7,500 *gdes*

Chapter 10

Work, Craftsmen, and Marketing Specialists

Introduction

As seen in chapter 8, agriculture and livestock rearing are the most important economic activities in Jean Rabel. Literally everyone is somehow involved in farming and, when asked to report the three most significant sources of household income, over 87 percent of Jean Rabel respondents reported agriculture, and 50 percent mentioned livestock. But these were not the only sources of income: 45 percent cited commerce as the most important source, 20 percent mentioned charcoal production, 15 percent mentioned manual labor, and 12 percent mentioned "professional," which here includes both skilled labor and teaching. In this chapter I deal with these other categories of income. Unlike farming strategies, which are relatively equal opportunities based on household organization strategies, these other income-generating activities are more akin to fishing in that they are performed outside of the household, and access to and success at such activities are based on political contacts, age, sex, skill, and work ethic. Differential economic opportunity and success create differentials in social power and it will be seen in a later chapter that in examining the behavior of these individuals, the most economically active who by dint of their control over others—or dint of others who control them—are a vital determinant of family structure and kinship patterns.

Specialization and the Flourishing Subsistence Economy

Rural Jean Rabeliens are highly independent with regard to providing for their daily subsistence. Farmers have recourse to hundreds of natural and homemade substitutes for items like soaps, shampoos, hair laxatives, water containers, lamps, ropes, beds, fasteners, and shoes. Virtually anything regarded as a necessity has its homemade and cost-free substitute. As shown with regard to the marketplace, the range of specialization takes on almost extreme dimensions. For example, individuals specialize in the following activities: making tin lamps from discarded containers of condensed milk; crafting graters and funnels from tin vegetable oil containers; making candles from local beeswax or tree resins with wicks woven from locally grown cotton; fashioning brooms from a

Table 10.1: Household income-generating activities

Income Activity	# (N=1,519)	Percentage
Agriculture	1,320	87%
Livestock	784	52%
Marketing	652	43%
Charcoal	348	23%
Manual labor	211	14%
School teacher	159	10%
Artisan	70	5%
Remittances	48	3%
Maid	35	2%
Other	146	10%

long stick with palm thatch lashed to the end; fashioning coffee makers from a sock of cloth and a loop of wire; producing juice strainers from screen scraps; making mortars and pestles of all sizes out of local woods, making switches to whip animals—and children—from the skin of bull testicles.[1]   These items are all made by part-time farmer-specialists. Lumber for houses and furniture is hewn by the local specialists who fell trees with axes and saw them into boards using hand saws. Furniture is made with hand tools. Chairs are made of sticks and palm thatch, sisal, or vine. Nails, hinges, latches, iron bed frames, and the bits on horse bridles are produced locally by smiths working with nothing more than a hammer, burin, pliers, and burning coconut shells for heat to work the iron.[2] There are also specialists who make nets, weirs, and boats, caulk the boats, and go into the hills to find buoyant *monben* tree seed pods for nets and poles for oars. There are specialists who make bread, sweet rolls, and coffee. Others sew shoes. There are those who go into the bush to find vines and *galata* poles for roofs. There are specialists who climb coconut and palm trees, who gather rocks, and who make lime and charcoal. There are specialists for fixing doors and roofs and there are children who specialize in fixing bicycle tires. Digging holes in gardens is another specialist activity, as is the castration of livestock. There are even specialists who castrate particular kind of livestock. Other specialists hunt cats or mongoose using trained dogs. There are specialist tomb builders, grave diggers, casket makers, and those who wash and prepare bodies for burial. There are health care specialists, herb specialists called leaf doctors who know hundreds of remedies made from local plants and trees to treat everything from colds to AIDS (not all of them are effective). There are masseuses, midwives, spiritual healers, magic practitioners, and card readers. There are prayer-saying specialists, and even those who specialize in saying particular prayers on particular occasions.

   Most specialists, men and women, work for the smallest pittance. For example, it costs 2 *gdes* (US$.12) for the sewing up of a pair of sandals, 1 *gde* (US$.06) for a sweet roll, 1 *gde* for a cup of coffee, 7.5 *gdes* (US$.45) for a session of sorcery, 6 *gdes* for a twenty-foot rope, 5 *gdes* for a lamp, and 25 *gdes* (US$1.50) for a chair. Basket and hat makers earn no more than 10 to 15 *gdes* per day (US$0.60 to US$0.89). Successful healers are often the wealthiest individuals in an area, but most herb doctors and midwives earn respect but little money. A midwife for example makes 50 *gdes* (US$3.00) per birth and is lucky to get one birth per month. A *manyè* (type of masseuse) makes two or three *gdes* a consultation (US$.12 to $.18) and is lucky to have one consultation per day—which will probably require a walk of several miles. One compensation for the low fees is that service specialists generally must be fed and men are given rum while they work. But the actual labor cost is usually very low. Specialists invariably also have their own home, livestock and gardens, the economic foundation of Jean Rabel, upon which they depend for survival.

Male Employment Opportunities

At the top of the Jean Rabel income ladder are tree sawyers, masons, and carpenters. These particular *bosses* (craftsmen) earn 100 *gdes* per day (US$5.95) and their workers earn 50 *gdes* per day (US$2.97).[3] But this assumes ideal conditions. Tree sawing, for example, is one of the most lucrative if arduous tasks in rural Jean Rabel. A tree sawyer can earn anywhere from 100–300 *gdes* per day (US$5.95–US$29.75). The pay is by the job and depends on unforeseeable conditions—sharpeners break and some trees have almost impenetrable knots in them, knots that can be discovered only after a pay scale has been agreed on and the sawing begins. Thus, when all things are considered, a tree sawyer probably averages less than 100 *gdes* per day. Masons make about 75 *gdes* (US$4.46) per day and a carpenter makes the same.

Table 10.2: Estimated wages for male workers

Type of work	Estimated income (*gdes*)
Boss	75
General laborer	43
Charcoal maker	35
Porters	30–90
Ag laborer	10–50
Hat and basket maker	10–15
Rural school teacher	10

Table 10.3: Reported wages for male workers

Type of work	Estimated income per working day (*gdes*)
Sawyer	40–300
Mason	40–100
Carpenter	40–100
Iron smith	35–250
Charcoal maker	35–150
General laborer	10–50
Ag laborer and porters	30–100

The principal benefit to being a *boss* is that the individual will find at least some work some of the time, occassionally much work, and the 75 *gdes* per day earned will be surplus beyond the subsistence earnings from farming livelihood strategies. Assuming work can be found two hundred days a year—accounting for weather, funerals, festivals, marriages, family reunions (called *gombos*), sickness, and Sundays off—the total possible annual income for skilled labor is probably no more than 15,000 *gdes* or approximately US$893 dollars per year, and at an average of 42.5 *gdes* per day (US$2.52), an unskilled laborer can make 8,500 *gdes* per year (approximately US$505.95). These are sums that significantly exceed the mean household income estimated by CARE International (US$350.00). Furthermore, *bosses* generally have the same number of livestock and gardens, if not more, than other farmers.

For the majority of men, however, well-paying wage opportunities are scarce. Porters who transport loads on their heads for money or who unload trucks in the village may make from 30 *gdes* (US$1.78) per day to a rare and strenuously earned 100 *gdes* per day (US$5.95).[4] Full-time charcoal makers can also earn as much as *bosses* but the work is hard and prestige low. If they can find enough wood to cut, a charcoal specialist makes two sacks of charcoal per day for a daily income of about 70 *gdes* (US$4.17) but they still have to haul the charcoal to the market or to a place where it can be shipped on boat or truck, something that can take another day per two sacks reducing earnings to 35 *gdes* (US$2.08) per day. When hoeing fields, men are paid 10 *gdes* per *bout* (thirty *bout* to an acre). An average worker typically hoes three *bout* per day but actual production may range anywhere from one to five *bout* per day, depending on environmental conditions and the abilities of the worker, resulting in maximal possible earnings of approximately 50 *gdes* (US$2.97) for a day's work. Rural schoolteachers, of which there are over six hundred in Jean Rabel, make 250 to 300 *gdes* per month (US$14.88 to US$17.86)—although they often get fringe benefits, such as opportunities to embezzle CARE food aid.

Men and Wage Migration

In Haitian cities, the most menial income opportunities are comparably high paying in comparison to opportunities men find in Jean Rabel. A man pushing a wheelbarrow in the not-too-distant city of Port-de-Paix, for example, can earn an average of 100 *gdes* per day (US$5.95). In Nassau, the lowliest male laborer can reportedly earn 330 *gdes* per day (US$20) and more commonly 660 *gdes* (US$40.00)—a fortune by Jean Rabel standards. Women also migrate to the city and overseas but the opportunities are fewer. In Nassau, the principal job open to Haitian women is reportedly prostitution. A few women have access to upper scale urban neighborhoods within Haiti where they work as maids earning as much as $1,250.00 *gdes* per month (US$75), but domestic service far more commonly pays wages of 150 to 500 *gdes* per month (US$9–US$30).

Table 10.4: Urban blue collar pay scales, Port-de-Paix (adjusted for rental fees)

Male earnings (Haitian dollars per month*)		Female earnings (in Haitian dollars per month)	
Driver	800–2,000	Domestic	40–150
Collector on bus/taxi	300–800	Seamstress	300
Loader on truck	200–600	Prostitute	5 per customer
Mason	30 per day		
Carpenter	1,500		
Welder	1,000		
Tailor	800		
Merchant marine	600		
Rowing boat at wharf	40 per day		
Tire man	50 per day		
Taxi driver (moped)	25 per day		
Wheelbarrow operator	30 per day		
Laborer	10 per day		

* 1 dollar = 5 *gdes*

The upshot is that men have considerably more experience and opportunities for traveling overseas and to work in the capital city of Port-au-Prince. As seen in chapter 4, seventeen of the sixty-six men (two missing) interviewed for the Opinion Survey reported having worked in a city or overseas for at least 30 of the 365 days preceding the interview. Similarly, in a community sample of forty-one male household heads in Famadou, a typical Jean Rabel farming community, twenty-one of the respondents had gone to the city to work before they married or entered consensual union—and only seven had been away since entering into a union.[5]

Further, eleven of the sixty-six Jean Rabel men interviewed in the Baseline Survey reported having been overseas, whereas no women reported having ever been abroad. Also, twenty-six men versus seventeen women reported having visited the capital in their lifetimes (see table 10.5).[6]

Table 10.5: The most distant place farmers have visited

		Men		Women		N
	USA, Bahamas, DR	11	17%	0	0%	11
The most	Port-au-Prince (capital)	26	39%	17	25%	43
distant	Secondary city	7	11%	9	13%	16
place the	Port-de-Paix	17	26%	30	45%	47
respondent	Regional market	5	7%	11	16%	16
has visited	Total	66	100%	67	100%	133

To put employment into perspective, most men in Jean Rabel would consider themselves very lucky to land a full-time job for 750 *gdes* per month (US$44) as a watchman for a local intervention organization. Rural men and woman scramble to secure a spot on road projects at the State minimum wage of 30 *gdes* per day (US$1.78). But it is also important to understand that this "scrambling" and interest in extra-domestic jobs rests on the expectation that employment will not impede the carrying out of farming activities. Intervention workers in the area are often mystified by Jean Rabeliens who, feeling overtaxed by a demanding employer, simply walk off their jobs in favor of tending to their gardens.

Female Employment Opportunities

There are no female *bosses*. Women do not work in jobs that require heavy lifting, and while many women, even young girls, might pick up a hoe (*manye wou*), a woman rarely performs heavy garden work, such as swinging a pick (*voye pikwa*) and digging holes (*fouye tou*). Woman can sometimes make 15 *gdes* per day (US$0.91) picking beans but usually a woman doing an agricultural job is lucky to earn anything more than a meal, some of the harvest, and a return favor owed for her efforts.

Women have a low representation in high prestige fields. None of the twenty-one *kasek* or sixty-five *asek* (rural political representatives) are women. Of the 53 (out of 3,925) individuals over eighteen years of age who were identified during the Baseline Survey as professional schoolteachers, only ten were female (19%). There are successful female healers, called *mambos,* and they are not uncommonly among the wealthier people in the region. Nevertheless, male shaman (*bokor*) outnumber their female counterparts ten to one. As seen, migrant opportunities for women are considerably less attractive than those available to men. Putting female employment opportunities into perspective, employed women are happy if they can earn the equivalent or somewhat lower wages (500–750 *gdes*) working six days a week cooking and washing clothes by hand. There is, however, one opportunity open to women that overshadows all others: marketing.[7]

Table 10.6: People who travel at least once per month

| | | Gender | | | |
		Women		Men	N
Does this person	No	30	45%	47 73%	77
travel at least once	Yes	37	55%	17 27%	54
per month?	Total	67	100%	64	131

Women and the Market

Marketing is, after agriculture and livestock, the most important source of household income in Jean Rabel. Every woman who has her own household and who is not sick or crippled visits a regional market center at least once a week, where she makes household subsistence purchases and sells the agricultural and animal products produced by the household. In the Opinion Survey, 72 percent (97 of 135) women household heads or the wives of male household heads reported also being involved in buying and selling products other than those produced in the family homestead. Women may specialize in selling anything from staples to used clothes to brewed coffee to machetes and schoolbooks. Even butchery is a female buying and selling enterprise. It is women who skillfully chop with a machete freshly slaughtered animals into smaller divisions and then sell the fresh meat on the spot. The only marketing enterprises in which men participate are the selling of live animals—and even this is an activity in which women are more prominent than men—and itinerant pharmaceutical and pesticide sales. An illustration of the near-absolute domination of the retail marketplace by women was garnered through a count of 612 nonlivestock marketers in Lacoma, Jean Rabel on October 22, 1998: 609 of the sellers were women and only 3 were men. Female market activity is so important to household livelihood that few people would dare save money by stashing it away. A person who has money will invariably "put the money to work" by giving it to a female relative or friend who will roll the money over in the market, for as they say in Jean Rabel, *lajan sere pa fe pitit* (stashed money bears no children). Of fifty-two husbands interviewed on the topic during the Opinion Survey, thirty-nine reported that their wives were actively engaged in itinerant marketing and, of these women, thirty-one traveled to urban centers at least once a month. Indeed, although men travel farther and stay away from home longer than women, intense female marketing activity means that women travel more frequently than men. Many of the women specialize in the sale of one or several commodities, such as chickens, goats, or straw handbags, which they spend several weeks purchasing from neighbors, friends, or in rural markets to sell in the urban markets. Others focus on seasonal produce and staples.[8]

Figure 10.1: Port-de-Paix *Marchann* cost of merchandise
y = 483, SD=751, N = 54

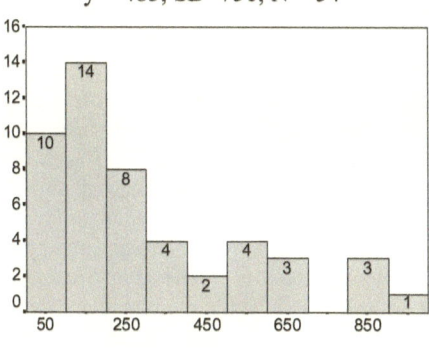

Cost of merchandise

Note: Six observations exceed the 1,000 *gdes* limit visible in the graph.

Figure 10.2: Port-de-Paix *Marchanns* profits on merchandise
Y = 234, SD = 165, N = 54

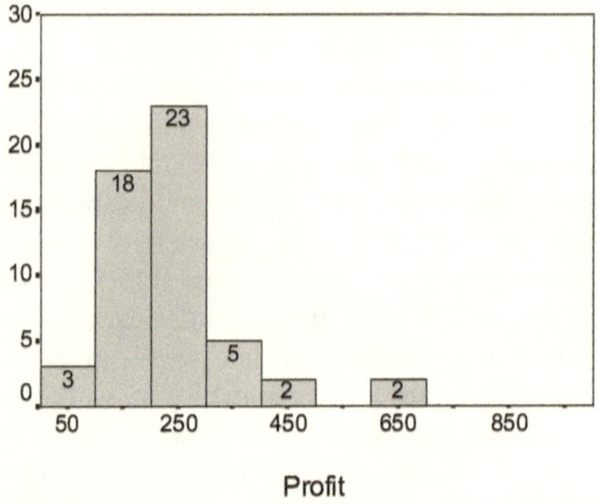

Profit

The most common ventures to urban markets are made to Port-de-Paix and 38 percent of husbands reported that their wives make the trip at least once per month. The voyage is invariably made on donkey or mule, since the cost of public transportation would consume too much of the profits, and the women usually travel in groups with other market women. They set out for Port-de-Paix in the late afternoon and walk behind their loaded animals all night, fording streams and winding their way down worn trails, some of which have not changed course since the Taino Indians trod them five hundred years ago. On a straight, flat stretch of road flanked by lush banana trees, the women come at last to their final obstacle, Trois Rivie (the Three Rivers). Normally a wide but meandering, crystal clear, knee-deep lowland stream, rainfall in the mountains can quickly turn this tranquil creek into a muddy, life-threatening torrent that woman and animal must wade across to reach the city. Once on the other side of the river, the women find themselves on the windswept dirt streets of Port-de-Paix. They sell their produce among decaying vegetable heaps in a bustling, tin-roofed, seaside market. Many then turn around and head home that very day, without ever having slept and without having purchased anything, because the Port-de-Paix market has little to offer that cannot be bought more cheaply in Jean Rabel from the handlers of imported food aid or from the *gran marchann,* who ply their trade with Port-au-Prince.

The money that an active market woman can earn compares favorably to male income earnings. In a sample of fifty-four women interviewed while they were en route from Jean Rabel to Port-de-Paix, the average woman was found to be carrying 483 *gdes* (US$28.75) worth of merchandise to be sold for 717 *gdes* (US$42.68), yielding an average profit on their merchandise of 234 *gdes* (US$13.93).[9] The norm, or modal value of merchandise a woman was carrying was between 100 to 200 *gdes* (US$5.95 to US$11.90), with a modal profit of 200 to 300 *gdes* (US$11.90 to US$17.85). There are no other incidental costs involved that reduce profit because the women carry their own food and water, and they cut grass along the way or carry fodder from home to feed their animals. They do not stop to buy cokes or ice cream, and their donkeys burn no gasoline and eat no store-bought feeds or supplements. The women simply take their profits and return.

The average number of voyages per woman per month is two (1.9 to be exact) and so an average market woman makes about 468 *gdes* (US$27.85) per month as a result of her excursions to Port-de-Paix. The enterprise requires a total investment time of between four and six days. These same women also trade in rural markets and sell goods out of their homes. An investigation of the twenty-four major commodities being sold revealed that the average profit margin for retail sales within the commune of Jean Rabel was 20 percent (standard error of the mean at 2.4%) with a 15.6 day average turnover rate for the major commodities. Thus, using an estimated working capital of 430 *gdes*—the average value of what women were carrying to Port-de-Paix—market women are probably earning another 172 *gdes* per month.

Totaling what an average *marchann* makes in her Port-de-Paix ventures with profits on the home front, a woman's average monthly income from marketing activities is about 640 *gdes* per month (US$38.00), more than 2.5 times the salary of the typical rural schoolteacher. The estimated annual total earnings is US$456, 29 percent greater than the regional income for a family of six as estimated in 1994 by CARE International (1996; 1997).[10] But these are modal and average income levels. It needs to be understood that as with *bosses*, some market women are more successful than others, some have access to greater amounts of capital, and some are simply shrewder. Six of the women interviewed (11%) are not even reflected in figures 10.1 and 10.2 because they were carrying more than 1,000 *gdes* worth of merchandise. One woman was leading 4,410 *gdes* worth of livestock to market and she was going to make a profit of 1,040 *gdes* (US$61)—four times the average rate. Furthermore, as shown earlier, eleven of thirty-one urban-venturing *marchann* (35%) travel to the larger cities of Gonaives and Port-au-Prince, where the most successful women sometimes build their trade revenue up to several thousand Haitian dollars per month. There are a special few rural women who by virtue of their marketing savvy have migrated to the village of Jean Rabel and led their entire families into the higher ranks of the village commercial elite. They buy land for their husbands to farm, they pay other men to work gardens for them, and they send their children away to urban schools and overseas universities.

Conclusion

Jean Rabel has a flourishing subeconomy of skilled craftsmen and female marketing specialists. The money paid for services and local products may appear pittances to outsiders but they are meaningful within the narrow bounds of the regional subsistence economy. In particular, skilled craftsmen such as tree-sawyers, masons, and carpenters are among men who have an exceptional local income-earning opportunity outside of the household means of production. For women, the most substantial nonfarm income opportunity is marketing, the third most important source of household income in the region, and an activity that most women strive to master. But whatever the occupation, a person is already a member of a household, the true foundation of livelihood and survival in Jean Rabel, a point necessary to understand other sources of income. Without being a governing member of a functioning household, one is not free to engage in these other activities. It is through ownership and management of a household that one is free to pursue other economic activities. But this assumes that someone is left behind to take care of the household, for the demands of the household as a production and income-generating unit and its role as the primary assurance against vicissitudes of the market and natural disasters implies immense labor demands, the subject of the next chapter.

Notes

1. Saddles and saddle blankets are made from banana and plantain stalks, saddle bags and sacks ranging from quart size to a hundred gallons are woven from palm thatch, baskets are made from slithers of bamboo, bridles are made from sisal and palm thatch rope and goat skin with scrap iron used to make the bit, and hats are woven from grasses.

2. The scrap iron is heated over a fire of dry coconut shells, a fuel that burns hotter than regular woods.

3. The exchange rate used is 16.8 Haitian *gdes* = one US dollar. Five *gdes* = one Haitian dollar.

4. Examples of porter opportunities: Carrying fish weirs from the village to Mole St. Nicolas, a four-hour walk (eight hours round trip). Depending on physical endurance, a person can carry one to three large weirs at H$6.00 each or three to four small weirs at H$3.00 to H$4.00 each for a total of H$6.00 to $18.00 per day. Porters in the village get 1 to 2 *gdes* for carrying and unloading one 110 lb sack of rice or flour—wheelbarrows are rare. These same porters report making about 100 *gdes* a day but abundant work is not often available—usually on the two village market days, Wednesday and Saturday.

5. It makes no sense to a Jean Rabel woman to go live with a man in a house he gives her if the man has no gardens or livestock; nor does it make sense to go live with the man's mother when the girl can more comfortably stay with her own mother, who will be happy to have the services of a grandchild. In the absence of a supportive husband, a Jean Rabel woman can begin bearing children while still living with her parents without suffering shame or ridicule. The higher rates of males in older age groups is possibly due to women with grown children going to live with the children in urban areas.

6. The chief advantage of domestic employment is that meals and sleeping quarters are usually provided by the employer. Some women go to the city for a year or two to earn the money to pay debts, buy land, or enter into marketing activities.

7. For the same wages as men, women fill some 33 percent of the places on road projects. But female involvement in roadwork is somewhat misleading because control of the lists is dominated by a few individuals and these people favor friends and family members. The outcome is that lists are stuffed with people, some of who never show up for work—a respectable man or woman of means would never actually work on a road project, although they might send a younger or less fortunate family member to work for them. When gardens are being planted, for example, one can expect to find only women working, no matter how many men are on the lists. In any case, for November 1998 to February 1999, 33 percent (3,289) of the 10,000 participants in a random one in three systematic sample of the AAA food for work lists were women. On lists made available by PISANO, 21 percent (234) of the 1,121 PISANO road workers were female although the proportion of females varied widely per *habitasyon*—between 4 percent and 67 percent female.

8. The most successful women are intermediaries in urban/rural exchange of staples between Jean Rabel and Port-au-Prince—the staples flow both ways depending on the season. These women develop extensive networks of local female clientele who depend on them for supplies that are

often provided on credit. Some of them become wealthy by local standards—many subsequently emigrate. Seven of the fifty-two women reported on in the followup survey regularly make the trip to Port-au-Prince.

9. The method of selecting women was not highly regimented or the sampling design sophisticated. Every morning for five days in January 2000, between the hours of sunrise and about 8:00 a.m., I sat by the roadside coming into Port-de-Paix, in a place called La Saline, before one arrives at Trois Rivie. All market women were stopped, explained the purpose and nature of the research and then interviewed regarding the type and quantity of merchandise they were carrying. Most women were friendly and cooperative. There were six refusals or rather six women who gave obviously false responses or who simply ignored me. To obtain sales prices in Port-de-Paix and purchase prices in rural areas, I personally visited the markets, haggled over prices, and consulted with market women I know as friends.

Concerning investments in pack animals: twenty-three of the women had only one donkey, seventeen had two donkeys, one woman had three donkeys, one had four donkeys, five women were on mules, and two were walking. An adult donkey costs about H$250.00 to H$350.00, a young donkey can be purchased for H$100.00 to H$250.00. A mule goes for H$800.00 to H$2,000.00, with H$1,200.00 being the most typical price.

10. I have not discussed credit in the main body of the text because I did not think it necessary. The analysis has to stop somewhere and the issue is how much women have invested and how much they can make—not how much they owe. Nevertheless, it may interest the reader to know that there is a well-established if indirect system of money lending. It works as follows: *Gran marchanns* (big vendors) and store owners sell sacks of staple foods—most often flour, rice, corn, and sugar—on credit to small vendors. Many of the small vendors then turn around and sell the sack or sacks of food for less than cost, using the money to buy and sell more profitable merchandise. The sellers give women a fixed amount of time to pay for the merchandise, usually twenty-two days (three market weeks). Some large vendors charge more money per sack but give as much as a two-month repayment period.

The reason large vendors prefer to give merchandise rather than simply loan money is not clear. The interest that can be demanded for money is reportedly as high as 100 percent per month. The interest charged through this "euphemistic" system of credit works out to be about 15 percent for twenty-two days (and this takes into consideration the loss to the borrower of selling the merchandise below cost).

Chapter 11

Labor Demands

Introduction

In the previous chapter I showed that in Jean Rabel a dazzling degree of specialization occurs in both the production of local material goods and the provision of services. For men, skilled craftsmanship and seasonal agricultural work are sources of additional income and most men at some point in their lives temporarily migrate to urban areas, overseas, or to the Dominican Republic, where they work as menial wage laborers in agriculture and construction sectors. Some women also go to the city and work as maids or cooks. The primary feminine opportunity is marketing, something that all rural Haitian women eventually engage in and something that has the potential to put women on economically equal footing with men. But all these activities presuppose the individual's participation in a household, for one must be a member of a household to assure survival in the unpredictable and harsh environment and to be free to engage in other income-generating activities.

In this chapter I want to show that the labor demands associated with technologically simplistic and low-risk household livelihood strategies are enormous. In later chapters it will be seen that it is precisely these demands that explain high fertility and the associated pronatal cultural patterns seen earlier. The role of household livelihood strategies in the face of an unpredictable economy, periodic drought, and the tremendous labor demands inherent in accomplishing these strategies is critical to survival in Jean Rabel. In tending gardens and livestock, fetching wood and water, cooking, cleaning, and childrearing, households need labor. The labor can be procured in three ways: (1) it can be purchased, as in hiring local or immigrant labor, (2) it can be traded, as in reciprocal work groups, and (3) it can be produced, as in pregnancy, childbirth, childrearing, and child labor (or as will be seen later, a child can also be "borrowed").

Jean Rabeliens are at a decided disadvantage when it comes to purchasing labor. As shown previously, Jean Rabel ranks among the poorest areas in Haiti and the pay that cash-poor farmers can offer workers is too low to attract migrant laborers. Local wage laborers are scarce because most households have access to land and animals through the tenure arrangements described in the previous chapter. The result is that even the few Jean Rabeliens who have money available to pay agricultural laborers frequently complain that labor cannot be found. Moreover, Jean Rabeliens consider performing chores for another household to be humiliating, and no household head would ever consider paying anyone to perform these tasks.

Labor can also be obtained through the use of reciprocal labor groups, the only functional suprahousehold organizations in rural Jean Rabel. Farmers often depend on membership in such organizations, called *kwadi*, to prepare fields for planting.[1] But as shown previously, agriculture is only one of the labor demands that must be satisfied to maintain a productive household, and reciprocal labor groups will not drop by the house to assist in the completion of the daunting number of chores that must be accomplished daily in every rural Jean Rabel household. For most labor needs, Jean Rabeliens must depend on themselves and their family.

The Organization of Labor and the Prominence of the Household

Members of Jean Rabel households resolve simple subsistence tasks with raw human labor and abundant amounts of time. Household chores must be accomplished daily, tasks such as traveling several miles to fetch water, purchasing food in rural markets, and collecting firewood. The simplest message must be entrusted to and sent via a person, and clothes must be carried miles to the nearest river or spring where they are washed and wrung out by hand. These tasks, necessary and basic to a sanitary and healthy existence, are accomplished within the sociostructural organization of the household, meaning they are carried out by a cooperating group of people who identify themselves as members of a particular household. Furthermore, it is through the labor-allocating organizational structure of the household that the overwhelming majority of people in Jean Rabel are able to succeed at making a living, however meager, in agriculture and animal husbandry.

Household Tasks

In every household, a minimum number of time-consuming tasks must be performed on a daily basis. Every day the house and yard must be swept (the rolled up and put away and the house dusted, tasks that take an average of one to two hours to accomplish. Food preparation and cooking involve starting and tending a fire, snapping beans, peeling plantains and sweet potatoes, and pounding beans and spices. If the fire is good—i.e., the wood is seasoned and hard—rice or sweet potatoes can be boiled in about one hour. Beans are a daily staple in virtually all Jean Rabel households. If fresh, they take only twenty minutes to prepare, but if they are dry they must be boiled for more than two hours. Under optimal conditions, therefore, a meal can be prepared in about two hours, but it can and usually does take considerably longer. If the fire is not hot, because the wood is too green or of a poor quality, cooking a simple meal without meat can take more than four hours. If meat is cooked it must be washed with sour oranges or limes, boiled, and then fried, adding another hour to the time it takes to prepare a meal.

Gathering firewood is a task that requires at least one hour per day, and where wood is scarce it takes as much as three man-hours per day. Triweekly picking of beans and digging sweet potatoes are also time-consuming endeavors. The average distance from the homestead to a garden is a forty-six-minute walk, but 45 percent of gardens are located more than ninety minutes from the house. The actual harvesting takes one to two hours. Water is necessary in the house for drinking, cooking, and washing dishes and to accomplish these tasks the typical household uses ten gallons per day, although small households with very young children may get by on as little as five gallons per day. In effect, someone must make at least one and typically two or three daily trips to fetch water, at an average of seventy minutes per trip. For bathing and washing clothes, people usually go to the water sources rather than carry water back to the house, but this also involves another time-consuming trek. Clothes are washed by hand. Women typically wash clothes on one in every three days, a task that, depending on the number of people in the household and the distance to the water, may consume from a half to one full day's labor (six to twelve hours). Someone in the household must go to the market at least twice a week, an average round-trip walking time of three hours per journey (twelve kilometers). Totaled, the minimum labor demand for a Jean Rabel household is an average of 74.2 adult hours per week, or 10.6 hours per day. Depending on where the house is located in relation to water, sources of firewood, and markets, and how many people live in the house, labor demands can exceed 155.4 adult labor hours per week, or 22.2 hours per day. And this is to say nothing about labor demands associated with livestock and gardens (see table 11.2).[2]

Table 11.1: Average daily labor requirements for principal household tasks

Task	Frequency per day	Days per week	Avg # hours per performance	Avg. time per week (hours of adult labor) Min	Max
Morning house cleaning	1	6	1–2	6.0	12.0
Weekly house cleaning	1	1	3–6	3.0	6.0
Water carrying	1–4	7	1.2	8.4	33.6
Morning meal	1	7	1–2	7.0	14.0
Afternoon meal	1	7	2–4	14.0	28.0
Gathering fire wood	1	7	1–3	7.0	21.0
Laundry	1	2	6–12	12.0	24.0
Walk to garden + harvesting	1	3.5	2.5	8.8	8.8
Trip to market	1	2	4	8.0	8.0
Total	—	—	—	74.2	155.4

In reality, a task-by-task tabulation of labor demands does not accurately depict time spent doing subsistence chores, because some household tasks can be integrated in such a way as to facilitate the realization of others. For example, one may fetch the water on the way back from the market or clean the house while breakfast is boiling. But, the primary objective of the analysis is to begin to illustrate the tremendous time demands required in rural Jean Rabel to accomplish simple subsistence tasks. A myriad of other routine household tasks not included in table 11.1 must also be accomplished. Goods and messages must be hand carried to other people and young children must be fed, washed, and supervised. Adults insist on ironing cloths, a task that involves using a charcoal heated steam iron. Coffee beans must be roasted and pounded into a powder, a task that may be done once a week but takes up an entire morning. Just making coffee, when one considers starting the fire, boiling the water, and straining the grounds, takes an hour. Dishes are always washed after meals and in many households they are washed again every morning as a sanitary measure—an activity that is virtually a Jean Rabel custom. On Saturdays everything is hauled out of the house, dusted and scrubbed, another Jean Rabel custom. Other occasional time-consuming chores not included in the calculations in table 11.1 include weaving rope and sleeping mats, and repairing thatch roofs and mud walls.

Agriculture Labor Demands

There are two planting seasons per year in Jean Rabel, one in October and November and another in April and May. Even before the seasonal rains arrive, farmers scramble to begin working their own plots before daybreak (~5:00 a.m.) and if there is a bright moon, some farmers may begin working as early as 3:00 or 4:00 a.m. They hoe the soil (*tchake*) until about 10:00 a.m., take a break, and return to their fields at around 3:00 p.m. when the sun is no longer directly overhead and the temperature begins to cool. After the soil is turned, and providing the rains have begun, planting begins. One to two months later, the garden is weeded (*sakle*), and after three months the harvests begin (*rekolt*).[3]

Table 11.2: Estimated labor inputs for average 5.7 acres of garden: One three- to four-month planting cycle (eight-hour work day) (see endnote 5)

{A}	{B}	{C}	{D}	{E}[a]	{F}[b]
				Days	Total days
Type of activity	Total # of bouts	Mean bout per day	# of adults	needed per task	needed per task
Hoeing	171	3.5	1	48.9	48.9
Planting	171	11	3	15.5	46.5
Weeding	171	2.5	1	68.4	68.4
Harvesting	171	8	3	21.4	64.2
Processing	171	24	5	7.1	35.6
Total	—	—	—	—	263.6

[a]$E = [B / C]$, [b]$F = [D * E]$

Virtually all rural Jean Rabel households are involved in agriculture. Only 2.5 percent of the Baseline Survey respondents claimed not to have any gardens. The mean amount of land farmed was 5.7 acres per household per year.[4] What this means to farmers in practical work terms is that if the gardens are to be planted and harvested, the average farmer will need 319 adult/days of labor per cycle to do it. Due to the fact that the seasonal rains do not wait for people to finish planting and that hungry birds do not wait for people to finish harvesting, the farmer will need access to all of these labor hours concentrated into a few weeks time (see figure 11.1 below).[5]

Figure 11.1 Rainfall by months (Cabaret Station 1965–1969, 1978–1996)

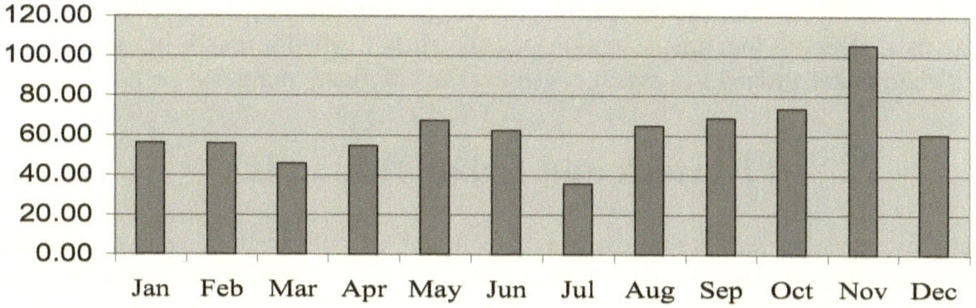

Complicating matters for farmers is the regional labor shortage mentioned earlier. Farmers in Jean Rabel may be poor, but 67.1 percent report owning some land and even this is probably a large underestimate resulting from the tendency for farmers, in anticipation of assistance, to portray themselves as totally impoverished. Furthermore, the 32.9 percent percent who reportedly do not own land enter into fifty/fifty sharecropping arrangements or employ some other strategy to attain access to a plot of land.[6]

Table 11.3: All types of land tenure (units of analysis = gardens)

Types of land tenure	Percentage (n=3,711)	Cumulative percentage
Owned	67.1%	67.1%
Sharecropped	19.1%	86.2%
Rented	11.0%	97.2%
On loan	2.2%	99.4%
Employed	0.1%	99.5%
Other	0.5%	100.0%
Total	100.0%	100.0%

The consequence is a labor squeeze. Everybody is working on their garden plots at the same time—hoeing at the same time, weeding at the same time, and harvesting at the same time. In the rush to get their gardens hoed lest they miss out on a good season, adults and even boys as young as nine and ten years of age form reciprocal work groups called *kwadi*. People with the money to pay local wages frequently complain they cannot find workers.

Fifty-one percent of household respondents reported reciprocal volunteer work groups as the principal source of garden labor, 25.7 percent reported family as the principal source, and 22.7 percent reported paid labor as the principal source. A time-consuming feature of planting not accounted for in table 11.2 on labor commitments is getting to the gardens. As farmers say, "there is mountain and there is plain" *(gen monn, gen plenn)*, meaning that in Jean Rabel, in the endeavor to avoid crop failure, the farming of multiple garden plots geographically distant from one another is, in the face of highly variable soil types, altitudes, and rainfall patterns, a practical and adaptive strategy. The average farmer has 2.8 gardens and, as mentioned earlier, the average garden is a forty-six-minute walk from the house, with 45 percent of gardens more than ninety minutes from the house. Some men and women migrate to gardens and stay there during planting and harvests, sleeping in a small, tent-shaped thatch hut called a *joupa*, but most make the daily commute, a round trip average walking time of ninety minutes.[7]

Livestock and Labor Demands

Virtually everyone in Jean Rabel owns livestock and, as with land, there is a livestock tenure system. People with many animals, especially people who live in the village, give animals to other farmers to raise and look after. The farmer turns the first offspring over to the owner and then takes the second for himself, and so on. Any profits from sales of the "shared" animal are split fifty/fifty.[8]

Labor demands associated with livestock are more constant and greater than those associated with agriculture, because tasks related to livestock raising must be performed several times daily without failure. In most areas, livestock are tethered. In some areas, however, goats and sheep are free ranged but this is risky as other farmers have a right to kill the animals should they venture into a garden. Nevertheless, even free-ranged goats and sheep require a daily checkup and owners need to take water to the animals to prevent them from straying into garden areas.[9] Animals particularly vulnerable to dog attacks (sheep), and animals popular with thieves (cows and mules), are brought back to the homestead in the evening. Goats are left tethered in the brush because they will bleat when approached by dogs, usually attracting the attention of people from nearby homesteads.

Animals are led to open pasture or checked before dawn. The animals are moved again at least once and sometimes twice during the day to areas with shade and fresh fodder. These times also serve to assure that the animals are not strangling on their cords, that dogs are not in the process of killing them, or that thieves are not in process of stealing them. Small animals such as goats and sheep do not need to be watered when there is abundant rainfall. But when there is not sufficient rainfall, as is common in Jean Rabel, the animals must be watered at least every three days and generally every day during the hot summer months. Rain or shine, large livestock such as cows and pack animals must be watered daily.

The amount of time invested in livestock obviously depends on the number of animals a household owns and the distance from the household to water sources and foraging areas. Animals are often tethered on the same land or in the vicinity of the garden and the average distance in time from the homestead to these grazing areas is thus a forty-six-minute walk. In cases where people use the *kadas* (the arid State lands) to free range, or more commonly to tether animals, the walk is considerably farther. When traveling through the *kadas* it is not uncommon to encounter boys two hours from home en route to or coming from checking livestock.

It is difficult and probably impractical to try to estimate the amount of time necessary to tend animals. To begin with, there is wide spectrum of intensity with which members of a household can care for their animals. Animals can be turned loose in the *kadas* and not checked for days, or tethered somewhere and moved only once a day. But these are risky practices that increase the chances of animals being lost, stolen, or killed by dogs. At the other extreme, a household head can see to it that animals are checked and moved at least twice during the day and brought into the yard at night, practices that increase the probability the animals will survive to reproduce and to be sold in the market. But that also requires significantly greater investments in time and labor.

Another factor that complicates the estimation of livestock labor inputs is the difficulty of determining how many animals can be moved or led to the water at the same time. A lone man or woman, for instance, can handle as many as six goats and an unlimited number of sheep. Only one sheep needs to be guided and the rest will follow. Goats will also follow but they are less cooperative. In summary, regarding the time and labor inputs required by a household for livestock raising, the general rule is that the more time and the more labor that is invested, the better.[10]

Hard Times

Yet another issue that should be factored into an understanding of labor demands in Jean Rabel is periods of climatic stress. A severe regional drought occurs in Jean Rabel on average one in every eight years. When a drought strikes, demands on household labor increase precipitously, and the principal feature that determines the success of a household in coping with and surviving drought is not how few mouths it has to feed, but how many able bodies it can put to work. Crop failure turns many households to charcoal production and, as a consequence, local wood supplies dwindle and household members must travel farther and farther to find wood for fuel.[11]

Table 11.4: Distance to and from water

	N	Min	Max	Mean	Std dev
		Round trip distance in minutes			
When there is rain	124	1.00	240	67	58
When there is no rain	124	1.00	360	120	80

Most problematic is the water supply. Water sources dry up and people have to travel farther to fill their buckets. In the followup survey, respondents reported that the temporal distance to and from the nearest secondary water source is 120 minutes, almost twice as far as during normal times. All households in the region are experiencing the same stress and this means that the fewer water sources are being visited by more people. The fewer springsare packed with crowds of pushing, shoving, and cursing women and children. People get up at midnight so they can arrive at a distant spring before it becomes too crowded and they spend hours waiting to fill a single water jug. Some people, particularly young children, return to the house teary-eyed, trodden and bruised, having failed to procure any water at all. Washing clothes during drought conditions becomes problematic as well. Women must travel great distances to find clean water and a vacant place to sit and scrub. Animals have to be watered more frequently since the desiccated fodder dehydrates them. Fodder itself becomes scarce, so farmers are traveling farther and farther into remote areas to graze their animals or to cut grass for them and then they must lead the animals more frequently in the other direction, into more peopled areas, where there are adequate water sources that have not dried up.

All of this additional effort translates into more labor and the need for more workers because, rain or no rain, people must eat and they must drink. Food still must be cooked, water found, clothes washed, and at least some animals must be kept alive so that when the drought finally does end there will be something with which to start producing again.[12]

Conclusion

In Jean Rabel, the household is the principal organizational medium for survival and, for the most part, the only enduring organizational structure. Being a member of a household is a prerequisite for survival. Virtually all tasks necessary for production and participation in the regional economy are accomplished within—or dependent on—the household. In this chapter, I showed that the actual time needed to accomplish the tasks that make a household viable are tremendous. There is also a feature inherent in the household economy that may not be readily visible to the casual observer. No matter how few members there are in a household, there is a minimum level of labor that must be accomplished. Distance to the water and the market does not change with the number of members in a household, nor does the time required to cook beans change as a result of the number of people eating them. The fundamental point is that the fewer people in a household, the more work there is to do for each member. On the other hand, with increasing numbers of household members, there is a relative decline in the workload required of each member (this was Chayanov's Rule). This is assuming of course that the size of the household is within reasonable limits, meaning that too many people concentrated in a single household would exhaust local resources.

What exactly is the happy medium between too few and too many household members will be dealt with shortly. But first, as will be seen in the following chapter, labor intensiveness of household tasks and the income- generating opportunities available outside the household give way to a sexual and age division of labor. A woman is usually the focus of the household and the manager of domestic tasks while men concentrate their energies on animal and garden activities. Children are a significant source of labor and, while they participate in agriculture, they more often can be found carrying out easily accomplished but tedious, time-consuming chores such as retrieving water, gathering firewood, cooking, and tending livestock. The role of children in this regard sets up the conditions that give way to the particular types of kinship and family structure found in Jean Rabe

Notes

1. While reciprocal labor groups are important, they are probably less important in Jean Rabel than in regions where farmers heavily depend on a few crops harvested over a very short period of time. The primary agricultural labor pinch in Jean Rabel comes during planting season and the significant advantage of reciprocal labor is that it resolves the need to accomplish particular tasks quickly, such as clearing a field that is grown over with small trees and brush, or turning the soil in a field so that it can be planted before weeds start growing. But in reality, there are few agricultural labor tasks that must involve reciprocal labor groups. Most crops in Jean Rabel are not harvested all at once, but rather over a long period of time and the few crops that do become ripe all at once, namely beans and corn, are easily harvested by a few people, typically women, who can manage the task alone. Furthermore, reciprocal labor groups are ultimately a zero-sum strategy of capturing labor because households get no more from participating in work teams than they contribute as members—i.e., one day of work in a neighbor's field begets one day of work on the farmer's own field.

2. A common mistake for development workers in the region is to assume that the limiting factor on meals is food availability, when in fact it is often time needed to cook meals.

The same observations were made in both the baseline survey of 1,586 households and the followup subsurvey of 138 households, in which the exact average was 67.19 minutes.

The estimates for distance to and between markets was based on the average cartographic midpoint of eight kilometers between markets. Four kilometers were added for altitude change and the fact that when it comes to traveling in rugged Jean Rabel, the shortest distance between two points—in this case the household and the market—is never a straight line.

3. The fall season is the highest yielding of the various seasons at low altitudes while the spring planting season is the highest yielding in the mountains.

4. This is a reference to total land farmed—not necessarily owned—and includes sharecropped property (see endnote 7 below). Seventy-six percent of all garden plots are .5 *kawo* (1.6 acres) or smaller, indicating the data is skewed by a few relatively large gardens.

5. Information is based on inputs per ¼ *kawo*, called *ka* and measured in Jean Rabel as *sink kout chen* (five lengths of a standardized surveyor's chain = 28 feet per chain length). The table below assumes 24 *bout* per *ka* (16 square *gol* per *bout*; 1 gol ~ 9 ft; or another measure is *bras* which is about 5.5 five feet; 1 *bout* = 7 – 10 *bras*). In the conclusion here and in the main text, the measure has been translated to acres for convenience (30 *bout* to an acre). Planting here includes all crops; harvesting only includes bean, corn and millet, crops that are harvested all at once. Farmers—and it is usually women farmers who do this task—harvest sweet potatoes, beans, and other crops the entire year round, making these difficult tasks to estimate. They have been included in household tasks. Thus, in this calculation, harvesting involves uprooting beans and millet or picking corn. Drying time is not included in processing; only threshing. Total time may be slightly overestimated because some gardens are not planted in grain or beans but rather in crops for which little processing is necessary (such as plantains). On the other hand, time devoted to plants subsequently intercropped is not included. Many tasks should have been measured in hours, such as processing crops, because people perform them until they are tired and then do something else, thus distributing the task over a longer period of time. The appropriate adjustments were made based on eight hour working days, typical during hoeing. The total labor input per garden *acre* is fifty-six adult/days—the estimate below is in units of *ka* ¼ kawo and there are 3.19 acres per *kawo*, .80 acres per *ka*.

Table 11.5: Estimated labor inputs for average 1/4 kawo garden

{A} Type of activity	{B} Total number of bouts	{C} Mean bout per day	{D} Number of adults	{E}1 Days needed per task	{F}2 Total adult days needed Per task
Hoeing	24	3	1	8	8
Planting	24	14	7	2	14
Weeding	24	6	1	4	4
Harvesting	24	-	2	2	10
Processing	24	—	5	1	10
Total	—	—	—	—	46

1{E} = {B} / {C}, 2{F} = {D} * {E}

Note: Harvests refers to grains only. One three- to four-month planting cycle, given an eight-hour work day.

6. Almost one third of respondents, 413 households, reported owning no land; 87.7 percent of households own 2 *kawo* or less; and a mere 1.1 percent of households claimed to own more than 5 *kawo* of land. This should not, however, be interpreted to mean that ownership of land is concentrated. The largest landholder in the sample owned only 12 *kawo* and the now infamous *gran dons* (big landowners) of Jean Rabel—who have been alleged by the Haitian State to have played a role in the 1987 massacre and who controlled much of the local irrigated State land—long ago gave this land in sharecropping arrangements to local farmers and more recently have disappeared from the scene (at least two are in prison for accusations relating to the massacre). There are people who control and collect rent for this land in the name of the families, but their influence is fading and with the recent presence of INARA—the agricultural reform arm of the new Haitian Government—the days of the *gran dons* appear to be drawing to a close.

7. Some development workers in the region explain the fragmentation of garden land as a consequence of inheritance, i.e., families dividing land into ever smaller parcels for the inheritors. That land is fragmented through inheritance is undeniable. But land could also be aggregated through sales and trades. Over 50 percent of gardens in the baseline survey were reportedly purchased, and even though much of this land was purchased from family—meaning it was still a type of inheritance—it nevertheless indicates the opportunity to aggrandize land. But there appear to be practical reasons why Jean Rabel farmers prefer instead to hold on to a multiplicity of small fragmented holdings rather than aggregating them into a single large garden: in the Opinion Survey not one of the sixty-eight male farmers interviewed explained land fragmentation as a result of inheritance; virtually all the farmers explained the multiplicity of garden plots as an adaptation to variable ecological zones, i.e., soil and rainfall patterns (which in Jean Rabel change dramatically over distances of only a few kilometers). None mentioned heredity or lack of market access; thirty-eight respondents (56%) mentioned the importance of different soil types or the position of the garden plot—such as bottom land versus plateau—and thirty respondents (44%) emphasized rainfall patterns.

It is also interesting to note that the number of gardens per household in Jean Rabel is identical to the national average (RONCO 1987), and the size of gardens as well as the number of gardens planted per household does not appear to have changed in at least the past fifty years (see the 1950 census). With all technological factors being equal, therefore, there appears to be a limitation on the amount of land and number of gardens that an average household can work. The mean garden size is .59 *kawo* (see table); about 50 percent larger than the national average of .5 hectares (1 *kawo* = 1.29 hectare). However, 75.5 percent of all gardens are .5 *kawo* or smaller.

8. With regard to tenured livestock, the Baseline Survey turned up many more people looking after animals for others (tenured in) versus people giving animals to other people to look after (tenured out). A logical explanation for the "missing" animal owners might be that people who

tenure animals out are fewer but wealthier—meaning a few tenure to many. However, a look only at the most highly tenured animals—cows (26.1% vs 3.8%), hogs (14.2% vs 1.1%), sheep (11.8% vs .7%), and goats (10.3 vs. 1.1%)—suggests this is not the case: assessing only households that have tenured animals, tables and below reveal the mean number of animals tenured in (1.58) is actually greater than the mean number of animals tenured out (1.11).

Table 11.6: Animals tenured-in vs. tenured-out

	N	Mean	Std. error	Std deviation
Tenured-in	220	1.58	.076	1.1220
Tenured-out	20	1.10	.069	.3078

This is probably a result of the way in which livestock tenure was measured: tenure was not recorded for every animal but rather the primary means of tenure by which households came into possession of each species of livestock. For example, if a household head reported being responsible for six donkeys, the question on tenure was "what is the primary means by which you have these donkeys?" Another reason for the disparity between people who "tenure out" versus "tenure in" animals is that many town-dwellers tenure animals out to people living in the countryside, thus they are not captured in the equation. The survey did not sample the village of Jean Rabel, which would have helped to clarify this point.

9. Damage done to gardens by roaming livestock is a principal source of conflict among farmers. Farmers who find goats or sheep foraging in their gardens sometimes exercise the right to kill the animal. The head is kept by the gardener, but the rest of the carcass is strung up in the nearest tree for the animal owner to come collect. Pigs found foraging in the neighbor's gardens are usually not killed for their crime, but owners must pay for damages. Pigs suffer, however, in cases where the owner refuses to indemnify the victim—a pig belonging to the author was once macheted to death by a woman fed up with the procine's repeated and uncompensated invasions of her kitchen (the pig had been "tenured out" to another neighbor). Roving cattle are never killed. However, owners must pay indemnities for damages to gardens. Failure to compensate for persistent intrusions into a neighbor's garden sometimes results in a machete wound across the rump of the animal or the severing of its tail. Roving donkeys, horses or mules are, compared to other animals, a rare sight, and seldom are the animals intentionally injured for their depredations. Owners must pay for damages to gardens.

10. As elsewhere, I want to document here a series of ethnographic observations that are relevant here, that might be important to other researchers but for which there is no place in the main text.

In Jean Rabel, there is system of rights regarding browsing livestock that is in various stages of evolution. In decades past, livestock in most areas was free ranged. In some areas today, particularly in the dry coastal region, farmers continue to free range goats and sheep on communal grazing lands owned by the State. Pigs are allowed to forage freely in seaside settlements and in large villages where there are no gardens to destroy. In other areas people are not allowed to free range livestock, but by consensus tether animals on any land not planted with crops. In still other areas landowners appear to be in the process of rebelling against free-tethering and are asserting their property rights by cutting loose livestock they find tied on their land. In more than 50 percent of communities—an educated guess—farmers now exclusively use private property to browse livestock.

11. Charcoal is bagged and sold to intermediaries who ship the product on trucks or by boat to urban centers, most notably Port-au-Prince. Rural Jean Rabeliens generally do not use charcoal themselves—they use wood. In almost any region one finds an ongoing production of charcoal with a handful of specialists and intermediaries engaged in the industry and they are considered among the poorest, lowliest people in an area, although the money earned at charcoal production

can compare favorably to other occupations (see chapter 8). But for most individuals charcoal production is something that occurs when a special need arises, as when someone wants to build a house or finance a new garden, and charcoal production is most conspicuously bound with times of drought and crop failure. Makab, for example, is a shipping point for charcoal and there are usually several dozen sacks stacked on the beach. But during the 1996–1997 drought, the entire beach was covered with thousands of sacks of charcoal stacked as high as the houses.

12. The same increased labor demand associated with crises is true of marginal regions. The poorest people usually live in the most marginal areas, which in Jean Rabel are by definition those areas farthest from water and markets, thus increasing household labor requirements.

Chapter 12

Gender- and
Age-Based Divisions of Labor

Introduction

In meeting the demands associated with maintaining a Jean Rabel household there is a sexual and age division of labor. Men perform tasks associated with gardening and livestock and women tend to focus on household chores such as cooking, carrying water, and marketing. Women are the focal point of households; they are thought of as the managers and they are more likely than men to cross the gender lines and perform tasks that fall in the sphere of men, particularly with regard to agriculture. Children are major contributors to household labor demands, particularly with regard to retrieving water and cooking fuel, and Jean Rabeliens recognize and emphasize the role that children play in assuring the survival of the household. Indeed, children and their contributions are so important to survival that, as will be seen, the drive to produce large numbers of offspring in order to meet domestic labor demands largely determines the structural organization of the Jean Rabel family, patterns of conjugal union, and the sociocultural fertility complex discussed earlier.

Gender-Based Division of Labor

Labor within the household is divided in such a way that the members of one gender depend on members of the other gender in a type of socially constructed symbiosis that makes life difficult for the lone woman and nearly impossible for the lone man. For example, when asked if they could live without a spouse, 119 of 136 respondents (87.5%) replied "no," with comments such as:

> No. We need each other. The man plants gardens and the woman, it is she who must harvest what the man plants. It is the woman who must sell the harvest too. It is the woman too who must wash clothes.[1]   (thirty-seven-year-old father of three)

> I can't do it because if I need a garden, it is my husband who must get to work. If I build a house, it is my husband who does it for me. You see, we need each other.[2] (forty-year-old mother of five)

> I cannot live without a woman. There are several circumstances, problems that women resolve. I cannot enter into some affairs. I cannot whip up a meal. I cannot wash clothes.[3] (thirty-eight-year-old father of seven)

> No. One enters into the other. Water enters into the sugar. Sugar enters into the water. You cannot throw out just the water. They are a single mixture.[4] (thirty-eight-year old father of seventeen)

Women take care of the house, clean, wash clothes, make meals, carry water, and purchase basic foods and necessities at the market. As shown earlier, women also sell garden produce, they sell staples out of the house, and they often work as itinerant traders who extend household revenues by rolling cash reserves over in retail marketing ventures. A woman with a husband who is present will typically not participate in preparing fields or weeding, but women are considered indispensable in planting and, more importantly, for the daily picking of produce and seasonal harvests. Indeed, harvesting is considered to be the exclusive domain of women and is typically coordinated by the ranking woman of the house. Men who do not have a wife will rely on their mother, sister, or a daughter to harvest and sell produce.

Table 12.1: Adult sexual division of labor (N = 1,482)

Task	Male	Female	Both	Male, female, and both	Neither	Total
Housework	5.4%	86.0%	6.7%	98.1%	1.8%	100.0%
Cooking	5.6%	87.6%	4.6%	97.8%	2.4%	100.0%
Childcare	5.3%	77.1%	7.4%	89.8%	10.3%	100.0%
Carry water	6.7%	79.1%	7.8%	93.6%	6.4%	100.0%
Sell produce	6.1%	75.2%	4.6%	85.9%	14.2%	100.0%
Sell livestock	24.4%	34.6%	22.3%	81.3%	18.8%	100.0%
Tend lvstck	58.4%	11.7%	16.4%	86.5%	13.5%	100.0%
Garden work	58.7%	13.8%	20.9%	93.4%	6.6%	100.0%
Wage labor	24.4%	5.8%	3.0%	33.2%	66.9%	100.0%

Note: Neither means no children in the household perform the task. Includes households with no children and only toddlers.

Men work in the gardens, care for livestock, make charcoal for sale to villages, towns, and cities, and gather firewood for their own households. The heaviest tasks, like hoeing (*voye wou*) and digging holes for plantain trees (*voye pikwa/fouye twou*) are considered to be men's work while light garden work, such as covering holes and collecting the debris from a weeded garden, are thought of as women's work. Men help process the food, such as flaying millet, beans, and corn or pulverizing the seeds with bat and bucket-size mortar and pestle. Men build houses, and all jobs involved in the building of a house, such as carpentry and masonry, are male jobs. The only task related to household construction that women do is plaster houses with white mud or lime—if the mud is not white then plastering house walls is men's work. As seen earlier, men, and to a far lesser extent women, migrate to the city in pursuit of temporary wage opportunities.

Perhaps the most significant and telling feature of the gender division of labor, and a point that will also be important later in understanding marriage patterns, is that men rarely engage in female chores while women can and sometimes do perform the full range of male activities. Men do not wash clothes, make meals, clean the house, or go to the market. Men seldom carry water. Women on the other hand can and often do tend livestock, weed gardens, and search for firewood. Some women, particularly older, economically independent women, hoe the soil and, in a few rare instances, dig holes for plantain trees. This versatility in job performance reflects the fact that women are more important than men in the day-to-day functioning of homesteads. Indeed, households are thought of as belonging to women and, as discussed in a later chapter, Jean Rabeliens are fond of saying, "men don't have houses" (*gason pa gen kay*), and people will typically refer to the homestead, even when a productive male is present, as belonging to the woman, as in "Ma Benita's place" or "Lili's house."

Age-Based Division of Labor

While men and women clearly report needing each other to survive, they report needing children even more. In the Opinion Survey there were 10.8 percent more respondents who said they could *not* live without children than those who said they could not live without a spouse (97.0% vs. 86.2%). Typical comments included:

> Oh, you must have children. If you don't have any you are in bad shape. You have too much to do.[5] (fifty-four-year-old mother of six)

> That is the biggest illness. I can't do it. I just can't live without children.[6] (sixty-two-year-old father of eleven)

> No. I can't live without children. . . . It's them that work, that give me water, fetch wood, make food.[7] (sixty-two-year-old father of fifteen)

> No. You can't do it. You need children. You need children. You understand? You need children to help you.[8] (fifty-four-year-old father of ten)

> No. Children are everything in a household.[9] (twenty-six-year-old mother of three)

Children of both sexes participate in every type of labor activity (see table 12.2).[10] In over 70 percent of households visited—including households with only toddlers or infants—children (primarily girls) carry water, cook, and perform housework. In over 50 percent of households, children (primarily boys) reportedly help in the garden and with livestock; in some 32 percent of households, girls, boys, or both, market produce; and in over 30 percent of households, children (mostly girls) sell livestock.

Table 12.2: Child sexual division of labor (N = 1,482)

Task	Male	Female	Both	Male, female, and both	Neither	Total
Housework	11.7%	49.2%	14.8%	75.7%	24.3%	100.0%
Cooking	12.4%	46.9%	13.5%	72.8%	27.2%	100.0%
Childcare	9.8%	40.4%	12.3%	62.5%	37.5%	100.0%
Carry water	13.4%	28.7%	31.5%	73.6%	26.4%	100.0%
Sell produce	10.9%	10.6%	10.1%	31.6%	68.4%	100.0%
Sell livestock	5.1%	22.1%	5.7%	32.9%	67.1%	100.0%
Tend livestock	40.7%	5.6%	10.2%	56.5%	43.5%	100.0%
Garden work	39.1%	4.4%	9.2%	52.7%	47.3%	100.0%
Wage labor	5.6%	1.2%	1.5%	8.3%	91.7%	100.0%

Note: Neither means no children in the household perform the task. This includes households with no children and only toddlers.

Who Cares for the Animals

Figure 12.1: First response question:
"Who takes care of the animals?"

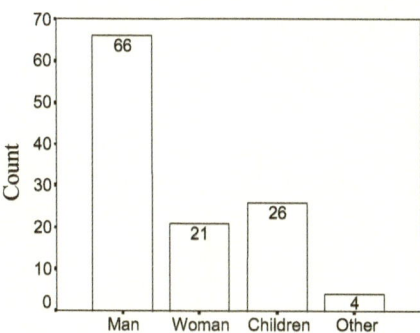

Figure 12.2: Second response question:
"Who takes care of the animals?"

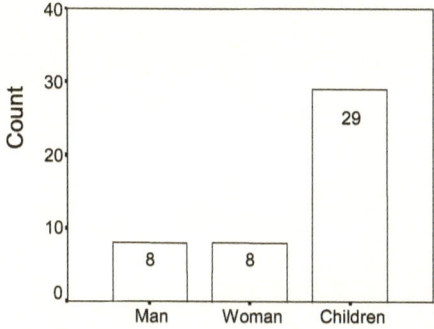

Who Carries the Water

Figure 12.3: First Response to Question
"Who Carries Water?"

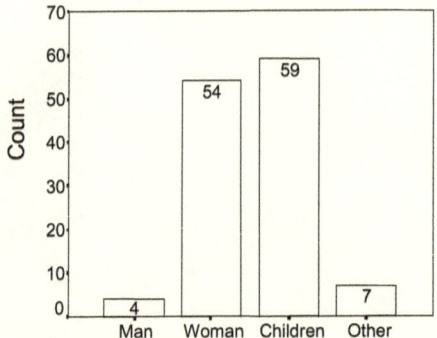

Figure 12.4: Second Response to Question
"Who Carries Water?"

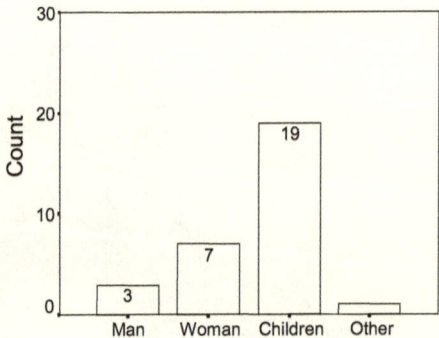

Relationship between Number of Children and Household Prosperity

As discussed previously, all people in the region, regardless of their poverty, have access to garden plots and animals through sharecropping and other tenure arrangements, something that makes the capacity to tend animals and gardens a significant factor in determining the actual number of each managed by a household. Capacity is determined by the availability of domestic labor. That means children.

The extent to which the number of children contribute to household productivity is evident in the relationship between the number of children living in a house and the number of gardens and animals belonging to households.[11] The Livestock and Gardens Survey, discussed in chapter 1, was designed to measure the relationship. I compared actual number of children sleeping full time in the household with the number of animals and gardens that belong to the household.[12]

Excluding the heads of households and their spouses, the number of seven- to twenty-five-year-olds present in the household was found to explain fully 32.6 percent of the variance in ownership of animals and 33.1 percent of the variance in the number of gardens planted (see figures 12.5 and 12.6). This relationship was expected to be a byproduct of the age of the household head. But when age of the household head was statistically controlled by adding it to the regression equation, the model still explained 32.0 percent of the variance in number of household gardens and 20.0 percent of the variance in number of household animals (see tables 12.4 thru 12.9).

The number of children present in a house is also a major factor in determining the likelihood that the principal woman of the household will be engaged in marketing activities. Controlling for age, a woman with more than four children is three to eight times more likely to be engaged in commercial activity than a woman with zero to three children.

Figure 12.5: Animals by children per household
(children = 106; seven- to twenty-five years of age)

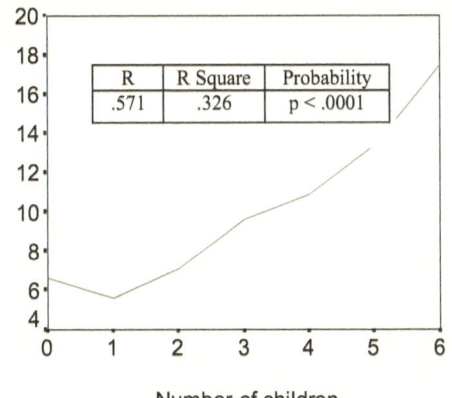

Number of children

Figure 12.6: Gardens by children per household
(n = 106; children seven- to twenty-five years of age)

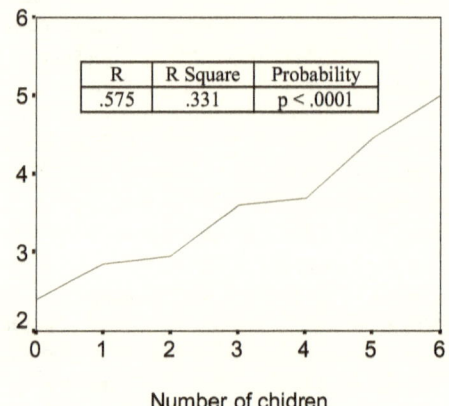

R	R Square	Probability
.575	.331	p < .0001

Number of chidren

Table 12.3: Number of children resident in house by whether or not woman is engaged in marketing (n = 132; children seven to twenty-five years of age)

				Does woman market		
				No	Yes	Total
	20–34	Children resident in the house	0–3	8	8	16
			4–6	4	12	16
			7+	0	2	2
			Total	12	22	34
Age categories	35–49	Children resident in the house	0–3	5	6	11
			4–6	4	18	22
			7+	0	13	13
			Total	9	37	46
	50+	Children resident in the house	0–3	8	11	19
			4–6	3	17	20
			7+	4	7	11
			Total	15	35	50

Statistical Results for Test of the Number of Household Gardens by the Number of Seven- to Twenty-Five-Year-Olds Controlling for Age of the Head of the Household

Table 12.4: Gardens by the number of seven- to twenty-five-year-olds controlling for age of the head of the household: R-square

Model	R	R-square	Adjusted R-square	Standard error of the estimate
Regression	.577	.333	.320	1.08

Note: Predictors: (constant), age of household head, children seven to twenty-five years old.

Table 12.5: Gardens by the number of seven- to twenty-five-year-olds controlling for age of the head of the household: ANOVA

Model	R	df	Mean square	F	Sig
Regression	57.028	2	28.5	25.4	.000
Residual	114.400	102	1.1		
Total	171,428	104			

Note: Predictors: (constant), age of household head, children seven to twenty-five years old
Dependent variable: gardens.

Table 12.6: Gardens by the number of seven- to twenty-five-year-olds controlling for age of the head of the household: coefficients

	Unstandardized coefficients		Standardized coefficients	Probability	
	B	Std. error	Beta	T	Sig
Constant	2.169	.375		5.8	.000
Children 7 to 25 yrs old	.388	.084	.553	6.1	.000
Age of household head	4.SE-03	.009	.048	.527	.599

Note: Dependent variable: gardens.

Statistical Results for Test of the Number of Household Animals by the Number of Seven- to Twenty-Five-Year-Olds, Controlling for Age of the Head of the Household

Table 12.7: Animals by the number of seven- to twenty-five-year-olds, controlling for age of the head of the household: R-square

Model	R	R-square	Adjusted R-square	Standard error of the estimate
Regression	.466	.217	.202	4.63

Note: Predictors: (constant), age of household head, children seven to twenty-five years old in house.

Table 12.8: Animals by the number of seven- to twenty-five-year-olds controlling for age of the head of the household: ANOVA

Model	R	Df	Mean square	F	Sig
Regression	607.1	2	303.6	14.2	.000
Residual	2187.1	102	21.4		
Total	2794.2	104			

Note: Predictors: (constant), age of household head, children seven to twenty-five years old in house. Dependent variable: animals.

Table 12.9: Animals by the number of seven- to twenty-five-year-olds, controlling for age of the head of the household: Coefficients

	Unstandardized Coefficients		Standardized Coefficients	Probability	
	B	Std. Error	Beta	t	Sig
Constant	4.8	.1.6		2.9	.004
Children 7 to 25 yrs old	1.3	.281	.445	4.5	.000
Age of household head	1.695SE-02	.039	.043	.430	.668

Note: Dependent variable: animals.

Table 12.10: Gardens by the number of seven- to twenty-five-year-olds for household head age categories

			Number of gardens			
			1–2	3–4	5 +	Total
Age of hshld head	15–29	Hshld members 7 to 25 years old				
		0	4	3	0	7
		1–2	1	2	0	3
		3–4	0	1	0	1
		Total	5	6	0	11
	30–44	Hsehld members 7 to 25 years old				
		0	6	4	1	11
		1–2	11	13	1	25
		3–4	2	3	2	7
		Total	19	20	4	42
	45 +	Hsehld members 7 to 25 years old				
		0	2	0	0	2
		1–2	4	8	1	13
		3–4	3	11	6	20
		5–6	0	7	8	15
		7 +	0	1	1	2
		Total	9	27	16	52

Table 12.11: Animals by the number of seven- to twenty-five-year-olds for household head age categories

			Number of Animals—					Total
				Livestock				
			0	1–4	5–8	9–12	> 13	
Age of hsehld hd	15–29	Hsehld members 7 to 25 years old						
		0	1	3	3	0	0	7
		1–2	0	2	0	1	0	3
		3–4	0	0	1	0	0	1
		Total	1	5	4	1	0	11
	30–44	Hsehld members 7 to 25 years old						
		0	0	1	6	3	1	11
		1–2	1	7	12	4	0	24
		3–4	0	1	3	1	2	7
		Total	1	9	21	8	3	42
	45 +	Hsehld members 7 to 25 years old						
		0	0	2	0	0	0	2
		1–2	0	4	6	2	1	13
		3–4	0	1	7	5	7	20
		5–6	0	0	2	4	9	15
		7 +	0	0	1	1	0	2
		Total	0	7	16	12	17	52

Conclusion

The value of child labor is evident in the correlations between the quantity of household livestock and gardens and the number of children resident in a particular household. Although, as shown, children participate in virtually all household and productive activities, the increased number of livestock and gardens may not be so much a result of children directly participating, as the result of contributions children make by carrying out small, time-consuming tasks such as fetching water, cooking, cleaning, and tending animals, contributions that free adults to focus on productive income generating activities such as gardening and commerce.

But none of this unequivocally demonstrates that children are a net asset to household livelihood. It is unlikely, given the data, that households with greater numbers of children are *more* impoverished than households with fewer children. However, the argument could just as easily be made that more children simply increases the demand for food and additional income, translating to the need for more gardens, more animals tended, and more wage-labor and market ventures. Thus, the question is, do children increase household prosperity? And very importantly, how are those contributions related to high fertility, the pronatal sociocultural fertility complex and particular values associated with Jean Rabel's sexual moral economy? These issues are the subject of the following chapter.

Notes

1. *Non. Nou toudè bezwenn lòt. Si gason ap travay, fi a menm se li pou ranmase rekolt ki gason ap fet. Rekolt ki fet la tou, se fi a menm ki pou al van ni. Se fi a tou pou al lave.*

2. *M pa kapab paskè si m bezwenn nan jaden an, se mari-m pou al travay. Si m-ap monte yon kay la , se mari mwen pou fe pou mwen. Ou we yon bezwenn lòt.*

3. *M pa ka viv san fi. Sa-k pase m pa ka viv san fi, gen yon seri de sikonstans, pwoblem se fi pou fe, paskè se pa tout bagay m ka antre andan. Ma pa ka nan fe ti manje rapid, m pa ka lave.*

4. *Non. Yon antre nan lòt. Dlo antre nan sik la. Sik antre nan dlo a. Sa di, ou pa ka jete dlo a. Sa di, se yon dosaj fet.*

5. *O, fo ou gen ti moun. Si ou pa genyen ou pa bon. Ou anbarase twop. Kounye-la m vin pran dlo la, oswa m sot nan jaden lè m rive se mwen pou mete ponyet atè, se mwen pou al nan dlo. Lè m vini, pou al nan bwa.*

6. *Pi gwo maladi, m pa kapab. . . . Telman m pa ka viv san ti moun.*

7. *Non. M pa ka viv san ti moun. Bondieu ba-m pitit la, se li ki bay ou travay, ki ba-m ti dlo, chèche ti bwa, vin fe manje.*

8. *Non. Ou pa kapab. Paske ou bezwenn ti moun, ou bezwenn ti moun, ou konprann. Ou bezwenn pou ti moun yo ed-o.*

9. *Non. Ti moun se tout eleman andedan kay.*

10. Only 5.4 percent of households (85 of the 1,523 reporting) had no children—compared to 12 percent of households with no adult woman present full time and 23 percent of households with no adult male present full time. Fifty-seven percent of these childless households (forty-seven of eighty-three for which the data is available) were in yards with other houses that do have children indicating that only 36 of 1,523 houses (2.4% of the total) are actually homesteads having no

children. Only seven of these latter households had a woman as household head.

11. There are obviously other factors that also determine the number of gardens and animals a household may own, specifically wealth. Differential access to land and capital and other sources of revenue such as remittances and money earned through skilled craftsmanship and marketing are clearly determinant of the number of animals and gardens a person can purchase. The periodic sale of animals and garden land to cover medical expenses and costs associated with funeral and wedding ceremonies are also prominent factors determining the number of animals and gardens a household might have at any given time. But the point regarding children and prevailing social and economic conditions in Jean Rabel is that they provide the next most important ingredient, the labor to manage gardens and animals.

12. The Baseline Survey included the same data needed to test the relationship between the number of children present in the household and the number of animals and gardens the household tended. The relationship is significant, even when controlling for age of the household head—which has no statistical influence—but as described in chapter 1, it was discovered too late that respondents in the Baseline Survey were tending to include in their enumeration of household members children who were away at school in the village or in the city. Because of drought conditions, there was also a problem with reporting on the number of animals. To address these shortcomings, the smaller survey used here was carried out in two Jean Rabel communities. This survey, called the Livestock and Gardens Survey, was conducted by a supervisor from the Baseline Survey (see the introduction).

Below are data from the Baseline Survey regarding the number of children reported as present in the household versus number of gardens and controlling for age of the household head. (The ages five to nineteen years was used in this test rather than the seven- to twenty-five-year-old range used in the other test. The decision was arbitrary.)

Table 12.12: Child present in house by number of gardens, model summary (Baseline Survey)

Model Summary

Model	R	R Square	Adjusted R Square	Std. Error of the Estimate
1	.141[a]	.020	.018	1.57

a. Predictors: (Constant), Age, Number of 5 to 19 years-olds in hshld

Table 12.13: Child present in house by number of gardens, ANOVA (Baseline Survey)

ANOVA[b]

Model		Sum of Squares	df	Mean Square	F	Sig.
1	Regression	71.944	2	35.972	14.646	.000[a]
	Residual	3551.589	1446	2.456		
	Total	3623.533	1448			

a. Predictors: (Constant), Age, Number of 5 to 19 years-olds in hshld

b. Dependent Variable: Number of Gardens Planted

Table 12.14: Child Present in House by Number of Gardens, Coefficients (Baseline Survey)

Coefficients[a]

Model		Unstandardized Coefficients		Standardized Coefficients	t	Sig.
		B	Std. Error	Beta		
1	(Constant)	2.589	.128		20.262	.000
	Number of 5 to 19 years-olds in hshld	.115	.022	.139	5.312	.000
	Age	-1.51E-03	.002	-.018	-.676	.499

a. Dependent Variable: Number of Gardens Planted

Chapter 13

What Parents Have to Say about the Economic Utility of Children

Introduction

In the previous chapter it was shown that children are important contributors to the labor-intensive household livelihood strategies that prevail in Jean Rabel. Children do household chores, they cook, they clean, they go for water and to market, they work in the garden, and they tend livestock. More children appear to translate into greater economic security and relatively greater household prosperity, i.e., more animals and more gardens, and greater resources to survive drought. The statistics may or may not convince the skeptical reader. However, in this chapter it will be seen that Jean Rabel farmers need no convincing. During the Opinion Survey, farmers overwhelmingly emphasized the fact that children are not just helpful, they are necessary; and they are necessary because they work.

What Farmers Have to Say about Children

The matter-of-fact explanation farming men and women in the Opinion Survey (N = 136) gave for producing children is simply because children are the single most important source of household labor. When asked "Why did you have children?" 76 percent of respondents made comments similar to the following examples:[1]

> Why does a person have children? To help. Right now for example, I would have to go get water. But I don't have to. It is here. I would have to go get wood. But I don't have to. It's right here.[2] (forty-year-old mother of five)

> If I did not have them, things would be worse for me. You need a little water, they go to the water. You need a little fire wood, they go get wood. The boys work in the garden for you. They look after the animals.[3] (thirty-three-year-old mother of eight)

Children are the biggest necessity. If you need something you tell a child. Like right now, I can say, "go look for some fire wood," or "some embers from the neighbor's house." "Go to the market."[4] (twenty-seven-year-old father of three)

Why did I have children? I don't understand what you are saying. Children are there to help you. Your children do your work. I don't know who takes care of things at your house.[5] (sixty-year-old father of thirteen)

The need for children is conceptualized first and foremost *not* in terms of love, companionship, or the security that grown children can provide to aging parents; the need for children is conceptualized first in terms of labor. When asked if they could live without children, only 4 of the 136 respondents (3%), 2 women and 2 men, replied "yes," yet 14 percent of respondents said they could live without a spouse. Almost without exception and without hesitating, 97 percent of men and women replied to the question in the manners exhibited in the following examples:

If you don't have children, dogs will eat you. If you have no children to fetch a little water and get some fire for you. If you hurt something or you are sick, you're finished.[6] (fifty-five-year-old father of seventeen)

No. Children are protection. You need children to help you work. It is children who save the household[7] (thirty-two-year-old mother of five)

Oh, a big never. Children don't tire. Children are animals. Children are never worn out. They do all the work. They go to the water. They do all the work.[8] (forty-year-old mother of four)

No. I cannot live without children. . . . If I need one to go to the village, I send him. If I need one to go for wood, I send him. They can't tell me no . . . . Not one of them can stand in front of me and say no. We pull together.[9] (thirty-nine-year-old father of six)

Me! Times the way they are? Me! If I didn't have children I wouldn't stick around here for a minute. I would leave. I would go play a different lottery. I would go look for another type of work. The type of work where they would pay me money.[10] (forty-year-old mother of five)

Only 7 percent of respondents indicated they wanted children for reasons of affection and only 14 percent indicated children were valuable foremost as adults (i.e., when the children are grown) to provide support during old age. This should not be interpreted to mean people in rural Jean Rabel do not love their children, nor should it be interpreted to mean that when their parents become aged, children are not at some level considered valuable sources of security. Farmers emphasized that children's support should be reciprocated; children "do" for adults and adults have a responsibility to "do" for the children.[11] Interviewers regularly received comments like *Yo itilite o. Ou pran reskonsab yo* (They make themselves useful to you and you feed and care for them) and *Ti moun ka ede-m. M ka ede ti moun yo* (Children can help me. I can help children). Beyond feeding and clothing children, the most important thing adults can do for children is put them in school. School is the single greatest nonsubsistence expense for Jean Rabel households and the second biggest reason for selling livestock (see chapter 7). Also, to some extent, school is thought of as an investment in the future security of parents: 25 percent of parents said they sent their children to school primarily so the child could better care for them in the future.[12]

But the point that farmers made more emphatically than any other is that it is the work children perform in their youth rather than after they are grown that is foremost in importance. Thus, children are important to their parents as they age but not for the reasons outsiders tend to anticipate—that they will provide for their parents—but rather for the contributions they make to the household labor pool in their youth and for the grandchildren they will provide as they mature, grandchildren who will also run errands and do the time-consuming and labor-intensive chores necessary for survival in Jean Rabel. This fact came through most clearly in the question, "If you had not yet borne children, and someone came along and promised you $500 per month, every month, for your entire life, with the single condition that you do not bear/father children, would you agree?" Respondents had no problem understanding the question, nor did they have a problem answering. Only five women and eight men said "yes," they would take $500 a month (an enormous sum for the farmer) for life rather than bear children. The other 123 respondents (90%) responded with an emphatic "no." The variety of responses revealed the appreciation with which people in Jean Rabel regard their children, especially young children, and the logic underlying this appreciation. In the following comments, take particular note of the importance of children versus money; the limitations of money; and the emphasis on young, rather than grown, children who can be sent on errands:

They give you $500 a month. OK. You are in the house by yourself. Fever takes you. And while you are sick, who is going to look after you? [13](forty-year-old father of three)

No. I would not agree. That couldn't help you at all. If I am getting $500 a month and I do not have a child to say, go there, take this gallon, go get some water for me. Look at me, I'd be making $500 dollars a month and all the time things would be getting worse. Not better. No. Not better. Worse. Things would be getting worse.[14] (fifty-one-year-old father of two)

No. Children are worth more than money.[15] (forty-year-old mother of three)

No. Because it doesn't make sense. . . . I would rather have children. As the old people say, children are the wealth of the poor.[16] (thirty-eight-year-old mother of seven)

No. Because I need children. I can tell you, you have money in your hand and you can't send it to do a single errand. Sometimes you have money with you and you lose it.[17] (fifty-year-old father of six)

Why don't I agree? Something happens. I get to the house. I lie there. I'm sick. Money? I can't send it to do anything for me. I can die lying there on it. It's something that can't do anything for me. It is a person you need to take the money, go with it, buy what I need and bring it to me. And if I don't have any children to give the money to? [18] (fifty-six-year-old father of one)

No. If I need a little water, money can't give it to me. I cannot send money on an errand.[19] (thirty-four-year-old mother of five)

No. Because I know that if I had no child, tomorrow, by God, I am sick, I would not find a child to help me.[20] (twenty-eight-year-old mother of two)

Ah, you can have money in the house but if you do not have children to do for you? A person can have money and you can lie down and die. If you do not have a child to stand there and do things for you that money can not do. Money! You can sleep on a pile of money. It cannot work for you. It is people who stand up and work for you.[21] (sixty-five-year-old mother of nine)

Oh. Children are wealth. If you don't have children, a dog is better than you. No. I would rather have children. Children are help. This morning, if you send one out there, he does his job, it's you who benefits.[22] (fifty-four-year-old mother of six)

I would not agree. Ahh, children. Money can't do anything for me. If I am sick, I need to take care of something, the children, if they are there, they will take care of it. If I am sick, I can't send money to do errands.[23] (forty-five-year-old mother of five)

No. Why. Because children are the wealth of the poor. Children are wealth.[24] (fifty-year-old mother of four)

Oh no. Children are wealth. It is children who are, who are the wealth of the poor. Money is not wealth.[25] (forty-two-year-old mother of three)

No. Because let's say you have money. You go find someone to do something for you. He doesn't do it. But children. As soon as I am sick, look at my child making food for me, washing clothes for me, doing things for me. And if it was money, it wouldn't be doing anything for me.[26] (thirty-year-old father of four)

I would ask for the chance to have one child. I find children necessary.[27] (forty-year-old mother of three)

Number of Children Desired

Of the 1,361 women reporting in the nutritional part of the Baseline Survey, the average number of children desired was 3.5 (missing = 183). Of the 124 men and women who were willing to respond in the Opinion Survey (missing = 12), the average number was 3.9 children. These figures are consistent with similar results reported by farmers all over Haiti (Stycos 1954, Murray 1972, Allman 1982b, Smith 1998). But perhaps the question is not specific enough to provide a clear understanding of the decision-making process involved in determining the number of children desired. For example, farmers distinguished between how many children they want to be responsible for and how many they need, or would be useful to them. Some individuals expressed a preference for few or no children but then added that they had no choice, that they must have children, that children were necessary to assure a minimal standard of living. Elsewhere in Haiti there is evidence that five people—two adults and three children—is considered an ideal sized household (Murray 1972, Smith 1998). But this implies that the ideal number of "working" children is three, and it does not consider that children grow up and leave the house and must then be replaced by other children. Furthermore, when respondents in the Opinion Survey were asked how many children they would want if they had a paying job, the average went from 3.9 to 4.2 children.

There is another good reason to question the results. When asked, "How many children do you want?" farmers everywhere in rural Haiti are typically reluctant to reply and responses are evasive (Stycos, 1954; Murray 1972; Smith 1998). In the Opinion Survey, respondents commonly replied first with a curt, "However many God gives me" (*mezi sa bon dieu bay mwen*). Others responded, "All children, all children. Both girls and boys. They are all good." (*Tout ti moun, yo tout bon, ni fi ni gason. Tout bon*). One thirty-four-year-old father of six said "two, three, or thirty" (*dè, twa, obyen trant*). A forty-five-year-old mother of five said "well, fifty is good, six is good" (*en ben, sinkant t-ap bon, sis la t-ap bon*). One man who did not want to respond at all explained that he knew a guy who asked God to give him five children; so God gave him ten and then killed five. After considerable prompting, one woman said she wanted six children. An appalled bystander was caught on cassette saying, "now you won't get any more at all" (*kounie-a ou pap fe menm anko*).[28]

To get around the problem of directly asking "how many children do you want," the question was asked, "Which couple is better off, a husband and wife with three children or a husband and wife with six children?" Respondents were clearly less reluctant about replying to the "three or six children" question. Only three men refused to respond, insisting that the matter was up to God: 59 percent of total respondents favored the couple with six children being better off.[29] But, the data indicated that a preference for the larger family is significantly influenced by the sex and age of the respondent. Thirteen of twenty-three women (57%) in the age range twenty through thirty-four years preferred six children, whereas in the over the age of fifty category, twenty of the twenty-three women (87%) preferred six children. Similarly, while only three of thirteen men (13%) in the twenty to thirty-four-year age group favored the family with six children, thirteen of twenty-seven men (52%) in the over fifty age group favored the larger family (see table 13.1).

Table 13.1: Preferred number of children by age and sex of respondent

			Age categories			
			20–34	35–49	50 +	Total
A couple with three children versus a couple with six, who is better off?	Men	Three	10	11	14	35
		Six	3	13	13	29
		Total	13	24	27	64
	Women	Three	10	6	3	19
		Six	13	16	20	49
		Total	23	22	23	68

Note: Missing = 4

Moreover, farmers who responded "three" usually did so with much discussion and evaluation of the choices. The biggest issue was school costs. Forty-three of the fifty-four respondents (84%) who chose three children explained that the cost of school was the principal reason for not wanting a greater number of children. Moreover, respondents spontaneously linked the importance of school with dwindling resources described as "hard times," "having nothing to stand on," and "necessity."

> Three would be better. Because things are hard nowadays. Education. Things are hard. It was not a long time ago you could have children. . . . Now, if you have ten children, you have to put all ten in school.[30] (fifty-year-old mother of four)

> Three. If I had six, put all six in school, I would spend more money. But if I have three, I spend less. It is there you find the advantage. But if God gives you six, you are obliged to put all six in school. It is not in your interest. But if God takes care of you, it can be in your interest. There are people who have ten children. They are no help at all because their parents have nothing to stand on, they don't have any way to get by. And then there are those who have fifty children and they are better for it.[31] (twenty-nine-year-old father of nine)

> Three would be better. Because sometimes you have all these children, the times are so bad you can not keep them in school.[32] (thirty-five-year-old father of five)

> Better you have six children. But you cannot educate all of them.[33] (thirty-four-year-old father of six)

In contrast, responses in favor of six children were usually clear and adamant declarations in favor of six.

> When you have six it is better for you. More people, more work, more things getting done. The work gets done faster.[34] (forty-year-old mother of three)

> Six. Because if for example you are going out this morning, you are going to work in the garden or the market, you take three with you and you leave three to do the work at the house.[35] (forty-three-year-old father of three)

> When you have six children it is better for you. Why? Because this morning, you are all by yourself, you send each child somewhere to do a job for you. Each job gets done at the same time.[36] (thirty-five-year-old father of six)

> All six are important. All six. You send one to the left, one to the right, and the rest in all four cardinal directions.[37] (forty-seven-year-old father of seven)

Sons vs. Daughters and Mothers vs. Fathers

Jean Rabel fathers favor daughters over sons at a rate of two to one. The principal reason given is that girls do more work, 20 percent of fathers also said that "girls are cooked food" (*fi se manje kwit*), a Jean Rabel expression that literally means that daughters are good to have because they maintain the homestead—they can make cooked food—and can fulfill the role of wives. But in clarifying, fathers often turn to the ability of daughters to obtain financial contributions and favors from men:

> The girls are better. Why? I could fall for one, this guy could fall for another. You yourself could fall for another. You understand? Prepared food. Women have more luck than men.[38] (thirty-eight-year-old father of three)

> When a daughter lands in a good situation, she's likely to come gather you up. You can be pale and all washed up. In three days you're another color. . . . Girls are cooked food.[39] (thirty-two-year-old father of three)

> Cooked food. . . . If you have a daughter and she takes a man, she takes the man and she goes and lives with him. She lives with the man, and that man regards you better than he regards his own father.[40] (sixty-two-year-old father of eleven)

> A guy who has daughters, he lives better. Because girls are prepared food. . . . If a jitney is coming down the road, the driver will put him in the front seat.[41] (seventy-five-year-old father of five)

Table 13.2: Reasons fathers gave for preferring daughters

	N = 62 (missing = 4)	% responses
	Girls help more	21%
	Girls are cooked food	21%
Why do	No preference	32%
you prefer	Boys help more	18%
girls/boys?	Boys cost less	3%
	Girls are more faithful	2%
	Boys are more faithful	3%
	Total	100.0%

Fathers favor their daughters, but daughters do not feel the same way about their fathers. The socially constructed gender behavior of men means that their lives are oriented outside the home as makers and tenders of distant gardens, tenders of livestock, professional craftsmen who often must voyage far from home as house builder, boat carpenter, sawyer, or as fisherman and migrant laborer in pursuit of wages to pay for homes, to afford gifts for lovers, and to pay for the education and upkeep of children, all necessary to rise above the label of *vakabon*. Thus, often absent from the homestead, men do not consistently participate in the upbringing of their children, they are seen as fickle, and they are correspondingly not, as seen in the *téat* song below, appreciated to the same degree as mothers.

On the other hand, Jean Rabel girls revere their mothers. Eight of the forty-two *teat* songs analyzed included refrains praising mothers—such as the above "I must caress her"—and designating gifts and money meant for the mother. And the relationship goes both ways: mothers reported favoring daughters over sons by a factor of four to one.

Table 13.3: Male and female, daughters vs. sons

| | | Respondent | | Total |
		Male	Female	
Which is	Five daughters	26	44	70
Better, 5	Five sons	17	8	25
daughters or 5	No difference	23	13	36
sons?	Mixture	2	3	5
	Total	68	68	136

Moreover, adult daughters take their mothers in to live with them at a much higher ratio than they take fathers in and they do so at a much higher ratio than their brothers do.[42] Of the seventy-eight parents identified as living in a household headed by one of their children, fifty-nine of them were mothers, and in forty-six of these cases the host was a daughter (see table 13.4 below).[43]

Table 13.4: Sex of child who is hosting resident parent (N = 1,521)

| | | Sex of host | | Total |
		Son	Daughter	
Sex of	Father	17	2	19
resident	Mother	13	46	59
parent	Total	30	48	78

But while mothers might occasionally live in homes with their daughters, the reason they favor them arguably has to with more immediate rewards. While some observers may object to a crass materialist approach, mothers themselves reported that the reason they prefer girls is because they are a tremendous source of help around the homestead: 62 percent of mothers gave this as the reason.

The value of girls means that women are eager to take in nieces, younger female cousins, and, in an institution known as *restavek,* less fortunate female offspring of other families—although the value of young girls also means they are seldom successful in procuring them. Girls learn young how to care for the household and how to perform tasks of the mother. By the age of twelve or thirteen years, Jean Rabel country girls can do everything their mothers can: cook, clean, take care of younger children, and sell in the market. Indeed, when arriving at homesteads in Jean Rabel, one often finds not the mother but a young teenage girl left in charge.

Conclusion

The bottom line is that despite a few concerns about school costs, farmers in Jean Rabel want children. They see children as valuable economic assets and more children are better than fewer children. Furthermore, while concerns that may be associated with old age, such as illness, are important, farmers were not referring to adult offspring. When a sixty-five-year-old Jean Rabel woman says she can not live without children, that she needs someone to do errands for her, especially when she is sick, someone to fetch water and run to the market, she is not referring to her adult children. She is talking about her grandchildren, nieces, godchildren, or the children of neighbors, something that, as will be discussed shortly, is critical to understanding high birth rates in Jean Rabel. Thus, statements like "children are the wealth of the poor" (*pitit se byen malere*) and "it is children who save the homestead" (*se ti moun ki sove kay la*) are direct references to the tasks that young children perform. These are burdensome time-consuming tasks thought of as humiliating for an adult, but tasks that, nevertheless, must be accomplished to maintain a viable and productive household and to free adults to engage in outside income-earning endeavors. Both mothers and fathers prefer daughters over sons and while the most immediate reason is for the labor contributions and greater involvement in the household, another reason discussed shortly is that daughters are capable of having more children, thereby contributing further to the household labor pool. In the following chapter, I show how the high demand for children that derives from their economic utility conditions kinship, conjugal union, and the rights, duties, and expectations associated with rearing children and benefiting from their labor.

Notes

1. In sixty-eight of the households the ranking male household member was interviewed and in sixty-eight of the households the ranking woman was interviewed. Unintelligible responses were omitted.

2. *Pou kisa yon moun fe ti moun, se pou li ka ed-o. Kounye-a la lè ou we-m pati se mwen k-ap al nan dlo-a, min lè ou we-m vini, mwen jwen dlo-a. Se mwen t-ap al nan bwa, lè m vini ke mwen jwenn bwa-a.*

3. *Bon dieu, Bon Dieu. Se pa mwen te vle fe yo, Bon Dieu. Tout ou jwenn sa, Bon Dieu fe yo. (Wi men gen anpil moun ki bezwenn fe ti moun). Wi. (Kouman ou ta santi si ou pa ta genyen). Si m pat genyen li t-ap pi mal pou mwen. (Men pou ki rezon ou we ou gen yo?) Ou bezwenn ti dlo, yo al nan dlo. Ou bezwenn ti bwa, yo al nan bwa. Ti gason yo al travay nan jaden pou ou. Yo fe bet pou ou, y-al lonje yo, al mare yo nan jaden.*

4. *Ti moun nan se yon bagay ki nesesè. Pase ou bezwenn voye ou ka di, ' pitit, koulye-a, pou mwen, al chèche yon ti difè pou mwen,' 'al chèche yon ti bwa,' 'al nan mache.'*

5. *Pou ki sa m fe ti moun? Mwen pa konprann. Ti moun la pou sevi ... Tout kondi sevis pa-ou. Pa-ou, kondi sevis pa ou. M pa ka konprann sa-k mennen lakay ou....*

6. *Si ou pa gen ti moun, chyen k-ap manje ou. Si ou pa gen ti moun yon kote pou bay ou yon ti dlo, pou ba ou yon ti dife. Si ou fe sa obyen ou gen yon bagay k-ap fe ou mal, moun fin ou ye.*

7. *Non, paske se yon pwotejman ti moun yo ye. Paske ti moun yo bezwenn ede o nan travay. Se ti moun ki sove kay la.*

8. *O gran janme. Ti moun an pa janm bouke. Ti moun se bet. Ti moun an pa janm fatigue. Y-ap fe tout travay. Yo t-al nan dlo. Y-ap fe tout travay.*

9. *Non, m pa ka viv san ti moun. Ou pa ka viv nan kay ou sel... Ti moun pa-m mwen. Yon m bezwenn nan bouk, m voye li. M bezwenn nan dlo, m voye li. M bezwenn nan bwa, m voye yo. Li pa ka di-m non. Alo, yè egzakmwen, ki zanimo mare la m voye al chanje, si m gon pitit yo chanje li. Yon pa ka kanpe devan mwen pou di-m non. En sel lavi grandi.*

10. *Mwen menm? Pou vi tann sa a? Mwen? Si m pa ta gen ti moun menm, m pa ta fe isit menm. M t-ap pati, m tap al deyè lòt boulet, ke m tap al chèche lot travay ke m fe pou yo peye-m kob.*

11. Actually, farmers expressed favoritism for girls (see chapter 15).

12. Adults expressed this debt to children, owed in the form of education;

"Me? I need children all the time because it is all the time that children are working for me ... [But] What I am going to tell you is no lie. In the month of October I send all five of these children to school. Then, lunch pail in hand, I take the hoe, and I set to weeding all by myself. I go the whole day without decent food. I weed the garden. It's the truth. No lie. Because these days children can't make it without school." (forty-four-year-old mother of five)

(Mwen menm, m bezwenn ti moun tout tann paskè mwen menm se tout tann ti moun yo fe travay pou mwen ... Sa m di ou se pa manti. Nan mwa oktob m voye tou le sink ti moun sa lekol. Kounye-a manje nan min um, m pran wou a, met sakle, kounye-a m oblije pase jounen san manje net, m-ap sakle. Vreman, se pa manti. Kounye-a la, pliskè ti moun an pa ka leve san li pa lekol...)

"School is the number one thing a parent can do for a child. [But] It was not a long time ago it was livestock that was best to give your child." (thirty-one-year-old father of five)

(Lekol se premiè byen ke yon paran ka fe pou yon ti moun. Se pa lontan se yon bet ou te bay ti moun ke fe yo byen.)

The data used in the main text to illustrate the importance of school was actually a subsample of eighty-four Opinion Survey respondents. The reason for the "subsample," and not the entire sample, was that question was added after the survey had begun. Twenty-five of the eighty-four respondents (30%) said they sent children to school only to help the child when he or she was grown and thirty-eight respondents (45%) indicated that educating children was in the interest of both parents and children.

13. *Y-ap bay ou 500 dola pa mwa, OK, ou nan kay ou sel o e lè lafyev pran ou e lè maladi pran ou, sa ka okipe ou?*

14. *Non. M pa ka dako, sa pa ka itil ou anyen. Wi, eskè m-ap touche 500 dola le mwa, epi m pa gen yon moun pou m di ale la, al pran ti gallon, al pran empè dlo pou mwen. Ala m-ap touche 500 dola le mwa, ala se pa desann m-ap desann, se pa grandi m-ap grandi. Tout tann,, m pap desann? . . . Premiè byen yon moun se pitit-o. Chyen ap manje o.*

15. *Non. Pitit gen valè pase lajan.*

16. *Non. Pase, li pa fe sans . . . M tap pito pitit, paske gran moun kon di, pitit se byen pou malere.*

17. *Non. Pase m bezwenn ti moun nan. M ka d-ou, ou gen lajan min ou pa ka voye lajan. Ou gen kob la, pa fwa, epi lajan asanm av-ou ou pedi yo.*

18. *Pou ki rezon m pa t-ap dako? Gen yon mwayen, m rive, m kouche la, m malad. Kob la m pa ka voye li, m-ap mouri sou li. Bagay ki pa ka fe anyen pou mwen. Se moun pou pran kob la, ki prale, achte avek, e pran sa m merite. E m pa gen ti moun pou met nan kob la.*

19. *Non. Si m bezwenn yon ti dlo la, kob la pa ka ba-m mwen. Mwen pa ka voye lajan.*

20. *Non. Paske mwen si m pa fe ti moun, demen si dieu vle, lè m malad m pa ta jwenn moun pou ede-m.*

21. *Ah, ou met gen lajan nan kay la min si ou pat gen moun pou fe pou ou. Ou met gen lajan. Kounie-a ou met kouche mouri, si se pa pou yon moun kanpe fe yon bagay pou ou, lajan pa ke fe. Lajan, ou met domi sou lajan, pa ka fe pou ou, se moun ki pou kanpe fe pou ou.*

22. *O, pitit-la se byen o li ye. Si ou pa fe pitit, chyen pi miyo pas-o. Non. M pito pitit la. Pitit la se yon ed pou ou. Maten a si voye pitit la la, li jwenn lavi se ou menm ki jwenn lavi.*

23. *M pa t-ap dako. E pitit la, kob la pa fe anyen pou mwen, non. Si m malad, m-ap regle yon bagay, ti moun nan si li la l-ap fe yo. E si m malad m pa ka voye lajan.*

24 *Non. Sa-k fe sa? Paskè pitit se byen pou malere. Pitit se byen.*

25. *O, non. (PKS). Lajan pa byen, se pitit ki ye, ki byen pou malere. Lajan pa byen.*

26. *Non. Paskè ou gen lajan la, si ou al jwenn yon moun pou fe yon bagay pou ou, li rete la. Min ti moun an, depi m malad la, gade pitit um ap bouye pou mwen, ap lave pou mwen, ap bagay pou mwen. E te lajan li te ye li pa tap fe anyen pou mwen.*

27. *M ta mande yon chans pou fe yon ti moun, m jwenn ti moun nesesè. M pa ta dako. Ti moun itil.*

28. There was also some reluctance to respond to any questions about children. Some respondents refused to give children's names and some refused to divulge how many children they have or gave false information. Some responded easily to questions about adult activities and then clammed up when the issue of children was introduced. The most widespread fear among farmers is that the identities of their children may be recorded and the children sacrificed in rituals of black magic, sold to demons, or put in a *jakout* (grass storage sack) and subsequently eaten. There is even a widely recounted myth of a white boogeyman called "three buckets" (*twa ti bokit*) who goes around gathering children up, cutting them into pieces, and then carries them back to the city to eat with his white friends.

29. Translation from: *Tout bon! (M d-ou twa m d-ou sis, fok ou di-m sa-k pi bon nan yo). Eh, si, eh. Bon. Nòmal. Sou afe ti moun nan, si bon dieu ba ou twa ti moun, li pa bay ou anko, w-ap rete sou sa bondieu ba ou-a. (Wi w-ap rete sou sa li ba ou, min se yon kesyon m-ap poz-o) Mwen la tou bon madanmmwazel. (Wi, m konprann, 'tout bon'. Min m t-ap mand-o, sou kesyon, twa sis, sak pi bon nan yo? Fok ou we si se twa obyen sis la). [Silans] Sis la. (pou ki sa). Li la, l-ap ba-m yon ed. (Min twa ka bay ou ed tou, min sis la?) Sis la, sis la ap ba ou ed. Gen sa-k kap al nan jaden., y-ap al nan dlo, y-ap al lave. (Silans). En ben, twa.*

30. *Twa ta pi bon. Paskè bagay la di kounye-a. Preparasyon. Bagay la di. Se pa lontan, lè lontan ou te ka fe ti moun. . . . Kounye-a si ou gen dis pitit, pou ou met tout lekol.*

31. *Twa. En ben, si m gen sis, mete tou le sis lekol, m ta depanse plis kob. Min si m gen twa, m depanse mwens kob. Se la avantay li ka genyen. Min si bon dieu bay ou sis la, ou oblije mete tou le sis lekol, li pa nan avantay ou. Min si bon dieu pran swenn ou, yo ka nan avantay. Gen moun ki fe dis, yo pa itil yo menm paskè pye yo pa bon, pa gen kote pou pase. Gen ki fe 50 pou yo ede paran.*

32. *Twa t-ap pi bon. Paskè dè fwa ou gen tout ti moun sa epok sitelman pa bon ou pa jwenn posibilite pou ou ka kontiue ti moun lekol.*

33. *Pito sis ti moun min ou pa ka fe edikasyon pa yo.*

34. *Lè ou gen sis la li pi bon pou ou. (Pou ki sa?) Plis moun, plis sevis, plis okipasyon. Travay la mache pi vit.*

35. *Sis. Paske si petet maten an w-wap pati, ou al nan travay, ou pat a twa, lòt twa rete lakay la ap ede lakay la.*

36. *Lè ou gen sis ti moun nan li pi bon pou ou. (Pou ki sa?) Pou ki sa? Kounie-a maten-a, ou sel la, kounye-a ou voye chak ti moun yon kote, fe yon sevis pou ou, kounye-a tout sevis regle ansanm.*

37. *Tou le sis toujou impotan (Non, si ou ta gen twa o di mwen sis, kies nan yo ki tap plis impotan?). Tou le sis. (Eskè se sis k-ap impotan obyen eske se twa k ap impotan). Tou le sis ap impotan w-ap voye yon adwat yon agoch, tou le kat fasad.*

38. *Fi yo pi bon. Pou ki rezon? Sa vle di, mwen menm m gen dwa we nan yon pitit fi nan yo. Myseu sa gen dwa we yon nan yo. Ou menm ou gen dwa we yon nan yo. Ou konprann. Manje pare. Fi gen plis chans pase gason.*

39. *Lè ou we pitit fi-a tonbe yon kote, li ka ranmase ou. L-ap ranmase ou. Ou te met blanch konsa, nan dè twa jou la-p vin yon lòt koulè. . . . Fi se manje kwit.*

40. *Manje kwit . . . Si ou gon pitit fi li pran gason, li pran myseu li rete ave. Lè lì rete a myseu, myseu a regade papa pi mal pase bopè.*

41. *Neg ki gen sink ti fi viv pi byen. (Pou ki sa?) Pou ki sa? Paskè, fi se manje tou pare. . . . Si se yon machinn ki sou wout, chofè ap monte-m mete-m devan.*

42. Indeed, looking at residence patterns in table 13.4, in which it is seen that only two fathers

are hosted by daughters, it is difficult to understand why fathers favor daughters and not sons.

43. As mentioned earlier, 12 percent of *teat* songs put together by female dance troops included refrains praising their mother and designating gifts and money meant for the mother, the most common of which has the girl returning home after going away, "If you see me carrying a gift, it is for my mother, Manman come it" (*Si ou we m pote yon kado se pou fe manman-m kado, Manman vin pran nan min*). Fidelity to mothers in this respect is one of the most conspicuous principles of a good daughter.

Chapter 14

Raising Children and Control
Over Child Labor Activities

Introduction

In prior chapters I illustrated the all-important role of the household and associated farming livelihood strategies, the division of labor, the economic utility of children, and the value that parents attach to children. In this chapter I look at the most immediate costs, behaviors, and relations that pertain to childbirth, rearing children, and control over children. I will show how the economic value of children conditions kinship and family patterns and how the nature of this conditioning hinges on the costs of pregnancy—most importantly in terms of the lost labor contributions from the mother—and the costs to *chape* children—meaning to get offspring through the critical infant and toddler ages.

Birth

When a child is born in rural Jean Rabel, the umbilical cord is tied off and cut. The newborn is wiped with a damp cloth, and the breast is given almost immediately. Purgatives are not given to the child, as they are in some other regions of Haiti. The infant stays completely confined in the house with its mother for the first five days of life. Jean Rabeliens are extreme in their encouragement of the use of supplements to nourish the newborn. By eleven to fifteen days after birth—and sometimes earlier—the baby is being given supplements in the form of tea and sugar-water, and some women even begin feeding a kind of homemade baby food, usually a paste made from a type of dried plantain called *kiyez*. Jean Rabeliens believe that girls develop physically faster than boys, and so at two months a girl is encouraged to sit up, *kase*, while a boy is not encouraged to do this until three months of age.

The Costs of Rearing Children

The cost of a child is not so much in money and remunerated medical care but rather the loss of the mother's time and contributions to the households. In rural Jean Rabel, there are few direct costs involved in caring for an infant. Parents do not use cribs or disposable diapers, nor do they provide children with a plethora of toys or baby clothes. They do not feed children with expensive baby formulas or pay for daycare services. The infant sleeps in bed with its mother, is changed with a couple of homemade and reusable diapers, wrapped in a Goodwill towel that costs about 15 *gdes* (US$0.90), and dressed in Goodwill shoes and clothes that together may cost 50 *gdes* (US$3.00). The infant is fed breast milk and homemade baby formulas, and is surrounded by a neverending throng of aunts, sisters, cousins, grandmothers, and male relatives that provide the kind of cost-free attention and care that only family members can provide.[1]

The approximately 50 percent of mothers and infants who visit local clinics can expect to pay a total of 41 *gdes* (US$2.50) for a checkup, vaccinations, and vitamins during and after pregnancy. Another 5 *gdes* (US$0.30) are paid for a birthing packet (included are a razor blade, a string for tying the umbilical cord, and sterile gloves).[2] Most women employ midwives at an expense of 50 *gdes* (US$3.00). All totaled, the maximum direct costs of pregnancy, birth, and the first six months of infancy are approximately 161 *gdes* (less than US$10.00). After the first six months, a child eats what his/her parents eat and wears cheap *pepe* (Goodwill clothing).

Paternity

The primary expenses associated with childbirth and childrearing come with caring for the mother. A man is typically expected to assume responsibility for these costs. When a woman becomes pregnant, and if she is not in union, she is expected to name a father. If a woman does in fact name a father (and she sometimes does not), and if the man accepts paternity (which he almost always does), then that man must help support the mother and child. In cases where a man denies paternity, it is difficult or impossible to force him to support the child. But such cases are extremely rare. In a review of the May 1999 Jean Rabel birth registry, only 5 of 469 (1%) of registered births were fatherless (called a *deklarasyon mere*). Unlike in the United States where "paternity suit" is synonymous with forcing a man to be responsible for a child, Jean Rabel paternity suits almost always involve a man suing a woman because he has been denied control over his child; or, the most common of all, mothers assigning paternity to multiple fathers, one publicly and one in secrecy.

These are critical points because they highlight the labor value of children seen in previous chapter, revealing a struggle for control over child labor that gives way to a series of anthropologically fascinating institutions in rural Haiti. Fathers, even men who know they have been cuckolded, rarely refuse to accept paternity. The man who is not the real father is said to have been given a *kout pitit*, literally translated as having been clobbered with a child. But he typically accepts the responsibility, if not eagerly, then without objections. Judges in the area report that this practice occurs commonly. As mentioned in chapter 6, in a farming community where I lived, 13 percent of men (seven of fifty-two) had at least one child who friends and neighbors reported was also secretly recognized by another man as his own. I also discussed in chapter 6 the fictive illness known as *perdisyon*, whereby gestation is thought to have become arrested and can remain in suspension for as long as five years, allowing women to dupe their present and former spouses and lovers into accepting paternity for children sired by other men; or perhaps, to rephrase, allowing men a face-saving mechanism for accepting paternity for children who do not biologically belong to them.

Far more common than men denying paternity are cases where a woman and her family do not approve of a particular father and refuse to recognize him. The family makes this denial legal by registering the mother's father (the child's grandfather) or another male relative as the child's natural father. Related to this is control wielded by mother's mother. As will be seen in greater detail in the following chapter, many of the first or first several children born in the home of the maternal grandmother become hers. By virtue of her superior economic position and influence, she commandeers them. The grandchildren refer to her, and not the biological mother, as *manman* or *momi*.

In the event a named father does not support the child, or the woman has refused him rights, the woman may accept support from another man during her pregnancy and the nursing period. This "father" is known as the *papa nouriti* (the nourishing father), and it is then him who has paternal rights to the child's labor and it is him who must be repaid if the biological father wishes to gain control over his child.

The man is expected to begin helping to provide for the mother as soon as her pregnancy becomes apparent. When the baby is born, the paternal grandmother brings ginger, plantains, and chickens or a goat to be slaughtered and fed to the postpartum mother. When mother and infant emerge from the customary five days of postpartum confinement, the "mother-in-law" again brings plantains and meat (a goat is brought and killed if none was slaughtered at the occasion of the birth). For the next two to three months the woman remains in semi-confinement and does little work. During this period, the man is expected to provide extra amounts of meat, and other nourishing foods.[3] The father must also plant a garden for the mother and child and allocate animals to them— animals that he cares for and the proceeds from which will go to help the mother *chape* the child (see below). When a child begins primary school, it is also the father who is expected to pay the 345 *gdes* a year (US$20.53) needed for tuition and the obligatory school uniform.[4]

The Working Child

The working child is, as seen, an important and necessary factor in household livelihood security. The most important stage in child development is that point when he or she becomes more of a benefit than a cost, a point denoted by the term *chape* (literally, "to escape"). A child is considered to *chape* "when he can do for himself" (*li ka fe pou kont li*), "when he can wash his own clothes" (*lè li ka lave rad pa li*), "when he can 'get by'" (*lè li ka boukannen*),[5] and "when he can go to the water by himself" (*lè li ka al nan dlo pou kont li*).[6] The word is also inverted to apply to the act and cost of bringing a child to the point where he can not only take care of his own needs, but also make contributions to the survival of the household. The notion of *chape* was mentioned recurrently during the followup survey as in the examples given below:

> Oh, why does a person have children? You have children. You struggle to *chape* them. . . .You raise them. They *chape*. Tomorrow God willing, if you need a little water, the child can get it for you. If you need a little firewood, he can carry it for you.[7] (fifty-five-year-old father of seventeen children)

> I had children, now I have a problem, now the children can solve the problem. Tomorrow God willing I cannot help myself, it is on the children I will depend. Today I *chape* them. Tomorrow God willing we struggle with life together.[8] (forty-one-year-old mother of four children)

In rural Jean Rabel, children as young as two and three years of age do small chores like fetching utensils and carrying messages to the neighbors. At three to four years of age they are going to the water with other children and returning with a gallon jug awkwardly balanced on their head. At five to eight years of age the child will *chape*, for it is at these ages he/she begins to go by himself to the water, start a fire, wash clothes, tend animals, find food in the garden, and go alone to make small purchases in the market. By the age of seven, boys are typically trusted to tend goats and sheep without supervision by an adult or older child. By the age of eleven a boy can hoe a garden and may even participate in reciprocal work groups composed of other prepubescent and teenage boys. Similarly, by eight or nine years of age a girl can sell goods during short absences of her mother, both in the market or the home, and she can wash most clothes—except for large bulky items like pants, which require considerable strength to wring out. By ten or eleven years of age most girls have already had the experience of taking the family donkey on a twenty- to thirty-mile trek to and from a market to make purchases for the household. At this age, the girl does not go alone but in groups with other young girls or with a neighbor. As seen above, by the age of twelve or thirteen, Jean Rabel country girls can do everything their mother can, making the labor value of girls, coupled with their ability to bear additional children, significant factors in parents favoring daughters over sons (see previous chapter).

The Parental Contract

In Jean Rabel households, there is a clearly defined system of mutual rights, duties, obligations, and benefits that are exchanged between parents and children and that continue from a child's youth into adulthood. The "contract" begins at the time of the mother's pregnancy when she acknowledges a man's paternity, thereby offering him the opportunity to share the right of co-parentage. As shown, fathers must subsequently earn their paternal rights by helping to care for the mother and helping to *chape* (raise) the child. The parents' most immediate reward for raising children is the access to needed labor. It is an inalienable parental right to govern the labor activities of their children.

However, as we will see in the following chapter, a major determinant of family patterns has to do with whether the child is born in the house of the mother's mother—as most first and many second and third children are—because then it is the grandmother who exercises primary control. Other people, such as godparents, also exercise control over children by virtue of their relationship to the parents, and a child owes obedience to family members and older friends.

In their turn, parents in Jean Rabel, like parents everywhere, have an obligation to feed, provide clothes, and generally care for their young children. Parents also increasingly have an obligation to educate their children, an obligation that family, friends, and neighbors enforce by criticizing a parent for not sending children to school. Children themselves will also pressure their parents, saying at very young ages things like "my father does not like us, he does not want to pay for school." (*Papa-m pa reme nou. Li pa vle peye lekol*). Parents begin giving their children animals when they are as young as four or five years of age, and an attempt is made to increase the child's stock as she or he grows. Parents are expected to give land, even if only a small amount, to both sons and daughters as soon as they are capable of farming or soliciting someone else to farm for them. Also, as they come of age and begin to start their own families, children have the right to claim a portion of their parents' property. With increasing population and declining availability of land, education has increasingly begun to supplant gifts of land and animals to children. Nevertheless, children who do not migrate pressure parents to begin ceding property as soon as they begin bearing children of their own and enter into a conjugal union. Children cannot be deprived of these rights on the whim of their parents or other relatives, and all legitimate children claim an equal share of the parental property. Should a man have several "wives"—which was found during the Baseline Survey to be true for 11 percent of male household heads—the children of one woman generally have no rights to property purchased by their father for another woman (see following two chapters). All of a woman's children have the same rights over her personal estate.

In return, children are socially and legally obligated to care for their parents in their old age. A parent or grandparent can never be refused food or care. Children bathe, feed, wash clothes, and clean up after their infirm parents and grandparents. Not caring for an elder is considered shameful, and community members will criticize and humiliate the irresponsible younger kin of the elderly individual. Should one family member take care of an elder and other family members refuse to assist, the considerate member has a right to call her negligent brothers, sisters, and/or cousins into court and force them to pay an indemnity.[9]

Godparents and their Rights and Duties

It is inconceivable that a child in Jean Rabel should be without godparents. The parents select godparents almost immediately after the birth of a child. The godparents sometimes are asked to name the child and their own names are written on the back of the child's birth certificate. Generally, a Catholic priest ceremonially consecrates the relationship of the godparents to the child during baptism, although if the parents are Protestant the godparents and parents may simply present the child to the pastor. In both cases, the formalization of ties between godparents and their new godchild is a happy and symbolically important event. A small *fet* (celebration) is held in honor of the occasion at the parents' or mother's house, complete with *kolas* (Haitian sodas), *gato* (cake), and *kremas* (liquor made with condensed milk, rum, and sugar).

The naming of godparents initiates important fictive kinship relations. A godchild addresses his godfather and godmother by the terms *parenn* (godfather) and *marenn* (godmother) and these take on the roles of surrogate parents. The biological children and all the other godchildren of the *marenn* and *parenn* become fictive brothers and sisters and are sometimes referred to as *sè* (sister) and *frè* (brother). The spouses of both godfather and godmother—as the two are seldom chosen as a pair of spouses—also take on the status of *marenn* and *parenn*, meaning that a child usually has two godmothers and two godfathers. The biological parents as well as all the godparents assume a relationship to one another of *kompere* and *kommere* (co-father and co-mother), meaning they are co-parents, and they all refer to one another and address one another with titles of *makompere* and *makommere* (my co-father and my co-mother). They also assume an incest taboo *vis a vis* one another—albeit the taboo is weak and easily violated.

The selection of a godparent is strategic. In large, economically secure families that have good land holdings, godparents are often chosen from among immediate relatives such as a brother, sister, uncle, or aunt, a selection that maintains control over the child and his labor within the family. Among the less fortunate, godparents typically have no kinship relation to the biological parents and are often chosen from the ranks of people who have higher socioeconomic status than the biological parents, something that can be viewed as a trade: the poor parents offer partial control of a child and his or her labor and in return they have special relationship with the more powerful godparents, a relationship that may benefit both them and the child.

Godparents have obligations to godchildren that at first glance make godparentage appear to be a burden, especially to outsiders who find themselves offered the privilege of being a godparent but have no need for the labor of the child—and therefore do not see the advantage. Godparents should, and usually do, contribute to the upbringing of their godchildren. They have a tacit obligation to help pay for the child's education. Godparents should also contribute to the child's marriage or any other major and costly life event. But despite the appearance, godparentage is considered to be a privilege and honor that is more often accepted than declined. One of the fundamental reasons for this is that there is the very tangible benefit of gaining access to the godchild's labor (a fact not generally emphasized in studies that have examined godparentage in Haiti and elsewhere in the Caribbean and Latin America: see Foster, 1969, 1953; Nutini and Bell 1980; Lowenthal 1987: 164; Mintz and Wolf 1950; Simpson 1942; and for an exception see Glenn Smucker, 1983: 197–200; the labor advantage of godchildren in Haiti is mentioned by MacKenzie 1830: 273).

A godchild, called a *fiyel,* should never refuse service to a godparent. Godchildren are obliged to visit godparents, they sometimes sleep over at their houses, especially when the godparent needs extra hands for a particular task, and they sometimes spend school vacations with godparents. If a godparent should need assistance, he or she has the right to summon the child and even has the right to whip the child should he or she disobey. As one Jean Rabel man jokingly explained, "you can whip a godchild all you want, only thing is you cannot kill them—they will put you in prison for that."[10] At least one person in the Opinion Survey responded to the question, "what would you do if you had no children," by saying:

> I would ask my co-mother or my co-father if I could get a child. That means, I would ask if I could take the child as mine because a godchild is the same thing as a child.[11] (thirty-one-year-old father of five children)

Friends, Relatives, and *Restaveks*

Twenty percent of Jean Rabel children live in households headed by grandparents or other relatives—either with or without their parents present. Furthermore, 25 percent of households in the Opinion Survey reported having at least one resident child who is not the offspring or grandchild of the household head (see table 13.1 and table 13.2).

Table 14.1: Child residence patterns: Relationship of child household members to head of household (Missing = 86; children under nineteen years of age)

	Freq.	Percentage
Child	4,866	79.74
Grandchild	609	9.98
Niece/nephew	180	2.95
Sibling	137	2.25
Cousin	69	1.13
Restavek	66	1.08
Stepchild	50	0.83
Godchild	18	0.29
Sibling-in-law	18	0.29
Friend	16	0.26
Total	6,029	100.00

Source: Baseline Survey.

Table 14.2: Unrelated children in the house

# of unrelated children in the house	# of households	Percentage of all households
0	102	75.0
1	19	14.0
2	9	6.6
3	3	2.2
4	1	0.7
5	1	0.7
6	1	0.7
Total	136	100.0

Source: Opinion Survey.

Role switching is not uncommon in these households. A female household head, no matter what her relationship to children, may be addressed as *momi* (a mother-like term) and where the grandmother is present, young children sometimes refer to her as *manman* (mother) while calling the mother by her real name, as if she were a sister. In some instances parents leave children with relatives because they cannot care for the children themselves. But children are welcome and in many cases it is not so much a matter of the child being left as it is a case of the child being requested. People who no longer have children of their own remaining in the house—because, for example, their own children are grown and have established independent households or have gone to school in the city—may ask a relative or friend for a child. Grandparents are especially likely to raise grandchildren, but uncles, aunts, siblings, cousins, and others take in children as well. Old people who live alone are almost always "given" a grandchild, niece, nephew, or godchild to sleep with them and to perform tasks around the house. There is also an institution that exists called *restavek* (literally translated as stay-with), through which a child is given to an unrelated person for the primary purpose of performing domestic chores (referred to elsewhere as the institution *ti moun*, see Herskovits 1937; Simpson 1942; Metraux 1951; Smucker 1983). The possibility of upward social mobility generally plays an important role in all of these arrangements, especially the *restavek*. People who take the children are invariably either of higher socioeconomic status or, because they have no or few other children, they can offer the child better care, better clothes, and better schooling. Indeed, there is an expectation, if not an explicit verbal contract, that the child will be educated when turned over to another household. For example, a man in the Opinion Survey explained:

> I went and took two kids from some people I know. I put both of them in school. Why? Why? It is so hard for me to live without children. . . . I need water. Right now I had one with me, he went to the house to get me some water. Tomorrow, God willing, he goes to school, I do all I can to give him shoes and clothes to put on. Food too.[12] (sixty-two-year-old father of eleven)

The practice of giving children away to family, friends, or acquaintances who are better off financially, and the fact that people need children to help with daily subsistence tasks

sometimes produce strange results. There are Jean Rabel households in which the natural offspring of the household head have all gone to live with better off relatives in the village or in a distant urban center. These have then been replaced in the household by nieces, nephews, cousins, or the children of unrelated acquaintances who come from less economically fortunate and usually more rurally located households. But it must be emphasized that true *restavek* in the village and distant cities may *come* from rural Jean Rabel but households that *have* them are statistically rare. Only 2 percent of children in the Baseline Survey were living in homes other than those owned and managed by their mother, grandmother, or another close family member.[13]

The value of children means there are few true orphans in the area in the sense of being without someone to care for them. In a study of all orphanages in the Northwest Department of Haiti, in which Jean Rabel population is about one-eighth of the total, I found that virtually all functioned in a manner similar to boarding schools in the United States: most children had parents, most were not from the ranks of the poorest farmers but rather the Haitian orphanage managers shared access to free books, education, and overseas contacts with offspring of wealthier farmers, their own family, and even with offspring of adults who had migrated to Miami. In some cases the orphanage owners had sent for their own young relatives in the city to be "orphans." In other cases farmers rented their children to the orphanage in exchange for part of the money sent by the child's overseas sponsor.

Children, Work, and the Whip

In the Follow-up Survey it was not asked *if* parents and guardians whip their children; it was asked *why* parents and guardians whip their children. None of the respondents replied, "I don't whip my children." Almost invariably the reason cited was work related. Twenty percent of respondents said they primarily whipped for failing to perform chores. Another 26 percent responded that they whipped principally for negligence if, for example, the child did not properly tether an animal or allowed a pig to raid the kitchen when left in charge of the household. Another 29 percent of the responses fell within the category of "disrespect." When children themselves were asked what "disrespect" meant, their answer invariably turned out to be related to work performance. For example, children explained that they show "disrespect" by not obeying, *lè yo fe ou fe yon bagay, tankou lè yo voye ou* (when they make you do something, like when they send you on an errand).

Whipping children is thought of as necessary and important in making children perform chores. A proud mother of a well-behaved child explained, "you know what makes that child work so hard? She is scared of the whip." Another Jean Rabel farmer explained the relationship between whippings and work as follows:

> When they say a child is afraid of the switch it does not mean that when the child sees the switch he starts crying. No. It means the child is always thinking about the switch in everything he does. This is what makes a child walk straight. [14]

People sometimes jokingly say, *Kale, kale, kale. Ti moun fet pou kale* (Whip! Whip! Whip! Children are born to be whipped!). But the whipping a child receives is generally no joke. The child is usually held by the hand and whipped about the bare legs with a *raso* (braided rope whip), a *rigwaz* (a strip of dried bull testicles also used on mules and horses), or a *fret* (a thin, flexible branch taken from a bush or tree). By Western standards the whipping is brutal. The child typically does much screaming and begs for mercy. Blood is sometimes drawn and many children bear scars on their legs. "Children" as old as their late teens and even into their early twenties are whipped across the palms by schoolteachers or made to kneel for hours at a time as punishment for not turning in homework or for speaking disrespectfully. Young women are sometimes switched severely for consorting with men of whom their parents disapprove (see Murray 1977: 172; and Metraux 1951 for descriptions of severity with children).[15]

Conclusion

Maternity, paternal obligations to support a pregnant woman or mother with a child who has yet to *chape*, earned paternal rights, and godparentage define who controls the labor activities of a child. These are reciprocal relationships in that everyone involved must also contribute to the child's growth and education. But the most significant feature of the relationships, the one that takes precedence above all else, is that the child must work, he must do as he is told by those who have a right to control his activities, and the recourse to corporal punishment assures that he or she will in fact cooperate. In this way the relationships described are conditioned by the distribution of rights over the control of child labor. In the following chapter the presence of children and control over their productive labor activities are shown to be principal factors in consecrating a conjugal union and defining rights and duties between spouses.

Notes

1. The most common baby formula is made with a banana-like plantain called a *kiyez*. Milk may be added as well as smashed crackers.
2. Even in the very worst case scenario when antibiotics, antifungal agents, antimalaria pills and antacid are called for, clinicians report that costs should not exceed 58 *gdes* (US$3.50). A Caesarean can cost as much as 1,000 *gdes* (US$60.00).
3. The duration of semi-confinement is the only custom discovered that bears on the difference between boys versus girls. If a woman has given birth to a boy she will not begin to do significant chores again and she will take extraordinary care not to immerse her body in cold water or expose herself to the cold for approximately three months. If the child is a girl, the time is usually two months. The explanation is that carrying and birthing a boy is harder on a woman. Similarly, girls will be encouraged to sit up (*kase*) at a younger age than boys—the same two versus three months.
4. The typical cost for primary school in rural Jean Rabel for the 1999–2000 school year was 35 *gdes* first payment, 25 *gdes* per month, and 75 to 100 *gdes* to make a school uniform, a school

year total of 345 *gdes* (US$20.53).

5. *"Lè li ka boukannen"*(when he can barbeque) is an expression that derives from children digging up and cooking sweet potatoes, something young children, especially boys, often do, and it signifies a child's ability to look after himself.

6. The term *chape* literally means to escape and in this literal sense of the word a person can *chape* a danger on their own or someone can *chape* them—save them. Similarly the term *chape* can be used to describe that point at which a child "escapes" the dangers of infant and childhood disease and, in this way, people in Jean Rabel sometimes use *chape* as a synonym for weaned. *Chape* can also be used to describe a child who has managed to finish school and find a well-paying job; such a person has *chaped* the "small" life of an impoverished farmer. By the same token, a mother may go barefoot to *chape,* in this instance to educate, her older children. But the most common connotation of the term *chape* and one that all adults interviewed were in agreement with denotes that point when a child is more of a benefit than a cost. In addition to the quotes already given in the body of the text, others include *Lè ou ka pran ti moun an e mete li kinpot kote epi l-ap viv* (when you can put a child anywhere and he will survive), *Lè li konnen kouman pou mande pou manje* (when he knows how to ask for food), *lè li gen lespri* (when a child achieves common sense), *lè li ka rete nan kay la pou kont li* (when he can get by without constant adult supervision), and *lè li ka retire min ni nan difè* (when he will take his hand out of the fire).

7. *O, pou ki yon moun fe ti moun? Ke vle di, ou fe ti moun nan. W-ap bat pou chape yo. ... L-ap grandi yo. L-ap chape. Demen si dieu vle, si ou bezwen ti dlo li ka ba ou. Si ou bezwenn ti bout bwa li ka pote li pou ou. Ou bezwenn ni konn ed.*

8. *Mwen fe ti moun, kounye-a m vin gen yon pwoblem, kounye-a ti moun ka redi pwoblem. Demen si dieu vle, m vin pa kapab, se sou kont ti moun m-ap vini. Kounye-a map chape yo. Demen si dieu vle yo ka bat ave-m.*

9. The second question a person in Jean Rabel asks, right after "Do you have any children?" is "Are your parents alive?" (*Mama ou la? Papa ou la?*). Then, "Where are they?" (*Kote yo ye?*) "Do they miss you?" (*Yo pa sonje ou?*), and finally, "Are you going to visit them?" *(Lè ou al lòt bo eskè ou pral vizite yo?*).Woe to those who reply that they do not visit their mother or send her money, "You should go see her. She misses you. She is the one who made you. You seem to be a bad person" (*Fo ou al we mam'o. L'ap sonj'o. Se li ki fe ou. Ou gen lè pa bon moun.*).

10. *Ou met kale li jan ou vle sof ou pa ka touye li—pou sa y-ap mete ou prizon.*

1. *Pa fwa ou we ou pa gen ti moun konsa, m te kapab fe deman a makomè oswa makompè epi pou m te ka jwenn ti moun sa. Ke vle di, pou li ka sevi-m. Paskè yon fiyel se yon pitit.*

12. *M ale nan min moun, m pran dè ti moun. M mete yo tou dè lekol anko. Pou ki, pou ki? Telman m pa ka viv san ti moun. ... M bezwenn dlo-a, kounye-a m te gen yon isit ave-m, li al lakay pou yo voye dlo pou mwen. Demen si dieu vle li al lekol la, m toujou bat pou li gen sandal li avek rad pou mete, ni pou li manje.*

[13]. The *restavek* institution is a rural-village and rural-urban phenomenon; rural farmers loan children to town and city people to gain sociopolitical and commercial contacts in village and urban areas and to attain educational opportunities for their children.

14. *Lè yo di yon ti moun krent fret se pa lè yo we fret yo krie, non, se lè yo toujou panse sou fret nan tout bagay yap fe. Se sa ki fe ti moun yo mache dwat.*

15. In contrast to whipping a child about the bare legs, slapping is considered brutal. There was an incident in the village in 1998 when a French nurse, scurrying two children out of an area where they were not supposed to be playing, slapped the child of a school supervisor on the side of the head. Within the hour, an outraged crowd of upper-level Jean Rabel school administrators, including the boy's father who had been in an nearby meeting, had gathered outside where the nurse was working. When the nurse tried to leave, they blocked her, harangued her, and ultimately convinced her to settle the issue by permitting the child to slap her in the face. One of the nurse's Haitan coworkers, a man who was also a Jean Rabelien, arrived just in time to witness the nurse being slapped and he entered into what nearly became a badly outnumbered brawl between himself

and the crowd of school authorities. The incident continued on the radio with the school supervisor using the nurse's behavior as an example of how offensive foreigners sometimes behave toward Haitians. The French NGO directors were equally outraged by what they saw as a forced and public humiliation of the nurse. There were calls to ministers and much complaining. In the end, the incident passed, nobody lost their jobs, there were no official public reprimands, nor did any apologies come from either side.

Chapter 15

Conjugal Union and the Formation

of the Household

Introduction

It was seen in the previous chapter that labor value of children gives way to a rigid defining of how children are treated and who has control over them. In this way the value of children as contributors to the household labor pool is a primary conditioner of consanguineal and fictive relations—such as godparentage. This important role of children and the institutionalized control over them is embedded in the petty farming and autonomous regional marketing economy seen in earlier chapters, and in the following chapter I show how children free women to engage in marketing. But particular emphasis must first be placed on the household because it is there that children make their primary contributions. In this chapter it will be seen that the indispensable role of children in household production couples with the infrastructural requisites of establishing a household to also determine the rules and expectations associated with conjugal union.

To illustrate the rights and duties that derive from demand control over household production, I draw on interviews with judges, farmers, and actual cases, in addition to survey data. In many instances, decisions made by judges in the Jean Rabel courthouse differ from official Haitian civil law, and in some instances, decisions handed down in the village courthouse differ from the expectations and actual behavior of locals. Child support, for example, is a paternal statutory duty whether the mother and father are married, living together, or not in union at all. Jean Rabel judges recognize this legal duty and even insist that they enforce it. But in practice a Jean Rabel woman rarely summons a man to court for child support and, if she does, the court cannot enforce a decision ordering a man to pay child support (more common are men who summon women to court because they are angry that the woman has assigned paternity, and hence rights of control over a child, to another man). Thus, where official civil law and local legal procedure differ, I have emphasized the local procedure; where local legal procedure and practice differ, I have emphasized the practice. I begin with the definition of a child to show how the status of child and concept of a household and control over production are, in the minds of rural Haitians, inextricably bound.

The Definition of a Child

The definition of a child in Jean Rabel reflects labor roles and derives from dependency on and control over the household, the primary and most important regional unit of production. People in Jean Rabel enjoy telling visitors—particularly childless visitors—that an individual remains a child, whatever his age, as long as he has no children himself. But this definition of a child is actually a corollary to another more overarching definition. When pressed on the issue, farmers explain that a person becomes a *gran moun* (an adult) not when the person becomes a parent but when he or she has ascended to the head of an autonomous homestead by building a house, rearing children, or installing children already born to the couple, to make the house productive. A person with children but still living under the roof of his or her parents does not have primary control over those children: the parents or grandparents own the house and it is they who have control over the young children and their labor activities. For example, as mentioned in the previous chapter, if a woman bears a child while still living in her mother's home, as do most with their first-born, the child's grandmother assumes the role of mother. The child is taught to call her *manman* (mother), not *gran* (grandmother), while the mother is called by her first name, as if she were the child's sister. Thus, the status of being an adult is directly related to both having children and owning a homestead. Neither is of any significance without the other. Moreover, as will be seen, the two together are the defining ingredients for a conjugal union between a man and woman; and all taken in sum—house, land, gardens, livestock, the woman who manages and the children who provide the labor that make it productive—that is what comprises a household.

The Conjugal Contract

There are two forms of conjugal union in Jean Rabel, legal marriage and what is called *plasaj,* referred to in anthropological terminology as consensual union and in colloquial terminology as common law marriage. Approximately 50 percent of couples in the Jean Rabel Baseline Survey reported being engaged in *plasaj* unions, with the remaining 50 percent legally married.[1] But whether consecrated by ceremony or an unconsecrated consensual union, there are two indispensable ingredients involved in legitimizing a conjugal union: a house and children. Absence of either one means that, while the couple may refer to themselves as in union, a full-blown contractual union does not exist, and neither customary nor legal sanctions apply.

Table 15.1: Marriage vs. consensual union (age >15; N=4,927)

Conjugal unions	Male	Female	Both
Consensual union	40.4%	43.8%	42.1%
Married	41.8%	37.0%	39.3%
Single	14.6%	10.6%	12.6%
Widowed	2.9%	8.5%	5.8%
Divorced	.1%	.1%	.1%
Total	100%	100%	100%

Legal Marriage vs. *Plasaj*

Married women and women with children have the same strength to fight.[2]
—(Jean Rabel proverb)

The first woman with whom a man bears children and enters into a *plasaj* union is typically known as his *met* (owner). She generally takes priority over any other woman with whom the man may subsequently enter into a union. Should a man who has already entered into a *plasaj* union and fathered children wish to marry another woman, he must formally cede over the property purchased or worked for the earlier wife or wives (although his and no other children of the woman by other men will inherit the property). After a formal marriage, the legally recognized wife becomes the man's unchallenged *met*, no matter what her prior status, and she is addressed by the term *madanm* (as in Mrs.). Only she and her children are entitled to use or inherit property purchased in the husband's name. Should a man purchase land or a house in his own name and allow another woman to reside on that property, the wife has the right to put the other woman out and to have the husband arrested and judged in court. Should a legally married man bear children with another woman, then according to Haitian law only the legal wife can make the children legitimate by adopting them as her own. This statute is meant to protect the property of the man and his legal wife and their children against the proprietary claims of outside women and their children.

But despite the laws and the enthusiasm with which legal wives often describe the dignity of their status as a *madanm marie*, marriage does not offer the Jean Rabel woman a great deal more security or even prestige than *plasaj*. No single word clearly distinguishes a married woman from a woman who is in a *plasaj* union. Both are referred to as *madanm* (wives). People are expected to address the married woman by the term *madanm*—as in Madanm Francois—but the same title is also used for a *plasaj* woman of high status. A married man can be sued by his legal wife for adultery, but only if he has sexual relations with another woman on property his wife is accustomed to visiting. Marriage also confers rights to the wife such as exclusive access to her husband's earnings and possessions, but these rights can and often are circumvented by married men who decide to take a *madanm deyo* (outside wife).

Case #1: Francois Bon-Homme

Francois Bon-Homme, a farmer, lived just outside the village of Jean Rabel. His wife had gone to work in Port-au-Prince with Francois's knowledge and consent, and had been away for over six months. In her absence, Francois entered into a *plasaj* union with another woman, Venucia, and rented a house for her near the village. The wife heard from a cousin that her husband had put Venucia in a house and so while Francois was away to Cape Haitian, Madanm Francois came back from Port-au-Prince, waited for Venucia to leave the house, and then took the door off the hinges and claimed possession of the house. Venucia sought out the local judge who said he could do nothing if the house was not in Venucia's name and that she would have to wait for the return of Francois. When Francois returned, the judge counseled him to make a new receipt putting the house in Venucia's name. That done, the judge subsequently ordered the wife out of the house.

House Building and Ownership

Whether marriage or *plasaj*, the building of a house is the single most important event that occurs in the legitimization of a conjugal union. A woman not legally married to a man who builds a house for her has nevertheless become the man's *madanm* (wife) and by moving into the house she has accepted him as her *mari* (husband). In contrast, a legal marriage or *plasaj* union in which the husband has not provided a house for the woman is not considered a consummated union. Even marriage, in order to gain legal and social recognition, requires children and a house. The woman may have produced several children with the man, but so long as the man and woman do not reside in a house together, their union does not get the full respect of friends and neighbors, particularly if it is a *plasaj* union; nor, according to local judges, does the union get respect from the local judiciary system—irrespective of whether or not this is actually codified civil Haitian law.[3]

Case # 2: Ti Frè and Lizanne

Ti Frè, a fisherman, lived in a small seaside hamlet. In 1996 he was twenty-eight years old, married, and had a child. He was also sexually involved with his twenty-one-year-old first cousin and childhood sweetheart, Lizanne, who lived three km from his own home. The mother of Lizanne gave her a small house in the yard where Ti Frè could comfortably sleep over. Lizanne became pregnant and in January 1997 bore a son. Ti Frè financially supported her and the child and he began to spend as much time sleeping with Lizanne in the house her mother gave to her as he did sleeping in his own house with his legal wife. In December 1997, Lizanne bore another child fathered by Ti Frè, a daughter. Ti Frè continued to support her and the children, but in October 1998 he and Lizanne had an argument. Ti Frè spent several weeks avoiding Lizanne and in the meantime Lizanne began to receive frequent visits from another cousin, Pijon—who also had a wife. Ti Frè became jealous, but did nothing against Pijon or Lizanne. People in the village explained that he had no right to intervene as Lizanne lived in her mother's house and could do as she pleased. In a subsequent event, Pijon's wife came to Lizanne's mother's house and cursed Lizanne publicly, standing just outside the fence and screaming accusations that Lizanne was having an affair with Pijon. Lizanne swore it was not true and a year later she continued to insist that she never had an affair with Pijon. She explained confidentially that she had only tolerated Pijon's short visits in order to make Ti Frè jealous (she in fact suspected him of seeing a third woman). Ti Frè, however, refused to believe Lizanne. He quit supporting their two children and moved back to his wife's house full time. Lizanne subsequently left the children with her mother—Ti Fre came and took the son—and migrated to Port-au-Prince where she went to work as a domestic servant.

Once a house has been built, there are inviolable rights and duties associated with the union and they carry the weight of both custom and law. For his part, the man must plant gardens and raise livestock for the household.[4] He may come and go as he pleases. He may even take other wives. But under no circumstances may he lead another wife or lover into the yard or share products of the homestead with another woman. Should a man fail to provide for his spouse and children, or at least fail to demonstrate that he is making a serious effort to plant gardens and raise livestock, the woman has the right to cuckold him without being expelled from the house.

Case # 3: Marco and Selest

Marco, thirty-two years old, and Selest, twenty-six years old, were in a *plasaj* union together. They had two children, a seven-year-old girl and a two-year-old boy. Marco took a second wife and began to financially neglect Selest. He allocated to the new wife a garden plot that was previously for Selest. When Selest objected, he beat her. Marco's brothers and even his father tried to intervene, talking to him, trying to get him to return the garden to Selest, but Marco ignored the advice and became increasingly abusive toward Selest, cursing her often and occasionally beating her. Selest subsequently began to have an affair with another man, Anel, and in June 1998, after a fight with Marco, Selest took the two children and went to live in a second unfinished house that Marco had been building for his new wife. In a rage, Marco beat Selest and destroyed the unfinished house, justifying his actions with the accusation of Selest's affair with Anel. Selest went to stay with her mother and, with her family's support, she had Marco summoned to court. In the courtroom, Marco countered that Selest's affair with Anel sacrificed her right to the house. Selest did not deny her affair with Anel. Instead, she pointed to Marco's financial neglect of her as a justification for adultery. Citing the importance of customary law, the judge agreed with Selest, ordered Marco to behave kindly toward his wife, to restore her gardens, to begin supporting her and the children, and he assured Selest that she had a right to live in her original house unmolested by Marco. The judge then sent the couple home to work out their differences.

Marco quit beating Selest but he continued to speak abusively to her and so one day Selest's uncle summoned her and sent her away to Port-de-Paix to stay with a sister. Several days after Selest's departure, Marco was coming home from the market when he was met by Selest's younger brother, the brother's wife, and one of Selest's sisters. The brother greeted Marco and then struck him over the head with a club. The sisters joined in, and together they severely beat Marco with clubs. Marco's skull was split and his collarbone and several ribs were broken. They then tied up their near comatose brother-in-law and sent for the acting local law enforcement official (the *kasek*) and Marco's family. In a clear acknowledgement of Marco's guilt, only Marco's father came and he made no defense for his son other than to say they should not have beaten him so badly. The brother and sisters then dropped Marco off at the local clinic. After several weeks of convalescence, Marco filed charges against his three assailants. Everyone involved in the incident was summoned to court. The judge, however, was unsympathetic. Citing Marco's abuse and the lack of support from even his own family, the judge ordered the brother-in-law to pay the cost of Marco's medical care and the case was dismissed. In the interim, Marco's second "wife" had taken up residence with another man and Marco returned to his house where Selest was again living with their children. In the fifteen months since the incident took place, Marco has reportedly behaved nicely to his wife.

People in Jean Rabel say *gason dwe fe kay, min gason pa gen kay* (men have a duty to build houses but they do not own houses). For a woman who has borne children with a man, all the property inside the house, all that is in the yard and all the gardens that men plant for the house belong to the woman. Or, as I will clarify shortly, they belong to the woman in the name of her children. As seen in the case of Marco and Selest above, custom and law reinforce the preeminence of the woman's right to the household. Should a man and woman argue, it is the man who must leave and he takes only his clothes with him—and, as Jean Rabeliens like to joke, his radio, if he has one.

The woman is thought of as the owner of the house, but in return she owes her husband absolute sexual fidelity—an obligation men are not required to reciprocate. She can justifiably violate this rule only if, as in the case of Marco and Selest, her husband is negligent in providing for her and their children. Should a woman whose husband is adequately supporting her have sexual relations with another man, especially on property belonging to her and her husband, she can be legally expelled from the homestead and deprived of her children. On the other hand, if a man is caught in *flagrant delecto* on property shared by the couple then, in theory, he can be beaten without fear of legal judgment and he can even be made to pay an indemnity. In practice, however, violence between men over women is rare.[5]

Case # 4: Selikè and Marlene

In 1994, Selikè, a mason, was twenty-six years old. His girlfriend, Marlene, was twenty years old, and she was pregnant with their child. For several years, Selikè had been going away for a month at a time to work in Port-au-Prince and he managed to save some money, so he built Marlene a house on property his father had given him and he and Marlene entered into a *plasaj* union together. The child, a girl, was born in June 1995. For the next four years Selikè continued to migrate to Port-au-Prince for one to several months at a time, working different jobs and supporting his small family. But in September of 1998, while Selikè was away in Port-au-Prince, his father discovered that another man had been sleeping in the house with Marlene. The father sent a message to Port-au-Prince summoning Selikè, who arrived several days later to find Marlene was still on the premises and apparently not intending to leave. Selikè locked himself in the house with his "wife" and beat her. He then sent her back to her parents and entrusted the now three-year-old daughter to his mother. Marlene did not contest Selikè's actions, nor did any of her family members defend her or attempt to claim the daughter. People in the area explained the lack of action on the part of Marlene and her parents as shame and an admission of guilt. Marlene subsequently entered into a public union with her alleged lover.

The Familial Contract

It is children that solidify a conjugal union and turn the conjugal contract into a familial contract involving not just the husband and wife, but the children as well. Cohabitation before a woman has conceived is rare—as is marriage. In the Polygyny Survey, for example, only five of three hundred women reported moving into a house with a man before becoming either pregnant by the man or bearing a child with him. In the event a man and woman do enter into union and then separate before any children are born, the woman must renounce rights to the house—provided it is on the man's property, as is usually the case (see table 15.2).

Table 15.2: Residence patterns

		Number of households	Percentage of households
On whose land is the house built*	Husband's family	100	73.5
	Wife's family	27	19.9
	Neither	9	6.6
	Total	136	100.0

Note: This land is often purchased from one or the other's family.

All other property is divided equally or according to the original purchaser. After the birth of a child the rules change. Even if a man and woman no longer wish to have sexual relations and separate, everything in and around the house remains with the household. It is in this sense that people in Jean Rabel say that a woman is the owner of the house in the name of her children. The woman is *sou dwa pitit li* (literally, on the rights of her children), and she has a right to remain in the house undisturbed by her husband or his family so long as she continues to care for the children and so long as she does not openly engage in a relationship with another man. As already mentioned, the man must continue to provide for the household by raising livestock and planting gardens that the wife will harvest, selling the produce in the local market to pay for household subsistence needs and to engage in further marketing activities. If the man fails to plant a garden, the woman may take over this role using his land.

Case #5: Renaud and Yoland

Renaud, thirty-two years old, married a twenty-four-year-old woman named Yoland who was pregnant with his child and who had no previous children or previous husband. Renaud already had three children by two other women with whom he continued to have relationships but for whom he had not built houses. Renaud built a house for Yoland on property adjoining his mother's house and adjoining another residence belonging to a sister. He also brought three acres of irrigated land into the marriage. Yoland subsequently bore three children with Renaud, two sons followed by a girl. But in 1980, when the oldest son was only six years old, Renaud boarded a *kantè* (illegal immigrant boat) and successfully immigrated to the United States. Friends of Yoland saw and visited with Renaud in Fort Lauderdale, Florida, but Renaud himself never responded to messages sent by Yoland. Nor did he send money, and he reportedly took up residence with yet another woman. Yoland, in the meantime, had begun farming the three acres of land by herself. Together with marketing activities and the help of her children she was able to get by financially without the assistance of her husband.

Then, in 1988, eight years after Renaud had left on the *kantè*, Yoland began having an open relationship with another man, Toma (who also had another wife and family). Yoland's mother-in-law and sister-in-law reacted angrily. They summoned Yoland to court in an attempt to have her expelled from the property. The judge decided in Yoland's favor, citing Renaud's abandonment of Yoland as just cause for her sexual freedom, the presence of Renaud's children as just cause for her to remain on the property, and the absence of children by any other man as lack of cause to expel her from the property. In 1990, however, Yoland became pregnant with Toma's child. For whatever reason, she subsequently ended the relationship with Toma. But, at the same time, growing antagonism from her mother-in-law and sister-in-law and the recognition that her new child would cause her to lose the right, in the eyes of the community, to remain in the house, compelled Yoland to leave. She built another house several kilometers away and continued to farm the three acres that are the inalienable property of her children.

Conclusion

I showed in earlier chapters that a household is the single most important unit of production in Jean Rabel. A household means food and shelter today, tomorrow, next year, and the years after. It is through ownership of a household and the presence of the working children that a man and woman are freed to engage in outside income-generating activities.

In this chapter I showed how the ability to reproduce and control over children give women institutionalized control over the household. The man and the woman aside, there are two ingredients for the formation of a *de facto* contractually complete conjugal union: a house—which is built by the husband—and children—produced by the woman and fathered, reputedly, by the man. In this way the conjugal contract in Jean Rabel can be thought of as a woman ceding a man partial rights over her reproductive capacity and domestic services in exchange for a house. Men subsequently must plant gardens and tend livestock. Women must subsequently manage the household and sell the garden produce and livestock, the proceeds from which are used to meet household subsistence expenses and to raise the children to the point where they become contributing members of the household. When their husbands are complying with their customary obligations, women are bound to absolute sexual fidelity. On the other hand, a man may engage in union with other women and father "outside" children without losing his rights in the original homestead—so long as he continues to provide financial support. In concluding, these may appear to be unfavorable conditions for women; a woman must abide faithfully by her spouse while men can do as they please. Anthropologists have commented on this and in the following chapter it will be seen that Haiti has often been represented as one of the most repressive countries for women on the planet. But with respect to rural Haiti this is an error. Control over households, obtained through their natural position as mothers, engenders a control over the local economy and individual autonomy that arguably puts women in a position of power superior to their spouses.

Notes

1. In a review of the commune of Jean Rabel's birth registry for May 1999, only 27 percent of 469 births were to legally married parents (*enfant legitime*) and 337 (72%) were born to unmarried parents (*enfant natiral*). Only 5 (1%) of the 469 children born did not have a man attesting to having fathered the child (*deklarasyon mè*).

2. *Madanm marie ak fi ki gen ti moun gen menm fòs pou goume* and alternatively, *Fi ki gen pitit ak fi marie se menm bagay: Tou dè gen menm kouray pou goumen.*

3. A man who has not built a house for a woman has no recourse to complain should the woman entertain other suitors—her response would likely be, "well build me a house."

4. Harvesting in Jean Rabel is thought of as a woman's right and most women will claim in the name of her children any garden not being planted in the name of another woman, so that even if a man were to attempt to plant a garden independent of his wife—married or *plasaj*—he must do so secretly for if she gets wind of it she is likely to show up for harvest time and there may be much cursing if he tries to stand in her way.

5. Although it is rare for a man to actually succeed in depriving his wife of her children, farmers and local judges are unanimous in insisting that a man has this right in the event of the woman's sexual infidelity. Also in theory, if a woman should leave the house in anger, she must go stay with her mother-in-law or her husband's otherwise closest relative and if she fails to do so, even if she goes to the house of her own mother, she has, according to local judges, legally committed adultery.

Chapter 16

Polygyny, Progeny, and Production

Introduction

In the preceding chapters I tried to show how the importance of child labor with respect to household livelihood strategies—specifically the negotiation and sharing of access between genders, parents, and friends to control over child labor—conditions childrearing practices, kinship, family patterns, and even gender roles and division of labor. Here I want to bring together the preceding observations to show how it is that these customs and behaviors, as well as the pronatal sociocultural fertility complex seen in chapter 5 and the values associated with the sexual moral economy described in chapter 6 come about, how they are perpetuated, whose interests they serve, and how they relate to the subsistence strategies and the regional economy. I begin with a look at another misunderstood issue in Haiti, female repression; then I use polygyny, an institution considered by many advocates and aid workers to be a defining indicator of female repression but which in Haiti arguably works to the economic advantage of women; and ultimately I show how the importance of household-based production and the child labor upon which it is based mean that middle-aged women play a determinant role in perpetuating the relations of production and reproduction.

Another Misrepresentation of Social Life in Rural Haiti: Female Repression

Gender status in Haiti is widely misunderstood. One notable exception notwithstanding (N'zengou-Tayo 1998), most researchers and aid workers who have focused on gender in Haiti highlight the commonality of domestic violence and repression of women. In doing so they cite discriminatory legal codes (Fuller 2005), political violence against women (Fuller 2005), high levels of mortality during birth (World Bank 2002), the feminine struggle for identity manifest in creative literature (Francis 2004), female involvement in onerous, labor-intensive, economic endeavors (Divinski et al. 1998), and even the overall deterioration of economic and political conditions as unfair and repressive to women (UNIFEM 2006). Summarizing these views, the UN's Gender Development Index (GDI) ranks Haiti at the very bottom in the Western hemisphere, making it seem to observers who do not carefully interpret the index that Haiti is the most female repressive country in all of Latin America, indeed the world, being considerably lower in ranking than even Iran or Saudi Arabia (United Nations Development Programme 2006).

Social scientists too have portrayed Haitian culture as strongly patriarchic, male-centered and by implication, female repressive. In a stark misrepresentation of rural life in Haiti first noted by Gerald Murray (1977: 263), the oft-repeated explanation for polygyny is that farmers use "extra" wives to tend additional gardens (Bastien 1961: 142; Courlander 1960: 112; Herskovits 1937; Leyburn 1966: 195; Moral 1961: 175–76; Simpson 1942: 656). As seen, this is not now and probably never was true. Women in rural Haiti do not work in gardens on behalf of men. Quite the contrary, rural Haitian women may sometimes work gardens on their own and their children's behalf, but when a man is present, the obligation to plant and weed falls to him. To reverse the situation would be, from the cultural perspective of a rural Haitian, absurd. And oddly enough it is almost a certainty that the cited scholars knew this. Why earlier anthropologists and sociologists said differently I can only surmise is due to Western expectations and the domino-type repetition of one scholar reiterating what was said by another that so often infects our research.[1]

The point is that, once again, these types of misrepresentations have left a generation of scholars, aid workers, and interested laypeople with an erroneous image of social relations and conditions in rural Haiti. The reality of the situation in rural areas— where 70 percent of the Haitian population live and where we find what Sahlins (1972) called the domestic mode of production (DMP)—is much different. In rural Haiti, it is women who typically have the upper hand in terms of control over the local and domestic economies; who control the household and its products and the money derived from them. Women are also more violent than men both with respect to other women and to their husbands.[2]

I do not want to be misunderstood on this point. I want to make it emphatically clear that I am not denying the importance of empowering women in Haiti; violence and repression of women in Haitian urban areas is a problem. This is, I believe, a consequence of the extreme differentials in urban income- earning opportunities seen in chapter 10 (table 10.4). My point is that as with so many issues pertaining to life in rural Haiti, information is selectively and erroneously grasped by representatives of aid agencies devoted to a particular objective, consequently distorting ethnographic reality and giving way to misguided and wasteful intervention efforts that do more to convince rural Haitians that *"blan"* is indeed a little bizarre, than it does to help fight poverty and repression.

Definition of Polygyny

Polygyny in Jean Rabel is not legal but it is different from the "extramarital affair" in that (1) it is public, (2) efforts are made to produce children in all of the unions, (3) the man continues to perform his role as provider, planting gardens and tending livestock for all of the women, and (4) the women are expected to remain sexually faithful to the man.[3]

All Jean Rabeliens recognize the institution of polygyny, and all women engaged in union with a particular man are referred to as his wives (*madanm*). There are, in fact, three interchangeable terms for women who share a husband—*matlot, rival,* and *koleg*—meaning co-wives or co-wife. Co-wives usually live in separate homesteads and the houses of the different wives are usually at least several kilometers one from the other. Among fishermen however, it is not unusual for wives to live in the same small hamlet. In Makab, for example, three fishermen had two or more of their wives living in the hamlet itself. *Bokor* (healers/shaman) are also an anomaly among polygynous men; they are notorious for having multiple wives living in the same compound and sometimes even in the same household and being able to maintain peace among all of them. The ability of *bokor* to manage this type of situation is something that even fishermen do not accomplish and that never ceases to amaze other Jean Rabeliens.[4]

Frequency

At any given time, 11 percent of male Jean Rabel household heads are engaged in a conjugal union with more than one woman (Table 16.1). This may not seem like a large number of men, but with age the likelihood that he is or has been engaged in a polygynous union increases. Forty percent of men over the age of fifty have been polygynous at least once in their lives (table 16.2).[5]

Table 16.1: Polygyny: Opinion Survey

		Men who are polygynous			
		No		Yes	
	Baseline (n=898)	806	90%	92	10%
Survey	Opinion (n=136)	107	88%	16	12%
	Polygyny(n=300)	266	89%	34	11%

Opinion survey missing = 13

Table 16.2: Male age groups by ever been polygynous

		Men who have ever been polygynous			
		No		Yes	
Male age groups	20–34 (n=48)	43	90%	5	10%
	35–49 (n=128)	100	78%	28	22%
	50 + (n=122)	73	60%	49	40%
	Total (n=298)	216	72%	82	28%

Missing = 2

The Economic Underpinnings of Polygyny

There can be no doubt that polygyny in Jean Rabel is also somehow related to wealth. The vast majority of polygynous men in Jean Rabel have a relatively high level of material resources in comparison to most other men in the commune. A random sample of ten polygynous males taken from the Baseline Survey revealed that seven were skilled workers—in addition to being farmers. Another man from the sample turned out to be a *bokor* and only two depended exclusively on farming for subsistence and income.

Similarly, in another survey conducted in two different communities, one located in a mountainous area and the other in a lowland area, fourteen of forty-one skilled workers (*boss*) reported having more than one wife (33%). A sample of sixteen *bokor* in the same regions revealed that seven (44%) were polygynous and of fifteen male school teachers, four (27%) were polygynous. Fishermen, who as discussed earlier earn as great or greater income than a *boss*, appear to display the highest rates of polygyny: fifteen of twenty-four fishermen in Makab (62%) reported having more than one wife. Farmers with relatively large landholdings also display a tendency to have multiple wives. When informants in three separate communities, two lowland communities and one mountain community, were asked to list the ten most productive local farmers who were engaged exclusively in farming without practicing any other income-generating activity, six out of a total of thirty (or 20%) were found to be polygynous (see table 16.3).[6]

Table 16.3: Male high income groups by ever been polygynous

	Men who have ever been polygynous			
	No		Yes	
Skilled workers (n=41)	27	66%	14	34%
Spiritual healers (n=16)	9	56%	7	44%
School teachers (n=15)	11	73%	4	27%
Fisherman (n=24)	9	38%	15	62%
Big farmers (n=30)	24	80%	6	20%
Population as a whole (n=1,319)	1,179	89%	140	11%

Female Interest in Male Wealth

It is clear that male wealth is a primary determinant of polygyny but this does not necessarily mean that polygyny is an institution that favors men. Nor does it mean that women passively enter relationships of acquiescence and servitude. In order to understand the role of male wealth it helps to return to the sexual moral economy discussed earlier.

As seen in chapter 6 women are very much interested in the wealth a man has to offer. In what Richman (2003: 123) called "gendered capital" and Lowenthal (1984: 22) called a "field of competition" women in rural Haiti attach a price to their sexual and domestic cooperation. Negotiations begin with courtship and extend throughout a relationship. The building of a house is the single most important event that occurs in the legitimization of a union. A couple may have several children but until the man has provided her with her own house they are not considered in union nor is the woman bound by obligations of fidelity. Even legal marriage is dismissed and legally vacuous if the man has not provided a house for his wife.[7]

Once a house has been built, the inviolable rights and duties associated with the union begin and they carry the weight of both custom and law. As long as the man is fulfilling his obligations, the woman, on her part, must be faithful. In this way a man's provision of a house, gardens, and animals can be understood as a type of contractual partnership in which in exchange for these material goods a woman cedes her ability to reproduce, the resulting children, and the labor of her and her children. But she is still in control. People in Jean Rabel say *gason dwe fe kay, min gason pa gen kay* (men have a duty to build houses but they do not have houses). Should a man fail to provide for his spouse and children, the woman has the right to cuckold him without being expelled from the house. The point cannot be understated. For a woman who has borne children with a man, all the property inside the house, all that is in the yard and all the gardens that a man plants and that is not tagged for another woman belong to her, or more specifically, they belong to her in the name of the children she has borne with the man. Custom and law reinforce the preeminence of the woman's right to the household and the associated production. Should a man and woman argue, it is the man who must leave and he takes only his clothes with him—"and his radio," as informants jokingly added, "if he has one."

For outsiders who think that Haitian men can violate these rules by physical intimidation and violence, the reality is usually different. Women in Jean Rabel can be and often are more ferocious than men. They also have their brothers, fathers, and sisters, all of whom will, if it is clear that the woman's rights are being abused by a man, join her in violent confrontation. In seventeen violent incidences I recorded while living in one Jean Rabel community, only four involved men only; eight began with a conflict between a man and a woman. In only three of these cases was the woman slightly injured and in four cases the man was severely beaten; in two he almost died (see endnote 2, this chapter). Women also have recourse to the legal system and judges enforce the rules described.

Thus, women in Jean Rabel tend to be tough and they aggressively assert their control over household expenditures. Husbands who impinge on their wives' sovereignty in the financial sphere are resented if not physically challenged. With this in mind, we can return to the issue of polygyny and whose interest it best serves.

Economic Independence

While wealth appears to facilitate polygyny, the most important determinant of polygyny is not wealth, per se, but rather whether or not a man has a source of income beyond the control of his first wife. Skilled workers build houses and collect their pay with no participation from their wives. *Bokor* do not depend on their wives to help serve their clientele. Schoolteachers instruct students and collect their pay independently and fishermen are not dependent on their wives for fishing or even for the sale of fish in the market.[8]

The most productive male farmers were also found to maintain multiple families, but a closer looks shows that here too the issue is not only the increased wealth of the man, but wealth beyond control of his first wife. A large landowner typically cannot and does not plant all of his land. More often, the man rents and sharecrops parcels of the land to less fortunate individuals, something that allows him to move beyond the influence of, and dependency on, a single wife. In contrast, the average farmer does not have multiple wives. Even men who reported owning irrigated and "fat" land—high-yield garden plots the ownership of even a small parcel of which unquestionably places a household in the category of economically elite farmers—were not found to be unusually polygynous until the amount of their reported landholdings reached levels beyond the control of a single household (see table 16.4). Thus, it appears that men are polygynous when they can get away with it. But again, this does not necessarily mean that polygyny is an institution in the best interest of men, a point evident when I asked them.

Table 16.4: Polygynous males by the amount of "fat" and irrigated land owned

		Polygynous			
		No		Yes	
Irrigated and	.15 –.49 (n=50)	44	88%	6	12%
"fat" land	.50 –.99 (n=32)	29	91%	3	9%
owned	1.00 – 1.99 (n=15)	12	80%	3	20%
(in hectares)	2.00 + (n=4)	1	25%	3	75%
	Total (n=101)	86	-	15	-

Male Attitudes toward Polygyny

When asked about polygyny, Jean Rabel men revealed a general disdain for the institution. At first glance this appears to be out of sympathy for women. Men commonly said that having more than one wife is immoral and wrong, that polygyny is cruel to the first wife, it causes her to starve herself (*bouch li p'ap gou*), to become emaciated (*l'ap chèch*), and sad (*l'ap kalkile*). When asked what a woman should do in the case that her husband takes another wife, 71 percent of men said the woman should leave him.

But there is more to male opinions than sympathy for the women. Ninety-one percent of men interviewed in the Opinion Survey reported that having multiple wives is a burden. When questioned about the advantages of polygyny, most men were hard-pressed to think of any at all, 95 percent responding that there are no advantages. Typical responses include the following examples:

Ahh, there is no advantage. Men don't understand, it brings you down financially. It's just one little wife who truly pushes you ahead.[9] (fifty-year-old father of twelve)

When you have several wives it is a bunch of work. . . . Right now this morning, if you work this wife's garden, you have to go work the other garden for the other wife.[10] (seventy-five-year-old father of seven)

There are no advantages. It is a disadvantage.[11] (thirty-one-year-old father of five)

Yes, there are advantages, because there are people who have several wives. But if it is food, or whatever, I don't know.[12] (forty-year-old father of five)

No there are no advantages. Because you must plant gardens for both of them so you can send them both to the market. There is no advantage.[13] (fifty-three-year-old father of nine)

So why have more than one wife? In the subsample taken of ten polygynous men, nine of the men explained that having more than one wife serves either to compensate for the absence of the first wife, such as when she is away on marketing trips, or to provide an alternative to spending time with an argumentative first wife. [14]

When your wife is not getting along with you . . . you have somewhere else you can go eat and drink.[15] (fifty-five-year-old father of seventeen)

If the first one is not good, you have to look for another.[16] (twenty-nine-year-old father of nine)

If one wife is not there, the man he goes, he goes to the head of the other house who left a little food for him . . . he goes and eats it. It is this, and after this it is a drain.[17] (forty-five-year-old father of five)

Even then, when men took second wives they rarely left the first one. Only one of the seven polygynous men in the Opinion Survey was no longer with his first wife (see table 16.5).

Table 16.5: Men who have ever been polygynous by men who
have left their first wife (missing = 16)

		Have you ever had more than one wife at the same time?			
		No		Yes	
Are you still with your first spouse?	No (n=7)	6	86%	1	14%
	Yes (n=45)	39	86%	6	14%
	Total (n=52)	45	86%	7	14%

In summary, it is not clear why some Jean Rabel men take second and even third or fourth wives. If we base conclusions on what men say, then perhaps the best explanation is because they feel they must, the first wife or wives are not living up to her/their end of the conjugal contract and the man having no means of forcing her to do so. In any case, a more illuminating issue is why women put up with the behavior in the first place.

Female Attitudes toward Polygyny

It may seem ironic at first but women expressed a greater tolerance of polygyny than men. As seen, when asked what a woman should do in the event her husband enters into a union with a second wife, 71 percent of men said she should leave him. In contrast, 62 percent of women said that a wife should stay. Only 3 percent of women said the wife had a right to subsequently engage in an affair with another man; 34 percent of men said she had this right (see tables 16.6 and 16.7).

Table 16.6: A man takes a second wife, what should the first wife do (missing male responses=15—see text)

		Gender		Men and women
		Men (n = 51)	Women (n = 68)	(n = 119)
What should the first wife do?	Leave	71%	32%	49%
	Stay	22%	62%	45%
	Other	7%	6%	6%
	Total	100%	100%	100%

Table 16.7: A man takes a second wife, may first wife be unfaithful (missing male responses=15)

		Gender		Men and women
		Men (n = 51)	Women (n = 68)	(n = 119)
Does the woman have a right to take another man?	No	66%	97%	84%
	Yes	34%	3%	16%
	Total	100%	100%	100%

What seems to be an attitude of passive toleration may arguably be consequences of norms that militate against female infidelity. There are not many choices open to a woman who refuses to accept her husband's taking another wife. She can leave her husband and return to her parent's house, but if she does so she sacrifices her own house and her right to claim support from her husband. If the woman engages in an affair with another man she may be required to give up considerably more than the house and support for, as seen in an earlier chapter, doing so would give the man the right to throw her off the property and keep the children, or at least give them to his mother.

Moreover, no matter how tolerant of polygyny women say they are, the ethnographic reality is that a Jean Rabel woman is likely and even expected to react strongly to her husband taking another spouse. She may go no further than harsh words. But with a woman who is *bandi* (a scrapper)—as many Jean Rabel women pride themselves on being—violence is common. Displaying little or no aggression toward the husband—indeed, wooing and sweet-talking him in private—a Jean Rabel wife will make violent statements to others of intent to physically attack the other woman. She will curse her in the street and in the market. It is not unusual for this wife to go to the other woman's house and stand outside screaming insults at her. She may stalk her. She may wait at crossroads and on paths to ambush and beat her. She may throw rocks at her, scratch her, or try to bite the other woman's lip in order to disfigure her face.

So it might be said that women are pushed into a situation where they have little choice but to conform to their husband's philandering. When a man is no longer economically dependent on the labor contributions of his first wife there is a great probability that he may enter into conjugal union with another woman and take on a second family. In this way it does appear that women are repressed victims of a patriarchal familial system. However, there is another side to it: Men need women more than vice versa.

The Need for a Wife

In contrast to women who fight other women for access to male resources and who sometimes are behind violent attacks on negligent spouses or fathers of their children, Jean Rabel men rarely fight or even argue over lovers or potential spouses; and it is not because they do not want a wife. The importance of a wife cannot be gainsaid. Entering union with a woman means a man can establish a homestead, he becomes a *gran moun*, an adult, an economically autonomous individual worthy of respect, the head of a household, no longer a dependent, and no longer a child who can be ordered around by older family members. Without a wife none of this is possible. Without a wife a man cannot establish a homestead independent of his parents.

A Jean Rabel man needs a woman. It is a woman who will wash his clothes, make his meals, sell garden produce and livestock, extend the budget by rolling the family savings over in the market, and it is a wife who will bear and raise the children whose labor will bring prosperity and respect to the household. When asked "does a husband need his wife more or is a wife in greater need of her husband?" only 3 percent of men reported a woman needs her husband more; 28 percent reported that a husband is in greater need of his wife—the remaining individuals said that both needed the other equally (see table 16.8).

Table 16.8: Who needs the other more, husband or wife?

	Respondents		
	Men (n = 69)	Women (n = 69)	Men & women (n = 138)
Husband needs wife more	28%	23%	26%
Wife needs husband more	3%	13%	8%
They both need the other equally	70%	63%	68%
Total responses	100%	100%	100%

Thus, to vulgarize the analysis, as, in fact, a Jean Rabelien might do, the simple truths are (1) getting a wife is the most materially rewarding alliance a Jean Rabel man can form with another person and (2) men do not fight over women because they know that what stands between them and a wife is not other men, but their own ability to provide.

Women understand the need men have for a wife, and, like men, they too think that a husband is in greater need of his wife than vice versa. Only 13 percent of women reported that a wife needs her husband more, but 23 percent of women reported that a husband is in greater need of his wife (table 16.8). When asked, "can you get by without your spouse?" 96 percent of men interviewed said no, in comparison to 77 percent of women interviewed who responded no (table 16.9 below).

Table 16.9: Could you live without your spouse?

		Respondents		
		Men (n = 69)	Women (n = 69)	Men & Women (n = 138)
Could you live without	No	96%	77%	86%
a spouse?	Yes	4%	23%	14%
	Total	100.0%	100%	100.0%

Moreover, women, much more so than men, chose their spouse for material reasons: forty-five of sixty-four men said they chose their spouse because of love; only twenty-seven of sixty-eight women said so. Twenty-six of the sixty-eight women said they chose their spouse because he was a good worker; only one man said so. Thirteen of the sixty-four male respondents said they chose their wife because it was the only one they could find; four of sixty-eight women said so.

Table 16.10: Why men versus women chose their spouse (missing=4)

| | | Gender | | |
		Men n=64	Women n=68	Total
	Love	70%	40%	55%
Why did	Good worker	2%	38%	20%
you choose	Only one I could find	20%	6%	13%
your	Good family	2%	0%	1%
spouse?	Other	6%	16%	11%
	Total	100%	100%	100%

The Bargaining Stick: Paternity

The de facto gender-power relations and primacy of women in Jean Rabel are expressed most clearly in an ethnographically striking complex of behavior relating to paternity touched on in chapter 6. Unlike women, Jean Rabel men often accept being cuckolded in silent shame, and almost without exception they quietly accept paternity for children commonly known to be sired by other men: 13 percent of men (seven of fifty-two) in Makab had at least one child that their wife told them was their own but who friends and neighbors reported was actually sired and recognized by another man. The *couvade*, while not of conspicuous importance across the population in a ritual sense, occurs. In the home in which I first lived I once sat and watched as the "wife" lay in a bed rather stoically bearing her fifth child, a child well known to all of us was the biological offspring of a man other than her husband. Meanwhile, her husband—not the father—lay in another bed making a great display of sympathetic pains, moaning and holding his stomach. And in the fictive illness known as *perdisyon*, the disease seen earlier in which women can carry a fetus for as long as five years, both men and women accepted the disease as legitimate, allowing women to dupe their husbands into accepting paternity for children that do not biologically belong to them and giving men a rationale for accepting paternity.

The reason that men accept paternity, and indeed, the reason that women have the upperhand in the domestic sphere, should be apparent from previous chapters. It is because the children are so valuable and because women bear and control children. Indeed, in paternity cases that make it to court, it is overwhelmingly men complaining that the wife has assigned paternity to one or more other men, meaning that he must share control over the child. As for women, they are less concerned about the husband than the money he provides. Going back to the issue of polygyny, when asked to explain why they do not agree with the prospect of having a *koleg*,

I am gonna be angry because I will lose some of what he gives me.[18] (thirty-five-year-old mother of four)

I will start stashing my money because he is going to be carrying it away.[19] (thirty-year-old mother of two)

I am not going to be comfortable because he is going to be giving the other woman money.[20] (thirty-three-year-old mother of eight)

I am gonna cuss him because he is going to make me lose money.[21] (twenty-seven-year-old mother of three)

But the fact is that the average wife of the average husband in Jean Rabel is not especially worried about the prospect of their husband entering into a union with another woman. Going back to the greater female vs. male tolerance of polygyny, the common response women gave to, "does your husband have another or other wives?" was not a simple, "No," but rather, "No, he is too poor" (*Non, pase li malere*). The average farmer's wife knows her husband cannot afford another wife, and perhaps more importantly, she knows he needs her and the children, and this was evident in responses many women gave when asked what they would do in the event their husband took another woman:

I would talk to him. I would not curse him because if the guy had something, if he had a good paying job, I would raise hell, I would have a serious little chat with him. But the guy has no job, he has no education, he has nothing.[22] (thirty-two-year-old mother of five)

Ah well, I would not do anything, it is not me who made him do it . . . He'll be back, he'll be sick and to the house he'll be coming. There is not anyone before me. It is me who is first.[23] (fifty-year-old mother of seven)

If he finds a woman who is brave, he goes and spends a couple days with her, let him go with the girl because he is not a child, you can't beat him.[24] (thirty-four-year-old mother of three)

If it is strength he feels, if he feels strong, I won't stop his strength.[25] (sixty-five-year-old mother of nine)

I would not do anything. If he listens to me, if I tell him "No, times are not good, you can not have two wives. For example, like today, it is only a single two dollars you have there, and if there are two of us, you can not give us each only a dollar." Ah, he can't do it.[26] (twenty-seven-year-old mother of five)

He cannot abandon me completely. He has to come sit there and help me *chape* [raise] the children.[27] (forty-year-old mother of four)

Just so long as I have a path to go down I would not pay any attention. I would look after my children. Especially with him, I can't leave him. We are married, I cannot leave him. It is an engagement we have together. I have a bunch of children with him.[28] (sixty-five-year-old mother of nine)

It is here with the women's tolerance of their husbands' infidelity that the argument merits returning to another factor that enters into the decisions made by women regarding the choice of a spouse: male wealth, for it is precisely male wealth that makes polygyny an attractive institution; but for women in pursuit of economic independence achieved throughout childbearing.

The Econo-Demographic Underpinnings of Polygyny

Early on in the chapter I examined male wealth from the perspective of men being able to afford the "luxury" of more than one wife. I subsequently presented data that showed that most men thought it was wrong to have more than one wife and that it was not so clear whether or not there were any advantages to having multiple wives. Here I want to present the issue from the perspective of the women to show that in the aggregate, polygyny in Jean Rabel is better understood as in the interest of women rather than men.

To begin with, it was seen that at any given time 11 percent of Jean Rabel men are engaged in union with more than one women and 40 percent will have more than one wife, at least once, at some point in their lives. However, looking at it from the other perspective, polygyny is a far more significant institution for women than it is for men. While 11 percent of men are engaged in polygyny at any given moment, at least twice as many women are engaged in a conjugal union with men who have at least one other wife.

Moreover, the demographic fact is that if conditions in Jean Rabel really compelled farmers to maximize birth rates—i.e., maximize the number of valuable child laborers under her control—then, all things being equal, the best way for a woman to achieve high fertility is within the socioeconomic comfort of an enduring conjugal union with a man who has no other wife and who provides the material support necessary to care for her during pregnancy and while she is breastfeeding infants. But all things are not equal. In Jean Rabel, a highly stable monogamous union would only be possible for a minority of women, because as seen there is a scarcity of eligible bachelors, a scarcity that is financially induced and that has both a physical and an artificial dimension. The "physical" scarcity is a direct consequence of a disproportionate number of men going to the city and overseas, often in search of money so they can find a wife and start a homestead. Male wage migration causes the proportion of males to females in Jean Rabel to drop by 7 to 10 percent for the twenty- to thirty-nine-year age group (see 16.11).[29, 30]

An "artificial" scarcity of men is caused by the fact that many of the young men who remain in Jean Rabel do not have the money necessary to enter into a union, and to build the house, plant the gardens, and purchase the livestock that, as seen in chapter 15, are necessary to establish a conjugal union. Thus, a typical Jean Rabel man would very much like to have a wife, but for the majority of young men the associated financial demands make it impossible. And so, rather than delay the onset of childbearing while waiting for male age cohorts to come back from the city or to become financially mature at home, many Jean Rabel women enter into unions and begin bearing children with men several years older than themselves, a trend that is evidenced by the fact that 48 percent of women versus 18 percent of men are in union at the age of twenty-four (see table

16.11 below). At least 15 percent of women's first unions are with men who already have a wife.[31]

Table 16.11: Women vs. men in union per five-year age group

Age categories	Males in union	Total male pop	Women in union	Total female pop	Sex ratio (m/f)
0–14	-	2,030		1,900	1.07%
15–19	2%	373	12%	387	0.96%
20–24	18%	343	48%	378	0.91%
25–29	51%	253	76%	285	0.89%
30–34	81%	183	85%	216	0.85%
35–39	90%	196	90%	214	0.92%
40–44	92%	158	89%	170	0.93%
45–49	88%	134	87%	144	0.93%
50-64	89%	586	76%	532	1.10%
Over 64	80%	222	55%	220	0.96%
Total	—	2,226	—	2,326	0.96%

Reproductive Reluctance and the Matriarch

Despite everything seen above, there is one catch: young Jean Rabel women are often not so eager to begin their childbearing career. As was seen in chapter 5, girls pregnant for the first time often disavow their condition right up until the time their bulging stomachs make denial impossible. Others tie ribbons around their stomachs to conceal their condition. Others try to abort pregnancies, taking desperate measures that sometimes end in death. But entrance into a childbearing career is not something that women decide by themselves. Elder women in control of homesteads frame the conditions that make pregnancy likely or, to put it another way, almost impossible to avoid.

In earlier chapters it was shown that children are highly valued and that slightly more than half of all farmers would prefer to have six rather than three children. But when the respondents were broken down by sex and age group, it was overwhelmingly women, and specifically middle-age and elder women, who most favored large numbers of children. Women over fifty were far more inclined than any other male or female age category to choose the couple with six versus three children: Fully 87 percent (twenty of the twenty-three women) chose the couple with six children (see table 13.1). The reasons have to do with the economic benefits that accrue to older women. With greater numbers of children, women begin to plant their own gardens and to raise more animals, activities that free a woman from dependency on men (see table 16.12; see also Schwartz 2000: 153–57). The women who said they could live without a man were precisely those with children in the ages when they made contributions to the household.

Table 16.12: Women who have gardens by number of children

		Do you plant your own garden?		
		No	Yes	Total
	0	1	1	2
	1	4	0	4
	2	2	2	4
Number of	3	4	5	9
children woman	4	6	4	10
has	5	6	7	13
	6	2	3	5
	7	3	5	8
	8+	9	5	14
	Total	37	32	67

Equally or more important than livestock and gardens, child labor frees a woman to enter more fully into a career in marketing. A Jean Rabel woman with four to eight children is four times more likely to be engaged in commercial activity than a woman with zero to three children (see table 12.3). Freed by the help of children, the most successful women sometimes build their trade revenue up to several thousand Haitian dollars per month. They buy agricultural land and animals, invest in a wide assortment of business ventures and sometimes even hire men to work gardens for them. Houses that have a woman in her 40s, 50s, and 60s are almost invariably known, not by the husband's name, but by the name of the woman, as in Madam Jean's house, or Lili's place. As women themselves explained:

> What makes me say I can live without a man? What I need to do to come up with a sack of food I can accomplish with my four children.[32] (thirty-year-old mother of four).

> If I have children, I don't need my husband at all. Children, hey! hey! I would like to have ten children. I don't need my husband.[33] (forty-one-year-old mother of seven).

> Why can I live without a man? I arrive at an age like this. All my affairs are in order. I don't need my husband anymore.[34] (fifty-six-year-old mother of eight)

But younger women often do not see these advantages. Moreover, the older woman who controls the activities of her nubile daughters is keenly alert not only to the importance of her daughter bearing children relatively early on in life for the sake of the younger woman's household and marketing career but also to the advantages that accrue to herself, as the grandmother.

The Matriarchic Market Woman and Grandchildren

Parents, especially mothers, take a keen interest in the suitors of their daughters. At first glance this interest appears to the outsider as a promotion of chastity. "Good girls" do not flirt with men while away from the homestead. Many prenuptial daughters who are not in school do not leave the homestead at all, not for any reason, not even to go for water. Some mothers physically probe their daughters' genitals to see if the hymen has been perforated. Girls who see men in secret may suffer severe whippings at the hands of their mothers. But while parents may appear to be discouraging sexual contact it is actually something quite different.

Prenuptial girls are carefully watched, not with an antagonism toward suitors, something that might thwart the approach of gift-bearing men and potential sires of grandchildren, but with intent to maintain a grip on the girl's flirtations. The girl is severely rebuked for encouraging the interested *vakabon* but suitors who parents find acceptable are promoted. The daughter, of course, has to consent, but if with the encouragement of her parents she does consent, the man is welcomed. He is invited to the house and in good humor teased for not stopping by more frequently. When he does visit the house he is joked with, fed, given a place to relax, and he is deliberately left alone with the daughter for increasingly lengthy intervals. If all goes well, he may eventually begin sleeping over at the girl's house. The girl is then watched carefully for signs of pregnancy. At the smallest indication that she is pregnant the *matwon* (mid-wife) or another specialist in these matters is summoned to the house to make a diagnosis, a diagnosis that, as seen in an earlier chapter, often comes up positive even when the girl is not pregnant; i.e., *perdisyon*. This is also a diagnosis that for several years tags the next child born to the woman as the offspring of that particular man, whether or not she is still in union with the man, and whether or not she continues to have sexual relations with him—unless a more eligible man comes along, in which case the *perdisyon* may pass to spontaneous abortion or the girl and her mother may profit from the opportunity to assign multiple fathers, one secret and one public. It is also worth emphasizing however, that the man, his parents, and other family members will spend more time thinking about the joy and benefits of acquiring a new family member than they will dwelling on the question of whether the child is really a biological relative.

Everyone, especially the mother's mother, is able to benefit. As seen in an earlier chapter, in the event a daughter becomes pregnant while living in mother's home, it is her mother, the child's grandmother, who assumes the role of mother. While the real mother only breastfeeds the child or does mundane tasks such as cleaning up after him, the grandmother refers to the child as her own. The child is taught to call her *manman* (mother), not *gran* (grandmother), while the mother is called by her first

Table 16.13: Union type by household residents under thirty years old (but over fourteen) who are not the head or spouse of head

	Gender		
	Male	Female	Total
Plasaj	107	237	344
Separation	59	70	129
Single	876	738	1,614
Widowed	11	30	41
Divorced	3	3	6
Other	1	0	1
Total	1,057	1,078	2,135

Note: Reference is to children-in-law and sibling in-laws. Parental in-laws are included in other.

name as if she were the child's sister. Even after the mother has moved out to *plase* with a man, the grandmother often keeps the grandchild or several of the grandchildren.[35]

I want to make clear that the concern parents display regarding the sexual activities of their daughters and the emphasis I have put on the economic aspects of paternity should not be interpreted as intrusive or even unusual. Like parents elsewhere in the world, parents in Jean Rabel want their daughters to make practical decisions regarding mates, and they encourage them to bear children with men who can support the young women economically and who will help pay for the cost to *chape* offspring. Moreover, as seen in chapter 13, daughters are a critical source of labor for the household. They tend to be the most productive, they can take over the role of mother, and both mothers and fathers significantly favor daughters over sons. A daughter's pregnancy represents a critical disruption in her life in that it reduces her labor contributions to the household. Yet, 49 percent (1,046 of 2,135) of women over fourteen but under thirty years of age and still living in their mother's home had born at least one child (figure 16.1); and twenty-two percent (237 of 1,078) of young women under the age of thirty who were reported during the baseline as being in the formative phase of a conjugal union—meaning they identified themselves as being in union with a man but had not yet acquired an independent homestead—were in fact still living in the home of their mother, father, or another relative (table 16.13). It is at this juncture that parents, particularly mothers, play a determining role in polygyny. As a civil judge in Jean Rabel explained:

> A lot of the time it is the parents themselves who *plase* girls. Sometimes the parents, they are so interested in money, their daughter loves a young man who is the same age as her, they could marry, but the parents don't accept it. They see that at that time in the young man's life he can not do anything. He cannot give money. Then the parents see by the way the girl is acting that she is going to *plase* with a married man. But the fact that the married man can give money causes them to close their eyes so the daughter can take the money from him. It is like this. Adults are behind it.[36] (Civil judge in Jean Rabel)

Figure 16.1: Children under thirty years old (but over fourteen),
who have children of their own but still living in parent's household
(N = 2,135)

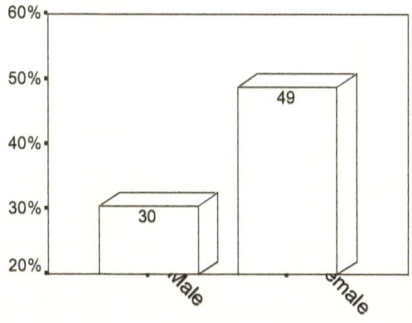

Gender

Whether the dynamics described above are to be construed as mothers exploiting daughters or as a partnership in the mutual interest of both mother and daughter is a matter of opinion. As seen, daughters revere their mothers, loyalty to mother is among the highest values, and the subsistence alliance between mother and daughter and the role of the mother in guiding a girl's sexual conduct are celebrated in *teat* songs, as in the following:

Heads together the time has already arrived	*Tet ansanm lè a deja rive*
Hand in hand until the time arrives	*Min dans la min jiskaskè lè a rive*
My mother sent me to the river (to get water)	*Se nan dlo maman-m voye mwen*
In broad daylight, this man came to bluff me	*La jounen myseu sa vin pou-l blofe-m*
My mother sent me to get water and told me to hurry	*Se nan dlo maman-m voye m byen prese*
The man came to fool me, he said	*Myseu vin pou chaba-m*
Sweetheart, I will give you a gold chain but you must not tell your mother so	*Ti cheri, m-ap f-o kado yon chen an lò fo-k ou pa di maman ou sa*
Sweetheart, I will give you a gold ring but you must not tell your mother so	*Ti cheri, m-a p f-o kado yon bag an lò fo-k ou pa di maman ou sa*
And so I said to him,	
Sweetheart, if you give me a gold chain I must tell my mother so	*Ti cheri, si ou fe-m kado yon chen an lò fo-k mwen ka di maman-m sa*
Sweetheart, if you give me a gold ring I must tell my mother so	*Ti cheri, si ou fe-m kado yon bag an lò fo-k mwen ka di maman-m sa*

Conclusion

Gender relations in Jean Rabel are not at all what they first seem to be. Men are more dependent on their wives than vice versa. After obtaining a homestead and entering a union, it is the woman who dominates the domestic affairs of the household. Women are more aggressive, they violently attack other women who try to engage in relationships with their husbands, and, while male violence against women does occur, the ethnographic reality is that Jean Rabel women—through their own efforts or a coalition of family members—more often hurt men than vice versa. As for polygyny, men might have the socially condoned option of having multiple wives but many women engage in outside relations, and they most often convince their husbands to accept as their own children sired by other men. Why men accept them is because they too are heavily dependent on the child labor that makes households productive.

As for why men take other wives, and why, if women are so powerful they are able to do so, it was seen that men in Jean Rabel are not really sure. The best answers any of them could come up with had to do with neglect by their first wife. Women, on the other hand, understood very well why they chose their husbands. Whether the man already had a wife or not, the principal reason women gave was to obtain labor, financial support, and children. As one woman explained, "He gives me money for the children, that is what makes me prefer having him around" (twenty-seven-year-old mother of five).[37]

It is children and the labor they provide, more than husbands and wives, who are the most important component of household livelihood strategies. And it is here that both an understanding of the superior control of women and the female role in determining polygyny begins to become apparent, for in the gender and age division of labor there is another critically important difference between men and women: by virtue of woman's ability to reproduce, her control over children, and the sharing of that capacity with men, she is able to gain institutionalized control over homesteads.

In conclusion, Jean Rabel women are best viewed not as bearing and rearing large numbers of children primarily to secure economic support from men, but rather as securing economic support from men primarily so they can bear and raise large numbers of children. Were all or even most Jean Rabel women to do otherwise, were they to behave like Hutterites and abide by ideals of chastity and monogamous Western marriage, many would be deprived of their principal avenue to economic autonomy: establishing a household. Jean Rabel women, as is typical of people who live so close to the margin of survival, make no pretensions about the raw material logic of conjugal unions and raising children:

If a person marries, why does she marry? She does not marry to be a big shot or anything like that. It is so she can have children... Why does a person want children? It is to help...to go to the water...to go get wood.[38] (forty-year-old mother of five)

What I am telling you is when you are young, you need a husband. What I mean is, if you haven't had children yet. So you can make a child.[39] (forty-two-year-old mother of three)

And so it all comes back to the prosaic fact that in the harsh and unpredictable environment of rural Haiti, children are extremely useful, a fact echoed in the poignant words of another woman:

The whole country can be full of money for women. But money is useless, because they will eat it all and take it. One little thing someone does for you because he knows you have no children, it can cost one hundred dollars. . . . In order for money to work you must have children. If you have no one, money can't work for you. Ahh, you can pay people to work. But if it ain't your child they will take all you have. They will load you up with lies. They will load you up with a bunch of things that are no good. But when it's your child, you always succeed.[40] (fifty-three-year-old mother of nine)

Notes

1. All the scholars cited in the main text did research touching on the division of labor in rural Haiti.

2. In over four years of following life in Makab, seventeen violent conflicts were documented. In only three of the conflicts did a woman suffer blows from a man and in an equal number of cases a man was beaten by a single woman or a group of women. The most brutal beatings involved women beating men or women and men beating a man on behalf of a woman.

Four of the seventeen conflicts involved men only, and five of the conflicts involved only women. In the eight remaining conflicts the principal combatants were a man and a woman. In three instances the woman was slightly injured. In one instance the fight turned into a small war. In another instance a woman kicked and slapped her drunken ex-lover and physically threw him out of her house. Another incident involved a relatively weak cuckolded man who tried to beat his wife but was hit by a large stick wielded by a neighbor woman who subsequently marched the man off to the police station. In another instance, a man was severely beaten and stabbed by his wife and four sisters-in-law. In another incident a man allegedly struck a woman and was immediately clubbed and kicked nearly to death by about a quarter of the village population.

Here are the most interesting cases, beginning with the oddest: A very aggressive and physically ugly woman aged thirty-two had stripped naked and flaunted herself before her mother-in-law whom she was angry with for having taken a fish given to her by her son—the angry woman's husband. Cursing and parading herself back and forth in front of her mother-in-law, the angry wife stopped, bent over and, slapping her naked buttocks, showed her anus to her offended mother-in-law. The wife's brother-in-law—another son of the now indignant mother-in-law—had been standing by looking on and he attacked his naked, buttock slapping sister-in-law, knocking her to the ground. (The son-in-law/husband was present but also took offense to his wife's behavior but he did not enter into the conflict, maintaining neutrality which is probably all that kept the incident from becoming a brawl between his and his wife's family.)

In five of the cases of physical conflict in the village, several women together, or several women and men, engaged in some configuration of combat. The most severe case occurred in the house in which I had recently been staying. The man's name was Rimmie (not his real name), undisputedly the strongest swimmer and deepest diver in the village. The conflict began over a bicycle. Rimmie had arrived in the village riding the bicycle, which belonged to his other wife— one that did not live in Makab. Two of his daughters, aged seven and eleven, borrowed the bicycle and went for a joy ride, which ended with the seven-year-old screaming and crying with a banged knee. An aunt came along (Rimmie's sister-in-law) and spanked both the girls. She then punctured the front tire of the bicycle with a thorn, making sure there were to be no more joy rides and undoubtedly also intending to make a statement about her feelings toward her brother-in-law's other wife. When Rimmie discovered what had been done, a screaming and shoving match erupted between him and his tire-poking sister-in-law. Being the stronger, Rimmie pushed his sister-in-law down and jumped on top of her. Unfortunately for Rimmie, his estranged wife and three other sisters-in-law had been standing by watching. The first sister-in-law to strike was the youngest, a fourteen-year-old girl, who with both hands lifted a small boulder over her head and hurled it into Rimmie's back. The other two sisters-in-law and the wife followed, slamming rocks into Rimmie's back. Rimmie's children, also witnesses to the unfolding events, danced around spastically in circles, little arms flailing, shrieking hysterically while their aunts and mother stoned their father. The sister-in-law who had originally been attacked managed to stab Rimmie in the cheek with a fork she had been holding, causing blood to pour down his face. My unfortunate friend was eventually saved by a neighbor who entered the fight and shielded Rimmie from his sisters-in-law while other neighbors pulled him to safety.

Another instance occurred on a brisk Sunday morning and it involved Pol, thirties, strong but a heavy drinker and a reputed cat burglar. (On at least two occasions while I was in the village, people awoke to find Pol tiptoeing across the floor of their thatch roofed huts and each time Pol got away by fleeing into the bush.) Pol was in a dispute with a women in her sixties, Maximine, to whom he owed money for rum he had bought from her. Maximine cursed Pol as he walked past her kitchen. Pol replied. More words were exchanged and Pol, who had been drinking kleren (rum), stepped into the kitchen and according to his subsequent assailants, slapped the older woman. It is questionable whether Pol really slapped Maximine because if he did, it was a very stupid thing to do. Pol has only one sister—she is cross eyed. His mother has mental problems, no one is sure who his father is, and Pol, by virtue of his thievery, is a near outcast in the village, albeit a tough one. In contrast, Maximine is a near matriarch. She is a mother of eight, and she lives in the middle of a cluster of houses in which also reside one of her sons and his six children, a brother in-law and his four children, a sister and her nine children, a daughter and her three children. Maximine also has a husband and two grown children living with her in her own house. And most unfortunately for Pol, one of these children, an Amazon-sized twenty-three-year-old daughter, was standing in the kitchen with her mother when Pol entered. She was pounding coffee with a pestle as big as a baseball bat and the first thing to hit Pol was reportedly that pestle. In moments, sons, nieces, nephews, grandchildren, and in-laws were kicking, pummeling, and clobbering Pol with whatever object they could find. I was not physically present and have not seen Pol since the incident, but people report he was almost killed.

The male versus female incident mentioned earlier in the main text, the one that became a small war, began when a twenty-year-old man slapped a thirteen year-old girl, thus instigating a battle between two lakous (family compounds). The thirteen year-old girl, Little-Bridget (Ti-Brijet), was filling her water bucket at the village spigot. Hot and thirsty from a just finished soccer game, Little-Demon (Ti-Djab), the obnoxious and insolent younger brother of the buttock-slapper mentioned above, came to get a drink of water. He rudely told Little-Bridget to get out of his way, and Little-Bridget, equally infamous for being insolent, just as rudely told him no. Little-Demon slapped her, knocking her to the ground. Standing only a few feet away was Little-Bridget's comparatively weak eighteen-year-old brother who leapt on Little-Demon, whereupon several other young men entered the fray. The fight might have passed had Little-Bridget's mother not launched a rock into the crowd, hitting yet another young man in the face. Very coincidentally—or perhaps not so coincidentally—the young man who was hit was the deadbeat father of another of the woman's daughters—Little-Bridget's sister. The man had not only neglected to care for the child but shortly after its birth had brought another woman, an outsider from the island of La Tortue, into the village. The new woman was also pregnant and she died giving birth to the child. Virtually everyone who was not immediately related to or good friends with Little-Bridget's mother agreed that she had killed her daughter's rival with sorcery. And now, after years of hushed accusations and seething hatred, Little-Bridget's mother had hit her estranged "son-in-law" in the face with a rock. As the people in the village said, guere pete—war exploded. The son-in-law's family, led by three sisters—three of the same four sisters who had stoned and stabbed Rimmie above—and accompanied by four brothers, bombarded Little-Bridget, her mother, and her two brothers with rocks. Little-Bridget's family did what they could to hold the attackers off, returning fire with stones and hurling threats of sorcery and retribution. But they eventually had to take refuge inside their house. The bombardment went on for some twenty minutes. The doors and shutters of the house were splintered by stones. The family stayed indoors that night. The next morning Little-Bridget's mother tried to pretend as if nothing had happened, coming out of the house, sweeping the yard, and then heading over to the water spigot. No such luck. The oldest sister in the opposing family had assembled a pile of rocks and was waiting. Seeing Little-Bridget's mother, she launched another all-out assault, hitting the older woman several times with rocks. Her sisters and brothers joined her in the attack and together they drove the entire family out of the village. Little-Bridget's mother subsequently secured a police mandate ordering the other family to allow her and her children to live peacefully in the village, but up to this day, three years later, the family has not been able to return.

Carol Anne Truelove, a missionary nurse with thirty years of experience in the region, reports having treated three men versus one woman for severed lips, a distinctively feminine form of retribution in Jean Rabel: biting her adversary on the lip in an effort to disfigure his or her face. The source of fights is almost without exception not that the man has another woman but the division of resources or the perceived loss of money, often after a period of financial familial neglect on the part of the man. Even in the other cases, those not between men and women, typically the source of the conflict is a struggle for financial access to a man. One fight erupted between a mother-in-law and one of her sons' wives over the ownership of a fish the man had caught. Another fight erupted over the presence of three nubile women who were competing for the financial attentions of men in the hamlet. In all but one of the seventeen cases—those involving men and women—the root of the fight was a conflict between men and women over resources.

In Haitian urban areas, domestic violence against women is widespread. I believe this is a consequence of the relative absence of family—parents, brothers, sisters, uncles, and cousins—who can protect or even seek revenge for the woman. I do not believe, nor do my personal experiences suggest, that violence against women occurs in rural areas to anywhere near the same degree. Indeed, as seen, women appear more violent than men. I believe this lower occurrence of domestic violence against women is a consequence of the exact opposite conditions found in the city: (1) women have higher economic status vis-a-vis men than their urban counterparts, and (2) family members are present and they often respond to violence against their daughters, sisters, mothers, and cousins.

Two community focus group studies revealed that men who beat their wives—and get away with it—are not your average male farmer but overwhelmingly men who have a source of income outside of the household mode of production and are wealthy compared to those around them. In one community, two of the four men who reportedly beat their wives were successful bokors, one was an employee for an international development organization and one of the wife beaters was the owner of a US$18,000.00 dump-truck—making him one the richest rural inhabitants in all of Jean Rabel. Carol Ann Truelove, mentioned else where, identified five men in her area who beat their wives. Two are bosses (skilled workers), one is a schoolteacher, one is mentally ill, and only one is a farmer. In short, three of five have income derived from a source completely independent of the household—and one is crazy.

Other stories that relate to domestic violence in rural farming areas include the story of Marco and Selest (given in chapter 15) in which Marco was eventually beaten severely by his wife's sister, her brother, and her brother's wife; and a Mare Rouge woman beaten by her husband and who subsequently repaid the abuse by feigning submission, feeding her husband dinner and then, while he was eating, throwing a pot of scalding water on him. Nobody defended the husband and he reportedly did not beat his wife again—or, at least, not yet. (For a similar discussion of the aggressiveness of rural Haitian women versus men see Murray 1977: 173).

Something that deserves mention here is the practice in rural Haiti of woman eating apart from men. Women typically eat in the kitchen, which is built apart from the house, and men eat at a table in the dining room of the house. Simpson (1942) took this as an indication of repression and surely many contemporary observers make the same assumption—I did. But this is probably a classic case of seeing an alien custom through one's own cultural lens. In developed Western countries, eating meals, particularly dinner, seated at a table in the company of others, has great symbolic value. We "break bread together" and "enjoy the family meal together," and the idea of eating in the kitchen while others are eating in the dining room smacks of discrimination. But in rural Haiti there is little value assigned to sitting around the table. Women make the food and they simply eat it in the kitchen. Why not? Why wait? In a country where most people do not get enough to eat, alone in the kitchen is a good place to be.

3. This description of the defining features of polygyny in Haiti was inspired by Gerald Murray et al. (1998)

4. There was a *bokor* in Makab with two wives in separate compounds, who both lived in the hamlet, and the *bokor* had also borne children with a mentally unstable sister of one of the wives. The sister lived in the same compound with the *bokor* and the wife, and they unashamedly explained the situation as necessary because the sister could not find a spouse with whom to bear children.

5.

Table 16.14: Ever-polygynous men in Kinanbwa Haiti

		Has the man ever been polygynous?		
		No	Yes	Total
Age	Under 35	77% (26)	23% (06)	100%
	35–49	70% (40)	30% (17)	100%
	50+	56% (35)	44% (27)	100%
	Total	67% (101)	33% (50)	100%

Source: Murray 1977: 263.

6. Data were gathered on all skilled workers (*bosses*) in both regions. There were forty-one in all. The argument that fishermen enjoy a higher income level is based on my own experiences and corroborated by data from CARE's 1994 baseline study in the northwest region, which found that fishermen enjoy on average ten times the income of local farmers (1996: 99). This latter observation does not reflect the fact that fisherman also spend much more on equipment, but the point nevertheless stands. Fishermen are relatively wealthier than farmers.

7. The value of a woman's sexuality is so closely linked to material exchange and house building that in cases of rape, marriage between victim and assailant is a possible penalty, particularly if the parties are young and particularly if the man is of higher socioeconomic status. In a case that occurred in a community where I was living, a twenty-five-year-old man was convicted of raping a fourteen-year-old girl. His punishment: to buy the girl a gold chain, earrings, and to promise marriage. The parents took the chain and earrings but citing the man's poverty "that good for nothing cannot provide anything for our child" (sansave sa pa ka regle anyen pou pitit pa nou), they insultingly sent the man a female dog in their daughter's stead. If the man is already married, a financial indemnity is the usual outcome. If the woman is married or in a consensual union with another man, the situation is different, and rare. The rapist is considered to have threatened the continuation of the marriage as the husband may leave his wife. Severity is the rule and the assailant will be going to prison—if the girl's family does not manage to kill him first—and his family will have to pay the woman and her husband a sum that according to local judges may include the loss of all or most of the man's property.

8. Fishermen are typically beset with marketing women whenever they reach shore with a fresh catch, which they sell immediately.

9. *Eh, li pa gen avantay. Desann gason pa konprann li desann ou, wi. Se en sel ti madanm ki vreman pouse ou monte.*

10. *Ah, lè ou gen pliziè madanm, se yon paket afè. . . . Kounye-a maten-a, si ou travay jaden sa pou madanm sa, fo ou travay lòt jaden pou lòt madanm.*

11. *Li pa gen avantay. Se yon desanvantay.*

12. *Wi gen avantay paskè gen moun ki gen plizyè madanm. Si se pou manje bagay sa yo m pa konnen.*

13. *Non, li pa gen avantay. Pasè fo ou ka fe jaden pou tou le dè, fo ou ka voye tou le dè nan mache. Li pa nan avantay.*

14. Only one polygynous man gave the expected and long-favored anthropological explanation for polygyny in rural Haiti: that a man can benefit from multiple wives because wives help him with the harvest and sale of garden produce. The man explained,

The advantage is, if you have the means, you work this little garden really hard, if it yields, you are working at the other woman's house on 2 or 4 *kawo* of land. If this harvest is good too, you have a money advantage. There is an advantage when days are good. But when days are not good, now you don't have jack and you have to give to both of them.

(*Avantay li gen ladan, si mwayen pèmet ou, ou travay telman travay ti kawo tè, si li bon, ou travay kay lòt fi-a dè o yon kat kawo tè. Si rekolt la repete, ou gen avantay kob la. Li gen avantay lè jou bagay yo bon. Lè jou pa bon, kounye-a ou sou jak. Bay fo ou bay tou le dè.*)

15. *Lè moun pa vin alez ave ou . . . ou gen kote ou ka al manje bwe.*

16. *Si premiè ba ou yon defo, ou oblije chache yon, min se pa avantay li ye.*

17. *Si gen yon madanm pa te la. Li ale, li ale kay lòt la, li al tet lòt la ki te kite yon ti mòso manje pou li, li al jwenn ni, li al manje li. Se sa, apre de sa se dekouraj. Apre de sa, pa gen avantay.*

18. *M-ap fache paskè w-ap pedi nan sa l-ap ba ou.*

19. *Map sere kob mwen paskè lap pran ladan pote li ale.*

20. *M pap alez paskè lap bay lot fi kob.*

21. *M-ap joure mari-m paske lap fe-m fe defisi.*

22. *M-ap pale ave li. M pap joure ave li pase si neg la gen yon bagay, gen yon djob nan min ni, m ka fe yon tenten, m ta ka fe ti dialog ave li. Min neg la pa gen djob nan min, li pa nan fe klas, li pa ka fe anyen.*

23. *En ben, m pa ka fe anyen, se pa mwen ki fe sa. . . . L-ap vini, l-ap malad, se andedan kay la l-ap vini. Se pa lòt la ki devan. Se mwen k-ap devan.*

24 *Si li jwenn yon fi ki brav, li al fe 2 jou a li, kite li al a fi akoz se pa ti moun li ye. Ou pa ka kale li.*

25. *M pa ta di anyen. Si se kouray li santi, si li santi kouray-a, m pap rete lakouraj li la.*

26. *M pap fe anyen. Si li koute-m, si m di non, moman pa bon li pa ka gen 2 fi. Tank si se jodi-a, se yon sel di goud li jwenn, e si se nou dè, li pa ka ba nou chak sink goud. E li pa kapab.*

27. *M-ap swiv neg la, paskè m gentan gen pitit ave-li. Li pa ka abandone ni net. Fo-k li vin chita la pou ede-m chape ti moun yo.*

28. *Depi m gen wout pou pase, m pa okipe-ou. M-ap okipe pitit. Sitel li menm, m pa ka lag-o. Nou marie ansanm, m pa ka lag-o. Se yon angajman nou gen ansanm. M gen ban pitit.*

29. The unnaturally higher rates of males in the 50 to 64 year age group is possibly due to women with grown children going to live with the children in urban areas.

30. It makes no sense to a Jean Rabel woman to go live with a man in a house he gives her if the man has no gardens or livestock; nor does it make sense to go live with the man's mother when the girl can more comfortably stay with her own mother who will be happy to have the services of grandchildren. Furthermore, as seen, in the absence of a supportive husband, a Jean Rabel woman can begin bearing children while still living with her parents without suffering shame or ridicule.

31. This is an inference drawn from the gender differences in age at entry into union, the differential rates at which women versus men separate from their first spouse, and the imbalance in the sex ratios (see chapter 5).

32. *En ben, ki fe-m ka viv san gason? Sa-m bezwenn m ka leve yon sak manje, se a kat ti moun um m ka rive.*

33. *Si m gen ti moun m pa bezwenn mari-m menm. Ti moun, hoy, hoy. M ta reme dis pitit, m pa bezwenn mari.*

34. *Pou ki rezon fe-m ka viv san gason. Ko-m rive nan laj konsa. Tout afe-m mache. M pa bezwenn mari-m anko.*

35. The tension between the desire to have a contributing "son-in-law" and the need for

grandchildren is manifest in rare but ideologically prominent and widely talked about incidences where impatient parents surprise eligible men copulating with their daughter. In local lore, parents found in such a situation do not run the man off their property with shotgun blasts of rock salt to his disappearing backside as a stereotypical U.S. farming father might be expected to do. That type of violence or even aggressive behavior against male suitors is rare. Instead, in local lore, the ideal Jean Rabel farmer will barricade the man into the house with his daughter, locking the doors and sending for the young man's parents and a pastor. With threats of violence and sorcery, the farmer tries to force the man to marry his daughter.

Two incidences of young men being locked in houses were recorded from reliable informants and I believe these incidences really do occur. But more salient is the ideology or the commonality with which people talk about such incidences. The image of rural parents eagerly waiting to trap a man in their house and force him to marry their daughter is very much a part of Jean Rabel lore. People will say things such as, "yea those people in La Montagne will call the preacher and marry you right there in your shorts" (Y-ap rele pastor epi marie ou nan bout chòt). In an interview with the Jean Rabel judge, he spontaneously began talking about marriages where men in rural areas were forced to marry at midnight and then challenged the legitimacy of the marriages in court. According to the judge, the marriages are not binding (but I have to add, midnight marriages probably never occur, people in the area would consider such behavior fit for demons).

36. *Gen anpil fwa se parann menm ki plase ti moun yo, ki plase yo. Gen dè fwa parann menm, telman se lajan ki interese-l, pitit fi konn reme avek yon gason ki gen menm laj ave li. Yo te ka marie. Li pa asepte. Pase lè gason sa li we li pa ka fe anyen, li pa ka bay lajan, etsetera. Pi devan li we ajè li pou plase a yon mouchè marie. Min de fe li konn mouchè marie sa ka bay lajan, gen lajan, li femen je-l pou pitit la ka pran lajan nan min zom sa pote ba li. An Ayiti se sa ki genyen kounie-a. Se granmoun kap minnin.*

37. *L-ap ba-m di goude pou ti moun, se sa k fe m ta reme sa.*

38. *Si yon moun marie, pou ki sa li marie? Li pa marie ni pou chef ni pou anyen. Se pou li ka fe dè ti moun. . . . En ben, pou kisa yon moun fe ti moun? Se pou li ka ed-o. . . al nan dlo-a . . . al nan bwa.*

39. *Non. Lè yon moun jenn, bagay sa m-ap di, ou bezwenn yon mari, komsi m di, si ou poko enfante, ou ka enfante yon ti moun.*

40. *Ou met gen tout peyi se lajan pou danm, lajan se unitil, paskè y-ap manje tout pran ni. Yon ti bagay moun t-ap fe pou ou konsa paskè li konnen ou pa gen pitit, bagay la ka koute ou 100 dola. . . . Pou lajan travay fok se pitit pou ou gen pou travay. Si ou pa gen moun lajan pap travay. AH, ou ka gen moun lajan ap travay, min depi se pa pitit ou y-ap pran tout. Y-ap vin chaje ou ak manti. Y-ap chaje ou anpil bagay ki pa bon. Min lè se pitit ou, ou toujou ap reyisi.*

Chapter 17

Caribbean Family Patterns

Introduction

In the introductory chapter of this book I pointed out that the anthropology of the Caribbean has been called "the battle ground for competing theories regarding family structure" (D'Amico-Samuels 1988: 785). Anthropologists were confounded by a distinct regional family structure similar to that seen in Jean Rabel—including, late age at marriage, high rates of births to single women, matrifocality, child dispersal, *de facto* polygyny, serial monogamy, and severe beting of children. Early scholars dismissed these patterns as "disintegrate" (Simey 1946), "uncivilized" (Matthews 1953: 302), "normless," "distorted" (see Smith 1996: 35, 54), "promiscuous," and "dysfunctional" (see Smith and Mosby 2003). Subsequently, no comprehensive and satisfactory explanation for the patterns was ever achieved.

In this chapter I revisit the literature and illustrate how the same patterns seen in Jean Rabel can be identified elsewhere in the Caribbean ethnographic record and can be explained with similar arguments, most importantly the value of the household in surviving a harsh natural and economic environment; the role of women as managers of these households; and the role of children as laborers in making them productive. It is this later point, the economic utility of even very young children—a point I demonstrated that many scholars documented but largely neglected and even denied—that completes the insights other scholars have made and makes Caribbean family patterns logical. In reinserting the importance of children into the analysis I believe that I can explain Caribbean family patterns as a logical outcome of the basic material challenges that face impoverished people of the region.

Dysfunctional Family Patterns

One of the patterns that most concerned and perplexed scholars was a seemingly contradictory complex of behaviors toward reproduction. Girls were kept in the dark about the processes of how pregnancy happens. Two-thirds of Blake's (1961) ninety-nine female Jamaican respondents said they knew "nothing" of sexual relations and pregnancy before their first union. Typical were women who said, "Me did know that boy and girl can do it. But I didn't know you would have baby" (Blake 1961: 52) and, "when I find myself with a child I never know what happen" (Blake 1961: 53). Young female Barbadians that Greenfield (1966) interviewed complained that "repeated admonitions about 'staying away from boys' never included a discussion of 'what to stay away from'" (Greenfield 1966: 109); many of the girls "were angry at their mother for not preparing them for motherhood" (Greenfield 1966: 109).

In contrast to the treatment of daughters—and similar to what was seen in Jean Rabel—Caribbean parents did nothing to punish the sexual aggressiveness of their sons or, for that matter, the sexual aggressiveness of men who seduced their daughters. Indeed, they encouraged it. As Wilson (1969: 71) noted early on, "almost every ethnographical report from the Caribbean mentions a double standard of sexual morality." In Jamaica, "the proof of a man's maleness is the impregnation of a woman" (Clarke 1966: 96). In Guyana, "for a man to have children all about is a matter of pride" (R. T. Smith 1956: 141). In Andros Island "boys are like dogs"; they are expected to have sex; if they don't they are "sissy;" and "in order to attain adult status a man must have premarital as well as extramarital sex relations" (Otterbein 1966: 67). In Martinique, fathers impress on their sons "expectations of masculinity" (Horowitz 1967: 64). In Trinidad, "It is a glory for a man to dupe a woman into having sexual intercourse with him. If you can't . . . you are not a 'famous man'" (Freilich 1968: 962; see also Clarke 1957: 91, 96; Smith 1956: 141, 1988: 137). The behavior is such that a UN report on the subject concluded that "it is reasonable to argue that in the Caribbean as a whole sexual harassment represents behavior which is largely normalized" (Lewis 2003).

Ignorant of the mechanics of conception and confronted by sexually aggressive males of all ages, young Caribbean women were left defenseless in preventing unwanted first pregnancies. For those who might try to "break the vicious circle" (Kerr 1952: 81; see also Freilich 1968: 52), there was censure, ridicule, punishment, and intimidation. Adolescent girls were terrorized with the specter of what could happen if they took contraceptives or resorted to abortion: contraceptive use was considered sinful and associated with physical and mental disorders (Buschkens 1974: 223; Kerr 1952: 25; Cohen 1956). *Coitus interruptus* was abhorred, as illustrated by Blake's informant who—as we saw in chapter 2—equated it with murder, "it is a sin, because you are destroying your blood, it is like killing a child" (Blake 1961: 201).

When young women did get pregnant for the first time, the "almost ritualized" reaction of her mother provided more evidence for those scholars who saw the entire process as dysfunctional (Senior 1991: 76). The discovery was accompanied by violence and quarrelling; and the girl was often thrown out of the house, but then quickly taken back in (for Barbados, see Greenfield 1966 and Handwerker 1989: 62; for Providencia, see Wilson 1961a: 128; for Suriname among the Paramaribo, see Buschkens 1974: 225; for

Guyana, see R. T. Smith 1988: 145; and for Jamaican examples, see Kerr 1952). Clarke (1966: 99) described the scenario in Jamaica:

> The discovery is greeted with noisy upbraiding, the girl is severely beaten, and in many cases turned out of the house. In the second stage the girl takes refuge with a neighbor or kinswoman. After a period, which may be quite short, the kinsfolk and neighbours intercede with the mother on her behalf, and the girl is taken back into her mother's home for the birth of her child.

It was precisely these types of seemingly contradictory behaviors—keeping girls in the dark about the mechanics of pregnancy, encouraging male sexual aggressiveness, and beating daughters when they did get pregnant—that early scholars were referring to when they described Caribbean family patterns as "dysfunctional." But what I try to show in the rest of this chapter is that in the context of the importance of households, children, and the challenges confronted by impoverished people of the Caribbean, these practices were anything but dysfunctional. On the contrary, the view of them as dysfunctional was the consequence of a presumption by social scientists that children were a material burden. For impoverished people of the Caribbean, quite the opposite was the case. As was seen in Jean Rabel, it was of the greatest importance that a woman have children. In St. Vincent it was believed that a woman who cannot have children is "tragic, sad, and pitiable" and similarly, "a man who could not have children is equally scorned, and his masculinity and virility are called into question" (Gearing 1988: 235). In Jamaica, "a child is God's gift," "nothing should be done to prevent the birth of a child," and "no woman who has not proved that she can bear a child is likely to find a man to be responsible for her" (Clarke 1966: 95–96). In summarizing the results of 1,600 interviews from the extensive Women in the Caribbean project (WICP 1979–1982), Senior (1991: 68) noted that "childless women are scorned," they are "mules" and "beyond the pale of society."

The "dysfunctional" behaviors described above evolved not as an aversion to high fertility, but as a mechanism of guaranteeing it. By keeping young women in the dark about the mechanics of reproduction, making them afraid of birth control, and encouraging male promiscuity, one could argue that impoverished people of the Caribbean, especially mothers, were setting up the conditions that made pregnancy unavoidable. By intentional design or simply the consequences of radical pronatalism, daughters were rendered defenseless against the processes that initiated their reproductive careers. As for the beatings mothers were arguably not punishing daughters so much as they were assuring their control of the newborn child. Indeed, as will be seen, throughout the Caribbean, elder mothers deliberately tried to commandeer the offspring of their nubile daughters. Similar to Jean Rabel, the behavior of parents can ultimately only be understood with respect to dependency on households, female control over those households, and the value of child labor in making the household productive. To begin assessing the pattern, I want to look at how changes in the plantation economy that dominated the region for more than four hundred years gave way to the primacy of the Caribbean household as a unit of production and survival.

History: The Plantation Economy and the All-Important Household

Plantations were so much a part of the Caribbean that anthropologist Charles Wagley (1957: 8) defined the region as "plantation America." In the colonial economic heyday of the region, massive importations of labor from Europe and Africa helped make small plantation-based colonies such as Haiti and later Jamaica and Barbados the most productive on earth. But in the shadow of the plantation emerged another economy, one based on the household. To lower costs of production, owners allotted provision grounds to slaves who planted staples for consumption and resale in local rotating markets. Mintz (1974: 130–55: 1985) called this the "slave proto peasantry" and it gave way to an economy so dynamic that in Jamaica, one-fifth of all the colony's currency was in the hands of slaves (Barickman 1994).

In most of the Caribbean the transition from proto to more developed peasant economy began in the 1830s postemancipation era. Through purchases, squatting, share-cropping, and government land reform programs, the impoverished semi-subsistence market producers acquired more land, the regional rotating market system expanded, and households became an important hedge against starvation, uncertain employment, and the economic vicissitudes of the plantation. As in the colonial times, plantation owners granted or rented workers "provision grounds" encouraging "peasant" production, but Caribbean low-income farming adaptation can be understood not only as a "mode of response" to the plantation system, it can also be understood as a "mode of resistance" as well (Mintz 1974b: 131–56). Not unlike what was seen in Jean Rabel, the household and regional subsistence economy provided a haven from onerous and low-paid plantation labor. In Haiti the process of transition from proto- to full-blown peasant economy began with the 1791 revolution and because the colonial French regime was defeated the transition became more complete.

But for the Caribbean in general, it was with emancipation that the transition began and with it a kind of struggle was born. On the one hand, the plantation economy, although weakened, continued to exist: managers continued to encourage workers to reproduce their own means of existence; they paid meager wages; recruited new migrants from India and Asia; and used vagrancy laws and restricted access to the most productive lands in an effort to force ex-slaves and the newer immigrants to work. On the other, many prospective workers retreated into the regional household-based farm economies. As in the case of Haiti, on some islands the farmers seemed to win with the full-blown "peasant" domination of regional rotating market systems and the near-total disappearance of plantations. But what emerged on most islands was a system where plantations still controlled the best and most productive lands while the impoverished ex-slaves were left with steeply sloped, rocky, and eroded marginal lands upon which they underwrote their own costs of reproduction. They planted survival-oriented crops such as those seen in Jean Rabel (sweet potatoes, yams, manioc, peanuts, millet, taro, and plantains); and they fished, foraged, hunted feral animals, tended their own small stocks of chickens, goats, pigs, cattle, and traded intensely with other households in weekly rotating markets.

Typical was the former British Caribbean, a region that included Antigua, Bahamas, Barbados, Belize, Dominica, Grenada, Guyana, Jamaica, St. Kitts, St. Lucia, St. Vincent, and Trinidad and Tobago. As late as 1988, plantations held the best lands while 70 percent of all people lived in rural areas on small plots (Heath 1988: 431; Sahlins 1972; Beckford 1972). The same pattern prevailed throughout the lower Caribbean Basin. Even in cases of Amerindians such as Miskitu in Nicaragua—traditionally dependent on fishing, foraging and swidden agriculture—classic Caribbean household subsistence strategies took hold (Nietschmann 1979). But the growth of the informal household-based economy was tempered by another major demographic trend: male wage migration.[1]

Male Wage Migration

Wage migration entered into the plantation versus household equation in a powerful way. Following emancipation in 1838, men in the Lesser Antilles migrated to Trinidad and Guyana to work in sugar cane plantations (Richardson 1975: 395–96). The period between 1880 and 1924 was what Brereton (1989: 101) referred to as "the great age of migration" when men throughout the islands migrated to work on the Panama Canal, first for the French (1880 to 1893) and then for the Americans (1903 to 1914); they built the trans-isthmus railroad (1851 to 1855, 1904 to 1912); they migrated to work in the massive U.S.-engineered fruit empires of Central America (1870s to present), the British sugar empire in Guyana (1800s to 1970s), the originally U.S.-engineered sugar empire of Cuba (1890s to 1950s), the Dominican Republic (1880s to present), and Florida (1960s to present); up until 1924 they migrated to New York and even as far away as Ontario to pick apples. Beginning in the 1940s they went to the oil fields of Maracaibo and refineries of Aruba and Curacao; those from the British Islands went en masse to rebuild Britain after WWII. They migrated to U.S. mining operations throughout the region, such in bauxite mines in Jamaica (1944 to present) and Guyana (1940s to 1970s). During the 1960s and up until the present they continued to travel to England to work in factories, dig tunnels, and lay pipe; to Guyana to work in bauxite mines; to the U.S. and British Virgin Islands to build hotels; and to the United States to work as itinerant agricultural laborers.[2]

Many if not most of the migration patterns continue and new ones have been added such that Deere et al. (1990) could justifiably write that today the Caribbean exports more of its people than any region on the planet. While the migrants were sometimes women—an increasing phenomenon in recent years (Aymer 1997; Barrow 1997; Springfield 1997; Quinlan 2005)—the vast majority were male. The result was that reproductive-age women remaining on Caribbean home islands often outnumbered men as much as two to one (see table 17.1).

Table 17.1: Sex Ratios Commonwealth Caribbean Islands 1881–1960

Country	Census date: Year					
	1881	1891	1911	1921	1946	1960
British Honduras	—	—	—	857	757	835
British Guiana	1,285	1,244	1,059	954	874	844
Trin. and Tob.	—	1,159	1,040	946	918	855
Antigua	759	763	553	486	745	747
Barbados	—	590	425	430	746	705
Dominica	—	579	647	716	735	714
Grenada	704	733	571	468	533	650
Jamaica	813	742	750	689	817	774
Montserrat	646	583	355	350	615	585
St. Kitts-Nevis	—	678	434	388	732	710
St. Lucia	—	847	722	719	766	708
St. Vincent	—	740	485	451	608	671

(Males/Females X 1,000); Source: Marino 1970: 163

An integral part of the social pattern that emerged was that men were expected to use migration as a source to underwrite the establishment of a family and homestead. Richardson (1975: 398) would write that in Carriacou "often a young man is not considered an appropriate suitor by parents of a prospective bride unless he has completed a sojourn working overseas"; and in Guyana, R. T. Smith (1956) reported that "if men wanted to fully participate in adult social life they often had to migrate." The outstanding manifestation of this trend was male house building.

Caribbean low-income households may sometimes have passed generation to generation in a matrilineal fashion, as with Solien's (1959) "consanguineal female headed households," but they came into being and only came into being in association with a union between a man and woman. Caribbean men were always the ones who underwrote the construction of the house and they held titular right to the homestead for life. The pattern was so consistent that we can elevate it to the status of a rule: in a review of twenty Caribbean ethnographies for twenty different Caribbean countries, Keith Otterbein (1965) found that in every case for which there was data (fifteen of twenty islands), the primary ingredient for conjugal union was that men provided a house (see also R. T. Smith 1956: 146; M. G. Smith 1961: 465; Philpott 1973: 120–21, 142; Sutton and Makiesky-Barrow 1970: 310).

Thus, what anthropologists found when they began studying family patterns in the mid 20th century was the consequence of over 150 years of adaptation to the weakening of the plantation economy, the importance of the household in surviving a harsh natural and economic environment, and the importance of male wage migration as a means to financially underwrite the household. These are points upon which anthropologists have always agreed. After all, it was not an argument; it was a description of Caribbean island economies. After that point, however, consensus crumbled such that social scientists were never able to agree on the determinants of Caribbean conjugal patterns and kinship.

I believe that I can show why scholars never agreed—and in the final chapter of this book I attempt to do so—but for the remainder of this chapter I want to show how seemingly dysfunctional behaviors such as keeping girls ignorant of the mechanics of pregnancy, encouraging male sexual aggressiveness, and ritual daughter beating, are linked to the plantation-peasant-migration economy, specfically through the critical role of children labor. The important thing is to keep our eye on the household. But in doing so, in showing the causal connection between the Caribbean household and the value of children in making it productive and family, courtship, and childrearing practices, it is also necessary to dispel a series of academic myths that have emerged over the more than fifty years of anthropological study in the region.

Matrifocality and the Myth of the Female Bread Winner

Caribbean men have sometimes been portrayed in the literature as failures (Blackwood 2005: 8–9); as "victims of their social environment" (Quinlan 2006: 476); as aggressive, sexist, and disrespectful (Lewis 2003); and as feckless and deadbeat fathers (Massiah 1982, 1983; Jackson 1982; Barrow 1986: 162; Brodber 1986: 46; Ho 1999). Certainly there are some Caribbean men, perhaps even many, who neglect their familial responsibilities, and in all fairness to feminist activists, this trend of male irresponsibility has without doubt increased with the recent transformation of the Caribbean economy from one based on traditional household-based subsistence strategies to one oriented toward industry and tourism, a transformation that was occurring precisely at the time that feminist scholars entered into the region (1960s to the present). But for the traditional Caribbean, the conditions were different.

The role of the Caribbean male not only as financier for the construction of homesteads but also as significant source of cash in the growth of the homestead and rearing of children should never have been in doubt. Barrow (1986: 161) found that all her informants "at some stage in their life histories received support from male partners." Senior (1991: 154) noted that "husband/partner is cited most frequently as a source of additional income." But it was much more than "additional income"; in most cases it was the principal source of "income."

Philpott (1973: 143) found that in the two communities he studied, fifty-four of eighty-one (66.8%) of female-headed households depended on remittances that came largely from men. George Cumper (1961) surveyed 1,296 Barbados households (5,364 people; a random sample of 2 percent of the Barbados population). In only two of Cumper's categories of female-headed households (White Collar and Landless Labor) did males contribute less than 50 percent of all income; and in no category of male-headed households did men contribute less than 75 percent of family income.[3]

Male spouses were important, but in lieu of late age at marriage and even conjugal unions, it was "baby fathers" who stood out most as monetary contributors to household upkeep. In Montserrat, Stuart Philpott (1973) found that fathers of young children in the household sent the most money; this meant fathers who had not yet set up an independent homestead with the mother and therefore the money was being contributed to the grandparents' household. Over 70 percent of female-headed households depended primarily on remittances from the parents of resident grandchildren. Even in male-headed households, 80 percent depended on remittances from parents with resident children in the household (Philpott 1973: 137, 141–42).

The importance of money from baby-fathers was such that a struggle between mothers and girlfriends was common. In Barbados, for example, mothers tried to break up their sons' unions. As one woman recounted to Penn Handwerker (1989: 63):

There is a saying—I've heard it *a lot*: 'Mothers-in-law break up most marriages.' The mother be tellin' the man he forgettin' her! And the wife be tellin' the man "when you going to grow up and cut the apron strings!"

As in most societies, the man's mother usually lost. Thus, similar to Jean Rabel, Caribbean parents found their interests best focused on daughters. Where scholars measured preference for daughters versus sons, daughters came out way ahead. In Jamaica, for instance, Sergeant and Harris (1992) found that 79 percent of mothers interviewed preferred to give birth to a daughter. As in Jean Rabel, the reason girls were favored was because they were a more dependable source of labor and physical assistance. Also, as in Jean Rabel, daughters were a source of child laborers (i.e., grandchildren), arguably the most important determinant of Caribbean kinship and family patterns. These are points taken up soon. But first, I want to finish with this other important issue, that of money from men, and the fact that the most efficacious way of getting it was via a daughter.

Parents, especially mothers, took a keen interest in prospective sexual partners of their daughters. Parents in Jamaica instructed the girl to, "tell her mother of his advances . . . he will then be investigated . . . and subsequently either be accepted or rejected" (Blake 1961: 69). In Barbados, men were selected at "meet-hims," church socials where parents could censor suitors. Upon approval, they subsequently had sex in the girl's home (Handwerker 1989: 62). Similarly, according to M. G. Smith, "Under the Carriacou regulation of mating, young girls may not reply to the addresses of their suitors without the permission of their parents or household heads" (M. G. Smith 1961: 468).

So important were financial contributions from men that there emerged what appeared to outsiders a type of institutionalized prostitution. As in Jean Rabel, women and their families conceptualized female sexuality as a commodity and were unwilling to allow daughters to engage in even casual relationships with men who could not afford to give them money or material gifts (Handwerker 1993: 45; 1989: 77,87; Hill, 1977: 279–80, 282, 305; Ashcraft 1968: 67-68; Freilich 1968: 52; Otterbein 1966: 105; M. G. Smith, 1962: 93,110–22, 226, 234–35; Stycos and Back 1964: 161).

The material demand attached to a girl's sexual acquiescence often meant that girls engaged in their first relationship with older men. Blake found that in her sample of sixty-five Jamaican women, at least ten of the first female sexual experiences were with a man from five to fifteen years older than the girl; in an additional eight cases the man was at least fifteen to twenty years older; and in thirteen cases Blake could not ascertain the age difference but nevertheless, "whereas for instance, she was only 14 or 15," the man was "already trained in a trade," "an itinerant laborer," "domiciled with another woman," "had many women," "and so on" (Blake 1961: 90–91). The pattern prevailed throughout the Caribbean, where men were on average six years older than their spouses (Roberts, 1957: 206–7; Massiah 1983).

On the other side of the equation, if men wanted to enter into relations with a woman or, as seen earlier, to establish a homestead with a woman, they had to find money. To do so they fished, raised animals, foraged, cultivated agricultural plots, built houses, and pursued virtually any gainful opportunity available to them. But as seen, wage migration presented itself as a fast way to bypass poverty on home islands and obtain the money to build a house and begin raising a family. Parents were primary agents in making this a norm; they often refused to allow their daughters to go with men who had not yet been abroad (R. T. Smith 1953: 108; see also Hill 1977: 281; Philpott 1973: 120–21; Ashcraft 1968: 67–68; M. G. Smith 1961, 1962: 113, 117; Wilson 1961b; Otterbein 1965; Kundstadter, 1963). And so, as seen, men migrated. They migrated such that by the latter 20th century Aaron Segal (1987: 44) could describe the Caribbean as having "borne the deepest and most continuous impact from international migration of any region in the world."

Thus, the reluctance to tell daughters or younger counterparts about the mechanics of pregnancy, the lack of censure of sexually aggressive males, and the beatings upon discovery of a first pregnancy and even male migration itself were arguably related to financial contributions from men. Children were an indispensable part of the equation in that it was the birth of a child that assured the continued flow of money. Suggestions of "secrecy" aside (Handwerker 1989: 62), parents were fully aware of what to expect when they allowed men to hang around their daughter: according to Senior (1991: 75), "pregnancy is expected." A Vincentian woman in her mid-thirties recalled, "the fella went home and speak with them so they expect anything. Because if somebody come home and you allow that child to go out with that person, you expect anything to happen" (Senior 1991: 75). "In other words," Senior clarifies, "if they allow the girl to go out with a boy they are tacitly acknowledging that she is a woman and ripe for womanly experience" (Senior 1991: 75).

Parents allowed girls to go out with specific suitors, but as seen, they did so with an eye toward his ability to provide. When girls did get pregnant, the parents, especially mothers, wanted to know who was responsible so they could demand support. Senior (1991) found that among the 1,600 WICP informants, it was the "greatest disgrace" that a father could not be named:

It's terrible, one of the worst things in life, it's a shame you having sexual intercourse with so many men and the next thing you get pregnant and you don't know who the father.

Do you know girls like that?

Yes, we have one like that. She has two children and she don't know who the father of both.

So she didn't call any names?

Yes, she called names. Names! A child got to have names. Somebody got to be the father. (Senior 1991: 79)

In effect, one reason mothers beat daughters upon discovery of pregnancy was so the girl would name a father. This tendency fed another anthropological myth, that of the deadbeat Caribbean father. But naming a father was not as difficult as some

Caribbeanists have suggested, for, feminist critiques of the traditionally negligent Caribbean male aside, men were eager to claim paternity.

The Caribbean Father

Caribbean children almost always had fathers. In Andros Island, "most illegitimate children used their putative father's name" (Otterbein 1966: 76). The same was true in Martinique (Horowitz 1967: 56) and St. Lucia (Crowley 1957); and in the Carriacou community, where M. G. Smith (1961: 470) found that out of more than two hundred children, only five had an obscure paternity. In his original formulation of the "matrifocal family," R. T. Smith (1956: 133) too dwelled upon the importance of the father's image; he found it was "inconceivable in British Guyana that a child should be fatherless," children almost always took the surname of their father, even when illegitimate, and "in the overwhelming majority of cases the father is known and recognized by the entire community" (see also Cousins 1935: 47; Cohen 1956: 668; Charbit 1984: 38). Lazarus-Black (2001), the only anthropologist to systematically study paternity suits in the Caribbean, observed only one case in nine years where a man denied paternity in court.

Just as in Jean Rabel, male eagerness to claim paternity and the associated prestige gave women power in that they could decide to which man they would assign paternity (Chevannes 2002). This sometimes gave way to a manipulation of the opportunity to choose who the father was; in Haiti this is known as a *kout petit*. In the British Caribbean, assigning paternity to a man who is not the biological father is known as "giving a man a jacket." Indeed, some women took the opportunity to assign paternity to two or more fathers, one publicly and the others in secret.

In short, contrary to what has emerged as an almost mythical image of the deadbeat Caribbean father, Caribbean men were often eager to claim paternity. Moreover, while abundant scholarly attention has been devoted to matrifocality, the role of man as underwriter and lifetime member of the household cannot be gainsaid. Otterbein (1965: 75) measured the association between female-headed households and male absenteeism manifest in male skewed sex-ratios and got a .81 correlation. Yves Charbit (1984: 32) got an almost identical correlation with data from surveys done in subsequent decades (.71).

The lessons to be learned are that a male spouse, while perhaps not always present, was the major financial underwriter of the Caribbean household, a household member as well, and if present, was considered the household head. Unless he was dead: when I added widowhood to Charbit's model above, the equation yielded a correlation of .92 (an R square of .84).[4] But as will be seen below, none of this is to say that Caribbean women did not play a dominant role in the governing of the homestead.

Figure 17.1: Plot of female household heads by sex ratios
(Legend: A = 1 observation; B = 2 observations; N = 15)

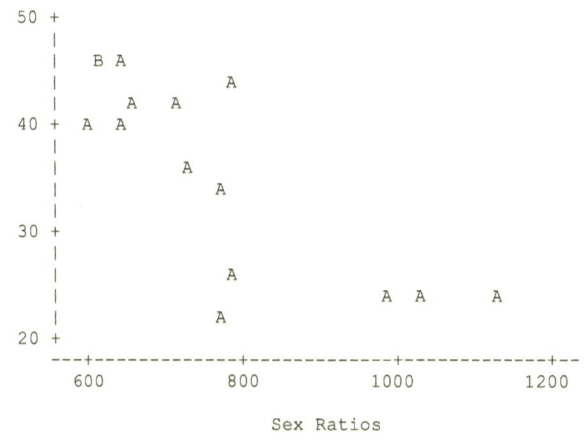

```
50 +
   |
   |    B A
   |            A
   |        A   A
40 +  A   A
   |
   |          A
   |            A
   |
30 +
   |
   |          A
   |                    A   A      A
   |          A
20 +
   ---+-------------+-------------+-------------+--
      600          800          1000          1200
```

Sex Ratios

Sex Ratios

Table 17.2: Analysis of variance for "female-headed household by sex-ratios" using Otterbein's (1965: 75) Caribbean data

Model (N = 13)	R	R-square	Adjusted R-square	Prob > F
Regression	.71	.633	.605	.0004

Table 17.3: Analysis of variance "female-headed household by sex-ratio" using Yves Charbit (1984: 32) and adding widowhood ratio from Massiah (1983:19)

Model (N = 13)	R	R-square	Adjusted R-square	Prob > F
Regression	.92	.84	.81	.0001

Autonomous Caribbean Households Controlled by Women and the Importance of Children

It is with women and their role as decision makers in Caribbean households that it becomes clear how and why the value of child labor played a determinant role in Caribbean marriage and kinship patterns. In Anguilla, "the woman is the family manager;

she is subordinate to her husband, but not subservient" (Walker 1968: 114); In Guyana, "the mistress of the house receives money and garden produce . . . she is solely responsible for its management once it has been handed over to her" (R. T. Smith 1956: 138). In Barbuda, "within the household, women take over exclusive management. . . . There are no tasks for men within the physical confines of the house" (Berleant-Schiller 1978: 259, 264). In Jamaica, "of most importance to a woman is her own yard" (Durant-Gonzalez 1976: 39). Even in Barbados, where Handwerker drove home the authority of the father, "authority . . . was not accompanied by men's participation in household affairs" (Handwerker 1989: 81). In summary, there really was something going on in terms of the prominence of Caribbean women in the domestic sphere: as a consequence of male migration and de facto absenteeism, women were left in control of households.

On many islands women also controlled local exchange. As in Jean Rabel where the *madanm sara* and *marchann* dominated both retail and intermediate exchange, female "higglers" and "hucksters" and small vendors from Jamaica to Guyana dominated both retail marketing of farm produce and much of wholesale interisland trade (Mintz 1955, 1971, 1974; Walker 1968; Pollock 1972; Massiah 1983: 12–17; Griffith 1985; Lagro 1990; Lagro and Plotkin 1990; Mantz 2007). And it is here that we can see the significance of children enter into the equation, for the critical component in the adaptation being described was child labor.

In St. John, "women were able to play such an active role in the extra-domestic activities partly because children were used as labor power as soon as they were old enough" (Olwig, 1985: 118–19). In Jamaica, "children lighten the work of adult women . . . by assisting in the easier tasks such as sweeping, watering the animals, collecting kindling, hauling water, picking fruit from the trees, and going to the neighborhood shop" (Davenport, 1961: 436–37). In Barbuda, "by the time a girl is eleven or twelve she can run a household and often does" (Berleant-Schiller 1978: 259). Even in the case of land-scarce Barbados, "growing children help reduce the woman's work load, and most women are well aware of this fact" (Greenfield 1966: 107).

Female control of the exchange economy was favorable in lieu of male absenteeism and wage migration. But as in Jean Rabel, what underwrote this particular configuration of marketing and male wage migration was the household; women were free to control the local retail marketing economy and men to migrate because membership in a productive household guaranteed their security, and what freed them from the tasks of the household were children and the labor contributions they made. Moreover, as seen in chapter 2, rather than being a commonsensical observation accepted by anthropologists, the importance of child labor to women is perhaps the most overlooked and consistently denied aspect of Caribbean family patterns, one that has led to a misunderstanding of the process. The point is thrown into stark light when one considers another behavior that social scientists considered "maladaptive" and "dysfunctional": violence exercised against children, largely by mothers.

Beating the Hell out of Children

As in Jean Rabel, the physical beating of children was common. In Jamaica Clarke (1966: 156) reported, "there was hardly a case where our informant did not expatiate upon what he called the 'floggings' he or she had received in childhood." In Suriname, "No part of a child's body is safe from blows. . . . In some yards it is not uncommon even for older children (especially boys) to be suspended naked by the arms from the branch of a tree and given a thrashing with a stick" (Buschkens 1974: 239). This violence against children has been called "repressive, severe, and abusive" (Leo-Rhynie 1997; Sharpe 1997) and "developmentally inappropriate" (Sloley 1999; see Smith and Mosby 2003 for a summary), but it too was part of adapting to harsh living conditions and it was a direct outgrowth of the critical role of children in household livelihood strategies.

In Curacao, "when a child reaches the age of five or six, parents begin to impose behavior by directing the child's chores and by using a belt or switch" (Hill 1977: 297). In St. Vincent, children are considered to misbehave if they are "lazy and shirk work," they receive "corporal punishment . . . discipline is taken seriously" (Gearing 1988: 194). In Barbados, "as the children grow older they help the mother with many of her duties. By the age of five, children have 'chores,' the neglect of which is punishable by beating" (Greenfield 1966: 107). In Haiti it was seen that the objective was for the child to be "thinking about the switch in everything he does."

In an anthropological projection of Western ideals, the Caribbean father was sometimes depicted as the sterner disciplinarian (Clarke 1966: 107, 159; R. T. Smith 1956: 134; Handwerker 1989: 86). But just as it was women who controlled the homesteads, it was women who most often disciplined children. In the Bahamas, "mothers are often the providers of discipline" (Bethel 1993: 7). Among the Black Carib, "the woman had the responsibility of raising the children, caring for their needs, disciplining them" (Solien 1959: 57). In Anguilla[4] "child discipline is in the hands of women" (Walker 1968: 114). In Suriname, "it is chiefly mothers who mete out punishments" (Buschkens 1974: 239). In Guyana, "fathers beat their children very infrequently and certainly much less frequently than do mothers and mother substitutes" (R. T. Smith 1956: 13). In Jamaica, "in all aspects of home training the mother is the principal actor . . . the authority of the mother is never questioned any more than the child's duty of obedience to her" (Clarke 1966: 118–20); and "this part of training is carried out almost exclusively by the mother" (Cohen 1956: 671). In Bermuda, "wives-mothers carry out the most part of the socialization of the children . . . and are also the disciplinarian figures" (Paul 1983: 100).

As the managers of households, women commanded children and they did so with the objective of making the household productive. Similar to Jean Rabel, what underwrote survival was the link between the household, female career as manager of a productive household, and the labor of children. Moreover, just as was seen in Jean Rabel, older women were at the height of their economic power as market women and heads of mature and productive homesteads stocked with working children. It was these older women who had the greatest interest in the reproductive behavior of their nubile daughters and in assuring the replenishment of the household labor supply.

Older Women

The stability of Caribbean economies and continuation of the homestead depended most heavily on the women who managed them. Because women also often controlled the local retail marketing economy of produce, because this economy was based on household production, and because children were a critical source of labor, they, children, were most critical to women. And they were most critical not as adults, as most researchers addressing the issue have argued (Handwerker 1989: 88; Smith 1962: 236; Otterbein 1963: 170; Philpott 1973: 123; Brittain 1990: 57; Murray 1977); they were most important as children. It is this issue of children that makes the rest of "dysfunctional" Caribbean family patterns understandable. Radical pronatalism, a complex of cultural beliefs and behavior from keeping girls in the dark about the mechanics of pregnancy to sending them off alone or leaving them in the house with sexually aggressive but financially capable older men, the entire complex is ultimately underwritten by the fact that children were not the burdens so often presented in the literature.

Even in the case of the mother's ritual beating upon discovery of a daughter's pregnancy, seen earlier, close examination reveals that what ethnographers where witnessing was more than simply assuring the identification of the father and procurement of child support; it was, as in Jean Rabel, part of an institutionalized struggle between mother and daughter for control over children. In Suriname, Buschkens (1974: 226) wrote of the grandmother's "refusing to part with these grandchildren, which she has come to regard as her property." In Trinidad, there was a custom for the first child of a marriage to "belong to the grandparents," something that Stewart (1973: 98) tells us "ensured the continued membership of young workers in each household" (see also Rodman 1971: 82). While calling the grandmother "ma" or " mama" or "muma," the children were taught to refer to their own mother by her pet name, as if she were another sibling (see Buschkens 1974: 226; Durant-Gonzalez 1976; Greenfield 1966; R. T. Smith 1956: 144–45). In Barbados, if the grandparents fostered the child, the couple was "relieved" of responsibility but they also "relinquished their parental rights" (Handwerker 1989: 63). Even Clarke (1966), who like many of her contemporaries saw children as a burden and the entire institution of high pronatalism, odd marriage patterns, and daughter beating as dysfunctional, went on to explain that, "we found no instance where the grandmother resented the presence of the child in her home . . . they 'gladden the home,' they are a source of companionship, they are useful" (Clarke 1966: 100, 180; see also Cohen 1956: 668; and see Philpott 1973: 140, for bitter competition over possession of children for their labor value).

The benefits that accrued to older women who controlled the process are manifest in the sheer demographic weight of grandchildren. Throughout the Caribbean, young women typically began bearing children while still living in their parents' household; 40 to 75 percent of all births on Caribbean islands are to single women; 25 to 40 percent of children lived in homes where neither parent is present and most of these were homes of grandparents (Philpott 1973: 137; Clarke 1966: 202–4; M. G. Smith 1961: 457,470–71; Cohen 1956: 668). Moreover, while money from men is a preeminent issue, the even greater importance of children is evident in the struggle between mothers and daughters-in-law for support from sons. While mothers tried to break up union and to get support from sons for themselves, it was the mothers of men's children—and the mother's mothers—who most often prevailed. Everywhere in the Caribbean, the value of young children to men and women who shared control over them overrode that of contributions from adult children and sons' loyalty to their own mothers. All of this brings up the question, why did men bother to cooperate with the system in the first place?[5]

Why Men Cooperated

One reason why men so readily conformed to demands of females for support was pressure. As seen, women and their families promoted a system in which female sexual acquiescence, motherhood, and domestic servitude were associated with remuneration from males. They selectively encouraged relationships with men who had money; and they attached similar values to male migration, encouraging if not compelling men to go overseas in search of money to invest in homesteads and families back home. And so men migrated; they did so in fantastic numbers; and they did so precisely so that they could give the money to the mothers of their children and invest in households. Those who did not, lost respect (Handwerker 1989: 80); they lost rights to inheritance (Philpott 1973: 127); their wives cuckolded them and assigned paternity for offspring to other men (Otterbein 1966: 70–75, 115); their own children refused to help them (Handwerker 1989: 91); they were censured (Philpott 1973: 178-179); they suffered "ridicule," "isolation" and "abuse" (M. G. Smith 1962: 70; see also Smith 1956: 158; Greenfield 1966: 119; Rodman 1971: 178; Senior 1991: 8).

But male conformance did not derive from pressure alone. Caribbean males had the option of never coming home. When away working as migrants, they could have stayed overseas. And some did. But for the many who returned, the most fundamental reason for conformance was quite simply because investment in a house back home, in the woman who would manage it, and in the children who would make it productive was the best shot most had at dignity, liberty, social security, and financial independence from a system in which corporate plantation enterprises sought to use them at the lowest possible cost. Industrial agriculture, mining, and massive building projects might have paid little, but when men migrated from the poorest regions to distant plantations or construction sites, they were able to save money by sleeping on the sites and bunking in barracks or sharing houses with other men and, in doing so, were able to return home with a sizable savings.[6]

Conclusion

Summarizing, while many young Caribbean women may have been reluctant to begin childbearing, the ethnographic record suggests that most often older women—and to a lesser extent their spouses—favored the idea of their daughter's pregnancy and they sought to arrange it so that it would happen with men who could and would provide support. These interests were expressed in the institutionalized complex of behaviors seen above, from encouraging male sexual aggressiveness, to encouraging migration, to keeping young women ignorant of the processes that would allow them to avoid first pregnancies, to censoring financially unsuitable suitors while permitting older, financially capable men to slip through. Moreover, it was precisely the drive to get money from men and male absenteeism that led to rates of illegitimate births as high as 70 percent of all births; it also led to "brittle unions" in the form of polygyny and to serial monogamy; and to the late age at entry into union.

But as we have seen, there was more to it than money. It was ultimately not migration or childsupport in itself that caused "peculiar" Caribbean family patterns. Money from men does not explain why women did not stick by one man, especially if the man was away earning money and sending back remittances. It does not explain why men and women bothered to get married toward the end of their reproductive careers, after all their children were already born. And it does not explain the high birth rates that until recently prevailed throughout the region. The answer to what ultimately drove pronatalism, distinct Caribbean family, kinship, and courting practices, as well as male conformance, and the pursuit of overseas employment to meet financial responsibilities associated with women and children was not money or sex, *per se*, but rather the same response to poverty seen in Jean Rabel: dependence on a livelihood strategy in which the household was the foundation and child labor the fulcrum point in making the strategy successful. It is also this causal concatenation of variables with the importance of children as labor at the base that explains one of the most counterintuitive phenomena in the demographic literature, why Caribbean women bore more children when there were fewer men present, i.e., fewer men, more babies, the subject of the next chapter.

Notes

1. For the transformation of islands from plantation economies to dual plantation/peasant economies, see Mintz 1974, 1985, Scarano 1989, Brereton 1989; for Dominica, see Gardner and Podolefsky 1977; for Martinique, see Baber 1982, Horowitz 1959; for Barbados, see Lowenthal 1957, Henshall 1966; for Carriacou, see Richardson 1975, Heath 1988; for Commonwealth Caribbean, see Heath 1988: 431, Beckford 1972; for St. Vincent, see Rubenstein 1977, Grossman 1997; for Antigua, see Augelli 1953; for Barbuda, see Berleant-Schiller 1978, Gaspar 1991.

2. For Caribbean migration, see Lowenthal and Comitas 1962, Foner and Napoli 1978; Frucht 1968; Crane 1971; Pollock 1972; Palmer 1974; Sutton and Makiesky 1975; Taylor 1976; Hill 1977; Midgett 1977; Green 1979; Rubenstein 1977, 1979; Plummer 1985; Perusek 1984; Pollock 1972; Richardson 1975: 396–98; R. T. Smith 1953: 93; McElroy and Albuquerque 1988; for U.S.-engineered plantations, Balch 1927; Millspaugh 1931; Montague 1966; Williams 1970; Castor 1971; Lundahl 1983; Perusek 1984; Segal, 1975; Saint-Louis 1988; for Jamaica, see Griffith 1985; Pollock 1972.

3. George Cumper (1961) surveyed 1,296 households with 5,364 people (a random sample of 2 percent of the population). Cumper broke his sample into eight occupational groups and male-versus female-headed households. In only two of Cumper's categories of female-headed households (White Collar and Landless Laborer) did males contribute less than 50 percent of all income and among male-headed households in only the category of Domestic Labor (58%) did men contribute less than 75 percent of family income (table 17.4 below).

Table 17.4: Percentage of household income from males: Male- vs. female-headed households

	White collar	Skilled labor	Self- employed	Nonfarm labor	Domestic labor	Peasant	Renter	Landless labor
Fem.-headed hshld	18%	77%	54%	64%	60%	72%	57%	49%
Male-headed hshld	88%	88%	80%	1%	58%	77%	76%	80%

Note: The sample is divided into occupational groups. On the top row is percentage of household income contributed by males to female-headed households. The lower row is male contributions to male-headed households [Cumper 1961: 388].

4. On average, Caribbean women marry younger and live longer than men. Average age for entry into common law or "consensual union" in the traditional Commonwealth Caribbean occurred at 29.9 for females and 36.4 for males (Roberts 1957; see also Massiah 1983: 14); and Caribbean life expectancy in 1960 was 66.3 for females versus 62.2 for males. These figures mean that compared to men, Caribbean women had 10.6 years more of life after union than their spouse. Congruently, Caribbean households headed by widowed females were high, ranging during the 1960s and 1970s from 11.4 percent in Guyana to 34.1 percent in St. Vincent (Massiah 1983: 19).

5. "These people work abroad for awhile and then return to Anguilla to plant crops, build houses, and work at whatever comes to hand. Lack of opportunities for employment, droughts and the slow pace on the island leads to economic need and a restlessness which results in another trip abroad . . . .

Despite the large disproportion of women on the island the role of the female is quite apparently subordinate to the man. . . . [But] the total responsibility for day-to-day home cooperation, care of financial resources and child discipline is in the hands of women. . . . As one respondent said, 'The woman is the family manager; she is subordinate to her husband, but not subservient'" (Walker 1968: 114).

6. Wages in Haiti or Jamaica at the turn of the 20th century were ten cents per day, one-tenth to one-twentieth the one to two dollars per day workers could make migrating to work the Panama Canal (Petras 1988: 179–80; Plummer 1985; Perusek 1984).

It should also be acknowledged that staying abroad was not always an option. In 1924, a new law cut off immigration to New York; in the 1930s the depression ended migration; in 1937 Cuba, the Batista government brutally rounded up and exported Haitians, and in the same year the Trujillo regime in the Dominican Republic massacred some twenty thousand of them (Balch 1927; Millspaugh 1931; Montague 1966; Williams 1970; Castor 1971; Lundahl 1983; Perusek 1984; Segal 1975; Saint-Louis 1988).

Chapter 18

Fewer Men, More Babies

Introduction

It was seen in chapter 2 that Chayanov's 1920s investigation of work regimes and birth rates among Russian small farmers (called "peasants" in the literature) culminated with anthropological studies of the 1960s and 1970s and Caldwell's (1982) theory of wealth flows: when wealth flowed from children to adults, birth rates would be high; when they flowed the other way, they would be low. Most subsequent scholars took a different course, veering away from concrete and measurable explanations. Even Caldwell began to talk of religion and culture as determinants of high fertility. Here I want to show that in one of the most important instances where social scientists tried to stick to a rigorous application of a mechanical model—in this case "the proximate and intermediate determinants of fertility"—the model was inconsistent with ethnographic reality. In doing this, in examining the fewer men, more babies phenomenon, I believe that I can provide a graphic example of the utility of the argument presented in the previous chapter while demonstrating the inapplicability of the "proximate and intermediate determinants of fertility." I believe that I can also show how the tension between the economic value of children to women and men and the need to get children through the critical early years determined the particular values associated with the sexual moral economy in the Caribbean and high birth rates.[1]

Proximate and Intermediate Determinants of Fertility

The first scholars to discuss the "the proximate and intermediate determinants of fertility" were Kingsley Davis and Judith Blake (1956), who identified fourteen determinants. Twenty-seven years later, Bongaarts and Potter (1983: 163–65) reduced the number to nine. The first four were the "proximate" determinants:

1. Fecundity—the ability to have sexual intercourse, the ability to conceive, and the ability to carry pregnancy to term,
2. Exposure to the risk of pregnancy— sexual unions, such as marriage, and the actual time that partners spend together,
3. Birth control methods—contraceptives, sterilization, *coitus interruptus*,
4. Abortion.

There were five "intermediate determinants" of fertility, those factors by which the "proximate determinants" are altered and that fall soundly in the realm of social behavior:

1. Postpartum taboos—such as sexual abstinence for new mothers,
2. Duration of breast feeding—nursing suppresses ovulation,
3. Delayed marriage—many societies have strong norms against young women engaging in premarital sex,
4. Disruption of union via male out-migration or military service, and
5. Attitudes toward contraceptives and family planning.

Over the ensuing three decades social scientists came to treat the "proximate and intermediate determinants of fertility" as demographic laws. Social scientists working in the Caribbean were no exception, particularly regarding male wage migration and the resulting male absenteeism so widespread in the Caribbean. They frequently assumed and even calculated—without empirical support—the dampening effect that male out-migration supposedly had on birth rates among the women staying behind (Murthy 1973; Blake 1961: 249–50, 1954; see also Denton 1979; Williams et al. 1975; Lowenthal and Comitas 1962: 197; Ibberson 1956: 99; McElroy and Albuquerque 1990; Brockerhoff and Yang 1994).

The problem is that while seemingly obvious, the assumptions underlying the "proximate and intermediate determinants of fertility" were based on Western middle and upper class courtship behavior, where marriage, or at least stable union, was the criterion for sexual reproduction. They do not always apply in other societies; in the impoverished Caribbean, they do not apply at all, as illustrated in the fewer men, more babies phenomenon.

Fewer Men, More Babies

Gearing (1988) in Guadeloupe, Marino (1970) in the Commonwealth Caribbean, Guengant (1985: 48, 70, 103) in Montserrat, and Brittain in St. Barthelemy (1990) and again in St. Vincent and the Grenadines (1991a) all demonstrated unequivocal, positive, time-ordered correlations between total fertility rates and migration-induced male absenteeism. In each case, fertility increments closely followed the onset of migration with lags varying from zero to five years. This phenomenon appears even more remarkable when taking into account the degree of male absenteeism; as seen in the previous chapter, male wage migration meant that there were sometimes as many as twice the number of reproductive-aged females versus males on home islands. Yet, women were having more and not fewer babies.[2]

To understand why, recall that the principal argument in the previous chapter was that children are highly valued for their labor. As in Jean Rabel, desire for many children and grandchildren, the cost of getting them through the early critical ages of childhood (zero to five years), and the scarcity of men caused by both physical migration and financial ineligibility—i.e., those men who did not have money were not considered eligible mates— gave way to a grey area between the ideal demands of monogamous union and matrimony and reality: eligible men were scarce. In resolving the problem, sexual norms regarding marriage were relaxed and parents, especially mothers, and eventually daughters themselves, emphatically linked financial contributions to sexual acquiescence. Thus, the more wealth available to men, the more disposed Caribbean parents, particularly older women, were to permit sexual access to younger women and the more disposed women already engaged in their reproductive career were to acquiesce themselves, providing the impetus that explains why in times of high wage migration, more women among the impoverished Caribbean class bore more children: the simple prosaic fact is that there was more money to meet the demands women and their families attached to sex and procreation and that was necessary to feed and care for a child until he or she became a contributing member of the household.

A look at child nutrition and mortality rates illustrates the gravity of the problem that faced lower-income Caribbean families dependent on child labor. As in Jean Rabel, where malnutrition levels approach 40 percent for children six to seventy-two months of age and 25 percent of children die before they reach five years of age, rearing young children to the ages when they are most likely to survive and when they begin to make contributions to household production was difficult. In 1890 Grenada, for example, half of all infants died before their first birthday; in 1896–1897 Jamaica, 17.6 percent of infants died in the first year of life and 26.8 percent of children died before the age of five; in 1952 Martinique, infant mortality was 23 percent (Brereton 1989: 103). The point is that for obvious reasons money made child survival more probable; money was used to support women during pregnancy, to help account for lost labor of the mother, and to nurture young children through to the ages where they were no longer extremely vulnerable and began to become net producers. And money could most readily be garnered from baby fathers—rather than uncles or grandfathers—because baby fathers were selected precisely for their capacity to provide financial support.

In understanding the importance of investments in young children, Jean Rabel serves as a valuable case where data not available in the past ethnographic record can be partially recovered. I showed in chapter 14 that the value of child labor and the stress that children experience prior to reaching the age where they begin to contribute to the household labor pool is captured in the term *chape*, a frequently used local term that conceptually integrates both the passage of the vulnerable years of childhood and the entrance into the age of productivity. *Chape* literally means "to escape," and in this sense connotes the danger that a child passes through early on in life. The child is considered to *chape* when he or she has passed that point where death from malnutrition is most likely. But it is also at that point in the child's life "when he can do for himself" (*li ka fe pou kont li*), "when he can wash his own clothes" (*lè li ka lave rad pa li*), when he can "get by" (*lè li ka boukannen*),[3] "when he can go to the water by himself" (*lè li ka al nan dlo pou kont li*), and just as importantly, when he or she begins to contribute to the sustenance of the household. Respondents in the 136-household survey of opinions regarding children and household labor tasks explained the process,

> Oh, why does a person have children? You have children. You struggle to *chape* them. . . . You raise them. They *chape*. Tomorrow, God willing, if you need a little water, the child can get it for you. If you need a little firewood, he can carry it for you.[4] (fifty-five-year-old father of seventeen)

> I had children, now I have a problem, now the children can solve the problem. Tomorrow, God willing I cannot help myself, it is on the children I will depend. Today I *chape* them. Tomorrow God willing we struggle with life together.[5] (forty-one-year-old mother of four)

And to recall women in Jean Rabel commenting on the importance of a husband,

> He gives me money for the children, that is what makes me prefer having him around.[6] (twenty-seven year-old mother of five)

> What I am telling you is when you are young, you need a husband. What I mean is, if you haven't had children yet. So you can make a child.[7] (forty-two-year-old mother of three)

> If a person marries, why does she marry? She does not marry to be a big shot or anything like that. It is so she can have children... Why does a person want children? It is to help...to go to the water...to go get wood.[8] (forty-year-old mother of five)

> He has to come sit there and help me *chape* the children.[9] (forty-year-old mother of four)

And once the children are there,

> What makes me say I can live without a man? What I need to do to come up with a sack of food I can accomplish with my four children.[10] (thirty-year-old mother of four).

> If I have children, I don't need my husband at all. Children, hey! hey! I would like to have ten children. I don't need my husband.[11] (forty-one-year-old mother of seven).

Why can I live without a man? I arrive at an age like this. All my affairs are in order. I don't need my husband anymore.[12] (fifty-six-year-old mother of eight)

If we accept the argument that children were considered critical to household production, that they were highly desired, that increased availability of money made successful pregnancies and child survival more likely—and women and their families more inclined to accept male consorts—then the question is how were women able to bear more children precisely when there were fewer men. *How* fertility increased during periods of high male absenteeism was precisely because of the types of conjugal unions seen in the previous chapter, polygyny and unstable unions, behaviors that Bongaarts and Potter (1983) and other researchers posited as lowering the "exposure to the risk of pregnancy," thereby precipitating a drop in number of births (see Wood 1995 for a review of conflict surrounding this issue).

Polygyny, although never legal in the Caribbean, was long identified as part of an informal "standard" whereby married men could assume responsibility for additional common-law wives. In these "extramarital" unions, the women lived in separate homesteads or, in a form not recognized as a consummated union, remained in the homesteads of their parents (known in the anthropology of the Caribbean as a "visiting union"). The men performed as de facto husbands, providing support and fathering children. This nonlegal, or de facto, polygyny made it possible for a greater number of women to gain socially accepted sexual access to and financial support from the fewer available but more financially capable men, thereby overcoming imbalanced sex-ratios caused by male migration (for Haiti, see Herskovits 1937: 114 –15; Simpson 1942: 656; Murray 1977: 263; for Carriacou, see M. G. Smith 1961: 469; 1962: 117–22, 463–65, 1966: xviii; Hill 1977: 281; for the Commonwealth Caribbean, see Otterbein 1965; Marino 1970; Sutton and Makiesky-Barrow 1970: 312–13: for Jamaica, see Clarke, 1966; for Trinidad, see Greenfield, 1966; for Providencia, see Wilson 1973: 79; for Belize, see Gonzalez 1969: 49; for St. John, see Olwig 1985: 125; for St. Vincents, see Gearing 1988: 219; for Montserrat, see Philpott 1973: 116, 119; for British Guyana, see R. T. Smith, 1988).

Greater numbers of births during times of male absenteeism were also made possible through a series of relationships, what can be called unstable union. Serial mating, or what is sometimes called serial monogamy (without the emphasis on legal marriage), was socially viable and acceptable in the Caribbean. Women often began childbearing while still living in the home of their parents (see Clarke 1966: 99; Blake 1961; Greenfield 1966; Freilich 1968: 52; Senior 1991); they waited to commit to matrimony until toward the end of their reproductive careers when they were in their thirties and forties (Massiah 1983: 14; Roberts, 1957: 206–7). The trend was manifest in the fact that up until the 1970s, 40 to 75 percent of all Caribbean children were born to unmarried women (Senior 1991: 82; Roberts, 1957: 202); and 50 percent of Caribbean women bore children by two or more partners over the course of their lives (Ebanks et al. 1974; Ebanks 1973; Roberts, 1957).

The extent to which it was in fact polygyny and serial mating that made increased birth rates in the Caribbean possible when fewer men were present is evident in the increasing incidence of illegitimate births during times of heavy male absenteeism, called a Caribbean "structural principle" by Hill (1977: 281; see also Otterbein 1965;

M.G. Smith 1962: 117–22; Roberts 1957: 220). The birth histories of individual Caribbean women also demonstrated the relationship. Those women with the highest fertility levels were not, as expected in Bongaarts and Potter's model, those who remained in stable union. Ebanks et al. (1974) in Barbados and Ebanks (1973) in Jamaica found that in contrast to conventional demographic theory, the number of children a woman gave birth to in her lifetime increased with the number of partnerships she had. This was the case even when the researchers controlled for present age, age at entry into first union, age at first pregnancy, time spent within sexual union, time spent outside of union, type of union, and contraceptive use (see also Wilson 1961, for a similar finding in Providencia, and Marino, 1970: 166, who compared age cohorts of women from eight different islands).

Conclusion

In this and the preceding chapter I have tried to show how Caribbean family patterns were a response to basic economic challenges that confronted impoverished people living in the region. The costs of households and the need for children to make them productive set up conditions that would give way to the familial patterns found in the Caribbean. Both women, parents, and, arguably, men subscribed in principle to elite values of marriage and monogamy. Indeed, in the Caribbean, female participation in the salaried labor force has been correlated with increased marriage rates and lower rates of illegitimacy, i.e., when women have a dependable source of extrahousehold income they marry (Abraham 1993). But it was not historically so easy. As in Jean Rabel, parents, especially mothers, wanted children and grandchildren, indeed needed them to make the household productive. But they wanted—and arguably needed—their daughter to father them with men who could provide income to at least help get the children through the early period of dependency, that critical zero to five years stage before children became contributing members of the household. Moreover, as women advanced in their reproductive careers, they depended on men to underwrite the costs of establishing a new productive homestead and the beginning of their marketing careers.

Thus, as in Jean Rabel, a particular configuration of a sexual moral economy emerged. Mothers tightly controlled daughters. They instilled them with fear of contraception and abortion, kept them in the dark about the mechanics of pregnancy, and monitored their sexual activities. On the other side of the equation, sons were encouraged to be sexually aggressive and ridiculed for not conforming. A man was not a man if he did not have premarital and extramarital sex and his status depended heavily on the number of children he sired. Not warned by mothers, not protected against men with financial resources, daughters were left defenseless against pregnancy.

On the part of males, the scarcity of cash and salaried jobs made it difficult for them to find the means to meet the demands of women and their families and most importantly of all, to finance a household. The primary way men got the money was by migrating. Wage migration became a male determinant of parenthood in much of the Caribbean, a veritable rite of passage. If men wanted to fully participate in adult social life they often had to migrate. But it was emphatically not an issue of men simply seeking the means to meet financial demands attached to sex. And it is here that we come back once again to the other side of the issue, the side often ignored in the literature: the dependency of Caribbean men on women and children, seen earlier; for economic autonomy, dignity, and respect ultimately accrued to impoverished West Indian men only through the co-ownership of the most important means of production and mechanism for survival in the Caribbean, a household.

The frequent absences of men, the increased income of those who were present, and the increased income through remittances from fathers, brothers, sons, and lovers, in combination with pressure from elders and ignorance of the mechanisms of childbirth, meant that many women were more likely not to marry until later in life, to keep options open to them, and to begin or to intensify their childbearing career during times of high male wage migration—when men were scarcer but had greater resources—resulting in the counterintuitive phenomenon of fewer men, more babies discussed in this chapter. When men and women did marry it was to consolidate exclusive ownership, rights to production, and heredity for an already long established and productive household— especially important to a woman in lieu of the probability that her now financially mature husband might engage in extra-marital unions that result in the birth of "outside" children, i.e. polygyny.

Moreover, although it struck most Western observers as bizarre, the fewer-men-more-babies phenomenon may be much more widespread than the Caribbean. Ethnographers in Polynesia (Larson 1981), in Thailand (Kunstadter 1971), in New Guinea (Taufa et al.1990), and in rural Spain (Reher and Iriso-Napal 1989) all found statistically positive relationships between increased birth rates and male absenteeism brought about by wage migration. Researchers analyzing large samples of cross-country data for developing regions have similarly noted that migration delays the transition to lower fertility (Bilsborrow 1987; Bilsborrow and Winegarden 1985); Bongaarts himself noted that in sub-Saharan Africa—an area characterized by high male wage migration—fertility-inhibiting effects expected from migration did not come about, the reasons for which he could only speculate (Bongaarts et al. 1984: 511). Indeed, what perplexed Bongaarts is an old and apparently much forgotten idiosyncrasy that vexed earlier students of the demographic transition. Even Kingsley Davis (1963), the original formulator of the proximate and immediate determinants of fertility and one of the most important demographers of the 20th century, noted that emigration often offset fertility decline (see also Friedlander 1969; Mosher 1980; Moore 1945: 119; Hawley 1950, particularly chapter 9). But as with so many other demographic trends that did not fulfill the expectations of social scientists, this issue of migration offsetting fertility decline was ignored. In the following chapter I want to deal with understanding why.

Notes

1. The landmark study supporting that migration—and hence male absenteeism— disrupted fertility in Caribbean communities was carried out by McElroy and Albuquerque (1990) who tested data from ten countries in the Commonwealth Caribbean. Using a Spearman's rank-order correlation coefficient, they measured the relationship between out-migration and fertility for the 1960–1965 and the 1965–1970 periods. Their results yielded correlation coefficients of -0.52 and -

0.39 (McElroy and Albuuquerque 1990: 792), respectively. Neither of the tests were statistically significant at the 0.05 level, the data nevertheless seemed to indicate that out-migration correlates negatively with fertility decline in Caribbean sending countries—the higher the out-migration the lower the fertility rate. But, rather than demonstrating that male wage migration disrupts fertility, their data can be interpreted as demonstrating the opposite.

First, although their argument that emigration during the 1960s is "dominated by females" (McElroy and Albuquerque cite Marshal, 1985:52), temporary wage migration was clearly dominated by men. Looking at Marino's sex ratio chart (in the main text) it can be seen that out of the ten Caribbean countries for which McElroy and Albuquerque provide data, men were in the minority in all but one; in most of the cases men were outnumbered by reproductive-age females three to two and in some cases there were almost twice as many reproductive-age females as men.

The most significant shortcoming in their argument has to do with attempting to identify the "independent influence of migration" that McElroy and Albuquerque claimed they had isolated (1990: 785). The researchers did not account for other variables affecting fertility, such as wage labor available to women. This neglect is understandable because, as the authors themselves point out, reliable cross-country socioeconomic data for the Caribbean is scarce (McElroy and Albuquerque 1990: 785–86). On the other hand, the failure to exercise socioeconomic controls damages the validity of their argument. And here is why:

Like other areas of the world, the Caribbean during the 1960s was experiencing dramatic socioeconomic changes. Specifically, in the countries included in McElroy and Albuquerque's sample, the percentage of the labor force engaged in agriculture declined by an average of 30 percent; the percentage of population living in urban areas increased by 24 percent; female enrollment in primary school increased by 44 percent; life expectancy increased by an average of 5.1 years; and in most instances, infant mortality declined precipitously—in Grenada, for example, infant mortality declined from 77.9 to 34 deaths per 1,000; all factors known to precipitate or at least be associated fertility transition (Caldwell 1982; Handwerker 1986). And indeed, congruent with changes in living standards and economic conditions, Caribbean Total Fertility Rates declined during this period by an average .351 births per women.

Table 18.1: Caribbean net migration by total fertility rate

	Total fertility rate (TFR)		Net migration	
	1960	1970	1960	1970
Barbados	2.000	1.630	-1.600	-1.180
Dom Repub	7.500	7.130	-0.150	-0.260
Guadeloupe	2.750	2.560	-0.180	-1.420
Guyana	6.490	5.740	-0.630	-0.530
Jamaica	2.660	2.650	-1.500	-1.730
Martinique	2.670	2.450	-1.230	-0.690
St. Kitts-Nevis	2.200	2.150	-3.460	-3.160
Puerto Rico	5.020	3.570	-2.480	-1.490
Suriname	3.200	3.200	-1.100	-1.280
Windward Isl.	3.050	2.950	-2.130	-1.860

Because of the dramatic changes in demographic, health, and socioeconomic conditions, the measurement of interest for McElroy and Albuquerque should not have been how much Caribbean out-migration correlated with fertility levels. The relationship that McElroy and Albuquerque should have measured is how much out-migration detracted from or sped Caribbean fertility decline, i.e., the average level of migration correlated with the change in fertility rates. When McElroy and Albuquerque's data is used to plot the changes in TFR (1970 TFR minus 1960

TFR) against the rate of out-migration, a very different picture emerges than that proposed by the researchers.

The amount of reduction in fertility levels for individual Caribbean countries correlated with the average rate of migration for the 1960 to 1970 period indicates an association between small or absent fertility decline and high levels of out-migration (see table 18.2). A Spearman's rank-order correlation coefficient yields a -.340 (without significance below the .05 level). In effect, the higher the migration the lower the fertility decline. When Puerto Rico is excluded from the data set, because it is an outlier and was experiencing large-scale economic and social intervention from the United States during this era, a Spearman's rank-order correlation coefficient takes on the value of -.628 (with significance below the .05 level. Thus, rather than stimulating fertility decline, it could more easily be argued that migration offset fertility decline. Moreover, the studies provided by Marino (1970) and Brittain (1990, 1991a, 1991b) demonstrate that before the onset of rapid fertility decline in the region, there was a correspondence between male absenteeism and increased birth rates.

Table 18.2: Correlations in average change in total fertility rate by net migration

	1960–1970	1960–1970
Barbados	-0.370	-1.390
Dom Republic	-0.370	-0.205
Guadeloupe	-0.190	-0.800
Guyana	-0.750	-0.580
Jamaica	-0.010	-1.615
Martinique	-0.220	-0.960
St Kitts-Nevis	-0.050	-3.310
Puerto Rico	-0.450	-1.985
Suriname	0.000	-1.190
Windward Islands	-0.100	-1.995

2. The fewer men, more babies relationship was also evident in Jean Rabel. With the first coup d'etat (1991) that deposed democratically elected Jean Bertrand Aristide and the ensuing three years of international embargo, the migration of men conspicuously intensified. An unprecedented wave of mostly young males left the area headed for the Dominican Republic, Jamaica, Suriname, Cuba, Panama, Honduras, Venezuela, Colombia, Mexico, the United States, and the nearby Bahamas. The migration was such that in 1997, Jean Rabel sex ratios for the twenty- to thirty-four-year age varied from eighty-five to ninety-two males for every one hundred females. Most of these missing men had left home in search of employment so they could remit income primarily to mothers, mothers of their children, wives, and girlfriends. Moreover, using clinic data from the Bon Nouvel Mission (a clinic in Jean Rabel), and comparing that data for the periods before and after 1992 suggests that birth rates during this period markedly increased. Comparing the seven year time period (1985–1992) with the six year time period (1993–1999), there was a 20 percent decrease in contraceptive use from 6.9 percent to 5.5 percent; a two-year decline in mother's age at first birth , from twenty-two to twenty years of age (P < .05); and a 5.9 month decline in the average length of a woman's first inter-birth interval, from 29.5 to 23.6 months (p > .05 but p < .10).

3. "Lè li ka boukannen" (when he can barbeque) is an expression that derives from children digging up and cooking sweet potatoes, something young children, especially boys, often do, and it signifies a child's ability to look after himself.

4. O, pou ki yon moun fe ti moun? Ke vle di, ou fe ti moun nan. W-ap bat pou chape yo. . . . L-ap grandi yo. L-ap chape. Demen si dieu vle, si ou bezwen ti dlo li ka ba ou. Si ou bezwenn ti bout bwa li ka pote li pou ou. Ou bezwenn ni konn ed.

5. *Mwen fe ti moun, kounye-a m vin gen yon pwoblem, kounye-a ti moun ka redi pwoblem. Demen si dieu vle, m vin pa kapab, se sou kont ti moun m-ap vini. Kounye-a map chape yo. Demen si dieu vle yo ka bat ave-m.*

6. *L-ap ba-m di goude pou ti moun, se sa k fe m ta reme sa*

7. *Non. Lè yon moun jenn, bagay sa m-ap di, ou bezwenn yon mari, komsi m di, si ou poko enfante, ou ka enfante yon ti moun.*

8. *Si yon moun marie, pou ki sa li marie? Li pa marie nì pou chef ni pou anyen. Se pou li ka fe dè ti moun. . . . En ben, pou kisa yon moun fe ti moun? Se pou li ka ed-o. . . al nan dlo-a . . . al nan bwa.*

9. *M-ap swiv neg la, paskè m gentan gen pitit ave-li. Li pa ka abandone ni net. Fo-k li vin chita la pou ede-m chape ti moun yo*

10. *En ben, ki fe-m ka viv san gason? Sa-m bezwenn m ka leve yon sak manje, se a kat ti moun um m ka rive.*

11. *Si m gen ti moun m pa bezwenn mari-m menm. Ti moun, hoy, hoy. M ta reme dis pitit, m pa bezwenn mari.*

12. *Pou ki rezon fe-m ka viv san gason. Ko-m rive nan laj konsa. Tout afe-m mache. M pa bezwenn mari-m anko.*

Chapter 19

A Reflexive and Critical Look at the Anthropology of the Caribbean

Introduction

At the beginning of this book, I showed how researchers and scholars have largely rejected the notion that economic benefits of children among small farmers are a significant determinant of developing country birth rates, kinship, and family and courtship practices. It is a rejection that permeates the literature; one that does not make sense in light of ethnographers' rigorous documentation of the utility of children; and it has impeded an understanding of the determinants of Caribbean familial patterns. But it was not the only misunderstanding of its kind in the literature.

Throughout the book, I touched on a series of other issues where scholars did not accurately appreciate the ethnographic facts. In chapter 8, I showed how estimates of per capita income were misleading and, in the case of Jean Rabel, based on faulty data collection; in chapter 16, I showed how scholars projected repression onto Haitian women when in fact rural Haitian women enjoy a level of economic autonomy that often rivals or exceeds that of their spouses; in chapter 17, I showed how male absenteeism gave way to inconsistent notions of "matrifocality" and how this was generalized to an erroneous conclusion that Caribbean women were financially independent of men; and in the previous chapter I showed how the "proximate and intermediate determinants of fertility" were projected onto the demographic behavior of impoverished Caribbean people when in fact they did not fit.

In addressing these issues and pulling together the work of other researchers I hope that I have shown that the causes of Caribbean family patterns are not complex. They derive from basic economic costs and benefits inherent in household livelihood strategies. Moreover, I am not the first to think so. Anthropologists began focusing on Caribbean family patterns in the 1930s, and among the first of them were scholars like Simpson (1942), who gave candid, economic explanations for Caribbean value systems and family structure, including recognition of the importance of the labor of children to the family. As will be seen in this chapter, others followed. Scholars such as Cohen (1956), Solien de Gonzalez (1961), Kunstadter (1963), and Otterbein (1965) made attempts to explain Caribbean family patterns according to practical material conditions, particularly male financial contributions to housebuilding and the male wage migration so prevalent in the Caribbean. But these explanations and trains of inquiry became overshadowed. A fog of research agendas, convoluted analyses, proposed ideational and cultural causes, and myths increasingly obscured the underlying determinants of Caribbean family structure.

In this chapter I want to present exactly what these research agendas were and I also want to deal with why. Why did researchers come to favor nonexplanatory explanations? I believe that I can demonstrate that the answer is that the research and conclusions were usually steeped in political discourse or government funded campaigns meant, not to understand the behavior of Caribbean people, but to rationalize, manipulate, exploit, or change it.

Historical Particularism and Civil Rights

Caribbean family patterns made their first entrance into the mainstream literature when Melville Herskovits—a student of Franz Boas—competed with Franklin Frazier, a sociologist, for what Freilich (1967: 239) called "The Explanation." Echoing sentiments of "separate but equal," Herskovits explained Caribbean family and kinship as reformulated cultural survivals from Africa. Upon visiting Harlem he was impressed by a "teeming center of negro life," complete with "hospitals and the social service agencies . . . lawyers, and doctors and editors and writers . . . capitalists, teachers, and nurses and students," what he called "the same pattern" as white society "only a different shade" (Herskovits 1925: 368; Gambrell 1997:104). As historian David Levering Lewis (1981: 116) quipped, Herskovits' arguments, popular with both white separatists and the wealthy blacks who dominated the NAACP, earned the white Jewish scholar the title "honorary New Negro"—a pun on Herskovits' essay "The New Negro."

Herskovits' nemesis, Franklin Frazier, was an African-American professor of sociology at Howard University and member of the civil rights intelligentsia that came to be known as the Howard Circle. Frazier insisted on the primacy of the slave experience and subsequent discrimination, poverty, and exploitation as determinants of Afroamerican/Caribbean family patterns. He and those close to him viewed Herskovits' arguments as an extension of that discrimination, charging that the ideas he promoted lent credence to white racist arguments, and that wealthy blacks accepted "unconditionally, the values of the white bourgeois world" because "they do not truly identify themselves with Negroes"—one implication being that they benefited from their positions as an intermediate elite negotiating the economic and political divide between whites and blacks (Frazier 1957). Addressing Herskovits in a speech in Harlem, Frazier summed the political implications of the Herskovits position:

If whites believe that the Negro's social behaviour was rooted in African culture, they would lose whatever sense of guilt they had for keeping the Negro down. Negro crime, for example, could be explained away as an "Africanism" rather than due to inadequate police and court protection"[1] (Tauheed 2003)

With the successes of the civil rights movement, the Herskovits-Frazier debate transformed. Afroamericans interested in motivating black ethnicity to politically consolidate power—and who may earlier have stood on the other side of the issue, that of equal rights and universal suffrage—soon embraced Herskovits' ideas. The 1960s was, as Cole (1985: 123) has described it, "the era of African dress, African hairstyles and adoption of African names"; and "The renewed interest in Africanisms . . . was clearly associated with the political climate of the Black Power Movement and the rise of black studies in academic circles" (Cole 1985: 121). The Africanism perspective of Caribbean family patterns continues among those scholars interested in identity (Sutton and Makiesky-Barrow 1975: 297; Crahan et al. 1980; Cole 1985; Barrow 1986; Yelvington 2001). But for most anthropologists, they are no longer of major interest.[2]

Structural Functionalism and Colonial Government Morality Campaigns

Concurrent with and following the Herskovits/Frazier debate—or, perhaps more accurately, the separation versus integration debate—was structural functionalism: a focus on the adaptive interrelations between social institutions. Once again, scholars were embedded in greater econopolitical processes, this one closely linked to colonial efforts to revitalize overseas protectorates through an "organized campaign against the social, moral and economic evils of promiscuity," and endeavor that included massive marriage campaigns (M. G. Smith 1957: iv). Among the leading structural-functionalists in the Caribbean were Edith Clarke—anthropologist, politician, and Jamaican aristocrat—and M. G. Smith—another Jamaican-born, English-educated aristocrat-anthropologist. Both Smith's and Clarke's viewpoints harked back to the earlier colonial regime attempts to capture "peasant" labor and illustrate the degree to which the endeavor was slanted toward modifying behavior to the advantages of state funding agencies. Specifically, the objective was to convert impoverished denizens of the Caribbean into productive taxpayers. In writing the introduction to Clarke's 1957 book, *My Mother Who Fathered Me*, M. G. Smith left no room for doubt:

> The material difficulties of West Indian economic and social development are compounded by instabilities and fluidities in the family organization on which the society depends both for the effective socialization of its young and for the adequate motivation of its adult members to participate vigorously in the social and economic life. These familial conditions affect labour productivity, absenteeism, occupational aspirations, training and performances, attitudes to saving, birth control, and farm development, and to programmes of individual and community self-help, housing and child care, education, and the like. (1957: vi-vii)

In the end, structural functionalists fulfilled the prophecies of the funding agencies so effectively—finding that the behavior of lower-income Caribbean people was indeed "dysfunctional," "uncivilized," and "disorganized"—that they were arguably a principal force in the destruction of the paradigm. Structural-functionalism could not survive the onslaught of "structural-less" and "functional-less" findings. As for the drive to modify the morality of impoverished denizens of the Caribbean, independence squashed it. Independence for Jamaica came in 1962; for Trinidad and Tobago, internal self-rule came in 1962 and full independence in 1976; for the Bahamas, internal self-rule came in 1964 and full independence in 1973; and most of the lesser Antilles' independence came in the 1960s to 1980s. With the end of the colonial regimes, came an end to the funding of social science research targeted to turn the impoverished people of the colonies into happy, ambitious, and legally married tax payers.

Post Functional-Structuralist Era

Beginning earlier on, with the structural-functionalists, and extending into the early 1970s, came a short period of scientific enlightenment when scholars began to test hypotheses and apply statistical methodology to resolve the causal puzzle of Caribbean kinship and family patterns. "Survivalisms" and a reification of cultural institutions typical of the structural-functionalists still lingered in the form of typologies, an attempt to break the culture of the Caribbean into specific patterns of behavior: Wolf typed peasants (1955); Solien (1961) typed migration; Richard Price (1966) wanted to type Caribbean fisher folk; Frucht (1971) made denizens of the Caribbean a unique social type altogether; almost everyone typed marriage patterns. But the arguments were nevertheless much improved over the preceding "survivalisms" and "diffusionist" interpretations.

With the work of scholars such as R. T. Smith (1953), Mintz (1955), Cohen (1956), Wolf and Mintz (1957), Clarke (1966), Blake (1961), Wilson (1961), Solien de Gonzalez (1961), and Kunstadter (1963), the foundation was laid for a statistically and qualitatively supported understanding of connections between male migration, households, and conjugal union. The causes of Caribbean family patterns began to unravel and, had they pursued the issue, anthropologists working in the region may well have overcome the ball and chain of typology (e.g., Otterbein 1966; Marino 1970). But they did not.

Instead of explaining Caribbean family patterns, independence movements throughout the Caribbean and changes in colonial policies meant less funding. Most scholars subsequently turned away from the region. Otterbein, for example, began to focus on warfare (1970, 1994, 2004) and capital punishment (1986); Kunstadter (1967, 1983, 1993, 2002, 2004) moved on to Asia, never to write anything significant about the Caribbean again. Anthony Marino completely fell off the radar screen. Of the most celebrated Caribbeanists, Sidney Mintz (1971, 1974, 1985) went on to focus on history, and Nancy Solien de Gonzalez (1969, 1970, 1979, 1984) and R. T. Smith (1988, 1996) went on to rehash the same information and the same arguments for half a century. And so scholars working in the Caribbean and interested primarily in explanations for the sake of science largely disappeared from the scene. Others less interested in explaining would take up the issue.

Feminists

"Feminists went to the Caribbean to correct ideological distortions by documenting and assessing women's economic, social and political roles" (Safa 1986: 1). They were funded by organizations such as USAID's Women in Development Technical Assistance Project (WIDTECH), a program deliberately targeted to empower women in the workplace and help them break with traditional gender roles, a worthy social goal in that many Caribbean economies were experiencing industrialization and almost all were being transformed by juggernaut growth in the tourist sector. But it was not conducive to academic understanding.

In analyzing and collecting data, feminists gave ample consideration to material conditions. Massiah (1983) showed that Caribbean women who head households were economically disadvantaged. Blumberg (1993) and Dehavenon (1993) both provided materialist models aimed at accounting for conditions that give way to female-headed households. Abraham (1993) showed how illegitimacy and marriage rates in Carriacou correlated with female access to wage employment. Another admirable feminist argument in regard to explaining female-headed/supported households was that women assume responsibility by default: when men were undependable providers, either because of marginal income opportunities, migration, or culturally ingrained apathy, women were forced to assume the role of household head and provider (Senior 1991: 36–37, 170–71; Massiah 1983: 10–12). A number of feminists, like Barrow (1986: 170), also documented Caribbean women as employing "strategies" to "manipulate a man thereby gaining materially and enhancing their economic autonomy" (see also Senior 1991).

But, while interesting and while they made notable contributions, feminist research was embedded in the movement to empower women. In pursuit of this endeavor it was eclectic, yielded no comprehensive explanation for family patterns, distorted the role of women in the other direction, largely ignoring studies carried out by men and women who preceded them, and often ignoring the existence of men altogether (see Greene and Biddlecom 2000 for a recent critique).

An example is the book titled *Where Did All the Men Go: Female-Headed/Female-Supported Households in Cross-Cultural Perspective* (1993), edited by Mencher and Okongwu, among the most notable feminist anthologies of causal investigations into Caribbean family patterns. Somewhat ironically, none of the authors investigated "where all the men went," what they were doing, if or how much money they sent back, or if female-headed households really meant "female-supported."

But worse regarding feminist contributions to causal understanding is that ignoring men gave way to one of the most obscurant myths that came to muddle a causal understanding of familial dynamics: that Caribbean women were financially and emotionally independent of men. Helen Safa (1986) a leading feminist scholar, typified the feminists in the Caribbean position when she declared in the introductory chapter for a major feminist anthology on the West Indies, "Caribbean low-income women have been fending for themselves and their families for a long time, and have learned not to depend on men for financial or even emotional support" (13–14). This poignant and often quoted misstatement was not only giving short shrift to the majority of impoverished Caribbean men—who in the endeavor to meet the demands women attached to sexuality and paternity found themselves far from home toiling in sugar cane fields, mines, and construction sites—it was not supported by research findings, not even, as seen an earlier chapter, by feminist research findings.

For many students and scholars the notion that Caribbean women were neither emotionally nor financially dependent on men became erroneously enshrined in the concept of matrifocality. R. T. Smith (1956; 1988: 8) first used the term to describe familial development sequences marked by unstable sexual unions, female-headed households, matrilocality, and strong mother-child bonds. Other scholars adopted the term and "matrifocality" became a widely used anthropological descriptive for the Caribbean family. But when Gonzalez (1970) tried to figure out what other scholars meant by "matrifocal" she found little agreement. Researchers used "matrifocal" to describe situations where women were "somehow" more important than the observer had expected: that women had influence in spending family income; as a reference to situations where women were the primary source of income; to designate female-headed households; to delineate female-dominated decision making in the domestic sphere; and at times matrifocality became confused with the consanguineal female-headed households (1970: 231–32, 236; see also Mohammed 1986: 171–72). Eventually, Gonzalez (1984: 8) herself decided that she was "no longer so sure" of her original distinction between consanguineal and matrifocal families "in either an etic or an emic sense." Even R. T. Smith (1988: 7)—who originally coined the term—came to describe "matrifocality" as "surrounded by a dense fog of misunderstanding," only to then admit to "some shifts in the meaning I now attach to it." Blackwood (2005) summed up the enduring confusion surrounding the concept when she wrote that during the 1980s the term "matrifocal" was "allowed to slink offstage without certain issues being resolved" only to return later in the form of "female-headed household." [3]

In short, feminist studies of the 1980s and 1990s were embedded in a campaign to empower women—to their credit they often admitted it—but they did little to advance the understanding of the causes underlying family patterns and kinship in the Caribbean. Indeed, authors such as Blackwood (2005) have criticized early feminists themselves for having overemphasized "matrifocality," thereby perpetuating patriarchic myths.

Contraceptive Campaigns

Many researchers who worked in the Caribbean Basin, especially since the early 1970s, were caught up in antinatal and contraceptive campaigns. Blake (1961), Stycos and Back (1964), Murray (1972, 1976, 1977), Ebanks et al. (1973, 1974, 1975), Handwerker (1983, 1986, 1989, 1993), Jennie Smith (1998), McElroy and Albuquerque (1990), Senior (1991), and Maynard-Tucker (1996) all went to the Caribbean under the tutelage or in association with internationally sponsored fertility reduction programs. The slant inherent in their research objectives are reflected in their conclusions: high birth rates are consistently portrayed as illogical and nonadaptive, the cause of economic hardship and burdensome to women.

As seen in chapter 2, Murray's (1977) otherwise excellent analysis of the reasons that Haitian farmers give for having large numbers of children was marred by an inexplicable division of the category "useful." Murray split into two separate categories those farmers who gave "useful" as an explanation for wanting children but did not explain what they meant from those who said "useful" and then specified "as workers." By dividing the response "useful," Murray was able to present farmers as favoring children for noneconomic ends; had he done otherwise, had he accepted the implication that "useful" meant to work, the small farmers in Murray's community would have overwhelmingly come out in favor of having children for economic reasons. Similarly, Maynard-Tucker (1996: 1381) inexplicably twisted her observations that Haitian children were economically useful into them being a burden and then blamed high fertility on causes such as values left over from slavery. Handwerker (1989,1993) focused on female repression in the domestic sphere and employment in the formal sector of Antigua and Barbados, a focus that echoed his earlier highly regarded cross-country test (1986) demonstrating that female involvement in the work force was the principal determinant of fertility decline throughout the world; a valid and well supported observation but one that ignored why fertility was high in the first place or, more specifically, ignored Caribbean women's traditional careers as managers of productive households, their roles as market women, and the importance of child labor in making them successful in these endeavors. Senior (1991: 67–69) blamed high fertility on causes such as "the need to feel like a woman" and "the biblical injunction to be fruitful and multiply." And Jennie Smith (1998: 11), began her discussion by saying that, with regard to poor Haitian farmers, proponents of contraceptive use "are simply proposing the preposterous!" But later, in an almost humorous parenthetical and self-reflective moment, she candidly wondered why she fell into the same trap: her exact parenthetical quote was, "Looking back over the pages above, I find that I myself, however unwittingly, also seem to hold that underlying assumption" (Smith 1998: 24).[4]

Beyond showing the otherwise inexplicable manipulation of categories (Murray), denial of their own observations (Maynard-Tucker, Smith, Senior), and the over-focus on the formal economy (Handwerker), it is perhaps impossible to unequivocally demonstrate the link between funding agendas and the thought processes of the researchers. But it could be argued that in their conclusions researchers eschewed the obvious importance of child labor contributions because it was a conclusion that meant funding agencies and the researcher-scholar who hoped to get another consultancy job could do nothing to change the situation. If impoverished people were having many children because children were important in the struggle to survive then what needed to be changed was the entire economic system, not a practical or feasible recommendation. If, on the other hand, it was only a matter of tradition, values, lack of knowledge, unavailability of contraceptives, and ineffective healthcare systems, something could be done about it. Seminars, education, and improved clinics could solve the problem. There is also the issue of the researchers' own values. Anthropologists themselves may have eschewed presenting Caribbean parents as wanting children primarily for work because it was an egregious violation of our own middle and upper class Western values, a point that brings me to the international campaign against child labor.

Child Labor Campaign

I mentioned in chapter 2 that the emergence of powerful pro-child institutions such as the United Nations Children's Fund (UNICEF), the International Labor Organization (ILO), Slavery International, and Save the Children coincides with an obsession with children. We come close to worshipping them. In Lancy's words, the transition went from preparing children to be "future farmers or factory workers—adding their critical bit to the household economy—to economically worthless but emotionally priceless cherubs"; "attitudes that have become enshrined in academic discourse as well" (2007: 278). These values were exported to the developing world through institutions such as UNICEF and Child Defense Fund. Perhaps more than in any other country, the campaign became vigorously executed and wildly exaggerated in Haiti.

The issue began to heat up with the 1984 and 1990 Conferences on Child Domesticity held in Port-au-Prince, Haiti. Participants at the conferences equated child domestic service with "slavery" and, in their zeal to please funding institutions and win support, presented it as epidemic. Lumping together every Haitian child between the ages of five and seventeen and not living with their parents in the category of child domestic servant, the experts came up with estimates of from 100,000 to 250,000, translating to 10 percent to 25 percent of all Haitian children in this age category (UNICEF 1993; Dorélien 1982; 1990; Clesca 1984).

The cry of slavery came to a head in 1998 with an autobiography titled *From Haitian Slave Child to Middle-Class American*, in which Jean-Robert Cadet (1998) recounted his life as a *restavek*, the creole word for child domestic servant. Subsequently appearing on National Public Radio and the Oprah Winfrey Show, Cadet precipitated a media hysteria. Prestigious journalists echoed the alarm with titles like "Haiti's Dark Secret" (NPR 2004) and "The Plight of Haiti's Child Slaves" (*Telegraph*, 2007). Frequently citing a 1996 UNICEF study, journalists upped the number of Haitian child servants to three hundred thousand, breaking the earlier records for inflated numbers and translating to about 30 percent of all Haitian children in the target age category. National Public Radio (2004) described the "slave children" as "trafficked," bringing to mind organized recruiters trucking rural children into the city to be sold. There were even descriptions of thousands of Haitian children annually "trafficked" across the border to the Dominican Republic (U.S. Department of Commerce. 2006; Bureau of Democracy, Human Rights, and Labor 2007; U.S. Department of State 2006).

In an attempt to put the issue into perspective and determine just how widespread the *restavek* problem was, an independent organization called Fafo (2002)— funded by UNICEF, ILO, and Save the Children—sent interviewers to visit a sample of 7,812 households throughout both rural and urban areas of Haiti. Defining *restavek* according to the criteria of parent-child separation, high work load, and lack of or low level of schooling, they estimated the number of Haitian *restavek* between the ages of five and seventeen years at 173,000 (8.2 percent of the population in this age group at the time of the research); and if the age of fifteen years and under is used, the number was 134,000 (7.7 percent of the population between five and fifteen years of age). They also presented a less dramatic picture of what was going on. The authors pointed out that one problem with the image of the slave-*restavek* was that most of the 60 percent of the

Haitian population that live in rural areas and towns have access only to primary schools that end at 6th grade or earlier and most village schools only go up to the 8th grade. Thus, families use connections in towns and cities to board their children and help them get educated so they can escape the spiraling rural overpopulation and land scarcity seen in earlier chapters (a point punctuated by Jean Rabel farmer responses seen in chapter 13). Many parents pay for their children to live with others so they can attend school. But for those who cannot afford to pay, the children do domestic work in exchange for room and board. So what earlier researchers had been doing was lumping informal boarding-school arrangements in with child slavery. Moreover, many of the child domestics were not the abused "slaves" recounted in the press. Fafo researchers found that parents tended to beat their own children more than the *restavek*; that the *restavek* had equal or greater sleeping time; and that as or more often than non-*restavek* children the *restavek* had his or her own bed, mattress, or mat. Another important finding was that contrary to the typical image of the vast majority of *restavek* being girls, 41 percent were boys; and contrary to the portrayal of them as missing out on education, at least 60 percent of all *restavek* were enrolled in school (Fafo 2002: 56–58).

But the Fafo findings did little to quell accusations of rampant child slavery or the misinformation that human rights advocates and agencies consistently latched on to. In its 2007 report, the U.S. Department of Labor ignored the Fafo data and cited instead an old and unsubstantiated UNICEF study (1997) to claim 250,000 to 300,000 *restavek* in Haiti, saying that 80 percent were girls under fourteen years of age, an absurd figure that places in the status of child servant one fourth of all Haitian girls in that age category. They also disregarded other Fafo findings, saying that "most" *restavek* worked from ten to fourteen hours per day and that "most" were not enrolled in school.

I am not saying that child abuse in Haiti is nonexistent or that the institution of *restavek* is not exploitative. What I am saying is that something peculiar is going on with respect to the presentation and interpretation of the data and that it is a manifestation of a deeply disturbing bias. Even Cadet—who eventually found himself testifying before the United Nations Commission on Human Rights (June 2000)[5]— was arguably not a *restavek*. He tells of his wealthy white father leaving him with a childless mistress who, a twisted, hateful, and perhaps jealous woman, abused him, leaving deep emotional scars. While sad, that could have happened anywhere. It could and does happen in developed countries. Moreover, unlike the classic media image of Haitian child slaves, Cadet's father was paying for his board, made sure he got educated, and then sent him to university in the United States, where he became a teacher and, after the child slavery issue became a hot topic, wrote a best-seller, became famous, and lent his name to a charitable foundation to aid *restavek*. When reading the Amazon reviews for Cadet's book I came across this commentary,

> As a child growing up in Haiti…I knew Mr. Cadet, I played with him, I saw him everyday for at least four years, and only thought of his adoptive mother as a strict disciplinarian. A lot of what my young eyes saw did not prepare me for what I read in this book. As they say in HAITI, nothing is what they seem.

> January 20, 2000; Amazon.com By "A Customer"

Charities, such as that Cadet represented, pursued the issue with gusto, further inflating figures and creating an image of Haiti as the largest slave state since Cuban emancipation--an ironic accolade for the country that evolved out of the only successful slave revolt in history. In the scramble to solicit donations, Internet sites for organizations like Haitian Street Kids Inc. (HSKI 2007), further inflated the numbers and lumped homeless street urchins with the *restavek* in even more absurd and self-contradictory claims such as "There are currently over 400,000 child slaves as young as 4 years old throughout Haiti," telling the reader that they "often times are beaten to death," and that if one were to go to Haiti—which few readers ever will—they can identify the *restavek* by "their torn rags and tattered clothes hanging from their strained and feeble limbs, often times begging for food and money" (HSKI 2007).

The main point that I am trying to make is that the reaction to child labor and the sensationalism of the presentations reflect the extremity of the mainstream Western view of children in which having children for the purpose of exploiting their labor is criminal. The fact is that, as we already know, Haitian children living with their parents also work, something that likely occurs among impoverished farmers throughout the world and certainly occurred widely in the 17th to early 20th century United States. In David Lancy's (2007: 280) ethnology of child-adult play he noted that pushing Western values of child-adult play on other societies and impoverished peoples is "tantamount to a condemnation of the child-rearing beliefs and behaviors of three fourths of the world's parents." Indeed, by definition of the 1956 UN Supplementary Convention on the Abolition of Slavery, the Slave Trade, and Institutions and Practices Similar to Slavery, the Haitian parents seen in earlier chapters are in violation of Convention 138 under the Child Labor Code (Fafo 2002: 33). Thus, the interesting point is not that rural Haitians are hard on their children or that they do not love their children. The interesting point is that mainstream Western conventions regarding children are so out of synchrony with the reality of poverty that it made the childrearing practices and goals of many impoverished peoples of the world illegal.

This 'discrimination' has an impact on the social scientist. Members of the Western educated elite but with a strong tendency toward advocacy on the part of those they study, anthropologists are subject to a definitive reluctance to bring attention to cultural values that Westerners regard as disparaging if not criminal. The Western anthropologist who reveals "his people" as thinking of their offspring first and foremost not in terms of love and companionship, but in terms of labor and material necessity has, by Western standards, done a disservice to his former hosts. He has portrayed them in the annals of the ethnographic literature as criminal, calloused and selfish.

In regard to child labor, the degree to which this bias and the pro-Western values that drive it have penetrated the anthropological literature is evidenced by the five articles of the June 2007 special edition of *American Anthropologist* focusing on children and reviewing the 20th century anthropological literature on child studies. There is only one, just one, passing mention of ethnographies of children at work. That reference was Lancy himself (2007: 277), who tersely summed up ethnographic references to child work, saying that "the primary reason adults [in the developing communities studied] are likely to take a jaundiced view of children at play is because they would rather see them working" (Lancy cited Bock and Johnson 2004; Munroe et al. 1984; and more specifically, for the Maya, Modiano 1973: 55; for the Yoruba, Oloko 1994:211; and for the Hadza, Blurton-Jones 1993: 317).

Other Value Campaigns and Agendas

The reflexivity and critical scrutiny I am trying to bring out with this review is not new to most anthropologists but is nevertheless seldom incorporated in our literature reviews: the conclusions made by scholars working in the Caribbean are readily linked to our own values, political policies, humanitarian decisions, and the funding sources that send scholars to the field. Moreover, this bias is consistently present. More recent investigations bolster the point. The most cited recent article on Caribbean family structure is Evelyn Blackwood (2005), who indicted both traditional anthropologists and feminists for reinforcing male bias with its hidden presumption that the prominence of women was somehow unusual. She is correct, at least in her basic point, but her own research and her demands for specific new directions in researching alternative forms of marriage and same-sex relationships are embedded in queer anthropology. Not that I object to her motivations; only to emphasize that as with almost every major work on the Caribbean family, the study is part of a value campaign. She made her indictments as an active member of the Society of Lesbian and Gay Anthropologists (SOLGA) and with the objective of promoting the recognition of same-sex marriage, even calling for—and obtaining—an official statement from the American Anthropological Association that marriage between a man and woman was not cross-culturally universal, the implication being that same sex marriage was not an unnatural state of human matrimony and calling for boycotts of presses that published books contradicting that position (see SOLGA website, www.solga.org).

There is also Quinlan (2006: 476), another of the most prominent contemporary Caribbeanists. He recently turned the earlier feminists on their head when he described Caribbean men as "victims of their social environment," but he did so as an agent of the growing and well-funded campaign against addiction and substance abuse.

It is this type of embedded-ness that led to a decided failure to develop a cohesive explanatory model for why Caribbean family patterns were different from mainstream Western ideals. Civil rights struggles underwritten by political parties, social welfare campaigns underwritten by colonial governments, research on the role of women underwritten by feminists organizations, contraceptive and female health campaigns underwritten by international organizations bent on reducing high birth rates, gay rights activists, AIDs awareness campaigners, and substance abuse programs came to have a decisive influence on the scholarly representation and explanations for Caribbean familial patterns. Most anthropologists were distinctly enmeshed in their own biases and the biases of the institutions that funded them. Those who were not—such as Otterbein and Kunstadter—lacked the resources, audience, or incentives to continue their studies.

I want to make it clear that I am not saying that the research cited above is bad research. Each of the researchers had specific objectives, most of the objectives meritorious, and most of the research of such a high quality that it can be used to detect other patterns or to disqualify certain conclusions made by the authors. But what I am saying is that the research objectives of the authors and the institutions that funded them undermined balanced interpretations. Moreover, before concluding, I want to show how the campaigns to change behavior, those in which anthropological research was embedded, also undermined the information given by informants in the field.

The Impact of Value Campaigns on Informants

Another aspect of the state-sponsored campaigns described above is that they create a proactive bias among church officials and agents of international institutions that, funded by the State and foreign and domestic NGOS, define their success by the degree to which they can convince constituents, clients, and students to adopt those values, if not in deed then at least in word. By dint of their control over the distribution of grades, jobs, food aid, used clothing, agricultural extension services, and life-saving medications, these practitioners in the field promote specific values. Police officers, aid workers, administrators, seminar specialists, health care workers, preachers, schoolteachers, justices of the peace, lawyers, professors, and, not to be left out, anthropologists themselves teach—if not force—their impoverished subjects, aid recipients, clients, patients, and dependents to espouse specific Western elite values, values that the impoverished people upon whom they are being thrust often do not in practice share.

An example of the insidious impact this promotion of values has on data can be garnered from the surveys I conducted in Jean Rabel. The NHADS survey upon which many of the conclusions in this study were based was largely targeted to give feedback regarding contraceptive and health campaigns being carried out by the NGOs that funded the survey. Assistants who helped train interviewers were Western-educated doctors, nutritionists, and agronomists. Moreover, many of the interviewers had been participants in past health and agricultural programs and they had already been sensitized to the values associated with these programs. This came out clearly in their active promotion of those values, specifically the priority placed on fewer children. While training them to conduct the interviews about fertility and how many children farmers wanted, we recorded the following exchange between a twenty-four-year-old high school-educated male interviewer and a thirty-five-year-old Jean Rabel farmer who is the father of six children:

Interviewer: What quantity of children is best to have?

Farmer: Okay. Quantity of children that is best? Ah, there, eh. . . . There are no children better than other children.

Interviewer: No. What quantity. As in number. I could say three, four children, five, six children. What quantity do you see as best?

Farmer: The biggest child. That's the one for me.

Interviewer: It is not the biggest or the smallest! Quantity! That means if you have a quantity of children, four children, five children. Which is best?

Farmer: It is best you have two, three, or six. If God gives them to you, it is best you take them.

Interviewer: Okay. Why do you say three children?

As exemplified in the exchange, our informants, similar to small farmers throughout Haiti, were stubbornly resistant to saying how many children they wanted—perhaps because they too knew that they were not supposed to want many. In contrast, the interviewers, high school-educated and seasoned participants in NGO seminars, tended to make the decision for them, consistently in the direction they thought proper (fewer children). Exchanges such as this, highly typical, destroyed any hope of directly measuring the number of children farmers really wanted; we could retrain the interviewer—at least we thought we could—but we could not make the farmers less elusive.

To get around the problem we introduced this question: "A husband and wife with three children versus one with six children, which is economically better off?" The problem, initially at least, did not end there. The following interview involved a twenty-six-year-old female university-educated interviewer questioning a thirty-four-year-old rural mother of five:

Interviewer: Who is better off, a couple with three children or the couple with six children?

Mother: All children are good.

Interviewer: No. I am asking you, respond three or respond six.

Mother: Eh, if, eh. Okay. Normally, concerning children, if God gives you three children, he doesn't give you any more, you just have to live with what God gave you.

Interviewer: Yes. You have to live with what he gave you. But it is a question that I am asking you.

Mother: I am following you *Madanmwazel*. Honestly.

Interviewer: Yes. I understand. "Honestly." But I am asking you, concerning this question, three or six, which is better? You must decide if it is three or six.

     (Silence)

Mother: Six.

Interviewer: Why?

Mother: They are there. They will help you.

Interviewer: Three can help you too. But six?

Mother: Yes, six. Six can help you more. Some will go to the garden. Some to the
                   water. Some will do laundry.

Interviewer: (Silence)

Mother: Okay. Three.

Conclusion

The trend toward a plethora of nondemonstrable explanations that contradict hard data
regarding causes of important issues such as high fertility, kinship, family, and courtship
practices has largely undermined an understanding of what motivates people in
impoverished or "under-globalized" areas of the world. In chapter 2 I showed that the
trend is especially evident in the Caribbean, particularly Haiti, where scholars have
provided excellent studies and abundant data showing the critical importance of children
to household livelihood strategies in a harsh economic and natural environment only to
then contradict their own data with conclusions that appeal to culture, tradition, and
ideational values without ever explaining why these values persist or how they come
about in the first place. More controversial than the fact that scholars downplay the
importance of child labor is why they have done this. Why, despite overwhelming
empirical evidence—evidence that many academics accepted in the 1960s and 1970s —
do recent scholars reject the importance of child labor as a determinant of high birth
rates? As I explained, I believe the answer is best found in the values of the
anthropologists and in the value campaigns associated with the organizations that fund
most anthropological studies.

What we see in this bias is the connection between social scientists, their own
system, and the most powerful developed governments in the world. Anthropologists are
one manifestation of Western and elite Judeo-Christian hegemony exercised through the
control of states and international organizations. Be it a campaign to reduce fertility, to
promote feminist values, democracy, or corporate interests, anthropologists issue forth
from the academies and scatter about the world collecting data precisely in response to
funds made available by the most powerful institutions in the world, institutions such as
the U.S. government, the Ford Foundation, the EU, the UN, and the World Bank.
Whether this is good or bad, right or wrong, is not the issue. Studies of birth rates or
substance abuse or marriage patterns or homosexuality are inextricably linked to the
promotion or repression of these practices. In addition to their own values, the agendas of
funding agencies and competition among scholars and NGOs for funding compel
anthropologists to bias their conclusions. Funding agencies' "value campaigns" also have
an impact on our informants, an impact beyond the reach of newly arrived
anthropologists but one that can determine the outcome and conclusions of our studies.
Haitians and other impoverished informants have been taught what we want to hear: that
beating children is wrong; that babies should be exclusively breastfed; that fewer
children are better than many children; that children must be sent to school. This makes it
difficult to reveal what impoverished people really believe and aspire to.

Notes

1. In his 1957 study, Frazier, himself African American, accused wealthy blacks of accepting, "unconditionally, the values of the white bourgeois world" because "they do not truly identify themselves with Negroes."

2. Herskovits came to be associated with explanations for Caribbean family patterns based solely on African survivals and Frazier became identified—somewhat unfairly—with a slavery origins argument. These theoretical positions persist in the literature today. In respect to family patterns, Barrow (1986), and Sutton and Makiesky-Barrow (1970: 297) emphasize both approaches. Abraham (1993) recently argued in favor of slavery as a primary condition for the emergence of modern Caribbean family patterns.

3. The problem with matrifocality and the misuse of the concept is also exemplified in another prominent work. Safa (1986), an excellent field researcher/anthropologist and a leading feminist scholar who was seen above saying that "Caribbean women learned not to depend on men for financial or even emotional support," expanded on this misrepresentation, subsequently titling a book *Myth of the Male Breadwinner* (1995), thus bequeathing to a generation of anthropologists the enduring image of Caribbean women being historically independent of financial support from men. She drove the point home in her introductions with sweeping conclusions and claims regarding the English Caribbean tradition of "matrifocality" as if it were a self-perpetuating institution, something that had little to do with reality or even with her own findings. Her studies were not about the historic Caribbean, nor were they about the English or French Caribbean; they were carried out in the Spanish Caribbean, an area so socioeconomically distinct that Safa herself is one of the few researchers to have ever made a comparison. Moreover, her studies in the Spanish Caribbean demonstrated not that there was a historic tradition of "matrifocality"—as she claimed—but rather the contrary, that "matrifocality" was a response to increasing urbanization and industrialization. Indeed, given her evidence for nonhistorical causation, a better title for Safa's book would have been Myth of Matrifocality (for a similar conclusion regarding matrifocality and feminism see Branche 2002: 89). As for the "mythical male breadwinner," it was seen in chapter 17 that in the traditional Caribbean he really existed. Or at least some version of him.

4. See Catherine Maternowska (1996) for an excellent investigation of the problems of insensitive health care workers and contraceptive distribution in the Port-au-Prince slum area of Cité Soleil.

5. Sub-Commission on the Promotion and Protection of Human Rights Working Group on Contemporary Forms of Slavery, 25th Session, Geneva.

Works Cited

AAA (AgroActionAllemande). 1998. Market Analysis of Jean Rabel Unpublished report by Thomas Hartmanship. Bonn: Germany.

Abraham, Eva. 1993. Caught in the shift: The impact of industrialization on the female-headed households in Curacao, Netherlands Antilles. In *Where did all the men go?*, ed. J. Mencher and A. Okongwu. Boulder, CO: Westview.

Adams, Lorraine. 1994. North didn't relay drug tips. *Washington Post*, Oct. 22: 1.

Allman, James. 1980. Sexual union in rural Haiti. *International Journal of Sociology of the Family* 10:15–39.

———. 1982a. Haitian migration: 30 years assessed. *Migration Today* (1):7–12.

———. 1982b. Fertility and family planning in Haiti. *Studies in Family Planning* 13(8/9):237–45.

Allman, James, and J. May. 1979. Fertility, mortality, migration and family planning in Haiti. *Population Studies* 33(3):505–21.

Alphonse, Henri. 1996. Haiti-agriculture: last battle of the coffee planters. Amsterdam: InterPress Third World News Agency (IPS).

Ashcraft, Norman. 1968. Some aspects of domestic organization in British Honduras. In *The family in the Caribbean: Proceedings of the first Conference on the Family in the Caribbean, St. Thomas, Virgin Islands, March 21–23*, 63–73. Rio Piedras, P.R.: Institute of Caribbean Studies, University of Puerto Rico.

Augelli, John P. 1953. Patterns and problems of land tenure in the Lesser Antilles, B.W.I. *Economic Geography* 29(4):362–67.

Aymer, Paula L. 1997. Coming from the Caribbean: Knowledge production and cultural transformations. In *Uprooted women: Migrant domestics in the Caribbean*. Westport, CT: Praeger.

Baber, Willie L. 1982. Social change and the peasant community: Horowitz's Morne Peasant reinterpreted. *Ethnology* 21(3):227–41.

Balch, Emily Greene. 1927. *Occupied Haiti*. New York: The Writers Publishing Company.

Barickman, B. J.1994. "A bit of land, which they call roca:" Slave provision grounds in the Bahian Reconcavo, 1780–1860. *The Hispanic American Historical Review* 74(4):649–87.

Barrow, Christine. 1986. Finding the support: A study of strategies for survival. *Social and Economic Studies* 35(2):131–77.

———, ed. 1997. *Caribbean portraits: Essays on gender ideologies and identities*. Kingston, Jamaica: Ian Randle Publishers.

Bastien, Remy. 1961. Haitian rural family organization. *Social and Economic Studies* 10(4):478–510.

Bazile, Robert. 1967. Demographic statistics in Haiti. In *The Haitian potential.* New York: Teachers College Press.

Becker, Gary. 1960. An economic analysis of fertility. In *Demographic and economic change in developed countries: A conference of the universities—National Bureau Committee for Economic Research*, 209–31. Princeton: Princeton University Press.

Beckett, Greg. 2004. Master of the wood: Moral authority and political imaginaries in Haiti. *PoLAR: The Political and Legal Anthropology Review* 27(2):1–19.

Beckford, George. 1972. *Persistent poverty: Underdevelopment in plantation economies of the third world.* New York: Oxford University Press.

Berggren, Gretchen, Nirmala Murthy, and Stephen J Williams. 1974. Rural Haitian women: An analysis of fertility rates. *Social Biology* 21:368–78.

Berleant-Schiller, Riva. 1978. The failure of agricultural development in post-emancipation Barbuda: A study of social and economic continuity in a West Indian community. In *Boletin de Estudiois Latinoamericanos y del Caribe*, Dec 25:21–36.

Bernstein, Dennis, and Howard Levine. 1993. The CIA's Haitian connection. *San Francisco Bay Guardian*, November 3.

Bethel, Nicolette. 1993. Bahamian kinship and the power of women. Master's thesis, Corpus Christi College.

BiblioMundo. 2006. Haiti La Diaspora. At www.bibliomonde.net/donnee/haiti-diaspora-293.html, accessed April 19.

Bilsborrow, Richard E. 1987. Population pressures and agricultural development: A conceptual framework and recent evidence. *World Development* 15(2):183–203.

Bilsborrow, Richard E., and C. R. Winegarden. 1985. Landholding, rural fertility and internal migration in developing countries: Econometric evidence from cross-national as data. *Pakistan Development Review* 24(2):125–49.

Blackwood, Evelyn. 2005. Wedding bell blues: Marriage, missing men, and matrifocal follies. *American Ethnologist* 32(1):3–19.

Blake, Judith. 1954. Family instability and reproductive behavior in Jamaica. Milbank Memorial Annual Conference:26–61.

———. 1961. *Family structure in Jamaica; the social context of reproduction.* In collaboration with J. Mayone Stycos and Kingsley Davis. New York: Free Press of Glencoe.

Blumberg, Rae Lesser. 1993. *Where did all the men go?* Boulder, CO: Westview.

Blurton-Jones, Nichol. 1993. The lives of hunter and gatherer children: Effects of parental behavior and parental reproductive strategy. In *Juvenile primates*, ed. Michael E. Pereira and Lynn A. Fairbanks, 309–26. Oxford: Oxford University Press.

Bock, John, and Sara E. Johnson. 2004. Subsistence ecology and play among the Okavanga Delta people of Botswana. *Human Nature* 15(1):63–82.

Bongaarts John. 1978. A framework for analyzing the proximate determinants of fertility. *Population and Development Review* 4(1):105–32.

———. 1982. The fertility-inhibiting effects of the intermediate fertility variables. *Studies In Family Planning* 13(6/7):179–89.

———. 1987. The proximate determinants of exceptionally high fertility. *Population and Development Review* 13(1):133–39.

Bongaarts, John, and Robert C. Potter. 1983. *Fertility, biology, and behavior: An analysis of the proximate determinants.* New York: Academic Press.

Bongaarts, John, O. Frank, and R. Lesthaeghe. 1984. The proximate determinants of fertility in sub-Saharan Africa. *Population and Development Review* 10(3):511–37.

Boserup, Ester 1965. *The condition of agricultural growth: The economics of agrarian change under population pressure.* Chicago: Aldine.

Bouwkamp, John C. 1985. *Sweet potato products: A natural resource for the tropics*. Boca Raton, FL: CRC Press.

Branche, C. 2002. Ambivalence, sexuality, and violence in the construction of Caribbean masculinity: dangers for boys in Jamaica. In *Children's rights: Caribbean realities*, ed. C. Barrow. Jamaica: Ian Randle.

Brereton, Bridget. 1989. Society and culture in the Caribbean. In *The modern Caribbean*, ed. Franklin W. Knight and Colin A. Palmer. Chapel Hill: University of North Carolina Press.

Britannica Concise Encyclopedia. 2007. www.answers.com/topic/french-guiana ?cat=travel.

Brittain, Ann W. 1990. Migration and the demographic transition: A West Indian example. *Social and Economic Studies* 39(3):39–64.

———. 1991a. Anticipated child loss to migration and sustained high fertility in an East Caribbean population. *Social Biology* 38(1-2):94-112

———. 1991b. Can women remember how many children they have borne? Data from the east Caribbean. *Social Biology* 38(3-4):319–32.

Brockerhoff, Martin, and Xiushi Yang. 1994. Impact of migration on fertility in sub-Saharan Africa. *Social Biology* 41(1-2):19–43.

Brodber, E. 1974. *Abandonment of children in Jamaica*. Kingston, Jamaica: Institute of Social and Economic Research, University of West Indies.

———. 1986. African-Jamaican women at the turn of the century. *Social and Economic Studies* 45:23–60.

Brown, Janet. 2002. Gender and family in the Caribbean. At www.kit.nl/exchange/ html/2002-4_gender_and_family_in_th.asp.

———. 2007. Fatherhood in the Caribbean: Examples of support for men's work in relation to family life. In *Gender equality and men: Learning from practice*, ed. Sandy Ruxton, 113–30. At www.oxfam.org.uk/what_we_do/resources/downloads/gem-13.pdf.

Buschkens, W. F. L. 1974. *The family system of the Paramaribo Creoles*. Gravenhage: M. Nijhoff.

Cadet, Jean-Robert. 1998. *Restavec: From Haitian slave child to middle-class American*. Austin: University of Texas Press.

Cain, Mead. 1977. The economic activities of children in a village in Bangladesh. *Population and Development Review* 3:201–7.

Caldwell, John C. 1976. Toward a restatement of demographic transition theory. *Population and Development Review* 2(3/4):321–66.

———. 1982. *Theory of fertility decline*. San Francisco: Academic Press.

Caldwell, John C., and Pat Caldwell. 1987. The cultural context of high fertility in sub-Saharan Africa. *Population and Development Review* 13(3): 409–37.

Camus, Michel-Christian. 1993. Filibuste et pouvoir royal. *Revue de la Société Haitienne d'Histoire et de Geographie* 49(175).

CARE. 1996. A baseline study of livelihood security in northwest Haiti. Tucson, AZ: The Bureau of Applied Research in Anthropology, University of Arizona.

———. 1997. An update of household livelihood security in Northwest Haiti monitoring targeting impact evaluation/Unit December. Port-au-Prince, Haiti: CARE International.

Castor, Suzy. 1971. *La occupation norteamericana de Haiti y sus consequencias*. Mexico: Siglo Veintiuno Editores.

CELADE (Centro Latinoamericano y Caribeño de Demografía). 2000. América Latina: Proyecciones de población urbano–rural population 1970–2025 [Latin America: Projection Of Urban–Rural Population 1970–2025]. Santiago, Chile: Centro Latinoamericano y Caribeño de Demografía (CELADE / CEPAL). Available at www.eclac.cl/Celade/publica/bol63/BD63.html, accessed April 30, 2006.

Census Records. n.d. Archives de France, Section D'outre-Mer, Aix-En-Provence, G1/509.

Charbit, Yves. 1984. WFS Scientific Reports no. 65. Voorburg, Netherlands: International Statistical Institute.

Chayanov, A. V. 1925. *Peasant farm organization*. Moscow: The Co-operative Publishing House.

Chevalier, George-Ary. 1938. Etude sur la colonisation francaise en Haiti: Origines et developpement des propriétès Collette. *Revue de la Société Haitienne d'Histoire et de Geographie* 9(31).

———. 1939. Etude sur la colonisation Francaise a Saint-Domingue. *Revue de la Société Haitienne d'Histoire et de Geographie* 10(33).

———. 1940. Un colon de Saint-Domingue pendant la révolution. Pierre Collette, Planteur de Jean Rabel. *Revue de la Société Haitienne d'Histoire et de Geographie* 12(36).

Chevannes, B. 2002. Fatherhood in the African-Caribbean landscape: An exploration in meaning and context. In *Children's rights: Caribbean realities*, ed. C. Barrow. Jamaica: Ian Randle.

Chomsky, Noam. 2004. U.S. & Haiti. *Third World Traveler Z*. At www.thirdworld traveler.com/Haiti/US_Haiti_Chomsky.html, accessed February 3, 2007.

CIA. 2007. *World Fact Book*. At www.cia.gov/cia/publications/factbook, accessed April 15, 2006.

Clarke, E. 1966 (originally published in 1957). *My mother who fathered me: A study of the family in three selected communities in Jamaica*, 2nd ed. London: George Allen and Unwin.

Clement, Christopher. 1997. Returning Aristide: The contradictions in US foreign policy in Haiti. *Race and Class* 39(2):21–36.

Clesca, Eddy. 1984. La domesticité juvénile est-elle une conséquence du sousdeveloppement ou le produit de la mentalité d'un peuple? In *Colloque sur l'enfance en domesticité*. Conference Report, Institut du Bien-Etre Social et de Recherche & UNICEF.

Coale, A. 1986. The decline of fertility in Europe since the eighteenth century as a chapter in demographic history. In *The decline of fertility in Europe*, ed. Coale and Watkins, 1–30. Princeton: Princeton University Press.

Cock, James H. 1985. *Cassava: New potential for a neglected crop*. Boulder, CO: Westview.

Cohen, Yehudi A. 1956. Structure and function: Family organization and socialization in a Jamaican community. *American Anthropologist* 58:664–87.

Cole, Johnnetta B. 1985. Africanisms in the Americas: A brief history of the concept. *Anthropology and Humanism Quarterly* 10(4):120–26.

Comhaire-Sylvain, Suzanne. 1958. Courtship, marriage and plasaj at Kenskoff, Haiti. *Social and Economic Studies* 7:210–33.

———. 1961. The household at Kenscoff, Haiti. *Social and Economic Studies* 10:192–222.

Comitas, Lambros. 1964. Occupational multiplicity in rural Jamaica. In *Proceedings of the American Ethnological Society*, ed. E. Garfield and E. Friedl, 41–50. Seattle: University of Washington Press.

Corbett, Bob. n.d. Haiti: Miscellaneous topics. At www.webster.edu/~corbetre/Haiti/misctopic/misctopic.htm, accessed April 6, 2006.

Coreil, Jeanine. 1980. Traditional and Western responses to an anthrax epidemic in rural Haiti. *Medical Anthropology* 4:79–105.

Coreil, Jeanine, Deborah L. Barnes-Josiah, Antoine Agustin, and Michel Cayemittes. 1996. Arrested pregnancy syndrome in Haiti: Findings from a national survey. *Medical Anthropology Quarterly*, New Series, 10(3):424–36.

Courlander, Harold. 1960. *The Hoe and the drum: Life and lore of the Haitian people*. Berkeley: University of California Press.

Cousins, W. M. 1935. Slave family life in the British colonies: 1800–1834. *The Sociological Review* 27:35–55.

Crahan, Margaret E., Franklin W. Wright, and Roger N. Buckley, eds. 1980. *Africa and the Caribbean: The legacies of a link*. Baltimore: John Hopkins University Press.

Crane, Julia G. 1971. *Educated to migrate: The social organization of Saba*. Assen, Netherlands: van Gorcum.

Cross, Gary. 2004. *The cute and the cool: Wondrous innocence and modern American children's culture*. New York: Oxford University Press.

Crowley, Daniel J. 1957. Song and dance in St. Lucia. *Ethnomusicology* 9 (January):4–14.

Cumper, George E. 1961. Household and occupation in Barbados. *Social and Economic Studies* 10(1):386–419.

Dalton, George. 1974. How exactly are peasants "exploited"? *American Anthropologist* 76(3):553–61.

D'Amico-Samuels, Deborah. 1988. Review of *Coping with poverty: Adaptive strategies in a Caribbean village* by Hymie Rubenstein. *American Ethnologist* 15(4):785–86.

Das Gupta, M. 1994. What motivates fertility decline? A case study from Punjab, India. In *Understanding reproductive change: Kenya, Tamil Nadu, Punjab, Costa Rica*, ed. B. Egero, M. Hammarskjold, 101–33. Lund, Sweden: Lund University Press.

Davenport, William. 1961. The family system of Jamaica. *Social and Economic Studies*, 4(1):420–54.

Davis, Kingsley. 1963. The theory of change and response in modern demographic history. *Population Index* 29:345–66.

Davis, Kingsley, and Judith Blake. 1956. Social structure and fertility: An analytical framework. *Economic Development and Cultural Change* 4(4):211–35.

Deere, Carmen, Peggy Antrobus, Lynn Bolles, Edwin Melendez, Peter Phillips, Marcia Rivera, and Helen Safa. 1990. In *The shadows of the sun: Caribbean development alternatives and U.S. policy*. Boulder, CO: Westview.

Dehavenon, A. 1993. Where did all the men go? An etic model for the cross-cultural study of the causes of matrifocality. In *Where did all the men go?*, ed. J. Mencher and A. Okongwu. Boulder, CO: Westview.

DeLancey, V. 1990. Socioeconomic consequences of high fertility for the family. In *Population growth and reproduction in sub Saharan Africa: Technical analyses of fertility and its consequences*, ed. G. T. F. Acsadi, G. J. Acsadi, and R. A. Bulatao, 115–30. Washington, DC: World Bank.

Denton, E. Hazel. 1979. Economic determinants of fertility in Jamaica. *Population Studies* 33(2):295–305.

Divinski, Randy, Rachel Hecksher, and Jonathan Woodbridge, eds. 1998. *Haitian women: Life on the front lines*. London: PBI (Peace Brigades International). At www.peacebrigades.org/bulletin.html.

Doggett, Hugh. 1988. *Sorghum*. New York: John Wiley.

Dorélien, Renand. 1990 [1984]. *Résumé de la communication sur « interprétation des données statistiques relatives à l'enfance en domesticité recueillies à partir des résultats d'un échantillon tiré du recensement de 1982.»* Atelier de travail sur l'enfance en domesticité. Port-au-Prince, 5, 6 et 7 décembre 1990. Port-au-Prince: Institut du Bien-Etre Social et de Recherche & IHSI.

Doyle, Kate. 1994. Hollow diplomacy in Haiti. *World Policy Journal* 11(1):50–58.

Driver, Tom. 1996. USAID and Wages (contribution to a dialog on Bob Corbett's Haiti list). At www.hartford-hwp.com/archives/43a/index-d.html, accessed September 3, 2008.

Duany, Jorge. 1984. Popular music in Puerto Rico: Toward an anthropology of "Salsa." *Latin American Music Review* 5(2):186–216.

Durant-Gonzalez, Victoria. 1976. Role and status of rural Jamaican women: Higglering and mothering. Master's thesis, University of California, Berkeley.

Eaton, Joseph W., and Albert J. Mayer. 1953. The social biology of very high fertility among the Hutterites: The demography of a unique population. *Human Biology*, 25:206–64.

Ebanks, G. Edward. 1973. Fertility, union status, and partners. *International Journal of Sociology and the Family* 3(1):48–60.

Ebanks, G. Edward, P. M. George, and Charles E. Nobbe. 1974. Fertility and number of partnerships in Barbados. *Population Studies* 28(3): 449–61.

Ebanks, G. Edward and Charles E. Nobbe. 1975. Emigration and fertility decline: The case of Barbados. *Demography* 12(3):431–45.

EMMUS-I. 1994/1995. Enquete Mortalite, Morbidite et Utilisation des Services (EMMUS-I). eds. Michel Cayemittes, Antonio Rival, Bernard Barrere, Gerald Lerebours, Michaele Amedee Gedeon. Haiti, Institut Haitien de L'Enfance Petionville and Calverton, MD: Macro International.

EMMUS-II. 2000. Enquête Mortalité, Morbidité et Utilisation des Services, Haiti 2000 (EMMUS-II). Cayemittes, Michel, Florence Placide, Bernard Barrère, Soumaila Mariko, Blaise Sévère. Haiti: Institut Haitien de L'Enfance Petionville and Calverton, MD: Macro International.

EMMUS-III. 2005/2006. Enquête mortalité, morbidité et utilisation des services, Haiti 2000 (EMMUS-II). Cayemittes, Michel, Haiti: Institut Haitien de L'Enfance Petionville and Calverton, MD : Macro International.

FAO (Food and Agricultural Organization of the United States). 2006. *The state of food and agriculture.* Prepared by a team from the Agriculture and Economic Development Analysis Division. F.L. Zegarra, team leader. At www.fao.org/docrep/ v6800e/V6800E02.htm, accessed May 2, 2006.

Fass, Simon. 1988. *Political economy in Haiti: The drama of survival.* New Brunswick, NJ: Transaction.

Feight, C. B., T. S. Johnson, B. J. Martin, K. E. Sparkes, and W. W. Wagner. 1978. Secondary amenorrhea in athletes. *Lancet* 2:1145–46.

Foner, Nancy, and R. Napoli. 1978. Jamaican and Black American migrant farm-workers: A comparative analysis. *Social Problems* 25:491–503.

Foster, George M. 1953. Cofradia and compadrazgo in Spain and Spanish America. *Southwestern Journal of Anthropology* 9:1–28.

———. 1969. Compadrazgo and social networks in Tzintzuntzan. *Southwestern Journal of Anthropology* 25:261–78.

Francis, Donette A. 2004. Silences too horrific to disturb: Writing sexual histories in Edwidge Danticat's *Breath, eyes, memory. Research in African Literatures* 35(2):75–90.

Frazier, E. Franklin. 1939. *The Negro family in the United States.* Chicago: University of Chicago Press.

———. 1957. *Black bourgeoisie: The rise of a new middle class.* Glencoe: The Free Press.

Freeman, Ronald. 1962. The sociology of human fertility: A trend report and bibliography. *Current Sociology* 11(2):35–68.

Freilich, Morris. 1967. Review of *The Andros Islanders: A study of family organization in the Bahamas*, by Keith Otterbein. *American Anthropologist* 69(2):239.

———. 1968. Sex, secrets and systems. In *The family in the Caribbean: Proceedings of the first conference on the family in the Caribbean, St. Thomas, Virgin Islands,* March 21–23, 47–62. Rio Piedras, P.R.: Institute of Caribbean Studies, University of Puerto Rico.

Friedlander, Dov. 1969. Demographic responses and population change. *Demography* 6(4):359–81.

Frisch, R. E. 1978. Population, food intake and fertility. Science 199(4324):22–30.

Frisch, R. E., and J. W. McArthur. 1974. Menstrual cycles: Fatness as a determinant of minimum weight for height necessary for their maintenance or onset. *Science* 185:949–51.

Frisch, R. E., R. Revelle, and S. Cook. 1971. Height, weight and age at menarche and the "critical weight" hypothesis. *Science* 194: 1148.

Frucht, Richard. 1968. Emigration, remittances, and social change: Aspects of the social field of Nevis, West Indies. *Anthropologica* 10(2):193–208.

———. 1971. Black society in the New World. New York: Random House.

Fuller, Anne. 2005. Challenging violence: Haitian women unite women's rights and human rights special bulletin on women and war. At acas.prairienet.org. accessed October 19, 2006. Originally published in the Spring/Summer 1999 by the Association of Concerned Africa Scholars.

Fund for Peace and Foreign Policy. 2007. The failed states index. *Foreign Policy.* At www.foreignpolicy.com/story/cms.php?story_id=3865.

Fuson, Robert H. 1987. *The log of Christopher Columbus.* Trans. by Robert H Fuson. Camden, ME: International Marine.

Gambrell, Alice. 1997. *Women, intellectuals, modernism, and difference: Transatlantic culture 1919–1945.* Cambridge: Cambridge University Press.

Gardner, Richard, and Aaron M. Podolefsky. 1977. Some further considerations on West Indian conjugal patterns. *Ethnology* 16(3): 299–308.

Gaspar, Barry. 1991. Antigua slaves and their struggle to survive. In *Seeds of change,* ed. H. Viola and C. Margolis, 130–37. Washington, DC: Smithsonian Institution Press.

Gearing, Margaret Jean. 1988. *The reproduction of labor in a migration society: Gender, kinship, and household in St. Vincent, West Indies.* Dissertation, University of Florida, Gainesville.

Geggus, David Patrick. 1982. *Slavery, war, and revolution: The British occupation of Saint Domingue 1793–1798.* Oxford: Clarendon Press.

Georges, Josiane. 2004. *Trade and the disappearance of Haitian rice.* Ted Case Studies Number 725. At www.american.edu/TED/Haitirice.htm, accessed April 4, 2006.

González, Nancie L. 1969 [1958]. *Black Carib household structure: A study of migration and modernization.* Seattle: University of Washington Press.

———. 1970. Toward a definition of matrifocality. *Afro-American anthropology: Contemporary perspectives,* ed. Norman E. Whitten and John F. Szwed. New York: The Free Press.

———. 1979. *La estructura del grupo familiar entre los Caribes Negros Guatemala,* Ministry of Education, 1st ed.

———. 1984. Rethinking the consanguineal household and matrifocality. *Ethnology* 23(1):1–15.

Graham S. 1985. Running and menstrual dysfunction: Recent medical discoveries provide new insight into the human division of labor by sex. *American Anthropologist* 87:878–992.

Green, Howard. 1979. Basin migration and dollar flows. Caribbean basin economic survey 5(2):12–15.

Green, William A. 1977. Caribbean historiography, 1600–1900: The recent tide. *Journal of Interdisciplinary* 7(3): 509–30.

Greene, Margaret E. and Ann E. Biddlecom. 2000. Absent and problematic men: Demographic accounts of male reproductive roles. *Population and Development Review* 26(1):81–115.

Greenfield, Gerald Michael. 1994. *Latin American urbanization: Historical profiles of major cities.* Westport, CT: Greenwood.

Greenfield, Sidney M. 1961. Socio-economic factors and family form: A Barbadian case study. *Social and Economic Studies* 10(1):72–85.

———. 1966. *English rustics in black skin.* New Haven: College University.

Griffith, David C. 1985. Women remittances and reproduction. *American Ethnologist* 12(4):676–90.

Grossman, Lawrence S. 1997. Soil conservation, political ecology, and technological change on St. Vincent. *Geographical Review* 87(3):353–74.

Guengant, Jean-Pierre. 1985. Caribbean population dynamics: emigration and fertility challenges. Conference of Caribbean parliamentarians, Heywoods, Barbados.

Hallward, Peter. 2004. Option zero In Haiti. *New Left Review* 27. At newleftreview.org/A2507.

Handwerker, W. Penn. 1983. The first demographic transition: An analysis of subsistence choices and reproductive consequences. *American Anthropologist* 85:5–27.

———. 1986. The modern demographic transition. *American Anthropologist* 88:400–17.

———. 1989. *Women's power and social revolution: Fertility transition in the West Indies.* Newbury Park: Sage.

———. 1993. Empowerment and fertility transition on Antigua, WI: Education, employment, and the moral economy of childbearing. *Human Organization* 52(1):41–52.

Harner, Michael J. 1970. Population pressure and the social evolution of agriculturalists. *Southwestern Journal of Anthropology* 26: 67–86.

Harris, Marvin. 1968. *The rise of anthropological theory.* New York: Harper & Row.

———. 1979. *Cultural materialism: The struggle for a science of culture.* New York: Random House.

Harris, Marvin, and Eric B. Ross. 1987. *Death, sex, and fertility.* New York: Columbia University Press.

Harrison, Lawrence E. 1991. The cultural roots of Haitian underdevelopment. In *Small country development and international labor flows,* ed. Anthony P. Maingot. Boulder, CO: Westview.

Hawley, A.1950. *Human ecology.* New York: Ronald.

Heath, B. J. 1988. Afro-Caribbean ware: A study of ethnicity on St. Eustatius. Dissertation, University of Pennsylvania.

Henriques, Fernando. 1949. West Indian family organization. *American Journal of Sociology* 55(1):30–37.

Henshall, Janet D. 1966. The demographic factor in the structure of agriculture in Barbados. *Transactions of the Institute of British Geographers* 38:183–95.

Herskovits, Melville J. 1925. The Negro's Americanism. In *The New Negro,* ed. Alain Locke. New York: Albert and Charles Boni.

———. 1937. *Life in a Haitian valley.* New York: Alfred A. Knopf.

Hill, Donald R. 1977. *The impact of migration on the metropolitan and folk society of Carriacou, Grenada 54.* Part 2, Anthropological Papers of the American Museum of Natural History. New York: AMNH.

Ho, Christine G. T. 1999. Caribbean transnationalism as a gendered process. *Latin American Perspectives* 26(5):34–54.

Hobart, Mark, ed. 1993. *An anthropological critique of ignorance: The growth of ignorance.* New York: Routledge.

Horowitz, M. 1959. Morne-Paysan: Peasant village in Martinique. Dissertation, Columbia University.

———. 1967. *Morne-Paysan, peasant village in Martinique.* New York: Holt, Rinehart & Winston.

Hostetler, John A. 1974. *Hutterite society.* Baltimore: The Johns Hopkins University Press.

Howell, Nancy. 1979. *Demography of the Dobe !Kung.* New York: Academic.

HSKI (Haitian Street Kids Inc). 2007. Family circle boys home: The solution. At quicksitemaker.com/members/immunenation/index.html.

Hugo G. 1997. Intergenerational wealth flows and the elderly in Indonesia. In *The continuing demographic transition,* ed. G. W. Jones, R. M. Douglas, J. C. Caldwell, R. M. D'Souza, 111–33. New York: Oxford University Press.

Ibberson, Dora. 1956. Illegitimacy and the birth rate. *Social and Economic Studies* 5:93–99.

Iverson, Shepherd. 1992. Evolutionary demographic transition theory: comparative causes of prehistoric, historic and modern demographic transitions. Dissertation, University of Florida, Gainesville.

Jackson, J. 1982. Stresses affecting women and their families. In *Women in the Caribbean project,* ed. J. Massiah, 28–61. Cave Hill, Barbados: Institute of Social and Economic Research, University of the West Indies.

Johnson, Allen W., and Timothy Earle. 1987. *The evolution of human societies.* California:

Stanford University Press.

Joy, Elizabeth. 1997. Team management of the Female Athlete Triad. *Round Table* 25(3):95.

Keen, F. G. B. 1978. Ecological relationships in a Hmong (Meo) economy. In *Farmers in the forest: Economic development and marginal agriculture in Northern Thailand*, ed. Peter Kunstadter, E. C. Champan, S. Sakhasi, 210–21. Honolulu: University of Hawaii Press.

Kerr, Madeline 1952. *Personality and conflict in Jamaica*. Liverpool: University Press.

Kundstadter, Peter. 1963. A survey of the consanguine or matrifocal family. *American Anthropologist* 65:56–66.

———, ed. 1967. *Southeast Asian tribes, minorities, and nations*. Princeton, NJ: Princeton University Press.

———. 1971. Natality, mortality and migration of upland and lowland populations in northwestern Thailand. In *Culture and population: A collection of current studies*, ed. Stephen Polgar, 46–60. Cambridge, MA: Schenkman.

———. 1983. Cultural ideals, socioeconomic change, and household composition: Karen Lua', Hmong and Thai in Northwestern Thailand. In *Households: Comparative and historical studies of the domestic group*, ed. Robert McC. Netting, Richard R. Wilk, and Eric J. Arnould, 299–329. Berkeley: University of California Press.

———. 1993. *Man in the mangroves: The socio-economic situation of human settlements in mangrove forests*. The United Nations University. Tokyo, Japan.

———. 2002. *Human population dynamics: Cross-disciplinary perspectives*. Helen Macbeth and Paul Collinson, eds. Cambridge, UK: Cambridge University Press.

———. 2004. Hmong marriage patterns in Thailand in relation to social change. In *Hmong/Miao in Asia*, ed. N. Tapp, J. Michaud, C. Culas, and G. Y. Lee. Chiang Mai, Thailand: Silkworm.

Lagro, Monique. 1990. *The hucksters of Dominica*. Port of Spain: United Nations Economic Commission for Latin America and the Caribbean.

Lagro, Monique and Donna Plotkin. 1990. *The agricultural traders of St. Vincent and the Grenadines, Grenada, Dominica and St. Lucia*. New York: United Nations Economic Commission for Latin America and the Caribbean.

Laguerre, Michel. 1979. *Études sur le vodou Haïtien: Bibliographie analytique*. Fonds St-Jacques: Centre de recherches Caribes.

Lancy, David. 2007. Accounting for variability in mother-child play. *American Anthropologist* 109(2):273–84.

Larsen Ula, and James W. Vaupel. 1993. Hutterite fecundability by age and parity strategies for fertility modeling of event histories. *Demography* 30(1):22.

Larson, Eric H. 1981. The effects of plantation economy on a Polynesian population. In *And the poor get children*, ed. Karen L. Michaelson, 39–49. New York: Monthly Review.

Lazarus-Black, Mindie. 2001. Interrogating the phenomenon of denial: Contesting paternity in Caribbean magistrates' courts. *Political and Legal Anthropology Review* 24(1):13–37.

Lee, B. S. and S. C. Farber. 1984. The influence of rapid rural-urban migration on Korean national fertility levels. *Journal of Development Economics* 17:47–71.

Lee, R. 1996. A cross-cultural perspective on intergenerational transfers and the economic life cycle. In *Seminar on intergenerational economic relations and demographic change: Papers*, 1–25. Liege, Belgium: International Union for the Scientific Study of Population [IUSSP], Committee on Economic Demography.

Lee, Y. J., W. L. Parish, and R. J. Willis.1994. Sons, daughters, and intergenerational support in Taiwan. *American Journal of Sociology* 99:1010–41.

Lenaghan, Tom. 2005. Haitian Bleu: A rare taste of success for Haiti's coffee growers. Development Alternatives Inc. At www.dai.com/pdf/developments/HaitianBleu-DAIdeasDec05.pdf, accessed April 20, 2006.

Leo-Rhynie, E. A. 1997. Class, race, and gender issues in child rearing in the Caribbean. In *Caribbean families: Diversity among ethnic groups*, ed. J. L. Rooparine & J. Brown, 25–56. Greenwich, CT: Ablex.

Lewis, David Levering. 1981. *When Harlem was in vogue*. New York: Alfred A. Knopf.

Lewis, Linden. 2003. Gender tension and change in the contemporary Caribbean. From expert group meeting on "The role of men and boys in achieving gender equality." DAW in collaboration with ILO and UNAIDS, 21–24 October 2003 Brasilia, Brazil.

Leyburn, James G. 1966 [1941]. *The Haitian people*. New Haven: Yale University Press.

Liebenstein, H. M. 1957. *Economic backwardness and economic growth*. New York: Wiley.

Lillard, L. A., and R. J. Willis. 1997. Motives for intergenerational transfers: Evidence from Malaysia. *Demography* 34:115–34.

Locher, Uli. 1975. The market system of Port-au-Prince. In *Working papers in Haitian society and culture*, ed. Sidney W. Mintz. New Haven, CT: Antilles Research Program, Yale University.

Locke, Alain. 1925. Foreword to *The New Negro, an interpretation*. New York: Albert and Charles Boni.

Lowenthal, David. 1957. The population of Barbados. *Journal of Economic and Social Studies* 6:471.

———. 1963. Occupational multiplicity in rural Jamaica. In *Symposium on community studies in anthropology*, ed. V. Garfield and E. Friedl. Proceedings of the American Ethnological Society. Seattle: University of Washington Press.

Lowenthal, David, and Lambros Comitas. 1962. Emigration and depopulation: Some neglected aspects of population geography. *Geographical Review* 52(2):195–210.

Lowenthal, Ira. 1987. Marriage is 20, children are 21: The cultural construction of conjugality in rural Haiti. Dissertation, Johns Hopkins University.

———. 1984. Labor, sexuality and the conjugal contract. In *Haiti: Today and tomorrow*, ed. Charles R. Foster and Albert Valman. Lanham, MD: University Press of America.

Lundahl, Mats. 1983. *The Haitian economy: Man, land, and markets*. New York: St. Martin's.

Mackenzie, Charles. 1830 [1971]. *Notes on Haiti, made during a residence in that republic*, Vol 1. London: Frank Cass.

Mamdani, Mahmood. 1973. *The myth of population control: Family caste and class in an Indian village*. New York: Monthly Review Press.

———. 1981. The ideology of population control. In *And the poor get children*, ed. Karen L. Michaelson, 39–49. New York: Monthly Review Press.

Mann, Jim. 1993. CIA's aid plan would have undercut Aristide in '87–88. *Los Angeles Times*, October 31.

Mantz, Jeffrey W. 2003. Lost in the fire, gained in the ash: Moral economies of exchange in Dominica. Dissertation, University of Chicago.

———. 2007. How a huckster becomes a custodian of market morality: Traditions of flexibility in exchange in Dominica. *Identities: Global Studies in Culture and Power* 14:19–38.

Marino, Anthony. 1970. Family, fertility, and sex ratios in the British Caribbean. *Population Studies* 24(2):159–72.

Marshall, Dawn I. 1985. International migration as circulation: Haitian movement to the Bahamas. In *Circulation in third world countries*, ed. R. Mansell Prothero and Murray Chapman, 226–40. Boston: Routledge and Kegan Paul.

Massiah, Joycelin. 1982. Women who head households. In *Women and the family*, ed. J. Massiah, 62–130. Cave Hill, Barbados: Institute of Social and Economic Research, University of the West Indies.

———. 1983. Women as heads of households in the Caribbean: Family structure and feminine status. United Kingdom: UNESCO.

Maternowska, Catherine. 1996. Coups d'etat and contraceptives: A political economy analysis of family planning in Haiti. Dissertation, Columbia University.

Matthews, Dom Basil. 1953. *Crisis of the West Indian family*. Caribbean Affairs Series. Port of Spain, Trinidad: University of the West Indies.

Maynard-Tucker, G. 1996. Unions, fertility, and the quest for survival. *Social Science & Medicine* 43(9):1379–87.

McElroy, Jerome, and Klaus Albuquerque. 1988. The impact of migration on mortality and fertility in St. Kitts-Nevis and the U.S. Virgin Islands. *Caribbean Geography* 2(3):173–94.

———. 1990. Migration, natality and fertility: Some Caribbean evidence. *International Review* 24(4):783–802.

McGowan, Lisa A. 1997. Democracy undermined, economic justice denied: Structural adjustment and the aid juggernaut in Haiti. Washington, DC: Development Group for Alternative Policies.

McPherson, Matthew and Timothy Schwartz. 2001. The Defeminization of the Dominican Hinterlands: Conservation Implications for the Cordillera Central. The Nature Conservancy: Arlington, Virginia.

Mencher, Joan P., and Anne Okongwu, eds. 1993. *Where did all the men go? Female-headed, female-supported households in cross-cultural perspective*. Boulder, CO: Westview.

Metraux, Rhoda. 1951. Kith and kin: a study of Creole social structure in Marbial, Haiti. Dissertation, Columbia University.

Midgett, D. K. 1977. West Indian migration and adaptation in St. Lucia and London. Dissertation, University of Illinois at Urbana-Champaign.

Millspaugh, Arthur C. 1931. *Haiti under American control: 1915–1931*. Boston: World Peace Foundation.

Mintz, Sidney. 1955. The Jamaican internal marketing pattern: some notes and hypothesis. *Social and Economic Studies* 4(1):95–103.

———. 1971. Men, women and trade. *Comparative Studies in Society and History*. 13:247–69.

———. 1974. *Caribbean transformations*. Chicago: Aldine.

———. 1981. Economic role and cultural tradition. In *The black woman cross-culturally*, ed. Filomina Chioma Steady, 513–34. Cambridge, MA: Schenkman.

———. 1985. From plantations to peasantries in the Caribbean. In *Caribbean contours*, ed. Sidney W. Mintz and Sally Price, 127–53. Baltimore: Johns Hopkins University Press.

Mintz, Sidney, and Eric R. Wolf. 1950. An analysis of ritual co-parenthood (*compadrazgo*). *The Southwestern Journal of Anthropology* 6(4):341–65.

Modiano, Nancy. 1973. *Indian education in the Chiapa highlands*. New York: Holt, Rinehart & Winston.

Mohammed, Patricia. 1986. The Caribbean family revisited. In *Gender in Caribbean development*, ed. Patricia Mohammed and Catherine Shepherd, 170–82. Mona, Jamaica: University of the West Indies.

Montague, Ludwell Lee. 1966. *Haiti and the United States: 1714–1938*. New York: Russel and Russel.

Moore W. E. 1945. *Economic demography of Eastern Europe*. Geneva, Switzerland: League of Nations.

Moral, Paul. 1961. *Le Paysan Haitien*. Paris: Maisonneuve et Larose.

Moreau, St. Mery. 1797. *Description de la partie Francaise de Saint-Domingue*. Paris: Societe de l'Histoire de Colonies Francaises.

Mosher, William D. 1980. The theory of change and response: An application to Puerto Rico, 1940 to 1970. *Population Studies* 34(1):45–48.

Munroe, Ruth H., Robert L. Munroe, and Harold S. Shimmin. 1984. Children's work in four cultures: determinants and consequences. *American Anthropologist* 86:369–79.

Murphy, Martin F. 1986. Historical and contemporary labor utilization practices in sugar industries of the Dominican Republic. Dissertation, Columbia University.

Murray Gerald F. 1972. The economic context of fertility patterns in a rural Haitian community. Report submitted to the International Institute for the Study of Human Reproduction. New York: Columbia University.

———. 1976. Women in perdition: Fertility control in Haiti. In *Culture natality and family planning*, ed. John Marshall and Steven Polgar, 59–79. Chapel Hill, NC: Carolina Population Center.

———. 1977. The evolution of Haitian peasant land tenure: Agrarian adaptation to population growth. Dissertation, Columbia University.

———. 1991. The phantom child in Haitian voodoo: A folk-religious model of uterine life. In *African creative expression of the divine*, ed. Kortright Davis, Elias Farajaje-Jones, and Iris Eaton. Washington DC: Howard University School of Divinity.

Murray, Gerald, Matthew McPherson, and Timothy T. Schwartz. 1998. Fading frontier: An anthropological analysis of social and economic relations on the Dominican and Haitian Border. Report for USAID (Dom Repub).

Murthy, D. 1973. Loss of potential fertility due to unstable unions in Haiti. Unpublished manuscript, Harvard School of Public Health.

Nag, Moni. 1971. The influence of conjugal behavior, migration and contraception on natality in Barbados. In *Culture and population: A collection of current studies*, ed. Stephen Polgar, 105–23. Cambridge, MA: Schenkman.

Nag, Moni, Benjamin N. F. White, and R. Creighton Peet. 1978. An anthropological approach to the study of the economic value of children in Java and Nepal. *Current Anthropology* 19:293–306.

Naval, G. 1995. Evaluation of the crisis program of the catholic relief services in Haiti. Final report. Port-au-Prince, Haiti.

Nene, Y. L., Susan D. Hall, and V. K. Sheila, eds. 1990. *The pigeonpea*. Andhra Pradesh, India: International Crops Research Institute for the Semi-Arid Tropics.

Newsom, Lee Ann. 1993. Native West Indian plant use. Dissertation, University of Florida, Gainesville.

Nicholls, David. 1974. *Economic dependence and political autonomy: The Haitian experience*. Occasional Paper Series No. 9. Montreal: McGill University, Center for Developing-Area Studies.

Nietschmann, Bernard. 1979. Ecological change, inflation, and migration in the far western Caribbean. *Geographical Review* 69(1):1–24.

Nonaka, K., T. Miura, and K. Peter. 1994. Recent fertility decline in Dariusleut Hutterites: An extension of Eaton and Mayer's Hutterite fertility study. *Human Biology* 66(3):411–21.

Notestein, F. 1945. Population—the long view. In *Food for the world*, ed. T. W. Schultz, 36–57. Chicago: University of Chicago Press.

NPR (National Public Radio). 2000. A restavec's tale: Jean-Robert Cadet. February 18. At www.npr.org/templates/story/story.php?storyId=1070500.

———. 2007. Haiti's dark secret: The restavecs: Servitude crosses the line between chores and child slavery. March 27, 2004 National Public Radio broadcast by Rachel Leventhal and Gigi Cohen, NPR Weekend Edition. At www.npr.org/templates/story/story.php?storyId=1779562.

Nutini, Hugo G., and Betty Bell. 1980. *Ritual kinship: The structure and historical development of the compadrazgo system in rural Tlaxcala*. New Jersey: Princeton University Press.

Nzeza, Koko. 1988. Differential responses of maize, peanut, and sorghum to water stress. Master's thesis, University of Florida, Gainesville.

N'zengou-Tayo M.J. 1998. "Fanm se poto mitan": Haitian woman, the pillar of society [Fanm se poto mitan: la femme Haïtienne, pilier de la société]. Mona, Jamaica: Centre For Gender And Development Studies, University Of The West Indies.

Oloko, Beatrice Adenike. 1994. Children's street work in urban Nigeria: Dilemma of modernizing tradition. In *Cross-cultural roots of minority child development*, ed. Patricia M. Greenfield and Robert R. Cocking, 197–224. Hillsdale, NJ: Erlbaum.

Olwig, Karen Fog. 1985. *Cultural adaptation and resistance on St. John: Three centuries of Afro-Caribbean life*. Gainesville: University of Florida Press.

Onwueme, I. C. 1978. *Tropical tuber crops*. New York: John Wiley.

Oprah. 2007. "Slavery" in Haiti and Ghana. From the show "A special report: The little boy Oprah couldn't forget." At www2.oprah.com/tows/slide/200702/20070209/slide_20070209_284_115.jhtml.

Otterbein, Keith. 1963. The family organization of the Andros Islanders. Dissertation, University of Pittsburgh.

———. 1965. Caribbean family organization: A comparative analysis. *American Anthropologist* 67:66–79.

———. 1966. The Andros Islanders: A study of family organization in the Bahamas. Lawrence: University of Kansas Press.

———.1970. *The evolution of war: A cross-cultural study*. New Haven, CT: HRAF Press.

———.1986. *The ultimate coercive sanction: A cross-cultural study of capital punishment*. New Haven, CT: HRAF Press.

———. 1994. Feuding and warfare: Selected works of Keith F. Otterbein. New York and London: Routledge.

———. 2004. *How war began*. College Station: Texas A&M University Press.

Oxfam. 2005. Food aid or hidden dumping? Separating wheat from chaff. Briefing paper. At www.oxfam.org.uk/what_we_do/issues/trade/bp71_foodaid.htm, accessed May 1, 2006.

Palmer, Ransord W. 1974. A decade of West Indian migration to the United States, 1962–1972: An economic survey analysis. *Social and Economic Studies* 23(4):572–87.

Paul, Max. 1983. Black families in modern Bermuda. Göttingen, Germany: Edition Herodot.

Perusek, Glenn. 1984. Haitian emigration in the early twentieth century. *International Migration Review* 18:4–18.

Petras, Elizabeth McLean. 1988. *Jamaican labor migration: White capital and black labor*. Boulder, CO: Westview.

Philpott, Stuart. 1973. West Indian migration; the Montserrat case. London, Athlone Press.

PISANO. 1990. Rapport relatif aux resultats de l'enquete de donnes de base de Jean Rabel. Theis, W, S. Lund, and T. Janssen, eds. Hindenburgring, Germany: Juillet Istrupa Consulting.

Plummer, Gayle. 1985. Haitian migrants and backyard imperialism. *Class and Race* XXVI, 4:35–43.

Polgar, Steven. 1972. Population history and population policies from an anthropological perspective. *Current Anthropology* 13(2):203–11.

Pollock, Nancy. 1972. Women and the division of labor: A Jamaican example. *American Anthropologist* 74(3):689–92.

Price, Richard. 1966. Caribbean fishing and fisherman: A historical sketch. *American Anthropologist* 68(6):1363–83.

Quinlan, Robert. 2005. Kinship, gender and migration from a rural Caribbean community. *Migration Letters* 2(1):2–12.

———. 2006. Gender and risk in a matrifocal Caribbean community: A view from behavioral ecology. *American Anthropologist* 108(3):464–79.

Reher, David Sven, and Pedro Luis Iriso-Napal. 1989. Marital fertility and its determinants in rural and urban Spain, 1887–1930. *Population Studies* 43:405–27.

Richardson, Bonham C. 1975. The overdevelopment of Carriacou. *Geographical Review* 65(3):390–99.

Richardson, Laura. 1997. Feeding dependency, starving democracy: USAID policies in Haiti. Boston: Grassroots International.

Richman, Karen E. 2003. Miami money and the home gal. *Anthropology and Humanism* 27(2): 119–32.

Roberts, G. W. 1957. Some aspects of mating and fertility in the West Indies. *Population Studies* 8:199–227.

Rocheleau, Dianne. 1984. Geographic and socioeconomic aspects of the recent Haitian migration to South Florida. In *Caribbean migration program*. Gainesville: University of Florida, Center for Latin American Studies.

Rodman, Hyman. 1971. *Lower-class families: The culture of poverty in Negro Trinidad.* New York: Oxford University Press.

RONCO. 1987. *Agriculture sector assessment: Haiti.* Marguerite Blemur, ed. Washington: RONCO Consulting Corporation.

Ross R. T., and M. Cheang. 1997. Common infectious diseases in a population with low multiple sclerosis and varicella occurrence. *Journal of Epidemiology* 50(3):337–39.

Rotberg, Robert I., and Christopher A. Clague. 1971. *Haiti, The politics of squalor.* Boston: Houghton Mifflin.

Rouse, Irving. 1992. *The Tainos: Rise and decline of the people who greeted Columbus.* New Haven, CT: Yale University Press.

Rubenstein, Hymie. 1977. Economic history and population movements in an eastern Caribbean Valley. *Ethnohistory* 24(1):19–45.

———. 1979. The return ideology in West Indian migration. In *The anthropology of return migration*, ed. Robert Rhoades. Papers in Anthropology 20:330–37.

———. 1983. Remittances and rural development in the English-speaking Caribbean. *Human Organization* 42(4):295–306.

Safa, Helen I. 1986. Economic autonomy and sexual equality in Caribbean society. *Social and Economic Studies* 35(3):1–21.

———. 1995. *The myth of the male breadwinner: Women and industrialization in the Caribbean.* Boulder, CO: Westview.

Sahlins, Marshall. 1972. *Stone age economics.* Chicago: Aldine.

Saint-Louis, Loretta-Jane Prichard. 1988. Migration evolves: The political economy of network process and form in Haiti, the U.S. and Canada. Dissertation, Boston University.

Sargent, Carolyn, and Michael Harris. 1992. Gender ideology, childrearing, and child health in Jamaica. *American Ethnologist* 19(3):523–37.

Scarano, Francisco A. 1989. Labor and society in the nineteenth century. In *The Modern Caribbean*, ed. Franklin W. Knight and Colin A. Palmer. Chapel Hill: University of North Carolina Press.

———. 1984. *Sugar and slavery in Puerto Rico: The plantation economy of Ponce, 1800–1850.* Madison: University of Wisconsin Press.

Schellekens, J. 1993. Wages, secondary workers, and fertility: A working-class perspective of the fertility transition in England and Wales. *Journal of Family History* 18: 1–17.

Schwartz, Timothy. 1992. Haitian migration: System labotomization. Unpublished master's thesis, University of Florida, Gainesville.

———. 1998. NHADS survey: Nutritional, health, agricultural, demographic and socio-economic survey: Jean Rabel, Haiti, June 1, 1997–June 11, 1998. Unpublished report, on behalf of PISANO, Agro Action Allemande and Initiative Developpment. Hamburg, Germany.

———. 2000. "Children are the wealth of the poor:" High fertility and the organization of labor in the rural economy of Jean Rabel, Haiti. Dissertation, University of Florida, Gainesville.

———. 2004. "Children are the wealth of the poor": Pronatalism and the economic utility of children in Jean Rabel, Haiti. *Research in Anthropology* 22:62–105.

SCID (South-East Consortium for International Development) 1993. Report: Farmer needs assessment exploratory surveys: CARE Northwest region 2, 3 & 4 South-East. Richard A. Swanson, William Gustave, Yves Jean, Roosevelt Saint-Dic, eds. Consortium for International Development and Auburn University. Work performed under USAID contract No. 521-0217-C-0004-00.

Scrimshaw, Susan. 1978. Infant mortality and behavior in the regulation of family size. *Population and Development Review* 4:383–403.

Segal, Aaron. 1975. *Population policies in the Caribbean*. Lexington, MA: D.C. Heath.

———. 1987. The Caribbean exodus in a global context. In *Caribbean exodus*, ed. B. Levine. New York: Praeger.

Senior, Olive. 1991. *Working miracles: Women's lives in the English-speaking Caribbean*. Bloomington: Indiana University Press.

Sergeant, Carolyn, and Michael Harris. 1992. Gender ideology, child rearing, and child health in Jamaica. *American Ethnologist* 19(3):523–37.

Sharpe, J. 1997. Mental health issues and family socialization in the Caribbean. In *Caribbean families: Diversity among ethnic groups*, ed. J. L. Rooparine & J. Brown. Greenwich, CT: Ablex.

Simey, T. S. 1946. *Welfare and planning in the West Indies*. Oxford: Clarendon.

Simmons, Alan Dwaine Plaza, and Victor Piché. 2005. The remittance sending practices of Haitians and Jamaicans in Canada. At www.un.org/esa/population/publications/IttMigLAC/P01_ASimmons.pdf.

Simpson, George Eaton. 1942. Sexual and family institutions in Northern, Haiti. *American Anthropologist* 44:655–74.

Singer, Merrill, Lani Davidson, and Gina Gerdes. 1988. Cultural, critical theory, and reproductive illness behavior in Haiti. *Medical Anthropology Quarterly* 2(4):379–85.

Skari, Tala. 1987. The dilemma. *Refugees* March:27–29.

Sloley, M. 1999. Parenting deficiencies outlined. *The Jamaica Gleaner Online*. At www.jamaicagleaner/1999117/news/n1.html, accessed April 2, 2002.

Smith, Delores E., and Gail Mosby. 2003. Jamaican child-rearing practices: The role of corporal punishment. *Adolescence*, Summer. At findarticles.com/p/articles /mi_m2248/is_150_38/ai_109027887/pg_1?tag=artBody;col1.

Smith, Jennie Marcelle. 1998. Family planning initiatives and Kalfouno peasants: What's going wrong? Occasional paper/University of Kansas Institute of Haitian Studies, no. 13. Lawrence: Institute of Haitian Studies, University of Kansas.

Smith, M. G. 1957. Introduction. In *My mother who fathered me: A study of the family in three selected communities in Jamaica*, by Edith Clarke. London: George Allen and Unwin.

———. 1961. Kinship and household in Carriacou. *Social and Economic Studies* 10(1):455–77.

———. 1962. *West Indian family structure*. Seattle: University of Washington.

———. 1966. Introduction. In *My mother who fathered me: A study of the family in three selected communities in Jamaica*, 2nd ed., by Edith Clarke. London: George Allen and Unwin.

Smith, R. T. 1953. Aspects of family organization in a coastal negro community in British Guiana: A preliminary report. *Social and Economic Studies* 1(1):87–112.

———. 1956. *The Negro family in British Guiana*. London: Routledge and Kegan Paul.

———. 1988. *Kinship and class in the West Indies*. Cambridge: Cambridge University Press.

———. 1996. *The matrifocal family: Power, pluralism and politics*. New York and London: Routledge.

Smucker, Glenn Richard. 1983. Peasants and development politics: A study in class and culture. Dissertation, New School for Social Research.

Solien, Nancie. 1961. Family organization in five types of migratory wage labor. *American Anthropologist* 63(6):1264–80.

———. 1959. The consanguineal household among the black Carib of central America. Dissertation, University of Michigan.

Sommerfelt, Tone, ed. 2002. *Child domestic labour in Haiti characteristics, contexts and organisation of children's residence, relocation and work.* A FAFO report to UNICEF, ILO, Save the Children UK and Save the Children Canada.

Springfield, Consuelo Lopez, ed. 1997. *Daughters of Caliban: Caribbean women in the twentieth century.* Bloomington: Indiana University Press.

Stepick, Alex. 1984. The roots of Haitian migration. In *Haiti—today and tomorrow,* ed. Charles R. Foster and Albert Valdman. Lanham, MD; University Press of America.

———. 1982. Haitian refugees in the U.S., Report No. 53. London: Minority Rights Group.

Stewart, John O. 1973. Coolie and creole: Differential adaptations in a neo-plantation village-Trinidad, West Indies. Dissertation, University of California at Los Angeles.

Stycos, J. Mayone. 1954. Haitian attitudes toward family size. *Human Organization* 23(1): 42 –47.

Stycos, J. Mayone, and Kurt W. Back. 1964. *The control of human fertility in Jamaica.* New York: Cornell University Press.

Sunday Telegraph. 2007. The plight of Haiti's child slaves. By Pete Pattisson, at www.telegraph.co.uk/news/main.jhtml?xml=/news/2007/02/11/wHaiti11.xml.

Sutton, Constance, and Susan Makiesky-Barrow. 1975. Migration and West Indian racial and ethnic consciousness. In *Migration and development: Implications for ethnic identity and political conflict,* ed. Helen I. Safa and Brian M. du Toit, 113–44. The Hague: Mouton.

———. 1975. Women, knowledge, and power. In *Women cross-culturally: Change & challenge,* ed. Ruby Roehrlich-Leavitt, 581–600. The Hague: Mouton.

———. 1970. Social inequality and sexual status in Barbados. In *Sexual stratification: A cross-cultural view,* ed. Alice Schlegel. New York: Columbia University Press.

Szwed, John F. 1970. Afro-American musical adaptation. In *Afro-American anthropology,* ed. Norman F. Whitten and John F. Szwed. New York: Free Press.

Taufa, Tukutau, Vui Mea, and John Lourie. 1990. A preliminary report on fertility and socio-economic changes in two Papua New Guinea communities. In *Fertility and responses,* ed. John Landers, 35–46. Cambridge: Cambridge University Press.

Tauheed, Linwood F. 2003. Brown—Then and now: Social science and the shifting Brown paradigm. Speech given January 25, 2003 at the University of Missouri—Kansas City School of Law.

Taylor, E. 1976. The social adjustment of returned migrants to Jamaica. In *Ethnicity in the Americas,* ed. Frances Henry, 213–29. The Hague: Mouton.

Toro, Julio Cesar, and Charles B. Atlee. 1980. Agronomic practices for cassava production: A literature review. In *Cassava cultural practices: Proceedings of a workshop held in Salvador, Bahia, Brazil, 18–21 March 1980.* Ottawa, Canada: International Research Development Research Centre.

Treco, Ria N. M. 2002. The Haitian diaspora in the Bahamas. Dissertation, Florida International University.

U.S. Department of Commerce. 2006. Haiti country reports on economic policy and trade practices—1998 key economic indicators. Trade Compliance Center. At trade.gov/mac, accessed April 13, 2006.

U.S. Department of Labor. 1998. Haiti: Child labor in Haiti. Bureau of International Labor Affairs. At www.dol.gov/ilab.

Ulysse, Gina. 1999. Uptown ladies and downtown women: Informal commercial importing and the social/symbolic politics of identity in Jamaica. Dissertation, University of Michigan, Ann Arbor.

UN Globalis. 2006. Global methodology for mapping human impacts on the biosphere . At globalis.gvu.unu.edu.

UN Supplementary Convention on the Abolition of Slavery 1956 Convention 138 under the Child Labor Code. At www.ilo.org/public/english/dialogue/actrav/genact/child/ part1_a/publ1_artic.htm.

Underwood, Frances W. 1960. The marketing system in peasant Haiti. In *Papers in Caribbean Anthropology*, ed. Sidney W. Mintz. New Haven, CT: Yale University.

UNICEF. 1993. Les enfants en situation spécialement difficile en Haiti. Port-au-Prince: Author.

———. 1997. *The state of the world's children*. New York: Author.

———. 2006. Fertility and contraceptive use: Global database on contraceptive prevalence. At www.childinfo.org/eddb/fertility/dbcontrc.htm, accessed May 3, 2006.

UNIFEM. 2006. UNIFEM in Haiti: Supporting gender justice, development and peace. UNIFEM Caribbean Office, Christ Church, Barbados. At www.womenwarpeace .org/Haiti/Haiti.htm.

United Nations. 1999. Human development report. New York: Author.

———. 2000. Indicators on income and economic activity. United Nations Statistics Division. At www.un.org/Depts/unsd/social/inc-eco.htm.

———. 2005. World population prospects. The 2004 revision population data base. At esa.un.org/unpp, accessed February 3, 2007.

United Nations. 2006. Demographic yearbook.At unstats.un.org/unsd/demographic/ products/dyb/dyb2.htm, accessed March 24, 2007.

United Nations Development Programme. 2004. Millennium development goals look out of reach for increasingly impoverished Haitians. At www.undp.org/mdg/news2. shtml.

———. 2006. Human development indicators 2003. At hdr.undp.org/reports/global/ 2003/indicator/indic_196_1_1.html.

UNOPS. 1997. Ministère de la planification et de la coopération externe (mpce) direccion departmental du Nord-Ouest July) Éléments de la problématique déparetmentale (Version de Consultation) Programme des Nations Unies pour le Développement (PNUD), Centre des Nations Unies pour les Établissements Humains (CNUEH-Habitat), Projet d'Appui Institutionnel en Aménagement du Territoire (HAI-94-016). Port-de-Paix, Haiti.

UPAN. 1982. Projections des besoins et services dans le domaine alimentaire et nutritionnel, Port-au-Prince, Haiti.

Vaessen, Martin. 1984. Childlessness and infecundity. Comparative Studies no. 31. Voorburg, Netherlands: International Statistical Institute.

Vassiere, Pierre de. 1909. *Saint Domingue la societe et la vie Creoles sous l'ancien regime (1629–1789)* Paris: Perrin.

Verschueren, J. 1984. Le Diocese de Port-de-Paix: La Mission Montfortaine de'Haiti 1871–1936. Informations & Recherches Mission Montfortain. Port-au-Prince, Haiti.

Veschuren R. 1955. La sucrerie Foache a Jean Rabel. In *Revue de la Société Haitienne d'Histoire et de Geographie* 27(97).

Victor, Rene. 1944. *Recensement et demographie*. Port-au-Prince, Haiti: Imprimie de l'Etat.

Wagley, Charles. 1957. Plantation America: A culture sphere. In *Caribbean studies, a symposium*, ed V. Rubin. Jamaica: Institute of Social Economic Research.

Walker, Della M. 1968. Family and social structure in Anguilla. In *The family in the Caribbean: Proceedings of the first conference on the family in the Caribbean*, ed. Stanford N. Gerber, 111–16. Rio Piedras: Institute of Caribbean Studies, University of Puerto Rico.

White, Benjamin. 1973. Demand for labor and reproduction in a Javanese village. Dissertation, Columbia University.

———.1976. Production and reproduction in a Javanese village. Dissertation, Columbia University.

———. 1982. Child labor and population growth in rural Asia. *Development and Change* 13:587–610.

WHO (World Health Organization). 1999. World Health Organization multinational study of breastfeeding and lactational amennorhea pregnancy and breastfeeding: World Health Organization task force on methods for the natural regulation of fertility III. In *Sterility and Fertility* 72(3):431–40.

Wikipedia. 2006. Economy of Haiti. At en.wikipedia.org/wiki/Economy_of_Haiti, accessed April 5, 2006.

Williams, Eric. 1970. *From Columbus to Castro.* London: Vintage Books.

Williams, S. J., N. Murthy, and G. Berggren. 1975. Conjugal unions among rural Haitian women. *Journal of Marriage and the Family* 4:1022–31.

Wilmsen, E. 1978. Seasonal effects on dietary intake on Kalahari Kung. *Proceedings of the Federation of American Societies for Experimental Biology* 37(1):25–32.

———. 1982. Biological variables in forager fertility performance: A critique of Bongaarts Model. Working Papers no. 60. Boston University: African Studies Center.

Wilson, Peter. 1969. Reputation and respectability: A suggestion for Caribbean ethnology. *Man* 4(1):70–84.

———. 1961a. The social structure of Providencia Isla, Columbia. Dissertation, Yale University, New Haven.

———. 1961b. Household and family on Provendencia. In *Social and Economic Studies* 10(1):511–27.

———. 1973. *Crab antics: The social anthropology of English-Speaking negro societies of the Caribbean.* New Haven, CT: Yale University Press.

Wolf, Eric. 1955. Types of Latin American peasantry: A preliminary discussion. *American Anthropologist* 57(3):452–71.

Wolf, Eric, and Sidney W. Mintz. 1957. Haciendas and plantations in middle America and the Caribbean. *Social and Economic Studies* 6:380–412.

Wood, J. W. 1995. *Dynamics of human reproduction: Biology, biometry, demography.* New York: Aldine de Gruyter.

World Bank. 1998. Haiti: The challenges of poverty reduction. Report #17242-HA Volume 1 1998. Poverty Unit and Economic Management Unit and Caribbean Country Management Unit. Latin American and Caribbean Region.

———. 2002. A review of gender issues in the Dominican Republic, Haiti, and Jamaica. Report No. 21866-LAC. December 11th , Caribbean Management Unit, Latin America and the Caribbean Region.

Yelvington, Kevin A. 2001. The anthropology of Afro-Latin America and the Caribbean: Diasporic dimensions. *Annual Review of Anthropology* 30:227–60.

Zelizer, Adriana. 1985. *Pricing the priceless child: The changing social values of children.* New York: Basic Books.

Zuvekas, Clarence Jr. 1978. *A survey of the literature on income distribution and the fulfillment of basic human needs in the Caribbean region.* Caribbean Regional Working Document Series #3. Washington, DC: USAID.

Index